Mothers in Law

Gender and Culture

Carolyn G. Heilbrun and Nancy K. Miller, Editors

Mothers in Law

Feminist Theory and the Legal Regulation of Motherhood

EDITED BY MARTHA ALBERTSON FINEMAN
AND ISABEL KARPIN

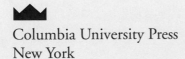

Columbia University Press
New York

Columbia University Press
New York   Chichester, West Sussex
Copyright © 1995 Columbia University Press
All rights reserved.

Library of Congress Cataloging-in-Publication Data

Mothers in law : feminist theory and the legal regulation of
   motherhood / edited by Martha Albertson Fineman and Isabel Karpin.
        p.   cm. — (Gender and culture)
     Includes bibliographical references.
     ISBN 0–231–09680–1 (cl.). — ISBN 0–231–09681–X (pa.)
     1. Women—Legal status, laws, etc.—United States—Congresses.
   2. Mothers—Legal status, laws, etc.—United States—Congresses.
   3. Feminist jurisprudence—Congresses.   I. Fineman, Martha.
   II. Karpin, Isabel.   III. Series.
   KF478.A5M68   1995
   346.7301'34—dc20
   [347.306134]   94–47019
                                                      CIP

Printed in the United States of America
c 10 9 8 7 6 5 4 3 2 1
p 10 9 8 7 6 5 4 3 2 1

TO OUR MOTHERS

CONTENTS

Part III: Regulating Mother

Part IV: Mother in Practice

PREFACE

MARTHA ALBERTSON FINEMAN

The experience of putting this book together illustrates the reluctance and ambivalence of legal feminists about the topic of motherhood. The essays in this book are based on papers presented at two conferences on Motherhood sponsored by the Feminism and Legal Theory Project, which is now located at Columbia University Law School. The first conference occurred in 1990 in Madison, Wisconsin, where a dozen papers were presented. Interestingly, almost all of the proposals received in response to this first call for papers on the topic of motherhood focused on abortion and birth control or on technology. A few suggested explorations of the phenomena of "bad" or abusive mothering. The focus on such topics was frustrating to me, since I had anticipated a more complex (and complete) examination of the issues surrounding motherhood. Nevertheless, I continue to feel that the limited nature of those proposals was consistent with the ambivalence surrounding the topic for feminist legal theorists at that time.

Fortunately, the call for papers for a second conference on the topic of motherhood, which was held more than three years later, brought proposals from wider perspectives. Bad and burdened mothers, along with issues pertaining to reproductive control, were certainly present in the pile of suggested topics, but the general tone of the proposals was less accusatory and defensive. As a group, the second set of authors seemed more familiar with, and accepting of, mothers—more realistic and less idealistic and therefore less judgmental about the failings and foibles of mothering. This sympathetic or empathetic mode complemented the earlier more negative forays into the topic. The political, legal, and practical aspects of the status of Mother were not only evident but central in the second set of papers submitted.

The essays in this collection are drawn largely from that second conference, although they are supplemented by three (Sanger, Siegel, and Woliver) from the earlier event. I have also included an essay of mine, even though it was not presented at either of the conferences. This essay, which was published in the interval between the two conferences, was the impetus for Dorothy Roberts's paper and is related to several others; I include it for those reasons.

Law as an institution—its procedures, structures, dominant concepts, and norms—was constructed at a time when women were systematically excluded from participation. Insofar as women's lives and experiences were (are) the subject of law they were (are) of necessity translated into law by men. Even social or cultural institutions such as motherhood that women occupy exclusively were what I call "colonized categories"—initially defined, controlled, and given legal content by men. Male norms and male understandings fashioned legal definitions of what constituted a family, what was good mothering, who had claims and access to children as well as to jobs and education, and, ultimately, how legal institutions functioned to give or deny redress for alleged (and defined) harms (Fineman 1995:38).

Mother is a universally lived experience with intimate and intensely personal content. We all have a mother; some of us are mothers. Our experience of Mother is pivotal in defining our understanding of our individual familial, sexual, and social circumstances. But Mother also has a social or political dimension. The meaning of the status may vary across, even within, cultures as Mother is placed in the context of other socially defined roles. The social and cultural dimensions of Mother are at least as significant in understanding the personal as are individual experiences. In many instances these generalized constructs are the most salient because they shape individual experiences and form the contours against which events are measured and given value.

Given its importance as a personal and a social construct exclusively operative on women, it is not surprising that motherhood has been a topic of exploration for feminist theorists. To a large extent, mothering has been perceived, and therefore theorized, as a "burden" or a problem for women—a set of obligations and responsibilities that must be managed if one is to allow the emergence of the "liberated" self. This self, as it is constructed in feminist discourse, is actualized or realized primarily through public (or nonmaternal) undertakings in the political or professional arenas.

The response of Simone de Beauvoir, the woman some feel is the mother of modern feminism, to a question about whether she felt deprived not having children clearly delineates the negative connotations of motherhood:

> I wrote in my memoirs about how children never held any attraction for me. Babies filled me with horror. The sight of a mother with child sucking the life from her breast, or women changing soiled diapers—it all filled me with such disgust. I had no desire to be drained, to be a slave to such a creature.   (Bair 1990:170)

Motherhood continues to be portrayed as burdensome, oppressive. Particularly relevant to the essays contained in this volume is the strain of contemporary American feminist theory in which Mother is typically cast as a problem-laden social and cultural institution.

Feminist legal theory is reflective of the treatment of Mother in other disciplines. In feminist legal theory, motherhood has primarily been presented as problematic for women. Mother embodies dependency at the same time that she is trapped by the dependency of others, marred by burdens of obligation and intimacy in an era where liberation and autonomy are revered. The focus of legal feminists has been on the marketplace and on the public aspects of equality and liberation (Sanger 1992:20).

The family is viewed as an institution in need of reform, but the solutions offered present little in the way of theoretical innovation. Women's difficulties are defined as primarily economic and political and presented as partly related to or caused by the distorting influence of motherhood on individual self-fulfillment. Reflecting the discourse in other areas, much of the legal reform discussion reaffirms the notion that the disabilities and disadvantages of motherhood must be overcome—the family refashioned so that the individual woman is left unencumbered.

The legal mechanism (and societal ideal) for accomplishing this task is "shared parenting." Fathers are envisioned (and empowered) as "equal" parents with corresponding rights and obligations within the egalitarian family. Feminist theorists thereby inadvertently romanticize the primacy of (hetero)sexual affiliation and, consequentially and inevitably, privilege the form of the patriarchal family. Social and legal policy is formulated with reference to this family as the paradigmatic core social institution.

Many legal feminists consider the topic of motherhood (or even family law) "dangerous" and are reluctant to address the issue. We are more comfortable with topics addressing sexuality and violence, where the issues and implications are clearer. To be a legal theorist concerned with mothering in any positive sense has been to risk the dismissive label of "cultural feminist," meaning that one's work is in danger of being relegated to the margins of feminist theory. To say that the status has "some" social value is often understood as a statement that it is the "only" thing of value for women. Speculation about the joys or pleasures of motherhood is often heard as a statement with coercive implications in which motherhood is mandated and inevitable. An interest in family and intimacy is often presumed by many to indicate some form of essentialistic reasoning or reaction regardless of the type of analysis employed.

But while legal feminists relegate motherhood to the margins of legal theory, the law coercively maintains antiquated, totalizing, overarching images of women that reflect beliefs and assumptions within society. And, in this regard, the law operates to shape and limit personal actions consistent with this embodied belief.

Motherhood as a colonized category has been given definition and content in the context of legal institutions that have historically excluded women from participation or relegated us to the "private sphere." Until fairly recently, in many states, women were not permitted to take part in or were discouraged from voting, serving on juries, holding office, or even practicing law. The exclusionary rules governing these practices have been formally altered. However, it is important to remember that the law is a conservative discipline, resistant to fundamental or dramatic changes. The law operates by establishing categories and proceeds by attempting to fit new situations into old paradigms. Rules such as *stare decisis* give content to the primacy of precedent and compel adherence to the status quo, thus ensuring that revolutions in conceptualization seldom occur.

 For these reasons, all women should care about the content of the social and legal construction of motherhood. Motherhood is central to the social and legal definition of woman. A woman who does not have children will still, in the context of law and legal institutions, be treated as though she is (or may become) a mother. Social construction and legal ramifications tend to operate independently of individual circumstances.

The representations of motherhood contained in these chapters are not essentialized, romanticized, or idealized. The authors are genuinely sympathetic to mothers and the difficulties in mothering, particularly as it is practiced within the confines of legal regulations and restrictions.

Many of the following essays place motherhood in a primarily political context—they address the maternal from a pragmatic and material perspective, restrained by law and other societal norms. Far from sentimentalizing mothering, the concern is with defining "good enough" mothering, a necessary endeavor if one is concerned with the excessive regulation and punitive laws currently directed at mothers. The contents of this volume are a necessary step in the exploration of the possibility of less-regulated mothering. Given the current attacks on mothers contained in discourses such as those associated with divorce and welfare policies, this project should be of paramount importance for feminist theory.

ACKNOWLEDGMENTS

We would like to thank Cynthia Hewett and Shary Crossfield, who contributed not only necessary labor but enviable humor and grace in assisting in managing the Feminism and Legal Theory Conference, from which most of these chapters are drawn. Rosemary Nidiry devoted many hours in the later stages of this project to ensuring that footnotes and text matched and that the bibliographic information was accurate and complete. She truly saved the day.

Mothers in Law

PART ONE

Resisting Mother

Mothers, Daughters, and
Autobiography: Maternal
Legacies and Cultural Criticism

NANCY K. MILLER

I begin with the death of a mother: the first, Carolyn
Steedman's in *Landscape for a Good Woman*, the second,
Annie Ernaux's in *A Woman's Story*.

She died like this. I didn't witness it. My niece told me this. She'd moved
everything down into the kitchen: a single bed, the television, the calor-
gas heater. She said it was to save fuel. The rest of the house was dark and
shrouded. . . . She had cancer, had gone back to Food Reform, talked to
me about curing it when I paid my first visit in nine years, two weeks
before her death: my last visit. . . . She complained of pains, but wouldn't
take the morphine tablets. It was pains everywhere, not in the lungs
where the cancer was. It wasn't the cancer that killed: a blood clot trav-
elled from her leg and stopped her heart. Afterwards, the doctor said
she'd been out of touch with reality.   (Steedman 1986:1)

Toward the end of this preface to her narrative, which she entitles "Death
of a Good Woman," Steedman goes on to invoke Simone de Beauvoir's
memoir, *A Very Easy Death*, framing her reference with these words:

Simone de Beauvoir wrote of her mother's death, said that in spite of the
pain it was an easy one: an upper-class death. Outside, for the poor,
dying is a different matter.   (2)

She then quotes Beauvoir directly:

And then in the public wards when the last hour is coming near, they
put a screen round a dying man's bed: he has seen this screen round other
beds that were empty the next day: he knows. I pictured Maman,

blinded for hours by the black sun that no one can look at directly: the
horror of her staring eyes with their dilated pupils.   (2)

Directly after this reference, Steedman concludes the preface to her narrative, with a brief paragraph, describing the moment of death:

> Like this: she flung up her left arm over her head, pulled her knees up,
> looked out with an extraordinary surprise. She lived alone, she died
> alone: a working-class life, a working-class death.   (2)

The following passages appear at the very beginning and end of
Ernaux's memoir, which is also the story of a working-class mother's life
and death:

> My mother died on Monday April 7 in the old people's home attached
> to the hospital at Pontoise, where I had installed her two years previ-
> ously. The nurse said over the phone: "Your mother passed away this
> morning, after breakfast." It was around ten o'clock.   (Ernaux 1991:1)

> She died eight days before Simone de Beauvoir.
>   She preferred giving to everybody, rather than taking from them.
> Isn't writing also a way of giving.   (91)

> It was only when my mother—born in an oppressed world from which
> she wanted to escape—became history that I started to feel less alone
> and out of place in a world ruled by words and ideas, the world where
> she had wanted me to live.

> I shall never hear the sound of her voice again. It was her voice, together
> with her words, her hands, and her way of moving and laughing, which
> linked the woman I am to the child I once was. The last bond between
> me and the world I come from has been severed.   (91–92)

Steedman's *Landscape for a Good Woman: A Story of Two Lives* and
Ernaux's *A Woman's Story* (*Une Femme*)[1] are contemporaneous accounts
of a mother's death. (Steedman's was published in 1986, Ernaux's written between 1986 and 1987, published in 1987.) At least this is their
point of departure. For both writers the mother's death becomes, to differing degrees, the occasion for a reflection about mothers and daughters, women and class, and more specifically about the ways in which
working-class identity shapes the stories of female development in postwar England and France. Like Beauvoir's monumental accomplishment
in *A Very Easy Death* (1964), both are acts of cultural criticism that
emerge from an autobiographical space. These are narratives insepara-

ble from a problem of definition, which is both a matter of genre and interpretation: a "cross [jointure] between family history and sociology, reality and fiction" as Ernaux puts it (1991:13); about "lives," Steedman writes, "lived out on the borderlands . . . for which the central interpretative devices of the culture don't quite work" (Steedman 1986:5).

Steedman's stated aim is to challenge two powerful bodies of thought: "the tradition of cultural criticism [in England]," which has no place for her mother in its "iconography of working-class motherhood" (6) and feminist "theories of patriarchy" (7), which ignore the class-consciousness of working-class children. By placing a biographical and autobiographical story at the center of her book, Steedman seeks to "*reverse* a central question within feminism and psychoanalysis about the desire to mother in little girls and replace it with a consideration of *women who, by refusing to mother, have refused to reproduce themselves or the circumstances of their exile*" (7; emphasis added). The story is told in its "difference and particularity," but told also for the effects of its representativity: "so that people in exile, the inhabitants of the long streets, may start to use the autobiographical 'I,' and tell the stories of their life" (6). Like Steedman, Ernaux sees identity as a process and autobiographical writing as a performance embedded in the social, but for her the task of testimony is more narrowly focused on the representation— we might even say the reproduction—of maternal experience:

> This book can be seen as a literary venture to the extent that its purpose is to find out the truth about my mother, *a truth that can be conveyed only by words.* (Neither photographs, nor my own memories, nor even the reminiscences of my family can bring me this truth.) And yet, in a sense, I would like to remain a cut below literature.   (tm, 13; emphasis added)

If we take seriously Beauvoir's achievement in making the maternal body—its wounds, demands, and desires—give voice to a culture's life and death narratives, what we can read here are further experiments in the construction of an autobiographical cultural authority. In all three instances embodiment is inseparable from the constraints and repercussions of materially located stories; but we also get to see the ways in which the figuration of that embodiment depends on the work, distortions, and gaps of individual memory.

Steedman argues that life stories like hers have not been told largely because they tend not to be heard; their specificity is tuned out because *as stories* they issue from a "structure of feeling" unavailable to middle-class readers, who by definition are assigned to a position of cultural centrality and domination. She writes:

> I read the collection *Fathers: Reflections by Daughters*, or Ann Oakley's *Taking It Like a Woman* and feel the painful and familiar sense of exclusion from these autobiographies of middle-class little-girlhood and womanhood, envy of those who belong, who can, like Ann Oakley, use the outlines of conventional romantic fiction to tell a life story. And women like this, friends, say: but it was like that for me too, my childhood was like yours; my father was like that, my mother didn't want me. What they cannot bear, I think, is that there exists a poverty and marginality of experience to which they have no access, structures of feeling that they have not lived within (and would not want to live within: for these are the structures of deprivation). They are caught in a terrible exclusion, an exclusion from the experience of others that measures out their own central relationship to the culture.   (17)

Steedman's mapping of this double exclusion is at the heart of her autobiographical project. On the one hand, you don't know us because you are the center from which, against which the borders are defined, and you don't know it. On the other, I know you but am not of you. The storyteller positions herself as irretrievably separate and set off from this audience; yet her tale is *also addressed* to other women, "friends" who think they speak the same language. Those readers must in turn confront Steedman's accusation of their failure to perceive the divide.

Having lived a "middle-class little-girlhood" I find myself in a predicament. I have just this projected reaction to Steedman's narrative. Like Steedman I tend to define myself in my life against the desire, as she puts it, to reproduce and its enactment as mothering, which she poses as the ground of her mother's and hence her own difference: their "sense of exclusion, of being cut off from what others enjoy" (18). But for me to insist autobiographically as a reader on resemblance—I felt cut off too, I didn't want to mother and my mother didn't either— would only seem to prove her point about middle-class mentalities: I can't see that however similar those feelings may seem to me, the structures of our experiences are fundamentally different. At the same time, I find myself protesting in turn against the assumption that simply by virtue of being middle-class—like Oakley—I automatically identify with the story of that life. My middle-class "womanhood" in no way resembles Oakley's; I identify not at all with the woman who defines herself as much by her child as by her writing. (It's not absolutely clear to me why Steedman "envies" Oakley her easy access to "the outlines of conventional romantic fiction." Like Steedman's, Oakley's account of growing up in postwar England interweaves personal narrative with feminist theory, autobiographical event with social analysis. What's different—Oakley's interleaving of that mix with pages from a love affair that parallels her family life in a poignant counterpoint—emerges, it seems, from Oakley's willingness to offer the reader, in a fictionalized mode, glimpses into the workings of her sexual desire. I don't understand this mode of self-disclosure as a function of class.) I read *Taking It Like a Woman*, resisting all the way, Oakley's account of her many desired pregnancies (five) and several children (three) whose needs and bodies figure significantly in her narrative.

Landscape for a Good Woman is powerful for me despite the differences in our original class assignments because of the ways in which it renders the maternal legacy that makes the daughter *not a mother*. Thus, reading as a middle-class girl now grown up, I meet Steedman autobiographically in a gesture of *counter-identification* (or as Eve Sedgwick puts it in "Axiomatic," "identifying with" [Sedgwick 1990:61]): I read *with* her—reader to writer, to writer—when I read "as a woman" who also lacked the desire to mother. And in that occasion of a possible encounter—"the autobiographical moment" de Man describes as "an alignment between the two subjects involved in the process of reading" (de Man 1979:921)—I reread, which is also to say rewrite, my history with hers. (This is what Susan Suleiman calls "autobiographical reading" [Suleiman 1994:8].)

Between the two passages of "Death of a Good Woman" excerpted above to frame this discussion, Steedman recalls an episode from her childhood in which a social worker, shortly after the birth of Steedman's baby sister, comes to inspect her mother's house and declares, "This house isn't fit for a baby" (Steedman 1986:2). Steedman describes her mother's reaction to the violence of that judgment, her tears of rage and bitter courage, and then adds:

> And I? will do everything and anything until the end of my days to stop anyone ever talking to me like that woman talked to my mother. It is in this place, this bare, curtainless bedroom that lies my secret and shameful defiance. I read a woman's book, meet such a woman at a party (a woman now, like me) and think quite deliberately as we talk: we are divided: a hundred years ago I'd have been cleaning your shoes. I know this and you don't.   (2)

As a four-year old little girl, Steedman bonds with her mother against the social worker: "We both watched the dumpy retreating figure of the health visitor through the curtainless windows" (2). The social violence of that scene in memory shapes the daughter's pattern of future identifications with women: with the mother, against all others. In the present of writing, the time of the memoir, the health visitor has been reconfigured as a published intellectual, or academic: a woman whose book Steedman will have read. A woman she puts into parenthesis, "now, like me." A woman, now *like me*. And I? Do I take up my position—like her now, not like her then? Or do I try to read across the divide otherwise through an identification with maternal rejection that flits through the particular zones of class boundaries unevenly; now you see it, now you don't. Although Steedman's theoretical project is to elaborate (which she brilliantly does) a *working-class* self-portrait, "a drama of *class*" (22), what I think this literary encounter can show are the twinned limits of class-based identifications: mine *and* hers: our predictable emotional blind spots, but also our unexpected intimacies. In that sense, my response pulls two ways at once in the two times of autobiography. "We are divided": on the one hand, as the daughter of the American postwar professional middle class, I would add even more specifically, New York Jewish professional middle class of the fifties (Ehrenreich 1990). And on the other, as a middle-aged feminist intellectual—"a woman now, like me"—who perhaps (also?) took Simone de Beauvoir too seriously, or at least too uncritically. If we talked at a party, would this give us something to say to each other?

Steedman's central question turns on the attempt to understand "*how* the wish not to have a child might come to be produced in a little girl, or in a grown woman" (Steedman 1986:85–86) and "what the refusal of a baby or a child is actually a refusal *of*" (84). She distinguishes in this between the "refusal to reproduce oneself . . . to perpetrate what one is . . . the way one understands oneself to be in the social world" and the refusal to be a mother.[2] "Some women of the recent past," she writes, "have been mothers," but not according to the official rules. She also emphasizes the kind of revolt that occurs *within* motherhood in a culture where "either socially or physiologically" women could not bodily refuse to bear children (84); this is how she understands her mother's performance. In both her mother's case and her own what's at stake is a rejection of the dominant social script. Despite the class differences between our mothers, and despite the lack of detail about *how* she came not to have a child, what attracted me to Steedman's story and what makes it (I guess I would have to say) thrilling to me—given the maternalism in and outside of contemporary feminism—is the conjunction of those intertwined repudiations, and in particular her defiant self-identification as a woman who has not had a child.[3]

Now I cannot like Steedman claim that I have *refused* to reproduce, since at various times in my life I flirted with the possibility and tried to conceive a child—strenuously, for three miserable years—at the borderlines of my fertility and failed a decade ago; rather, by virtue of a tenacious ambivalence and treacherous propensity for deferral I have not had a child, and probably never really wanted to in the first place. For me, as for many women of my generation in the United States who modeled our identities on Beauvoir's famous split—intellectual accomplishment *or* babies—it might be more accurate to say that like Steedman we refused to reproduce *as women*, as though anatomy were our destiny instead of history, on schedule as though we had no say; only some of us then changed our minds (or thought we did in a frenzy of belatedness), and it turned out that for some of us "nature" (or maybe it really was history) would have the last word after all (Jardine 1986). There's a poignant irony in the coexistence at the end of the twentieth century of a massive infertility that has given rise to dizzying adventures in reproductive techniques, and the ongoing challenges to women's reproductive rights. Choosing motherhood or refusing it has proven to be more complex than seventies feminists had imagined.

Our Bodies, Our Selves, the title of one of the most important collective projects to emerge out of seventies feminism, nicely glosses the conviction of that moment: the comma, rather than the copula—our bodies *are* our selves—meant that we would decide on what relation of apposition best described the relation between our bodies and our selves (Boston Women's Health Book Collective 1971). We were not *just* our bodies, but we authorized ourselves to have the decisive role in deciphering their meaning and adjudicating their circulation in the world. (The update of the volume, by the way, for women over thirty-five is called *Our Selves Growing Older*. I guess without bodies. Which might actually be an improvement.) Whatever our respective singular and collective intents about reproduction, however, the effects—wished for or not—are shared; for to be a "nonprocreative adult," as Sedgwick puts it, winds up being a marker of social difference more important, I'd like to argue, to a cultural critique of marginalities and dominations than one might think (Sedgwick 1990:63). I'm very taken with Michael

Warner's definition of "repro-narrativity" as "the notion that our lives are somehow made more meaningful by being embedded in a narrative of generational succession" (Warner 1991:7). What we might think of as "compulsory repro-narrativity" has everything to do with the radicality of Steedman's formal and theoretical project: what it refuses.

When I was a little girl I had a dollhouse, which I loved with an intensity perhaps peculiar to urban children whose experience of space is an apartment and a shared bedroom. The dollhouse was a present on the only Christmas my sister and I succeeded in getting our guilty assimilationist parents to celebrate (no tree, of course, but stockings hanging from the mantlepiece of the non-working fireplace); after that we returned to the more parsimonious installments of Hanukkah. I played for hours on end with my white-frame house and enlisted my mother's labor in the requirements of my scenarios for its inhabitants. She made doll's clothes—tiny knitted red snowsuits for my five (!) children. There was also a miniature tea set. I'm not sure I actually knew anyone who lived in a house (not to mention with five children), but it didn't seem strange at the time. Most of my playtime was spent either rearranging the furniture, or coming up with names: Cheryl, Beryl, and Meryl. I can't explain the rhyme. Maybe they were triplets. I don't remember actually doing anything with the girls, but I have always been able to remember those three names; maybe the other two were boys. In any event, this failure of imagination—the children's reality was limited to the rooms they would occupy—may have something to do with my subsequent failure actually to conceive.

Recently I revealed the existence of my imaginary children to a colleague with whom I had also been plotting about job negotiations. He said, so when you discuss salary, tell them all the kids are in college now, and you need more money. I laughed because I was amused by the way he reshaped the material, but also because it reminded me how abstract (oddly the word I want here is conceptual) the idea of children or motherhood had always been for me: in my fantasy, they never left their rooms; they certainly never grew up to go to college.

In much the same spirit, Steedman recalls the stationary existence of her two imaginary children, Joan and Maureen, who lived in the flat with her in their blue and green gingham dresses: "I don't know what I did with them when I conjured them up," she writes, "but they were there, behind the mangle all through the summer and winter of 1950–51, as my mother carried my yet-to-be-born baby sister" (91). Following Winnicott, Steedman takes the existence of these "fantasy children" as proof that she had received "good enough" mothering when she was a small child (95). (In Steedman's construction of her history, she had four years of this good-enough-mothering [perhaps directly inspired by her mother's listening to Winnicott on the radio], and then "expulsion from the garden" with the birth of her baby sister, and the concomitant failure of her mother to attach Steedman's father to her and their family by that birth [92].) She associates the cut between Eden and after with her mother's breasts, with the breastfeeding of her little sister, and she comments: "It was with this most familiar part of my mother's body that I came to symbolize her ambivalence towards my existence. What came free could be given freely, like her milk: loving a baby costs very little" (93). Typically, Steedman locates ambivalence in her mother not in herself, but the association, as we will see in a moment, of her mother and knives is open to interpretation. Elizabeth Abel reads the casting of the imaginary children to resemble her mother and herself as "a longing to repair insufficient mothering by remothering both her mother and herself" (Abel 1990:194). Why then did Steedman not go on (as her sister did) ultimately to wish for real children of her own?[4]

Here, close to the center of the book, toward the conclusion of the chapter called "Reproduction and Refusal," is a tantalizing opacity. Steedman seems to tie the wish for a child to a mimetic relation between the mother's and the daughter's body; she thus begins by explaining the difficulty she had accepting her mother's adult female body as her destiny: "My refusal of my mother's body was, I think, a recognition of the problem that my own physical presence represented to her; at the same time it was a refusal of the inexorable nature of that difficulty, that it would go on like that, I would become her, and come to reproduce the circumstances of our straitened unsatisfying life" (95). She then moves on, with no articulated transition, from this class-bound maternal economics to a more general psychological view: "Part of the desire to reproduce oneself as a body, as an entity in the real world, lies in conscious memory of someone approving that body" (95). And again her mother—in memory—fails her. But she moves on to make the wider point of maternal "coldness towards daughters," which draws its power from its conjunction with the daughters' assessment of "the attitude of the social world towards them." In this moment of a double "exclusion"—always a key word for Steedman— the failure of "self-love," which she places "at the root of the wish for a child" (96), takes on its fullest meaning and leads to the refusal to "reproduce."

Now what's tricky in this characteristic moment is the oscillation operating in Steedman's arguments between an economic (class-based) and a psychoanalytic (gender-based) explanation. (These don't have to be incompatible positions—elsewhere in her writing Steedman refers to herself as a "good Freudian"—but they tend to be competitively polarized here [Steedman 1992:615].) On the one hand she garners support for her views from working-class autobiographies; on the other, she acknowledges that daughters' "exile" from maternal attention is recorded in many "literary and autobiographical sources" (Steedman 1986:95), including fairy tales like "The Little Mermaid" and "The Snow Queen," which are foundational in her accounts of childhood fantasies. Nonetheless, throughout the memoir when Steedman seeks to analyze maternal rejection—" 'If it wasn't for you two,' my mother told us, 'I could be off somewhere else' " (39); "Never have children dear, they ruin your life" (85)—she insists on the working-class base of this (her) not-wantedness and in turn on its essential difference from a middle-class, Chodorowian repertoire of relatedness.   ·

Here Steedman footnotes Chodorow's "Afterword" and there takes up objections to her argument: "Some friends and colleagues have said that my account is too unqualified. In fact all women do not mother or want to mother, and all women are not 'maternal' nurturant." Chodorow answers the complaint by saying: "I agree that all claims about gender differences [the point of her book] gloss over important differences within genders and similarities between genders." "Indeed," Steedman writes, "Nancy Chodorow is well aware of the limitations of her account, and knows that it is class and culture bound. Were it not so bound, then the darker social side of the primary relationship between mothers and daughters . . . would have to emerge" (87). Yes, darker, but why locate the breakdown of maternal care, "the removal of the looking-glass," exclusively in the specific scene of material deprivation? What about other styles of maternal ressentiment? (Suleiman 1985; Hirsch 1989).

Steedman's concomitant insistence on her father's distance from the phallus—having a "father who wasn't a patriarch" (Steedman 1986:16)—is crucial to her refusal of what she takes to be a monolithic psychoanalytic discourse that doesn't speak to the experience of working-class girls and women; in particular the desire not to reproduce one's circumstances. But if it is possible to bracket paternal authority (The Name of the Father), at least as the culture's dominant representation of hierarchies of violence, it's less easy to dispose of its familiar symbolics, even when displaced onto the fantasy power regime of the Good Mother.

> A father like mine dictated each day's existence; our lives would have been
> quite different had he not been there. But he didn't *matter*, and his sin-
> gular unimportance needs explaining. His not mattering has an effect like
> this: I don't quite believe in male power; somehow the iron of patriarchy
> didn't enter my soul. I accept the idea of male power intellectually, of
> course (and I will eat my words the day I am raped, or the knife is slipped
> between my ribs; though I know that will not be the case: in the dreams
> it is a woman who holds the knife, and only a woman can kill).   (19)

How are we to understand this linking of a knife between the ribs with
rape in a parenthesis that comes to comment on the failure of patriarchy
to penetrate (the iron of a sword?) one's soul? Who is the woman wield-
ing the knife?[5]

Later in the narrative, Steedman describes a fantasy in which as a
seven-year-old reader of fairy tales, she imagines her parents sitting
naked, cutting each other and "making thin surface wounds like lines
drawn with a sharp red pencil, from which the blood poured." And she
comments, "She was the most cut, but I knew it was she who did the
cutting. I couldn't always see the knife in my father's hand" (54).
Despite the contradictory "evidence" of the fantasy, the daughter maintains her belief in the murderous power of the mother she seems to
eulogize: "Death of a Good Woman."

Playing the gender card against class, and the class card against gender, Steedman set out to challenge both male Marxist readings of autobiography in which "working-class boys . . . grow up to write about their
mother's flinty courage" (17)—and a mythified, motherist, largely
American feminist theory that takes the Persephone/Demeter story as its
foundational myth (86–88). In her refusal of that story as *not true*,
Steedman emphasizes its failure to account for "non-mothering" and the
"economic circumstances and . . . social understanding" in which it
occurs. I want to give both pieces of that intervention their due, but at
the same time I want to try and unhook the motherism under assault by
Steedman—the assumed wish for a child—as well as maternal coldness
from their specific class assignments. This is not to say that there aren't
important local and institutionalized class and racialized differences at
work in the structures of maternal experience; rather that not-wantedness and relatedness are *not only* a matter of class and material deprivation (as Steedman herself sometimes seems to know). What Steedman's
insistence on the detail of maternal experience *as material*—her mother's
longing for a New Look coat—can lead us to do, however, is to cross-
hatch maternal subjectivity with the full spectrum of class activity. For

every class context there's a range of responses inside the mother/daughter/mother/not mother narrative. The consequences (in life, as well as in feminist theory) of the identification/repudiation model we see at work in *Landscape* do not unfold against a unified horizon, even within a national working-class identity (Spence and Holland 1991). If as Adrienne Rich famously declared in *Of Woman Born*, "the cathexis between mother and daughter—essential, distorted, misused—is the great unwritten story," it is not one story either (Rich 1976:225).

It's in this sense that I want to turn now to *A Woman's Story*; for if like Steedman's case study, Ernaux's memoir is an account of two lives, it places them within a very different emotional landscape. Ernaux weaves the trajectory of her mother's life with her own in a double and overlapping chronology of complicity and struggle: her mother's movement out of the peasantry into the life of small shopkeepers; her own, encouraged by her mother, out of that world into a professional class. The end of the mother's life is shaped by the hideous drama of Alzheimer's disease; the daughter's midlife entails a coming to terms with that illness, the death of both her parents, and the confirmation of her new class identity. Ernaux also "reproduces." She has two sons who appear in the narrative primarily in relation to her mother; they allow her mother to assume the identity of a middle-class grandmother. Like her husband, Ernaux's children function primarily as placeholders; they are background figures in the mother/daughter plot.

In Ernaux's memoir the violence of the mother/daughter plot is located in the familial dramas of adolescence; the mother's disgust at her daughter's developing female body becomes explicit in outbursts of rage over clothes: "You're not going out like *that*!" "We both knew," Ernaux writes, "what to expect from each other: she knew I longed to seduce the boys, I knew she was terrified I would 'have an accident,' in other words, that I would start to sleep around and get pregnant." The daughter's evaluation of this struggle takes the succinct form of a remembered guilty wish: "Sometimes I imagined her death would have meant nothing to me" (50).

Although she does not, like Steedman, include references to psychoanalytic and feminist theory within her narrative, Ernaux seems to work out of the Kleinian categories that inform Steedman's reflection: the "good" and "bad" mother, violence and reparation. Writing within the year immediately after her mother's death, Ernaux talks about the difficulty of getting her mother straight.

To get away from these oscillating views, which come from my earliest childhood, I try to describe and explain her life as if I were writing about someone else's mother and a daughter who wasn't me. Still, though I try to write as neutrally as possible, certain expressions, such as "If you ever have an accident . . . " [*s'il t'arrive un malheur*] can never be neutral for me, while others, for instance, "the denial of one's own body and sexuality," remain totally abstract. When I remember these expressions, I experience the same feeling of depression I had when I was sixteen, and fleetingly, I confuse the woman who influenced me most with an African mother pinning her daughter's arms behind her back while the village midwife slices off the girl's clitoris.   (tm, 50–51)

While the reference to clitoridectomy is a relative commonplace in certain kinds of feminist discourse (Steedman's, for instance), it's quite startling in this writerly rememoration.[6] Ernaux, whose mother's fear that her daughter's pregnancy would keep her from the bright and open future she wishes for her, seems to conjure the maternal assault on the clitoris as a local struggle, not a global one (its displacement onto an African mother notwithstanding).

In the memoir, this violent moment is followed by a passage in which Ernaux returns to the past and evokes her crisis of separation, her social disidentification from the mother, which is the dominant and guiding thread of this story. It begins: "I stopped trying to copy her" (51).[7] In the blank between the paragraphs lies the unsaid logic connecting maternal violence, sexual pleasure, and the terms of the daughter's autonomy: "Until I married, I still belonged to her, even when we were living apart" (57).[8] The price of that separation is the recognition of a double split: the daughter both is still and is no longer like the mother; the daughter both is and isn't like herself. The divide is double: separating mother and daughter, disjoining the autobiographical subject from her childhood self.

Ernaux's rage against her mother is located in the body and this body ties (without permanently binding) her to class.

I was ashamed of her brusque manners and speech, especially when I realized how alike we were. I blamed her for being someone who I, by moving into new circles, no longer wanted to be. I discovered that there was a world of difference between wanting to be educated and actually acquiring that knowledge.   (51)

The growing abyss separating the child from the parent produced by education and the acquisition of new knowledge that compounds the

difference is a commonplace of contemporary American autobiographical writing in which the child moves into another world by virtue of
the education the parent has wanted the child to have. But here that
passage is figured—at least through juxtaposition—by the confusion of
images that results in the doubling of intellectual distance by sexual violence. And as in Steedman's memoir, the violence to the daughter comes
from the weapon in the mother's hand. Ernaux, however, does nothing
directly with this image, which cuts the book close to its center; within
the next two pages, the daughter leaves home to go to "boarding
school," and her departure is preceded by a summary of the mother's
view of her daughter in social terms: "Sometimes she saw her own
daughter as a class enemy" (tm, 53). What the mother seems to want to
cut off, then, in her language—"If you ever have an accident"—is the
possibility of a betrayal woven of sex and class.[9] On the one hand she
fears that the daughter's adolescent rebellion, with its bourgeois over-
tones of scorn for social convention, will subvert the education plot, the
Bildung out of the working class into the middle class. On the other, she
demands class loyalty: recognition by the daughter of the mother's values, authority, and vision.

As the daughter who is leaving the mother behind, Ernaux also fears
the inexorability of class betrayal, precisely through an education that
gives her access to new language, new powers of interpretation, and new
models of self-conscious behavior. The last third of the memoir, which is
marked by the death of Ernaux's father, describes the attempt of the two
women to live together in the daughter's house. The experiment of their
life together reveals the complicated ways in which class alignments can
shift within a family over the time of its own history. At her daughter's
house, the mother feels out of place: "I don't think I belong here" (64).
This is not cast, as it might be in an American context, as a psychological
problem. For Ernaux it's a social one in which her mother looks for work
to do in the house to help out, in order, she says jokingly, to pay her way:

> It took me a long time to realize that the feeling of unease my mother
> experienced in my own house was no different from what I had felt as a
> teenager when I was introduced to people a "cut above us." . . . I also
> realized that in pretending to act like the hired help, she instinctively
> translated the real cultural domination of her children's reading *Le
> Monde* or listening to Bach into an imaginary economic domination of
> boss to worker: her form of revolt.   (tm, 78)

In Ernaux's account, despite her identification with her mother's body/story/desires, class differences come to structure the mother/ daughter relation within the family and under the same roof.

The story of what those differences finally mean is inseparable in Ernaux's narrative from the memoir project itself; we could even say that those shifting class divides are Ernaux's subject: to memorialize her mother is to map the passage from the "dominated world" into which her mother was born to the "dominant world" of words (tm, 92).[10] It is in this mapping that we read most clearly the dissonance between Steedman's vision of maternal legacy and Ernaux's. Steedman takes up these issues within (at least between) the lines of her history as well, but she differs from Ernaux in two crucial areas: on the one hand, the stakes of separation; and on the other, in her reluctance (if not her failure) to acknowledge class change within herself, in her own life in the "dominant world" of words as an academic and writer. Steedman's attempt to separate from her mother displays an almost ontological resentment radically unlike Ernaux's essentially adolescent rites of passage: "There exists a letter that I wrote to a friend one vacation from Sussex . . . in which I described my sitting in the evenings with my mother, refusing to go out, holding tight to my guilt and duty, knowing that I *was* her, and that I must keep her company" (19).

Despite this overidentification that would seem to freeze the daughter into immobility, like Ernaux, Steedman has in fact moved on: she has become a social historian, and it is in part, at least, as a historian that she researched the materials of *Landscape*. The University of Sussex, to which she had gone as a student in 1965, is the scene of another vantage point from which she can view her mother's story; even if, as she claims, the cultural narratives available to the women of her generation and class do not feature their scenarios. "And should I have met a woman like me (there must have been some . . .) we could not have talked of escape except within a literary framework . . . ignorant of the material stepping-stones of our escape: clothes, shoes, make-up" (15). In this sense, *Landscape* sets itself the task of producing that missing text: supplying a women's working-class cultural criticism through the autobiography of her childhood as it can be reconstructed through the biography of her mother's.

Steedman acknowledges directly the effects of the process she names as "embourgeoisement and state education" (20), the passage into the "dominant world" Ernaux poignantly invokes, only when she refers to her professional identity as a historian. Beyond that, as readers we come up against a silence, which, following Raymond Williams, Steedman describes negatively as the "cancellation of a writer's present" for the writer who has left (and not left) the working class (Steedman 1986:20; Williams 1989). This silence has everything to do with the elusive quality of her narrative. How can we understand the ways in which the childhood stories continue to be lived in the writing present if the adult story of conflict and desire is completely suppressed?

For instance, as we learned in the passage with which we began, when Steedman goes to visit her dying mother, this is the first time they have seen each other in *nine years*, except, she specifies later in passing, at her father's funeral. This break is not explained—another one of many important silences that underpin (or undermine) the narrative—and the reader is left to conjecture about what's happened. Steedman alludes to their separation obliquely: her father, she writes, "was genuinely shocked when, at twenty-seven, I wrote to my mother and said that I didn't want to see her for a while because she upset me so much" (60). Why? What has happened between them?

If Steedman refuses to supply a motive for their separation, she says only this about their final scene: "An hour later I came away believing that I admired a woman who could, in these circumstances and in some pain, treat me as if I had just stepped round the corner for a packet of tea." This was, Steedman remarks in a tone that is eerily jubilant, the way things had always been: "We were truly illegitimate, outside any law of recognition: the mirror broken, a lump of ice for a heart" (142). Without the mirroring of Winnicottian mothering that allows the daughter to want to reproduce, any form of continuity and social exchange seems permanently damaged. Or is it the other way round? Perhaps we should interpret the daughter's admiration for her mother's indifference as confirmation of their ultimate bond: not their identity, but the daughter's will to identification.[11]

In the late seventies, my sister, who at the beginning of the sixties had set out to declass herself through her relations and activities and to separate herself from our middle-class parents, decided to quit her job as a day-care worker and try to earn her living as a potter. What stood between this desire and her ability to put it into practice was the price of a kiln, a basic element of a potter's studio. My mother offered to stake her to the equipment, and by way, she thought, of encouragement, added jokingly: "Don't worry, if it doesn't work out I can take it as a business loss on my taxes." A few days later, she received a note from my sister in which she announced that in view of our mother's lack of confidence in her ability to make a go of it—she always "rained on her parade"—she would not be seeing her for a while. And she didn't. Almost five years later my sister reluctantly came to see our mother who was rapidly dying of cancer. Our mother, who in response had written my sister out of her will, like Steedman's, betrayed neither anger nor surprise when her daughter showed up, but the wounds remained open on both sides.

This kind of violence between mother and daughter, which attests to the shattering of the mirror, crosses class identities as it shatters any comfortable motherism.[12] There's a particular rage, I think, *in and between* mothers and daughters that comes precisely from women's inability to *choose* motherhood, in the sense that they/we cannot possibly know *what* they/we are choosing. And of course, in not choosing it to know *what* has been refused.

Ernaux's memoir offers another kind of story about separation, identification, and attachment. If Steedman's account is fueled by "matrophobia," the fear "of *becoming one's mother*,"[13] Ernaux's is punctuated by "matrophilia," the desire to become her mother (or at least one with her), despite, or even through, the displacement a university education entails, and her transformation into a writer. "Throughout the ten months I was writing this book," Ernaux reveals toward the end of her memoir, "I dreamed of her almost every night. Once I was lying in the middle of a stream, caught between two currents. From my genitals [*de mon sexe*], smooth again like a young girl's, from between my thighs, long tapering plants floated limply. The body they came from was not only mine, it was also my mother's" (89–90). The book called *Une femme* is an act of emotional reconnection that passes through two bodies joined in resemblance. Nonetheless, the book depends on their separateness: "I believe I am writing about my mother because it is my turn to bring her into the world" (32).

The memoir of the dead other is both for oneself and for others: "Over the past few days," Ernaux explains in the writing notes that shape the memoir, "I have found it more and more difficult to write, possibly because I would like never to reach this point. And yet I know I shall have no peace of mind until I find the words which will reunite the demented woman she had become with the strong, radiant woman she once was" (76). But this separation is not only for her. When her mother starts talking to imaginary people, Ernaux first puts her hands over her ears not to hear. Then, "to make the thought bearable," she describes what's happening on a scrap of paper: "Maman's talking to herself." Finally, she explains toward the memoir's close, "I'm writing those same words now, but for other people, so that they can understand" (tm, 80).[14] Can they?

In the frame to *Landscape*, the two-page prelude entitled "Death of a Good Woman," Steedman, we saw, enlists Beauvoir's internal gloss on her mother's final suffering. "Simone de Beauvoir wrote of her mother's death, said that in spite of the pain it was an easy one: an upper-class death. Outside, for the poor, dying is a different matter" (2). Because she is so determined to maintain the difference class always makes, however, Steedman cuts out the heart of Beauvoir's irony. She omits the original appearance of the phrase, which occurs in Beauvoir's description of the actual moment of agony:

> Maman had almost lost consciousness. Suddenly she cried, "I can't breathe!" Her mouth opened, her eyes stared wide, huge in that wasted, ravaged face: with a spasm she entered into coma. . . .
>
> Already she was no longer there—her heart was beating and she breathed, sitting there with glassy eyes that saw nothing. And then it was over. "The doctors said she would go out like a candle: it wasn't like that at all," said my sister, sobbing.
>
> "But, Madame," replied the nurse, "I assure you it was a very easy death."   (Beauvoir 1965:88)

Beauvoir's commitment to demystifying human experience, to seeing identity as the effect of a construction, compels her to refuse the clichés of death—"there is no such thing as a natural death"—just as she famously refused them of life: "one is not born, rather one becomes a woman." Although Beauvoir's vision therefore necessarily includes self-consciousness about the socially situated nature of experience, her project in this memoir is not uniquely focused on that aspect of a failing body's reality. Rather, she scrupulously charts the tension between the living's caretaking and the dying's suffering: "Without our obstinate watchfulness she would have suffered far more. For indeed, comparatively speaking, her death was an easy one" (94). But "comparatively speaking" does not erase the death work of the body as a "defenseless thing," which gives Beauvoir, we might say, her material, and her text. The memoir graphs this body in pain, a body located, even rooted in class distinctions (and Beauvoir is merciless in her critique of hospital hierarchy, on the one hand, and her mother's snobbery on the other); and yet in the end, what we retain are less the ways in which class markers divide bodies—the screen that blocks the gaze of the dying poor—than the ways in which bodies demand our attention despite the protection or vulnerabilities of class.[15] Steedman's misreading of Beauvoir is critically productive, however, for it gives us another metaphor with which to figure the blindness of her insight as a writer: is not class the screen, the "good mother" screen that stands between a daughter and the rage at work in her own project? Elizabeth Abel makes the point clearly: "What the class configuration consistently inhibits is the direct articulation of anger and the endorsement of psychoanalytic accounts of childhood ambivalence that might seem . . . to blame the victim" (1990:194). The ambivalence Steedman refuses herself—and her mother—traverses her texts by its silence. Ernaux names the ambivalence and incorporates it. Steedman seems to remain a prisoner of past rage.

In the same way, despite the announced transparency of the "curtainless bedroom" (2) in which the origins of this story are said to be located, screening her own class displacements from view, Steedman refuses all allies (Yeo 1988:44).

Let us return now to two images I think we can take as emblems of what's at stake in both these daughters' memoirs, indebted in their different ways to Beauvoir's: Ernaux's of her mother "confused" with the African mother whose constraint enables the daughter's clitoridectomy; Steedman's of patriarchy's force as the woman with the knife. But what do they tell us?

To the extent that the maternal memoirs tell the story of a daughter's emergence out of her class culture and by the act of writing itself mark her difference from that place, perhaps we should understand the threatened knife cut not only as a metaphor for the mother's resistance to the daughter's autonomy but also for the daughter's rage to be free, her need to leave the mother behind. I want to suggest that the violence is mutual, and these images its signature. This is not to say that the rupture is always fatal, although it seems to have been for Steedman. Here we can speculate that it was only by breaking class patterns of attachment and violently tearing the bonds that tied mother and daughter to each other that she could move into the writer's space. By making herself into a case study, however, we might argue that she did reproduce herself, especially if we understand, as Barbara Johnson suggests, that the "autobiographical desire par excellence" is "the desire for resemblance, the desire to create a being like oneself" (Johnson 1987:146).

Is this the necessary path of a daughter's authority? There is, of course, no single answer, but I think that these violent embodiments of mother/daughter engagement supply powerful allegories for contemporary autobiographical writing by women who wish to perform a cultural analysis. Like *Landscape* and *A Woman's Story* their texts will be marked by a double specificity: this will entail the representation of both the local material culture in which all childhood scenarios are rooted, and of the heavily freighted passage that characterizes a daughter's negotiation with maternal power: this will include betrayal and mutilation, hatred, and sometimes love. This may mean that to some the testimony will not seem to bear the weight of (universal) authority because it feels too particular, too close to the maternal body, too monstrous. That, of course, is also its challenge.

In closing I recur to *A Very Easy Death* for another, more ambiguous image of these legacies. In her final, delirious moments, Françoise de Beauvoir speaks incoherently: "I should have liked to have the time to bring out my book. . . . She must be allowed to breastfeed whomever she likes" (tm, 88). I want to suggest that Beauvoir's text becomes that source of nurturance, severed, so to speak, from its metaphor of maternal nourishment. What I'm sketching here is the position of giving separated from a natural body and recast in a writer's repertoire. Beauvoir had the time to bring out her book. We've had the time to read it. But what kind of readers are we? And what kind of daughters?[16] The figure Ernaux assigns herself in this project is that of "archivist" (16): it is to her that falls the task of recording the end of a certain tradition: of "household tips which lessened the strain of poverty"; of a certain maternal lore that was passed on from mother to daughter. But there is also another task besides ending a tradition. By virtue of changing classes, Ernaux transforms its household materials. "Isn't writing," she asks toward the end of her memoir, "also a way of giving?" (91).

These memoirs (and I include Beauvoir's) embody a daughter's knowledge about women and class: lived and retrospective, of it and at a distance from it. But not only. Or rather they show how talking about class *also* allows us to talk about that which is both most us and what escapes us, since it is where we come from, and not necessarily, in these instances, where we remain, what Steedman calls elsewhere "the lost past within each of us" (1992:616). It is only because we have left those childhood places—the places we were made to occupy—that we can write of it. Writing this past is implicitly to acknowledge our own self-division; the nostalgia for, inseparable from, the loathing of identity as a cultural fact. This knowledge, therefore, is a source of loneliness—we are cut off from the origin stories, the bond is broken—and at the same time a possible reconnection: since the memoir is a form of testimony that posits an addressee, we get to retell these stories so that our version of "pastness" gets to be heard. This also takes us, however fleetingly, out of the very family history has allotted us.

The inevitable price of writing *out* of the family is that it stays *in* the family, but because autobiography always operates in the tension between the writer's published family plot and the reader's private one, readers are likely to respond with a story of their own, like hers and also different, with other hearts of darkness, and other screens.

Cultural criticism cannot do without these stories. What remains to be seen is what it can do with them.

Coda, in which I add an autobiographical death to the list.

Like Annie Ernaux's, my mother died on April 7. It was more than ten years ago. She had been in a coma for several weeks and finally her heart ceased beating. She died of lung cancer that had spread to her bones, throughout her body. The odd thing was that after a while she didn't seem to be in pain and had stopped taking all medication. The night she died we all went as usual to the Seder at her sister's house. No one cried or even said anything; it was as though nothing had happened, and I suppose in a way nothing had: she had already left us behind with her body; the doctor said she'd been out of touch with reality. The next day my father and I, like co-conspirators, trudged through the snow, unexpected so late in a New York spring, to the vault where I retrieved the jewelry she had left me in her will. No more than Steedman's, my mother did not die alone; she had a middle-class death, which resembled her life. At the funeral, the rabbi, counting the house, said it was a really good turnout, especially considering the weather.

NOTES

I'd like to thank Elizabeth Abel, John Brenkman, Rachel Brownstein, Mary Childers, Elizabeth Houlding, Alice Kaplan, and Sally O'Driscoll for their comments on earlier versions of this essay. I'd also like to express my gratitude to the audiences at the English Institute, the University of Wisconsin-Madison, SUNY Buffalo, the Center for Twentieth-Century Studies at Milwaukee, the Center for Literary Studies, Harvard University, the University of Rochester, and the Feminism and Legal Theory Project at Columbia University for their questions and responses to the work in progress.

1. I have occasionally made changes in Leslie's translation of Ernaux and have indicated this by the symbol *tm*.

2. Steedman seems to have assumed, as did Beauvoir and her sister, and my

sister and I, that to have children was necessarily to reproduce one's mother's life in the gender and number of one's children: to wit, that one would have girls (never boys) who would have the identical—negative—feelings about their parents (us).

3. I was startled to read in the brief author biography that accompanied an early and embryonic, so to speak, version of *Landscape*, which Steedman published in Liz Heron's collection of autobiographical writing, *Truth, Dare, or Promise: Girls Growing Up in the 50s,* that Steedman was married: "I got married in 1971—already an established relationship. No children," she writes, "nor shall I have any now, I think." She goes on to quote Hannah Cullick speaking of her baby nephew, as she does in *Landscape* at some length (Heron 1985:85–86).

4. It's curious that Steedman doesn't feel the need to explain why her sister took another path, since she seems to have had even less compassion for her mother than Steedman. "My sister," Steedman writes, "with children of her own and perhaps thereby with a clearer measure of what we lacked, tells me to recall a mother who never played with us, whose eruptions from irritation into violence were the most terrifying of experiences; and she is there, the figure of nightmares, though I do find it difficult to think about it in this way" (46).

Again, the author biography in *Truth, Dare, or Promise* tells us more than the autobiography: "My sister had her first baby at seventeen, her second nine years later. She's done it all by herself on social security. We're both daughters of the state, but she's poor and I'm not" (Heron 1985:125).

5. Elizabeth Abel discusses Steedman's absolute refusal to theorize either her ambivalent feelings toward her mother or the division of feeling between her father and mother in which her father's failures are poignantly lamented (Abel 1990:194): "But daddy, you never knew me like this; you didn't really care, or weren't allowed to care, it comes to the same thing in the end" (Steedman 1986:61). This title chiastically echoes Germaine Greer's autobiography: *Daddy, We Hardly Knew You.*

The metaphor of penetration returns at the end of the chapter dedicated to her father: "But daddy, you never knew me like this. . . . You shouldn't have left us there, you should have taken me with you. You left me alone; you never laid a hand on me: the iron didn't enter the soul. You never gave me anything: the lineaments of an unused freedom" (61).

6. Steedman, in the course of her critique of Nancy Chodorow's on the whole cheerful account of "gendered identification" between baby girls and their mothers in the (white, American) middle classes, remarks: "For it is women who socialize little girls into acceptance of a restricted future, women who used to bind the feet, women who hold down the daughter for clitoridectomy, and who, in more familiar and genteel ways, fit their daughters for self-abasement" (1986:87).

7. This phrase in French—"*elle a cessé d'être mon modèle*"—recalls Colette's famous celebratory self-identification with her mother: "*Imaginez-vous, à me*

lire, que je fais mon portrait? Patience: c'est seulement mon modèle." This is the epigraph to *La Naissance du Jour* [*Break of Day*] and provides us with the euphoric countertext of the daughter's identification with the mother. She describes the cost of separation in her late memoir: *Mes Apprentissages.*

8. These become the subject of Ernaux's novels; *Les armoires vides* (1974) opens on the scene of an abortion.

9. The daughter's pleasure is translated into the mother's anxiety about reproduction, which in turn codes an anxiety about class identity. Ernaux takes up this same expression in *La Place* (1987a:100) as well as her parents' sense of their own future: "He had learned the essential condition for not reproducing the misery of the previous generation: not to forget oneself in a woman" (65, my translation). Ernaux's parents determine not to reproduce their parents' poverty by having only one child; when their first child dies, they replace her with Annie.

10. The editor of *La Place* for the Methuen text, P. M. Wetherill, connects Ernaux's project here to that of Pierre Bourdieu (24–25); I think there's a parallel to be worked out here between Ernaux's relation to Bourdieu's thought and Steedman's to that of Raymond Williams: gendering the class analyses through their literary experiments.

11. I am indebted to my conversation with Ruth Perry for this reading.

12. This style of separation is described interestingly in Wini Breines's *Young, White, and Miserable: Growing Up Female in the Fifties* (Boston: Beacon, 1992) as a form of cultural dissidence.

13. The term is developed by Adrienne Rich in *Of Woman Born*, but in fact it was coined by Lynn Sukenick, another poet (1976:235). Rich defines it this way: "Matrophobia can be seen as a womanly splitting of the self, in the desire to become purged once and for all of our mothers' bondage, to become individuated and free. The mother stands for the victim in ourselves, the unfree woman, the martyr. Our personalities seem dangerously to blur and overlap with our mothers'; and, in a desperate attempt to know where mother ends and daughter begins, we perform radical surgery" (236). In *The Mother/Daughter Plot*, Marianne Hirsch reads matrophobia as "the underside of the feminist family romance" (1989:136).

14. In describing the writing she elaborated for *La Place* Ernaux talks about a flat style [*l'écriture plate*], the style of observation [*constat*] she used in answering her parents' letters: "They would have experienced any stylistic effects as a way of keeping them at a distance" (*La Place* 91). In some way, the writing of *A Woman's Story* is about refusing that distance; it functions like a letter meant to be opened and read.

15. Is it necessary to say that I'm not arguing that bodies transcend class? Rather that insistence on their class origins is not the only path to take in the emotional disarray produced by the urgency of death work.

16. In a talk at the CUNY Graduate Center (May 1992), Christie McDon-

ald remarked on the persistence of the maternal/filial metaphorics: "Beauvoir would set the example of a woman whose achievements depended upon and were articulated around the refusal of biological motherhood, yet she became the symbolic mother of the feminist movement. " And she goes on to observe: "Although she could probably not have predicted how complex and paradoxical the question of the mother was going to become, Beauvoir's own private discourse on the mother, as demonstrated in *A Very Easy Death*, shows to what extent she depended on that very person (her mother) whose status . . . she was to reject" (ms.).

In a 1992 British public television program called "Beauvoir's Daughters," Ann Oakley claimed that for women of her generation (she was born in 1944), Beauvoir was like a mother: "In that way, she's been the Mother, the mother we wished we'd had." Despite the fact that as a teacher of feminist theory I certainly think of Beauvoir (like Woolf) as a precursor or "foremother" of modern feminism, even a Symbolic Mother, I was actually quite surprised by that view of Beauvoir as a "real" mother, coming in to cheer one on and say the sorts of things you wished your mother would say. I took Beauvoir's refusal of motherhood seriously enough not to "matromorphize" her into my own. Or perhaps I've always taken her as a dead mother, which is to say an authorizing word, or as some have put it recently, the "Law of the Mother." See Julia Creet's "Daughter of the Movement: The Psychodynamics of Lesbian S/M Fantasy" in *Differences* 3, no. 2 (Summer 1991): 135–59.

2 | Mother from Child: Perspectives on Separation and Abandonment

CAROL SANGER

In J. M. Barrie's *Peter Pan*, Peter implores a hesitant Wendy to come with him to Neverland as a much needed surrogate mother for his band of followers, the Lost Boys. As part of his recruitment effort, Peter explains to Wendy that the Lost Boys are "children who fall out of their perambulators when the nurse is looking the other way. If they are not claimed within seven days they are sent far away to the Neverland to defray expenses" (Barrie 1985:28). To modern sensibilities, this practice by the mothers of London may appear less like reasonable fiscal policy than like a triple abandonment: mother consigns child to nurse; nanny loses child overboard; neither files a claim so the state dispatches the child to Neverland.

While certain aspects of *Peter Pan* may seem old-fashioned or culturally dated (the redskins, for example), one feature remains remarkably vivid. The theme of children being lost by careless mothers or abandoned by willful ones has nestled itself comfortably and, as far as one can tell, permanently into the culture. Of course, apart from movies like *Home Alone*, mothers today do not lose their children quite as literally as in *Peter Pan*, failing to notice the children are even missing. Still, children are currently designated as "lost" or motherless in a great range of circumstances: their mothers may work or attend school; they may be in prison or on vacation; they may have lost custody in a divorce; they may have died.

Indeed, the modern approach is often to designate the *mother* as the one who is missing instead of the child. *She* is not where she is supposed

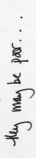

they may be poor . . . .

to be, which in many cases means simply that she is not at home. While she may have good reasons to be elsewhere, the reasons for the mother's absence are often of less interest to her children (of whatever age), to their teachers or therapists, or to judges and social workers making custody determinations than the simple *fact* of her absence.

The result is that while mothers and children may be separated from one another in response to a broad range of economic and social circumstances, maternal absence is often characterized less as a separation than as abandonment. But while the two terms are often used interchangeably, separation and abandonment are not the same. Physical separations between mothers and children are familiar, often ordinary occurrences. Mothers separate from children when they leave them with baby-sitters or hospitalize them for illness. A separation can be voluntary (mother places child in day care) or involuntary (child starts kindergarten). In contrast, abandonment connotes a separation that is brought about deliberately and intended to be permanent. In its more judgmental uses, it implies a kind of recklessness; one who abandons gives little thought or care to the fate of those left behind.

In this essay I want to explore the way differences between these two concepts—separation and abandonment—depend on the perspective from which the mother's act is viewed. My argument is that at levels ranging from individual complaint to social policy to legal rules, we have gotten too cozy with the child's perspective regarding absent mothers. From that vantage, especially in an age when terms such as "bonding" and "abandonment" are tossed around on playgrounds (Eyer 1993), physical separations between mothers and their children are often experienced, or at least articulated, by the child as abandonment.

It is time, however, to develop a maternal perspective on separations between mothers and their children. One of feminism's achievements has been its insistence on multiple perspectives. That practice now includes viewing and reviewing issues (or statutes or novels) from the point of view of those whose behavior is being regulated or described but who in many instances are rarely consulted. The investigation of separation and abandonment here expands the field of inquiry to include the perspective of mothers.

The endeavor has several dimensions. The first is to focus less on the consequences of separations for the child and more on the circumstances under which separations occur in the first place. Why is the mother leaving her child? What is in it for her? For her child? I want also to question the accuracy of the consequences of separation as we have come to understand them. Despite the legacy of John Bowlby's foundational work on institutionalized children during the Second World War (Bowlby 1951), maternal absence is not always maternal deprivation and not all separations result in separation anxiety. Nonetheless, the theme of the absent mother and abandoned child is a familiar feature of modern life. In popular culture, for example, motherless sitcom families became a staple of television programming in the early 1990s (Horowitz 1991); a decade earlier, viewers had been introduced to the disappearing mother in the movie *Kramer vs. Kramer* (Kaplan 1992).

I focus here on two other areas, one representational, the other real, in which the absent mother has established a formidable presence. The first is a genre of contemporary fiction in which maternal abandonment appears as a regular, almost predictable phenomenon or complaint from the child narrator. The second area is law, which defines the term *abandonment* with relative clarity. Abandonment is "the conscious disregard of parental obligations" or a parent's "consistent failure, over a substantial period of time, to communicate with the child, to support him, or to take any real interest in him" (Clark 1988:895–96).

The legal definition of abandonment attempts to govern behavior; that is law's usual task. In contrast, the literary accounts are less concerned with regulating a mother's behavior than with chronicling its emotional consequences for her child, often as expressed by the child her- or himself. There is, however, an increasing blurring of jurisdictional lines as the law moves out from the apparently secure terrain of applying a definition to the more contested business of telling a story. Mothers regularly separate from their children in ways that fall far short of a consistent failure to provide parental support. They may be motivated by civic duty (mother works for a ballot initiative or for the PTA), economic need (mother works for pay), or patriotism (mother volunteers for active service during Persian Gulf War). In each case, however, claims of abandonment, not always faint, are registered even when the strict definition would obviously not apply.

This is in part because the idea and the vocabulary of abandonment now has tremendous currency within the culture. Widows and widowers express a sense of intense abandonment upon the death of a spouse; patients feel abandoned by their psychiatrists during the month of August; baseball fans work up claims of abandonment whenever their team eyes another city. None of these complaints is inauthentic. At the same time, we would be unlikely to characterize the spouse, the psychi-

atrist, or even the team as consciously disregarding obligations to partner, patient, or fan. No doubt anyone who has been left behind may
experience something close to the feeling of abandonment. However,
the issue here is the dissonance between how the act is experienced and
an accurate description of what the actor has done.

In the case of mother-child separations, the situation is complicated
by the demographics of the relationship itself. We start with the fact of
adult and child, the latter by definition requiring care and supervision,
the former by statute required to care. More significant, the separations
under discussion here are between not just any adult and child, but
between *mother* and child. Her affection and care are understood as natural duties compelled by instinct and love, not law.

This assumption of devotion was, however, unmatched by traditional measures of power. Until the late nineteenth century mothers
were not even entitled to custody of their children. The twentieth century has compensated for this historical imbalance in parental legal
authority with a vengeance. The combination of a late-nineteenth-cen-
tury, romantic-religious image of (at least) white motherhood with
twentieth-century Freudian culture has established mothers as all-powerful beings with regard to their children, responsible not just for raising them but for how they turn out as well. The law's view is that a
mother, like any all-powerful being, must be sufficiently constrained by
legal rules to ensure that her power is used appropriately.

Mothers leaving children is now understood as a transcendent and
highly charged moral issue. This was not always the case. Historian
Linda Gordon explains:

> [I]n the nineteenth century a mother's attempt to place out her children
> was often encouraged and even applauded as evidence of an appropriate
> and rational commitment to the child's good. By the mid-twentieth cen-
> tury a mother making such a request would almost certainly be viewed
> as unloving, unmotherly, forfeiting her future credibility as a mother.
> (Gordon 1989:162)

There are, of course, certain circumstances where maternal decisions
to separate from her children are not only applauded but assumed. One
example is the dramatic evacuation of schoolchildren from London
during the Second World War. Mothers were expected as a matter of
national duty to send their children away on a day's notice to unknown
destinations, for an indefinite period, and with no assurance of reunion.
The historical circumstances of the Blitz eased any judgment about

mothers who sent their children away to strangers. (Indeed, only recently has attention been paid to the experiences of the children themselves, most now in middle age and many having suffered greatly at the hands of their hosts [Wicks 1988].) Under such circumstances we seem, perhaps reasonably, to have a greater tolerance for the public good than for the mother's.

The wartime evacuations introduce class as well as historical circumstance among the factors used to judge maternal separation decisions. By the fall of 1939, the children of many upper-class Londoners had already left the city, not in response to the evacuation plan but as part of their annual departure to public school. Despite the tearful nature of these partings, recorded in such fictional works as A. N. Wilson's *Incline Our Hearts*, it was a matter of duty and maturity on the part of mother and child alike to overcome the trauma of separating. Although the practice had been long established as a custom among the English ruling class, there was considerable surprise by senior evacuation administrators when some working-class mothers resisted the evacuation plan, some refusing to participate altogether.

As this wartime example most sensibly suggests not all separations are abandonments, at least in the legal sense of a "conscious disregard of parental obligation." Nonetheless, when the two terms are confused with one another, the costs to the mother whose behavior is under review are often quite high. If courts conclude a mother has abandoned her children, she may well lose custody of them. As a 1994 Michigan custody case made clear, maternal absences far short of what anyone would consider abandonment, such as putting a child in day care while the mother attends class, disqualify mothers in circumstances that would seem normal—indeed commendable!—were a father the one not at home. At least with regard to white middle-class families, there is nothing worse a mother can do than to leave her child. Her absence itself is understood as the injury.

This "fact" was put in place through the influential work of British psychiatrist John Bowlby's on "maternal deprivation." According to Bowlby, the result of maternal deprivation was that "the child's development is almost always retarded—physically, intellectually, and socially" (Bowlby 1951:15). Bowlby's study focused the agenda for much subsequent research on the relationship between child development and attachment. As one critic points out, despite the fact that "two decades of empirical research have failed to document the negative consequences predicted by the maternal deprivation-attachment theory

ex: The Queen Mother

hypothesis . . . the quality of the child's attachment to mother continues to be defined as *the* essential characteristic of infant emotional
development" (Silberman 1991; Eyer 1993).

Without question, the message has gotten through to mothers. As a
television critic recently explained, "the rash of [current] shows without
mothers can be traced to a confluence of psychological, sociological,
and economic factors, including the exploitation of every working
mother's most basic guilt about deserting her children and the flip side
of that—a child's fear of abandonment caused by women's changing
roles in society" (Horowitz 1991:23, col.1).

But this view of maternal absence, whatever its prevalence, too readily accepts the child's perspective. I do not want to deny that some children are actually abandoned or that others suffer from their mothers'
absence in circumstances that fall short of the legal definition of abandonment. At the same time, children are not always our best sources of
authority. They may feel injured anytime they get less of their mother's
time. Consider the arrival of a new sibling. Despite common grievances
on this score by the firstborn child, most parents do not let that articulation of loss determine family planning policies. More important, the
child's complaint rarely takes account of why the separation occurred,
or why the mother chose to negotiate the circumstance as she did. The
child's perspective is rooted in the immediate present; the child may be
unable to grasp the medium or long-term advantages to his or her own
interests, let alone the interests of others.

To understand the tenacity and power of what I have labeled as the
child's perspective, I propose a list of recent novels, each about and from
the perspective of a teenage girl whose mother has left her, whether
through death, divorce, drunkenness, emotional distance, or actual
abandonment. The novels are Louise Erdrich's *The Beet Queen*, Nora
Gibbon's *Ellen Foster*, Josephine Humphreys's *Rich in Love*, Susan
Minot's *Monkeys*, Joyce Carol Oates's *Because It Is Bitter and Because It
Is My Heart*, Jane Vandenburgh's *Failure to Zigzag*, Margaret Atwood's
Cat's Eye, and P. D. James's thriller *Innocent Blood*. The collection functions as an antidote to the peculiar gender imbalance found in Neverland where there were no Lost Girls but only Boys, girls being "much
too clever to fall out of their prams" (Barrie 1985:28).

Of course, lost or motherless girls are not unique to twentieth-century fiction. Jane Austen's heroines were rarely raised by mothers—and
almost never by mothers with any sense. Susan Peck MacDonald
explains the absence of mothers in Austen as a response to the com-

bined demands of the novel and of adolescence: "In order for these girls to mature as successfully independent adults—and in order for the novels to focus centrally upon them—the most powerful outside personality, the person who could best facilitate the adolescent's social rites of passage, but who could in doing so upset the balance of the adolescent's precariously sought selfhood, the Mother, must be kept at some sort of distance" (MacDonald 1980:68).

The absence of mothers in contemporary novels may serve a similar function, a form of compulsory individuation. There remains, however, at least one difference. These modern daughters are angry about their missing mothers and quite vocal about it. They know perfectly well that the cause of their distress has nothing to do with carelessness in a perambulator. In contrast to Austen's heroines, the daughters here do not acquiesce in the separation, especially when they know full well that the mother herself has brought it about. We get a sense of this from the opening paragraph of *Rich in Love* by Josephine Humphreys:

> On an afternoon two years ago, my life veered from its day-in day-out course and became for a short while the kind of life that can be told as a story—that is, one in which events appear to have meaning. Before, there had been nothing worth telling the world. We had our irregularities; but every family has something out of whack. But nothing about us was story material. Until the day, May 10, when one of us betrayed the rest and set off a story worth telling.   (1)

The traitor was the teenage narrator's mother; the betrayal was the mother deciding to end her marriage and move out of the family home.

While the daughter's indictment seems severe, philosopher Judith Shklar makes the connection between the vice of betrayal and the fact of maternal absence seem obvious and inevitable. Shklar returns us to the stories of childhood and argues:

> The fairy tale of Hansel and Gretel derives a great part of its enduring hold on the imagination because it is the epitome of what children fear most: that they will be abandoned by their parents. Contemporary psychology has shown us over and over again how deep and enduring and significant for our whole lives this earliest of terrors is. Whenever our friends desert us that unquenchable uneasiness wells up in us, and we, however momentarily, are infants again.   (Shklar 1984:139–40)

A stunning example of this terror occurs in an early scene from Louise Erdrich's novel *The Beet Queen*. A destitute, Depression-era mother of three wanders with her children to a local charity fair, The

Orphan's Picnic. The family joins a crowd of other onlookers to watch a dashing stunt pilot, the Great Omar, do flips and spins above the fairground. Readers then join the "narrator-daughter," who explains:

> I was not prepared for what came next.
>
> Without a backward look, without a word, with no warning and no hesitation, [my mother] elbowed through the people collected at the base of the grandstand and stepped into the cleared space around the pilot. . . . After he helped my mother into the passenger's cockpit and jumped in behind the controls, he pulled a pair of green goggles down over his face. And then there was a startling, endless moment, as they prepared for the take-off. . . . The plane lurched forward, lifted over the low trees, gained height. The Great Omar circled the field in a low swoop. [After a time] the crowd thinned. People drifted away. . . . By the time I looked into the sky, the Great Omar was flying away from the fairgrounds with my mother. Soon the plane was only a white dot, then it blended into the pale blue sky and vanished.   (12)

The scene depicts abandonment in abrupt and terrifying form. The scene evokes a range of emotions: sympathy for the children, anxiety and horror as the mother vanishes, and perhaps relief that this is, after all, just a novel.

Little relief is provided by my last example, taken from P. D. James's best-selling novel *Innocent Blood*. The story compares the depth of children's anger toward mothers who leave them with their anger toward any other crime the mother may have committed. The central innocent is Phillippa, a ferociously bright eighteen-year-old adopted as a child by a professor and his wife. Phillippa has applied under Britain's adoption records act for her original birth certificate in order to identify and locate her natural parents. As Phillippa tells the social worker during the compulsory counseling session, she knows only that her natural mother had been an unwed servant girl at a grand country house who died shortly after Phillipa's birth and that her father was an unnamed aristocrat who had visited the country house briefly.

The birth certificate reveals a very different sort of lineage. Her mother and father had been married after all and listed their occupations as "housewife" and "clerk." More crucially, following some simple detective work, Phillippa learns that both parents were criminals; her father raped and her mother then murdered a twelve-year-old girl. Phillippa now understands that she was put up for adoption not because of her mother's death but because of her mother's imprisonment. In fact, her mother is still alive, serving out the end of her sentence for the raped child's murder.

Once these facts are uncovered, the plot of *Innocent Blood* becomes a race of sorts: Phillippa's efforts to build some sort of a life with her mother, newly released from prison, competing against the efforts of the murdered girl's father to find and kill his daughter's murderer.

Although rape, murder, and revenge initially seize the reader's attention, the twist in *Innocent Blood* centers on the difference between separation and abandonment. On a short visit to her adopted father, Phillippa learns that her natural mother had given her up long before the murder or imprisonment. Her mother had beaten Phillippa throughout her early childhood, and after one particularly serious hospitalization, the mother had finally agreed to place the child for adoption.

This news—her mother's *voluntary* decision—to give her up, presents Phillippa with a form of maternal rejection she cannot absorb. She confronts her mother in an uncomprehending fury: "Was I such a nuisance, so much trouble? Couldn't you have tried with me a little longer?" Her mother then asks, *"Is what I did to you so much more difficult to forgive than what I did to that child?"* Phillippa responds with a curse: "I don't want to see you ever again. I wish they'd hanged you nine years ago. I wish you were dead" (318–19). Phillippa storms out, calms down, and comes back, only to discover that her mother has killed herself.

For plot purposes, the suicide deprives the victim's father of his chance for retribution. For our purposes, the exchange between mother and daughter underscores the utter intolerability of a mother voluntarily leaving her child, whether the mother's departure was in the child's interest or not. This feature is common to each of the fictional vignettes presented. Each mother made a deliberate, intentional move away from her daughter. Each mother *could* have stayed but chose not to. No one *had* to fly away, get divorced, or put a child up for adoption.

Of course, this description is not quite accurate. In *Innocent Blood* the mother agreed to her child's adoption because she knew she would continue to harm her; for whatever reasons, the mother knew she could not care for her child and decided they were better off without one another. In *Rich in Love*, the mother could have stayed in her meaningless marriage "for the sake of the children," as earlier generations of parents have done. Instead, she moved out, though not very far away, leaving her teenage daughters under the care of their father.

In *The Beet Queen*, the mother does abandon her children and, acting for the moment as child-protective service workers, readers might reasonably seek to terminate her parental rights on the ground of abandonment. We might also register a series of other facts: that the children were illegitimate, that their natural father died suddenly leaving neither the mother nor children with support or any claim on his estate, that the family had just been evicted and had no food, and that the previous night the deeply depressed mother has considered smothering her infant because she had no milk to feed it. Of course, awareness of that history might *not* change the outcome of a hearing on termination; the argument here is not mothers are justified in whatever they do with their children so long as maternal circumstances are sufficiently dire. The point is rather that the fact of maternal separation alone does not provide us with enough information to decide what a responsible social or legal response might look like.

For this we might turn again to literature. Novels cause us to see familiar phenomena in new and disconcerting ways. We read not just for escape or entertainment but, as it is often said, to "enrich our lives." The enrichment comes about through a process of deepening our perceptions, "thickening" them, in Geertz's sense of the word, through an imaginative investment in fictional observations and descriptions. Using literature to capture experience, to try out a different perspective, is particularly satisfying around the issue of motherhood, where there has been profound dissatisfaction by women with other accounts of what mothering is like or should be—the endless and aggressively imposed opinions of professional experts, for example (Ehrenreich and English 1978).

How then might we begin to think differently about the issue of separation? How might the *mother's* position, at times her predicament, be included in the calculation? Here I return to *Peter Pan*, though not to Peter Pan the Avenger, but to Wendy. One of the reasons Peter needed Wendy was so that the Lost Boys would have a mother to tell them stories. This aspect of motherhood in Neverland appealed to Wendy; when Peter first started to fly away from the nursery, she entreated him not to go, promising, "I know such lots of stories."

For all her coyness, Wendy was on to something important. Mothers, and writers on behalf of mothers, have begun to write the stories that mothers know. Most of these works differ from the Lost Boys' favorite story, *Cinderella*, in that happily ever after is rarely the finale to most maternal experience. Nonetheless, the project is already underway, as indicated by several recent anthologies of essays about mothers and daughters in literature (Davidson and Broner 1980; Pearlman 1989; Daly and Reddy 1991; see also Hirsch 1989).

The undertaking is not easy. Even in a forum structured for mothers, the filial viewpoint sometimes obscures the maternal; as the editor of one collection explains:

> Most of the novelists—and the critics—in this collection are between the ages of thirty-five and fifty-five, the years in which mature women, novelists or otherwise, must finally understand their own relationships with their mothers or be condemned to a lifetime of daughterhood, to a "girls'" angle of vision, to a dependent emotional space within a mother's parameters. Even if the original intention of the writer was to solve the enigmas and puzzles of motherhood, we find her discussing most fully the problems and solutions for daughterhood.   (Pearlman 1989:7)

Nancy Chodorow and Susan Contratto argue that many feminist writers and theoreticians not only discuss "daughterhood" but often weigh in with the daughter against the mother in the process. They explain that the perpetuation of maternal culpability is rooted in infantile fantasies about mothers as the source of all satisfactions and that feminists too "magnify the impact of one individual, the mother, and when the child in us suffers the inevitable frustration of living, we blame the mother" (Chodorow and Contratto 1982:64–66). Other feminist literary critics have also noted that "few fictional or theoretical works begin with the mother in her own right, from her own perspective, and those that do seldom hold fast to a maternal perspective." Yet there are important exceptions that do not "suppress the centrality of mothering" (Daly and Reddy 1991:2–3; Hirsch 1989).

I want to suggest two novels where maternal perspectives on the profound issue of separating from one's child takes center stage. They are Toni Morrison's *Beloved* and Doris Lessing's *The Fifth Child*. I have elsewhere presented a more sustained analysis of these two novels and their relation to the legal regulation of maternal-child separations (Sanger, forthcoming). My aim here is simply to introduce them as stories involving mother-child separation that stand in dramatic contrast to the "daughter-centric" list of novels discussed earlier. To be sure, the heroines of both *Beloved* and *The Fifth Child* are also daughters, aware of and influenced by what they have witnessed of their own mothers' lives. Nonetheless, the dramatic power of the two novels comes from the circumstances and decisions the two women make as mothers.

Although *Beloved* and *The Fifth Child* are set in different centuries, cultures, and countries, the two novels pose a common dilemma. In each, a mother must decide whether to separate permanently from her child. In *Beloved* a Kentucky slave mother escapes North with three of her children. The family is surprised by slave catchers bent on returning them South. In response to the family's imminent capture the mother begins to slaughter her own children, determined that her children will not suffer lives of slavery. She successfully kills her baby daughter and wounds the others before she herself is seized.

In *The Fifth Child* the circumstances of the separation around the mother's decision to separate are somewhat less brutal. A modern suburban mother of four gives birth to a fifth child, a monstrous, slow-witted, vicious boy who cannot be controlled. He strangles the family pets and would happily strangle his weaker siblings as well were he not kept in a barred crib in a locked room. Recognizing that this child is destroying the happy family life she and her husband have worked so hard to create with their first four, the mother agrees to institutionalize him. She understands that by this decision, the boy will die. He is sent to an isolated institution for severely deformed and deranged children where they are heavily drugged so that sooner or later, they die.

The two stories are the more complicated in that despite the profoundly difficult decision made by each mother, neither is quite able to get rid of her child. Both the murdered baby and the institutionalized boy come back—the first as a ghost and the second rescued by his mother to the great disgust of her family. The returning children take over their mothers' lives with a vengeance, commandeering the mothers' full attention, time, and energy. Worn to the bone, each mother must then decide a second time what to do with her child. In *Beloved*, the ghost-child is finally chased away by compassionate neighbors; the mother no longer haunted. In *The Fifth Child* the mother finds she cannot banish the boy, now an even more vicious young man. He goes off for periods of time with a gang of other thugs; she simply awaits his eventual arrest and imprisonment.

These novels present the case of maternal separation from children in its most drastic form: infanticide. Happily, Western mothers rarely face separation decisions of such stark dimension. With the exception of severely disabled newborns, mothers rarely envision lives for their children so bleak that death seems a rational alternative. Yet while the circumstances presented in the novels are particularly severe, many mothers commonly face decisions about leaving their children that require analyses not wholly unlike those of the two fictional mothers. Homeless mothers must decide whether their children are better off with them on the streets or without them in foster care. Mothers of disabled children continually face institutionalization decisions, often weighing the needs of one child against those of their other children. In other countries, historically and at present, mothers decide whether to evacuate their children—whether from Nazi Germany in the 1930s, from Vietnam in the 1970s, or from Sarajevo in the 1990s— or to keep their children with them even in the face of danger and death.

To comprehend how mothers themselves absorb and resolve such choices we might usefully turn to fiction: What are the balances of harms for the child? What does the child's continued presence mean for the rest of the family, for the distribution of resources, for maternal time and affection? What are the practical alternatives? What are the consequences to the mother if she separates from the child? If she does not? How is the issue of separation posed?

But comprehending the mother's position—her motives and circumstances—is a matter of legal reform as well as literary criticism. As I develop more fully in the larger project from which this essay is drawn, in most cases voluntary maternal separations from children are disapproved, discouraged, and often penalized at law. Consider just the matter of surrogacy, an intentional, indeed financially profitable decision to separate from a child conceived for the very purpose of parting from it. That description alone makes the increasing statutory restrictions on surrogacy seem sound and inevitable, although we might entertain alternative descriptions of surrogacy that focus instead on maternal autonomy and altruism as underlying her decision.

Here I want to provide two final examples of maternal separation decisions that illustrate the simplistic severity with which such decisions are met at law. The first concerns a mother circumstantially not so unlike the desperate mother in *The Beet Queen* except that the mother in *The Matter of Harlem Dowling Children's Services* (77 A.D.2d 115 [1992]) does not fly away. Instead, she works. As the New York appeals court explained, "the respondent-mother, Laverne F., came to the attention of the authorities for having left her three children [then ages 10, 6, and 21 months] for 'extended periods of time,' while she worked two jobs in a valiant, if losing, struggle to provide them with support and proper housing" (in *The Matter of Harlem Dowling Children's Services*, [at 116]). After an anonymous report that the children were being left unattended, the police removed them into emergency foster care. Their mother then consented to leave them in foster care voluntarily—an agreement often reached after the official assurance that the children will be removed involuntarily if consent is not given. In this case, the agreement was that the mother would get her children back after she had found a more suitable, three-bedroom apartment.

The arrangement was followed by a series of administrative mistakes and personal tragedies. Just after the mother found a three-bedroom apartment for $500 a month, her caseworker was replaced. The new caseworker decided that the $500 rent was too high and that the children should not yet be returned. The city ended one of the programs in which the mother was employed. She became ill; her own mother died. Throughout all of this, the mother continued to visit and correspond with her children, who looked forward to being reunited with their mom. Nonetheless, the Family Court ruled that the mother's parental rights should be terminated on the basis of her "permanent neglect" of the children.

The appellate court reversed this finding, holding that

> although some degree of irresponsibility in dealing with her predica-
> ment may perhaps be attributed to respondent . . . these failings do not
> constitute permanent neglect. . . . It cannot be too strongly emphasized
> that, to the extent that respondent fell short of ideal standards for par-
> enting, it was largely due to her economic condition and the despair to
> which she plummeted because of it. Indeed, it is to respondent's credit,
> that despite enormous difficulties, she has persisted in her attempts to
> regain the custody of her children.   (Citations omitted)(119)

The case was then remanded for a new hearing on the issue of custody.

The second case in which a mother "voluntarily" left her children and lost them as a result arises in the context of a custody dispute. In *Dempsey v. Dempsey* (1983), both the father and the mother claimed the benefit of West Virginia's primary caretaker presumption. Under this rule, the parent who was "primarily responsible for the caring and nurturing of the child" before the divorce is awarded custody. The idea behind the presumption is that past performance of parental duties is a more reliable indicator of where the child will be better off than speculating prospectively about the child's "best interests." The presumption applies unless custody of the child during the marriage has been "shared in an entirely equal way."

The son in the *Dempsey* case was born in Delaware in 1974. His mother stayed home and cared for him and for a child from her husband's first marriage. In January 1978, the father left the mother and the two children and moved to West Virginia. For the next three years the mother received less than $300 in total support for the children from the father. By October 1980, she "had fallen so far behind on her bills that she felt she could no longer care for Jay or Jennifer." She therefore sent them to West Virginia to live with their father and his parents until she could get back on her feet.

The father then quickly filed for divorce and for custody of the boy. He argued that because he had custody of the boy for the eleven months immediately prior to the divorce hearing, the primary caretaker presumption did not apply. The West Virginia court agreed and awarded custody to the father on the grounds that local testimony showed the child had become more obedient in West Virginia. The mother appealed the custody order but lost.

Dempsey turns the issue of separation and abandonment on its head. Characterizing the majority decision as "a singularly inequitable result," the dissenting appellate judge observed that the evidence

> clearly shows that the mother was the primary caretaker until she relinquished temporary custody to the father. The reason for the relinquishment was that Mr. Dempsey had abandoned her and the child in Delaware. . . . We should not permit a primary caretaker to lose her favored status simply because her husband abandons her and his child without any meaningful support, thereby forcing her to give up physical custody of the child.   (421)

Even outside the primary caretaker context, mothers in our society are understood to have a "favored status" of sorts. Mothers are celebrated annually on Mother's Day. Athletes mouth "Hi, Mom!" before every television camera. But the favor and attention last only so long as mothers behave as we imagine mothers should. Leaving one's children, even when the reasons for doing so are compelling, is often enough to end the official celebration. And even when a mother's reasons fall short of compelling, the verdict from the child's point of view can be more severe.

J. M. Barrie understood all this. At the end of *Peter Pan*, after Wendy decides to leave Neverland and return home, Peter devises one last plan to keep her. He and Tinker Bell fly to London ahead of the others and bar the window to the Darling family nursery so that when Wendy arrives "she will think her mother has barred her out." While Peter ultimately relents and opens the window, the scheme might well have worked. The injury felt by children in consequence of the fact or per-

ception of maternal absence is real. When mothers appear to have a
choice in the matter, the injury is all the greater.

It is time for a change in texts. Like the fictional mothers in *Beloved*
and *The Fifth Child*, real mothers who separate from their children are
often haunted by their decisions, even if the ghosts are less physically
robust. At a personal level, relations between mothers and their children
are always complex. Sorting out the causes and effects of separations
may now be an inevitable part of what the modern Western mothers
and children will spend time working out. This may be especially so in
a society where economic realities increase the likelihood that many
mothers will separate from children on account of work or poverty and
where considerable effort has gone into making maternal guilt a cultural norm.

But the *legal* response to separations between mothers and their children is another matter. In law we want to know more than how badly
everyone may feel about a particular separation. We want to know
whether the mother's actions reveal a sustained indifference to the
child's welfare. Mothers do not lightly choose to leave their children,
even if on occasion it is their preference to do so. Incorporating a maternal perspective into the calculation sharpens the legal inquiry. It illuminates background social circumstances that are too often obscured
once the mere fact of separation has been established. And so, if we were
to learn from facts well within our grasp that mothers not uncommonly
decide to separate from children in order to improve their children's

lives, we might shift our own perspective and concentrate less on punishing mothers and more on inventing policies to address the hardships
and difficulties that at present necessitate such hard decisions.

3 Abortion as a Sex Equality Right: Its Basis in Feminist Theory

REVA B. SIEGEL

T he abortion right is generally discussed as a negative liberty, a right of privacy, a right to be let alone. This conception of the right is consistent with certain libertarian traditions in feminism, but it is also at odds with other important aspects of feminist thought. Conversations about the abortion right typically occur within a framework that is individualist, anti-statist, and focused on the physiology of reproduction—that is, on matters of sex, not gender. This mode of speaking about the abortion right shares important features in common with the framework the Supreme Court adopted in *Roe v. Wade*.[1]

The abortion right is also sometimes discussed as an issue of equality for women, both in feminist circles and in the community at large. The Court's opinion in *Roe*, however, is generally oblivious to such concerns; indeed, *Roe* defines the abortion right in such a way as to make it difficult to speak about in sex equality terms. Recently, as judicial criticism of *Roe* has mounted, a growing number of scholars have attempted to reconceptualize the abortion right in a sex equality framework, developing arguments that draw upon diverse aspects of feminist legal and social theory. This essay situates the emergent sex equality argument for abortion rights in jurisprudential context and in an interdisciplinary field.

In the years since *Roe* was decided, feminist scholars have developed a sophisticated body of theory exploring the social organization of reproductive relations. The first wave of social construction theory demonstrated how much that was seemingly natural in reproduction was in fact the product of social relations legitimated as expressions of nature (Ehrenreich and English 1978; Gordon 1974; Leavitt 1986; O'Brien 1981; Rosaldo and Lamphere 1974). A second wave of social construction theory appearing in the 1980s began to explore the body itself as a terrain of cultural signification and contestation (Jacobus, Keller, and Shuttleworth 1990; Laqueur 1986, 1990; Martin 1987; *Representations* 1986). Much of this work has focused on abortion. Scholars have explored the history of abortion regulation and provided a rich account of the sociology and iconography of abortion disputes, past and present (Condit 1990; Luker 1984; Petchesky 1984, 1987; Smith-Rosenberg 1985:217–44). These developments in social construction theory, when combined with more recent work in feminist jurisprudence, enable a variety of new approaches to analyzing reproductive regulation.

Since the mid-1980s a growing number of lawyers and legal academics have begun to analyze abortion restrictions in an equality framework; these arguments are quite various in style, focus, and intellectual tradition (MacKinnon 1983a, 1987:93–102, 1991:1308–24; Law 1984; Ginsburg 1985; Tribe 1988:1353–59; Olsen 1989:117–35; Colker 1991; Siegel 1992; Sunstein 1992:29–44, 1993:270–85; see also Karst 1977:53–59; Regan 1979).[2] I will discuss the theoretical basis of one such argument, developed in my article "Reasoning from the Body: A Historical Perspective on Abortion Regulation and Questions of Equal Protection" (Siegel 1992). The equality argument I present in the following sections builds upon and contributes to social construction theory as it situates abortion-restrictive regulation in a new jurisprudential framework.

Analyzing Abortion Restrictions as Gender Status Regulation

Legal and popular debate over abortion tends to focus on matters concerning the physical relations of reproduction. But, as feminist scholarship in the humanities and social sciences demonstrates, the ways a society regulates reproduction and the reasons it advances for doing so are part of the *social* relations of reproduction. This paradigm shift has significant jurisprudential consequences. When abortion restrictions are analyzed in sociohistorical perspective, it is possible to identify constitutionally significant features of such laws otherwise obscured by the naturalistic framework in which courts now analyze them.

America's criminal abortion laws were first enacted in the nineteenth century, the product of a campaign led by the medical profession, then in its infancy. Doctors urged the enactment of laws criminalizing abortion and contraception for a variety of reasons. They argued that it was important to prohibit abortion and contraception in order to protect the unborn, to ensure that married women performed their duties as wives and mothers, and to preserve the ethnic character of the nation. Obstetricians and gynecologists drew upon the discourse of their profession—the discourse of reproductive physiology—to advance these arguments against birth control practices, thereby infusing social arguments for criminalizing birth control with the authority of science.

Analyzing the record of the nineteenth-century criminalization campaign reveals how social discourses concerning women's roles have converged with physiological discourses concerning women's bodies, as two distinct but compatible ways of reasoning about women's obligations as mothers. As I will show, the physiological discourses that currently dominate the abortion debate have roots in the nineteenth-century antiabortion campaign, where they were employed interchangeably with arguments emphasizing the need to enforce women's duties as wives and mothers. Simply put, in debates over abortion, issues we habitually conceptualize in terms of women's bodies in fact involve questions concerning women's roles. An examination of the nineteenth-century criminalization campaign thus provides a new basis for analyzing abortion-restrictive regulation, illuminating its lineage and function as gender-caste regulation.

The Nineteenth-Century Campaign to Criminalize Abortion

At the opening of the nineteenth century, abortion in the United States was governed by the common law; under this regime, abortion was allowed until "quickening," the moment in gestation when women first perceive fetal movement, typically in the fourth or fifth month of pregnancy (Mohr 1978:3–6). By mid-century, obstetricians and gynecologists of the newly founded American Medical Association (AMA) had inaugurated a campaign to criminalize abortion and other methods of birth control, which they undertook for reasons involving both social morality and professional status (Siegel 1992:282–84; Smith-Rosenberg 1985:217–44). In response to this campaign, a growing number of states prohibited abortion induced before quickening—although many conditioned more severe criminal penalties upon proof of quickening. During this same period, many states banned contraceptives and abortifacients, as well as the distribution of information about them; federal legislation enacted in 1873, popularly known as the Comstock Act, classified information concerning contraception and abortion as obscene, and prohibited its circulation in the U.S. mails (Comstock Act, ch. 258, 17 Stat. 598 (1873) [repealed 1909]; Siegel 1992: 314–15). To understand how the AMA persuaded social elites, who in the early years of industrialization were increasingly interested in limiting family size, to adopt laws criminalizing one of the most reliable methods of birth control of the era, it is necessary to examine the diverse arguments doctors marshaled against the practice. The profession's antiabortion arguments focused on the physiology of reproduction, the structure of the family, and the dynamics of population growth.

Doctors' Antiabortion Arguments The doctors who led the criminalization campaign sought, first of all, to discredit the customary and common law concept of quickening. Considered from the standpoint of medical science, the doctors argued, human development was continuous from the point of conception; therefore, quickening had no special physiological significance. The doctors then sought to use this scientific critique of quickening to demonstrate that life begins at conception, and thus that abortion at any point after conception was tantamount to murder.

As doctors sought to equate abortion with the murder of a born person, however, they invested physiological facts with particular social significance. Doctors observed that the embryo/fetus had the physiological capacity to develop into a human being, and pointed to this capacity for physical growth as evidence that the embryo was an *autonomous* form of life. Doctors also cited the embryo's physical separation from the pregnant woman as evidence of its autonomy. Thus, Dr. Jesse Boring argued:

> [T]he fecundated ovum is not only the embryonic man, already vital, but it is, in an important sense, an independent, self-existent being, that is having in itself the materials for development, being actually separated from the mother, as well as from the father, though maintaining a connexion in utero by the vacular arrangement repeatedly referred to; there is, *really*, as has been fully demonstrated, no actual attachment of the placenta to the uterus.   (Boring 1857:266)

Dr. Horatio Storer, leader of the criminalization campaign, contended that the embryo/fetus was for all practical purposes *outside* of the woman bearing it—even going so far as to compare the embryo/fetus to a kangaroo gestating in its mother's abdominal pouch. As he explained in his popular antiabortion tract *Why Not? A Book for Every Woman*, "The first impregnation of the egg, whether in man or in kangaroo, is the birth of the offspring to life; its emergence into the outside world for a wholly separate existence is, for one as for the other, but an accident in time" (Storer 1866:30–31; Storer and Heard 1868:10–11). In their effort to demonstrate the autonomy of unborn life, physicians discussed the embryo's capacity for growth as if it could be exercised outside the womb; the doctors' arguments confused categories of time and space so that unborn life seemed to have scant relation to the woman bearing it.

Yet the doctors' most powerful strategy for demonstrating the autonomy of unborn life did not require confusing the facts of human development; instead, doctors depicted the facts of human development in a highly selective manner, emphasizing the physiological continuity of human life but omitting all reference to the physical and social work of reproduction women perform. Dr. Hugh Hodge traced the path of human maturation without once mentioning women's role in reproduction when he invited his audience to imagine the fertilized ovum developing into the highest form of social life—a fully matured man:

> [T]he invisible product of conception is developed, grows, passes through the embryonic and foetal stages of existence, appears as the breathing and lovely infant, the active, intelligent boy, the studious moral youth, the adult man, rejoicing the plenitude of his corporeal strength and intellectual powers, capable of moral and spiritual enjoyments, and finally, in this world, as the aged man.
>
> (Hodge 1869:35, quoted in Smith-Rosenberg 1985:242)

To defend the claim that life begins at conception, nineteenth-century physicians offered a "scientific" account of human development that treated women's role in reproduction as a matter of minor consequence—from the point of conception onwards. This description of the maternal/fetal relationship appeared only in debates about abortion, just as it does today. It was otherwise wholly at odds with the "separate spheres" tradition—regularly controverted by medical and popular authorities of the era who emphasized that mothers had a unique capacity to shape a child's development, during gestation and after (Siegel 1992:292).

When doctors criticized quickening, they depicted the reproductive process in ways that obscured women's role in gestating and nurturing human life. But other arguments advanced against abortion and contraception emphasized women's family role. Doctors repeatedly argued that women had a duty to bear children. Implicitly or explicitly, they were discussing *married* women. The AMA's 1871 "Report on Criminal Abortion" denounced the woman who aborted a pregnancy: "She becomes unmindful of the course marked out for her by Providence, she overlooks the duties imposed on her by the marriage contract. She yields to the pleasures—but shrinks from the pains and responsibilities of maternity" (O'Donnell and Atlee 1871:241). A woman's duty to procreate was dictated by her anatomy, as the leader of the criminalization campaign explained:

> Were woman intended as a mere plaything, or for the gratification of her own or her husband's desires, there would have been need for her of neither uterus nor ovaries, nor would the prevention of their being used for their clearly legitimate purpose have been attended by such tremendous penalties as is in reality the case.   (Storer 1866:80–81)

It followed that a woman who shirked her duty to bear children committed "physiological sin" (Pomeroy 1888:97). In this compound concept of physiological sin, the profession translated religious, legal, and customary norms of marital duty into therapeutic terms. As doctors repeatedly argued, abortion and contraception both threatened women's health (Siegel 1992:294–95, and nn. 123, 125, 126). The only way that a wife could ensure her health was to bear children, pregnancy being "a normal physiological condition, and often absolutely necessary to the physical and moral health of woman" (Hale 1867:6n.).

By defining the obligations of marriage in medical terms, doctors claimed special authority to mediate between a married woman and the state, thereby appropriating a role the common law of marital status otherwise defined as a husband's. The profession's claim of expertise justified the so-called therapeutic exception to birth control laws that vested in physicians authority to determine whether their patients might have legal access to abortion and contraception. In this way, a woman was made legal ward of her physician; a woman's choices regarding birth control were made subject to a man's consent, where no such requirement existed at common law before.[3]

Just as doctors translated concepts of marital duty into physiological terms, they also analyzed matters of civic governance in reproductive paradigms. Another commonplace argument against abortion compared the birth rates of the white Anglo-Saxon middle class to that of the European-immigrant and African-American lower classes. In such arguments, the same doctors who condemned abortion as "feticide" condemned abortion and contraception as a form of "race suicide" (Calhoun 1919:225–54). Dr. Augustus Gardner dedicated a polemic against masturbation, contraception, and abortion, entitled *Conjugal Sins*, "To the Reverend Clergy of the United States who by example and instruction have the power to arrest the rapid extinction of the Native American People" (Gardner 1870:5). Dr. H. S. Pomeroy made the preoccupations of the criminalization campaign explicit when he observed: "[I]t is coming to pass that our voters—and so our lawmakers and rulers, indirectly, if not directly—come more and more from the lowest class, because that class is able and willing to have children, while the so-called better classes seem not to be" (Pomeroy 1888:39). Horatio Storer, who led the campaign, was equally blunt in describing the doctors' concerns:

> [T]he great territories of the far West, just opening to civilization, and the fertile savannas of the South, now disinthralled and first made habitable by freemen, offer homes for countless millions yet unborn. Shall they be filled by our own children or by those of aliens? This is a question that our own women must answer; upon their loins depends the future destiny of the nation. (Storer 1866:85)

As Storer made abundantly clear, political power resided in control of those citizens who would bear citizens. The doctors' physiological arguments against abortion thus channeled wide-ranging social concern into the act of reproduction itself. The claim that life begins at conception was but one of many arguments that identified the reproductive process as the basis of social life. Individually and collectively, these arguments suggested that regulating the physical act of reproduction was necessary to ensure reproduction of the social order.

Antiabortion as Antifeminism The campaign against abortion and contraception was quite specifically concerned with controlling the conduct of women. This is apparent in many of the physiological arguments the campaign directed against birth control practices, but it was also expressed in openly political terms. Physicians suggested that women's interest in controlling birth was incited by feminist advocacy, and depicted abortion and contraception as an expression of women's resistance to marital and maternal obligations (Smith-Rosenberg

1985:217–44). The same doctors who called abortion feticide also described the moral evils of abortion in the following terms:

> Woman's rights and woman's sphere are, as understood by the American public, quite different from that understood by us as Physicians, or as Anatomists, or Physiologists.
>
> "Woman's rights" now are understood to be, that she should be a man, and that her physical organism, which is constituted by Nature to bear and rear offspring, should be left in abeyance, and that her ministrations in the formation of character as mother should be abandoned for the sterner rights of voting and law making.   (Pallen 1869:205–6)

Or, as another doctor put it:

> There are lecturers "to ladies only" who profess to be actuated simply by good-will toward their unfortunate sisters, who yet call woman's highest and holiest privilege by the name of slavery, and a law to protect the family from the first step toward extinction, tyranny.
>
> There are apostles of woman's rights who, in their well-meaning but misdirected efforts to arouse women to claim privileges now denied them, encourage their sisters to feel ashamed of the first and highest right which is theirs by the very idea of their nature.
>
> There are advocates of education who seek to deter woman by false pride, from performing the one duty she is perfectly sure of being able to do better than a man! And there are those who teach that their married sisters may save time and vitality for high and noble pursuits by "electing" how few children shall be born to them.   (Pomeroy 1888:95–96)

As these polemics suggest, doctors who opposed abortion and contraception were engaged in a wide-ranging debate with the feminist movement of the era. It was not feminist support for abortion rights that drew the physicians' ire; the nineteenth-century woman's rights movement in fact condemned abortion. But the movement did seek reproductive autonomy for wives, in the form of a demand for "voluntary motherhood": the claim that a married woman was entitled to refuse her husband's sexual advances (Gordon 1976:108–11). To understand how physicians and feminists—who together opposed abortion—were nevertheless engaged in far-ranging conflict about abortion, it is necessary to consider their strikingly divergent views of marriage.

When nineteenth-century feminists demanded voluntary motherhood, they were attacking customary and common law concepts of marriage (Siegel 1992:304–5). Feminists demanding voluntary motherhood hoped to secure for wives "self-ownership": control over their daily lives in matters of sexuality, reproduction, and work (ibid., 305–8; Siegel 1994:1103–7). Indeed, the movement's criticisms of the legal and customary structure of the marriage relationship were sufficiently far-reaching that, while the movement did not openly support abortion, many feminists of the era tacitly condoned abortion as an act of self-defense under prevailing conditions of "forced motherhood" (Siegel 1992:307).

By contrast, physicians used antiabortion arguments to *oppose* the demands of the woman's rights movement. Antiabortion arguments explicitly and implicitly associated the practice of abortion with feminist efforts to reform the laws and customs of marriage and to expand women's participation in the nation's economic and political life, thus investing abortion with explosive social significance. In short, doctors urged legislators to criminalize abortion in order to preserve traditional gender roles in matters of sexuality and motherhood, education and work, and affairs of suffrage and state.

Even this cursory examination of the arguments advanced by the nineteenth-century criminalization campaign reveals that opposition to abortion was powerfully shaped by judgments rooted in relations of gender, race, ethnicity, and class. Those who sought to criminalize abortion were interested in protecting unborn life; yet it is equally clear that they viewed protecting the unborn as a means to control rebellious middle-class women and teeming immigrant populations, and it is in this context that their judgments about the morality of abortion and contraception must be understood. Concerns of gender, race, ethnicity, and class were not peripheral to this ethic, but were instead an integral part of it.

Criminalizing Birth Control: A New Mode of Regulating Gender Status
The campaign to criminalize birth control had significant effects on law, inaugurating a method of regulating women's social status unknown at common law. Restrictions on abortion and contraception were enacted at a time when state legislatures were liberalizing the marital status doctrines of the common law, modifying ancient restrictions on wives' conduct in an effort to accommodate the needs of a market society and to blunt criticisms of marriage advanced by advocates of woman suffrage (Basch 1982; Siegel 1994).[4] It is illuminating to consider the social preoccupations of the criminalization campaign against this backdrop. In advancing their case for criminalizing birth control practices, physicians offered the American public a *new* way of regulating wives' conduct, one that deviated in method and preoccupation from traditional doctrines of

marriage and family law. Laws against abortion and contraception enforced relations of social status by regulating the physical act of reproduction, in this respect resembling antimiscegenation laws and other eugenics legislation adopted in the postbellum period (Siegel 1992:319–20). Just as antimiscegenation laws of the era played an important role in maintaining a particular regime of racial status, laws that criminalized birth control played a crucial role in enforcing a particular regime of gender status. Considered in retrospect, the criminalization campaign can be understood as modernizing both the means of regulating gender status and the mode of its justification.

To appreciate the campaign's role in transforming discourses of gender status, it is helpful to examine the 1908 case of *Muller v. Oregon*.[5] In *Muller*, the Supreme Court upheld protective labor legislation regulating women's employment and justified this result on unprecedented constitutional grounds. To explain why the state of Oregon could restrict women's freedom of contract as it could not men's, the Court pointed to women's "physical structure," invoking women's bodies as the basis for gender-differentiated regulation of women's conduct in a fashion that no court of the early nineteenth century ever would. The Court understood that it was discussing matters of gender status in a fashion that broke with the conventions of the common law. The Court began its analysis in *Muller* by noting that Oregon had recently reformed the common law to allow wives to form binding contracts, yet the Court ruled that the state could impose new restrictions on women's capacity to form employment contracts, for reasons relating to their reproductive role:

> Though limitations upon personal and contractual rights may be removed by legislation, there is that in her disposition and habits of life which will operate against a full assertion of those rights. . . . [Woman's] physical structure and a proper discharge of her maternal functions—having in view not merely her own health, but the wellbeing of the race—justify legislation to protect her from the greed as well as the passion of man. . . . Many words cannot make this plainer. The two sexes differ in structure of body, in the functions to be performed by each. . . . This difference justifies a difference in legislation and upholds that which is designed to compensate for some of the burdens which rest upon her.   (*Muller*, 422–23)

In *Muller*, the Court employed claims about women's bodies to reach a result that some decades earlier it might have justified by invoking the common law of marital status.[6] The campaign to criminalize abortion did not supplant marital status law, nor did it eliminate the use of marriage concepts in explaining women's social status. Instead it gave them more "modern," scientific sense. As the *Muller* opinion illustrates, the campaign enabled the Court to repudiate traditional norms of gender status and still find reasons for enforcing women's roles—reasons now rooted in immutable facts of nature rather than transitory and contestable social norms.

Comparing the Abortion Debate, Past and Present

If one compares the contemporary abortion debate to the nineteenth-century campaign, certain commonalities and differences are immediately apparent. Arguments about human physiology continue to play an important part in the abortion controversy; yet today one does not commonly hear claims about women's roles of the sort openly voiced in the nineteenth century. In this section, I will examine the role of physiological discourses in the contemporary abortion debate, demonstrating how they simultaneously obscure and facilitate gender-based reasoning about the equities of reproductive regulation.

Today, secular arguments about abortion are conducted in a medical framework, just as they were in the nineteenth century. In fact, one can discern the legacy of the criminalization campaign in *Roe* itself. *Roe* recognizes that a woman has a privacy right to make decisions about abortion, and describes this right in medical terms: it is a right to be exercised under the guidance of a physician (*Roe*, 153–63, 165–66). *Roe* also allows the state to regulate a woman's abortion decision, in order to protect potential life. The opinion derives the state's interest in protecting potential life from a purely medical definition of pregnancy:

> The pregnant woman cannot be isolated in her privacy. She carries an embryo, and later a fetus, if one accepts the medical definition of the developing young in the human uterus. See Dorland's *Medical Illustrated Dictionary*. . . . The situation is therefore inherently different from [all other privacy precedents].   (ibid., 159)

Recognizing both a woman's right to make decisions about abortion and the state's prerogative to regulate those decisions, *Roe* reconciles the conflict by means of its trimester framework, with the strength of each constitutional interest determined by temporal progress of gestation itself (ibid., 163).

The medico-physiological reasoning that supports *Roe* also undergirds secular arguments opposing the right *Roe* recognized. To take one example, an editorial in the *New York Post* urged its readers to examine a photo essay depicting the formation of a human being, observing:

> Here in graphic color is living, thrilling irrefutable proof that within hours of conception, a unique distinctive human being has been formed. The magazine says that within 20 hours of conception, when the sperm enters the ovum, "the result is a single nucleus that contains the entire biological blueprint for a new individual, genetic information governing everything from the length of the nose to the diseases that will be inherited."   (Kerrison 1990:2)

The editorial asserts, without more, that these photographs "virtually render obsolete the whole abortion debate" (ibid., 2).

In debating the abortion question today, we reason within a physiological framework that abstracts the conflict from the social context in which judgments about abortion are formed and enforced. To understand the reasons why women seek to have children or to avoid having them, as well as the reasons why their choices are communally acceptable or not, one has to examine the social relations of reproduction and not merely its physiology. But the naturalistic rhetorics of the abortion debate deter this. As a consequence, we conceptualize the abortion question as a question concerning women's bodies, not women's roles. That women are the object of abortion-restrictive regulation is considered to be a matter of physiological necessity: women are where the embryo/fetus *is*. Indeed, as the *New York Post* editorial illustrates, medico-physiological discourses often present the fetus as if it were an autonomous form of life, depicting the process of human development as if it scarcely involved women at all (Petchesky 1987). Thus, today, as in the nineteenth century, antiabortion arguments use narratives of human genesis that omit all reference to women's work as mothers in order to condemn women who seek to avoid becoming mothers. An antiabortion pamphlet observes, "[n]othing has been added to the fertilized ovum you once were except nutrition" (Willke, n.d., quoted in Olsen 1989:128), just as Horatio Storer once argued that the "total independence" of the unborn could be discerned in the fact that "its subsequent history after impregnation is merely one of development, its attachment merely for nutrition and shelter" (Storer and Heard 1868:10–11).

While opponents of abortion no longer make claims about women's roles of the sort that dominated the nineteenth-century campaign, gender-based judgments do continue to inform arguments for regulating women's reproductive conduct; *today these judgments can be articulated in the physiological modes of reasoning the campaign inaugurated.* To appreciate how gender-based judgments can be expressed in physiological terms, it is helpful to consider the Court's reasoning in *Roe.* In *Roe,* the Court held that the state has an interest in protecting potential life that becomes compelling at the point of fetal viability, when this interest is strong enough to support state action prohibiting abortion (*Roe,* 163); critics of *Roe's* trimester framework contend that the state's interest in protecting potential life "exists throughout the pregnancy."[7] This proposition bears consideration. Considered in social rather than physiological terms, the state's "interest in protecting potential life" is a state interest in compelling women who are resisting motherhood to bear children. Of course, legislators would dispute this characterization of the state's interest in regulating abortion. To do so, they would invoke the discourse of reproductive physiology, that is, they would argue that the state has no interest in the pregnant woman, save for the fact that she is where the embryo/fetus is. But this rejoinder does not alter the fact that a state forbidding abortion to protect potential life *is* forcing women who are resisting motherhood to bear children. Should legislators protest that they wish to prohibit abortion out of concern for the unborn and entertain no thoughts about the women on whom they would impose motherhood, such a defense would reveal that the policy was premised on gendered assumptions with deep roots in the nineteenth-century campaign: that the embryo/fetus is somehow "outside" women, like a kangaroo gestating in its mother's pouch—or that women are little more than reproductive organs. Alternatively, if legislators attempted to explain why they believed they were justified in forcing a pregnant woman to bear a child, each of the putatively gender-neutral explanations they might provide (e.g., consent, fault) could in turn be traced to a set of status-linked judgments about women.[8]

In short, claims about abortion that focus on the physical relations of reproduction often express judgments about abortion rooted in the social relations of reproduction. In *Abortion and the Politics of Motherhood,* Kristin Luker traces value judgments about protecting unborn life to value judgments about the structure of family life, contending that "[t]he abortion debate is so passionate and hard-fought because it is a referendum on the place and meaning of motherhood" (Luker 1984:193). As Luker persuasively demonstrates, divergent modes of reasoning about the unborn correlate with divergent modes of reasoning about the nature of sexuality, work, and family commitments in women's lives (ibid., 192–215). Thus, while the separate spheres tradition no longer receives official public sanction, the sex-role concepts it fostered continue to play a crucial role in the abortion controversy, supplying norms of sexual and maternal comportment for women that inform public judgments about the propriety of abortion. A 1990 poll of Louisiana residents indicated that 89 percent favored providing women access to abortion when pregnancy occurred because of rape or incest, while 79 percent opposed abortion "when childbirth might interrupt a woman's career" (J. Hill 1990). The most widespread support for abortion depended on a judgment about the sexual relations in which unborn life was conceived, and the most widespread opposition to abortion reflected a judgment about women's pursuit of career opportunities in conflict with the maternal role.

We can thus recharacterize the interest in regulating abortion. Those who seek to protect unborn life want to regulate the conduct of women who fail to act as good mothers should. Judgments about women's conduct as mothers are expressed by those interested in protecting unborn life outside the abortion context, as well. One commentator surveying a hospital ward of babies born to drug-dependent women angrily warned his readers that "[t]he sins of the mothers are apt to become the burden of society for generations to come," and then applauded a female journalist and six other women who had volunteered to hold the "damaged babies" with the exhortation, "Good for Victoria. Good for the women who cuddle babies" (Martinez 1991).

Yet this analysis remains incomplete. Certain forms of fetal-protective regulation are overwhelmingly directed at pregnant women who are poor, of color, and on public assistance (for example, forced surgical treatment, or drug-related prosecutions and custody deprivations; see Roberts 1991:1421 n. 6, 1432–36; Siegel 1992:335 n. 301). Clearly, such regulation does not reflect gender-based judgments alone. As the nineteenth-century criminalization campaign richly illustrates, judgments about women's reproductive conduct may be intersectional in character, reflecting concerns rooted in relations of gender, race, and class. Public authorities may focus their regulatory efforts on poor women of color because their lives diverge most sharply from the white, middle-class norms that define "good" motherhood in this society (see Fineman 1991b). Or, as the history of the nineteenth-century criminalization campaign suggests, regulation nominally undertaken to protect the unborn may in fact be driven by antipathy to poor women of color and the children they might bear. Dorothy Roberts interprets the criminal prosecution of pregnant drug-dependent women in just this fashion. Roberts observes that criminal prosecutions provide no assistance to children, while punishing poor women of color for reproducing; she analyzes the prosecutions in light of the history of sterilization abuse in order to illustrate their underlying social logic (Roberts 1991:1442–44). The same analysis might be extended to other forms of birth-deterring regulation, such as recent welfare reform proposals that contemplate imposing "family-caps" on recipients of Aid to Families with Dependent Children (AFDC) (see L. Williams 1992:720 and n. 7, 736–41), or proposals that would make use of Norplant a condition for receipt of public assistance or for receipt of reduced criminal sentences (see Arthur 1992; Hand 1993).

The injuries fetal-protective regulation inflicts on women are most often justified as unfortunate incidents of a benign regulatory intention to protect children. But the structure of the regulation suggests otherwise. If one considers the means conventionally employed to protect the unborn, one finds ample evidence that fetal-protective policies do in fact reflect judgments about women, as well as the unborn life they bear. For example, a state criminalizing abortion to protect the unborn could nonetheless assist the women on whom it would impose motherhood. Why, then, is it that antiabortion laws do not assist pregnant women in coping with the social consequences of gestating and raising a child? Would every jurisdiction interested in prohibiting abortion do so if it were obliged to make women whole for the costs of bearing and raising a child? Do jurisdictions that wish to prohibit abortion employ all available *noncoercive* means to promote the welfare of unborn life, assisting those women who do want to become mothers so that they are bear and rear healthy children?

The same analysis of regulatory means can be extended to fetal-protective policies outside the abortion context. As evidence accumulates that toxins injurious to the unborn can be transmitted through men as well as women, is it likely that employers will decide to prohibit fertile men from working in substantial sectors of the industrial workforce? Would this society so readily contemplate criminal prosecution, "protective incarceration," or custody deprivation as responses to maternal addiction if the policies were to be applied to privileged women rather than the poor? An analysis of the means this society employs to protect the unborn reveals that fetal-protective policies reflect judgments rooted in relations of gender, race, and class, whose normative sense can

be elucidated by examining status concerns expressed in the nineteenth-century campaign.

Analyzing reproductive regulation in historical perspective thus yields
several critical insights that might be used in studying the regulation
from a variety of disciplinary perspectives:

1. *In the abortion debate, the discourse of reproductive physiology functions
as a discourse of gender status.* The ways in which the nineteenth-century
medical profession addressed the abortion question still shape the way it is
analyzed today, in legal and popular fora. Modes of describing the mater-
nal/fetal relation and the process of human development that would seem
to be purely empirical are in fact specific to the abortion debate; they have
a rhetorical history and a conceptual bias consistent with this history.
These rhetorics of the body are part of a discourse of gender status, long
used to justify regulating women's reproductive conduct. Consequently, in
contemporary debates about abortion, gendered judgments can be articulated in the physiological discourses the nineteenth-century campaign
inaugurated. (The "state's interest in protecting potential life" is an expression of this discursive tradition; the Court's reasoning in *Roe* unfolds
within, and not against, the logic of the criminalization campaign.)

2. *Laws criminalizing abortion and contraception compel motherhood,
and from an historical perspective can be understood as a form of gender
status regulation.* In the nineteenth century, the criminalization of abortion and contraception was advocated as a method of ensuring that
women performed their duties as wives and mothers. Laws criminalizing birth control enacted in this period can be understood as a new
form of gender status regulation, adopted in an era in which the older
common law regime of marital status was under feminist attack and
undergoing liberalization. Today, as in the past, public interest in regulating women's reproductive conduct has grown as older forms of patriarchal regulation have declined in legitimacy. Now, as then, new forms
of reproductive regulation are justified with reference to "facts of
nature" rather than to relations of social status, a justificatory stance
necessitated by the waning legitimacy of overtly patriarchal discourses
and the enshrinement of a "genderless" citizen subject. (With the
appearance of modern equal protection doctrines forbidding discrimination on the basis of sex, arguments grounded in reproductive physiology constitute one of the strongest constitutional rationales for class-
based regulation of women's conduct.[9])

3. *The nineteenth-century campaign to criminalize birth control was*

shaped by concerns of gender, race, and class—notwithstanding the apparent universality of its physiological polemics; the same is true of contemporary interest in reproductive regulation. In the nineteenth century, the "native" American middle class responded to the populationist "threat" posed by immigrant and African-American families by regulating the reproductive conduct of its own women. Today, with the growth of the state apparatus, reproductive regulation has multiplied and diversified in form. While all modes of fetal-protective regulation are aimed at women, such regulation may vary in class and race salience. An integrated approach to analyzing reproductive regulation will attempt to ascertain the gender, race, and class salience of such regulation, whether birth-compelling or birth-deterring in form.

4. *All regulation directed at women's reproductive conduct reflects judgments about women and the children they might bear; to determine whether such regulation is animated by benign judgments, judgments infected by gender, class, or racial bias, or some amalgam of both, it is necessary to analyze the structure of the regulation in light of the social, as well as physical, relations of reproduction—an inquiry that should include an examination of the historical lineage or antecedents of the practice.* Reproductive regulation has served to enforce or maintain caste relations in times past. For this reason, examining past regulatory practices can illuminate tacit forms of bias structuring present regulatory practices; Mary Becker and Dorothy Roberts have recently demonstrated how such historical analysis can be used to illuminate the status logic of fetal-protective regulation that restricts women's employment and that criminalizes women's use of drugs during pregnancy (Becker 1986; Roberts 1991). Thus, in attempting to determine whether contemporary regulatory practices are benign or biased in motivation, justification, and/or structure, it is helpful to consult the history of reproductive regulation. Such an historical inquiry might consider: the regulation of abortion and contraception; antimiscegenation laws; the eugenics and sterilization movements; laws governing adoption, custody, and other aspects of family structure; welfare laws; and diverse modes of regulating women's labor force participation, including restrictions on the employment of married women and sex-based protective labor legislation.

The Legal Context: Developments in Feminist Jurisprudence Since Roe

The foregoing analysis of abortion restrictions draws upon and contributes to social construction theory—the body of feminist theory exploring the social organization of reproductive relations. But this method of analyzing reproductive regulation shares little in common with the framework the Supreme Court employs in interpreting the Constitution. To appreciate the distance between the critical premises of social construction theory and the interpretive assumptions of the Court, a brief examination of constitutional doctrine is required.

This section reviews privacy and equal protection doctrine concerning the regulation of women's reproductive conduct. It then demonstrates how feminists have challenged equal protection doctrine in the years since *Roe*. Feminist jurisprudence now offers an alternative constitutional framework for analyzing restrictions on abortion—one that can draw on social construction theory in ways the prevailing constitutional framework does not.

In *Roe v. Wade*, the Supreme Court held that the right to privacy protects women's decisions about abortion; at the same time, the Court recognized the state's interest in regulating such decisions. *Roe* explains women's right to choose abortion and the state's right to regulate that choice with reference to the physiology of gestation (*Roe*, 163). Women have the liberty to control matters of bodily integrity and medical care; and the state has the prerogative to regulate matters affecting the genesis and physical development of future citizens ("the state's interest in potential life"). *Roe* reconciles the conflict between individual right and state regulatory prerogative in a "trimester framework" providing that a woman's privacy interest in making the abortion decision wanes over the course of gestation, while the state's interest in regulating the decision grows.

Roe protected women's right to make the abortion decision as a right of privacy not equality. In fact, when *Roe* was decided in 1973, the Court had not yet interpreted the equal protection clause to require government adherence to principles of sex equality. As important, *Roe* could not be easily incorporated into the constitutional sex discrimination tradition that would develop shortly thereafter. The modern equal protection tradition defines equality as a relation of similarity and discrimination as an illegitimate act of differentiation (Tussman and tenBroek 1949:344).[10] Roe, however, analyzed abortion restrictions in physiological terms. Considered from a physiological standpoint, no man is similarly situated to the pregnant woman facing abortion restrictions; hence, state action restricting a woman's abortion choices does not seem to present a problem of sex discrimination.

In the mid-1970s, shortly after *Roe* was decided, the Court began to apply the equal protection clause to questions of sex discrimination. In a series of precedent-setting decisions, the Court declared that it would scrutinize sex-based regulation closely and invalidate the legislation if it was premised on "old notions of role typing" or other vestiges of the separate spheres tradition[11] (such as the assumption that women are "child-rearers"[12] or the assumption that "the female [is] destined solely for the home and the rearing of the family"[13]). But the Court refused to analyze legislation regulating women's reproductive role similarly. In *Geduldig v. Aeillo*,[14] the Court ruled that a law governing pregnancy was not sex-based state action for purposes of equal protection doctrine, and thus did not warrant heightened constitutional scrutiny; on other occasions, the Court observed that the reality of reproductive differences between the sexes justified their differential regulatory treatment.[15]

While feminists protested the *Geduldig* decision, few were concerned about its implications for the abortion right. Initially, at least, neither legal academics nor litigators were interested in translating the abortion right into a sex equality framework. Feminist activists had little incentive to question *Roe* when the opinion represented an enormous victory for the movement—in result, if not in reasoning. In addition, so long as the movement was still seeking ratification of the Equal Rights Amendment, *Roe*'s silence about issues of sex equality had certain advantages, serving to isolate two controversial items on the feminist agenda (Law 1984:985 nn. 114–15, 986–87). Finally, it is not clear that in this period feminist lawyers had the critical tools necessary to translate *Roe* into an equality framework.

During the 1970s feminist legal theory substantially adhered to the comparative logic of the constitutional tradition. Advocates devoted their efforts to demonstrating the similarity of the sexes (Law 1984:975–82), even in those circumstances where it was necessary to deal with questions concerning pregnancy. For example, when the Court applied its reasoning in *Geduldig* to the nation's civil rights laws, holding in *General Electric Co. v. Gilbert*[16] that employment discrimination on the basis of pregnancy was not discrimination on the basis of sex, feminists sought to reverse the decision by amending Title VII of the Civil Rights Act of 1964[17] in accordance with principles of comparable treatment. The feminist lawyers who supported the Pregnancy Discrimination Amendment of 1978[18] argued that it was possible to identify certain forms of discriminatory bias by comparing the treatment of the pregnant employee to others similarly situated in their ability to work (W. Williams 1984–85:351–56). This model of functional comparability provided a standard that could protect pregnant employees from overtly exclusionary treatment in the workplace.[19] But because this standard of comparable treatment defined equality and discrimination in such a way as to obscure the distinctive physical and social characteristics of pregnancy,[20] it had little to say about protecting women's decisions concerning abortion.

By the 1980s Roe was engulfed in legal and political controversy, and the decision appeared increasingly vulnerable to reversal. An administration openly hostile to Roe was elected, and announced its commitment to select Supreme Court justices from the growing body of jurists and scholars who questioned the constitutional basis of the privacy right on which Roe rested (Tribe 1990:17–21). As jurisprudential criticism of the Roe decision mounted, legal academics began to explore alternative constitutional foundations for the abortion right.

During this same period there were developments in feminist jurisprudence that facilitated a new conceptualization of the abortion right. A number of feminist legal scholars began to repudiate equality theory focused on issues of similarity and difference and to argue for an inquiry focused on issues of hierarchy and subordination (MacKinnon 1979; West 1990:57–62). This approach removed a crucial stumbling block to analyzing abortion in a sex equality framework. No longer was it necessary to demonstrate sex discrimination by comparing the treatment of women to a group of similarly situated men; instead, as Catharine MacKinnon argued, it was enough to show that "the policy or practice in question integrally contributes to the maintenance of an underclass or a deprived position because of gender status" (MacKinnon 1979:117). Indeed, as MacKinnon conceptualized the problem of inequality, gender-differentiated practices such as rape, pornography, and abortion-restrictive regulation played a central role in women's subordination (MacKinnon 1983a; 1983b:646–55; 1987:40–45). This paradigm shift facilitated equal protection challenges to abortion restrictions. For example, in 1984 Sylvia Law drew on MacKinnon's work in one of the first major articles to explore the abortion right in a sex equality framework, "Rethinking Sex and the Constitution." Law argued that because women's capacity to bear children represented a real and significant biological difference between the sexes, reproductive regulation should be evaluated under an anti-subordination framework; at the same time, she contended that the traditional comparative treatment approach to equal protection analysis should be retained for all other forms of sex-based regulation (1984:1007–13).

From Privacy to Equality: Analyzing Abortion Restrictions as Caste Regulation

A growing number of constitutional scholars now defend the abortion right on sex equality grounds. This section will briefly consider the new sex equality arguments for abortion, and then analyze their judicial reception to date.

Sex Equality Arguments for the Abortion Right

As it is currently interpreted, the equal protection clause imposes virtually no restraints on state regulation of women's reproductive lives. Together, the Court's physiological view of reproduction and its comparative understanding of equality present formidable obstacles to equal protection analysis of abortion restrictions. Yet, analyzed in historical perspective, it is clear that restrictions on abortion are deeply at odds with the values and commitments informing the constitutional guarantee of equal protection. As our analysis of the nineteenth-century criminalization campaign reveals, laws restricting abortion do not just regulate women's bodies; they regulate women's roles. Because abortion restrictions can enforce caste or status relations, such laws implicate constitutional guarantees of equality as well as privacy.

While the Court often reasons comparatively in interpreting the equal protection clause of the fourteenth amendment, it has also drawn upon a cluster of concepts associated with social status or caste.[21] As Kenneth Karst observes: "[T]he equality that matters in our Supreme Court is not the simple abstraction that likes should be treated alike. . . . The equal citizenship principle that is the core of the fourteenth amendment . . . is presumptively violated when the organized society treats someone as an inferior, as part of a dependent caste, or as a nonparticipant" (Karst 1983:248; see also Karst 1977:48; Lawrence 1990:439).[22] Other scholars have employed the concept of caste to criticize the Court's interpretation of the equal protection clause as excessively formalist. Cass Sunstein argues that "understanding . . . the equal protection principle as an attack on irrational differentiation—treating likes differently—has been a large mistake for constitutional law, which might instead have understood the principle as an attack on caste legislation. This understanding draws firm support from history" (Sunstein 1992:39 n. 143). Commentators who would replace the "equal treatment principle" with a mediating principle focused on issues of group subordination also invoke concepts associated with caste to describe the practices prohibited by the fourteenth amendment (Fiss 1976:157; MacKinnon 1979:117; Tribe 1988:1520).[23]

As this paper demonstrates, restrictions on abortion are readily analyzed as a form of caste regulation. In the nineteenth century, restrictions on abortion and contraception were enacted for the explicit purpose of forcing married women to bear children. Abortion restrictions were used to enforce the gender status norms of the separate spheres tradition; they perform a similar function today. Today, no less than in the past, restrictions on abortion force women to assume the status and perform the work of motherhood (Siegel 1992:371–77). Such restrictions do not merely inflict status-based injuries on women; they reflect status-based judgments about women. While the gendered judgments informing abortion restrictions are often obscured by the physiological discourses employed to justify the regulation, it is possible to see how gendered judgments shape the regulation by considering its justifications and structure in light of its social history (ibid., 359–68). For these reasons, the history of abortion-restrictive regulation calls into question its legitimacy under prevailing equal protection jurisprudence, which specifically condemns regulation of women's conduct rooted in archaic gender-based judgments about women's roles.[24] At the same time, because an historical analysis of abortion-restrictive regulation reveals its lineage and function as gender-caste regulation, this approach renders the regulation more amenable to review within the antisubordination framework proposed by critics of prevailing equal protection law.

An increasing number of scholars have advanced equal protection arguments against abortion restrictions. While these equality arguments do not specifically invoke the history of criminal abortion laws or analyze the regulation in a caste framework, they do emphasize that abortion restrictions are (1) a form of class legislation that (2) reflects status-based judgments about women and (3) inflicts status-based injuries on women. The new equal protection arguments point out that:

1. *Abortion restrictions single out women for an especially burdensome and invasive form of public regulation* (Law 1984:1015; Tribe 1988:1353–54; MacKinnon 1991:1321; Regan 1979:1623; Siegel 1992:354; Sunstein 1992:32–33).

2. *Abortion restrictions are gender-biased in justification and structure, reflecting diverse forms of status-based reasoning about women's roles.* When justifications for abortion restrictions are considered in a larger social context, it appears that they rest on a distinctive set of judgments about the unborn, not consistently expressed in other social settings and often controverted by other social practices (Tribe 1988:1354; Olsen 1989:126–30; Siegel 1992:318 n. 236, 365–66). The regulations are selective, imposing a duty of lifesaving on pregnant women not otherwise imposed on citizens or family members who have the capacity to save the life of another (Olsen 1989:129–30; Regan 1979; Siegel 1992:335–47, 366; Sunstein 1992:33–36). The selectivity of the compulsion is rarely noted because women are expected to perform the work of motherhood, and this role expectation makes reasonable, or invisible, the impositions of forced motherhood. Thus, in justification and structure, abortion restrictions reflect stereotypical assumptions about women's roles (Tribe 1988:1354; MacKinnon 1991:1320–21; Siegel 1992:361–68; Sunstein 1992:36–37).

3. *Restrictions on abortion injure women by compelling motherhood, forcing women to assume a role and to perform work that has long been used to subordinate them as a class.* The injuries inflicted on women by abortion restrictions are not attributable to nature, but instead reflect institutional practices of the society that would force women to bear children (MacKinnon 1991:1311–13; Siegel 1992:372–77). Because abortion-restrictive regulation coerces women to perform the work of motherhood without altering the conditions that continue to make such work a principal cause of their subordinate social status, it is a form of status-reinforcing state action that offends constitutional guarantees of equal protection (MacKinnon 1991:1319–21; Siegel 1992:377–79).

4. *Too often, legal restrictions on abortion do not save fetal lives but instead subject women, especially poor women, to unsafe, life-threatening medical procedures* (Olsen 1989:132; Sunstein 1992:37–39; cf. Tribe 1988:1353 and n. 111). If the state is genuinely interested in promoting the welfare of the unborn, it can and should do so by means that support women in the work of bearing and rearing children (MacKinnon 1991:1318–19; Siegel 1992:345–47, 380–81).

Judicial Reception of the Sex Equality Argument

In the years since *Roe* the Court has grown to better appreciate the gendered character of the abortion conflict. In part this is because the

Court has acquired experience interpreting the federal law prohibiting pregnancy discrimination in employment (Pregnancy Discrimination Act, 42 U.S.C. §2000e[k] [1993]).[25] But the Court's understanding of the abortion conflict has also been shaped by sex equality arguments for the abortion right.

In its most recent pronouncement on the abortion right, *Planned Parenthood of Southeastern Pennsylvania v. Casey*,[26] the Court upheld waiting-period restrictions on abortion, insisting that the state has the power to protect the sanctity of human life by requiring women who seek abortions to meditate on the consequences of their act. But it also reaffirmed women's privacy right, under *Roe*, to abort such pregnancies after due deliberation. In the *Casey* opinion, the Court identified constitutional reasons for protecting this privacy right not discussed in *Roe*. The Court observed that the state was obliged to respect a pregnant woman's decisions about abortion because her "suffering is too intimate and personal for the State to insist . . . upon its own vision of the woman's role, however dominant that vision has been in the course of our history and our culture. The destiny of the woman must be shaped to a large extent on her own conception of her spiritual imperatives and her place in society" (*Casey*, 2807). In short, the Court ruled that laws prohibiting abortion offend the Constitution because they use the power of the state to impose traditional sex roles on women.

For similar reasons, the Court struck down a provision of the Pennsylvania statute requiring a married woman to notify her husband before obtaining an abortion. The Court was concerned that, in conflict-ridden marriages, forcing women to inform their husbands about an abortion might deter them from "procuring an abortion as surely as if the Commonwealth had outlawed abortion in all cases" (ibid., 2829), and it ruled that the state lacked authority to constrain women's choices this way. But the Court also condemned the spousal notice rule as a traditional form of gender-status regulation. The notice requirement "give[s] to a man the kind of dominion over his wife that parents exercise over their children" (ibid., 2831) and thus reflects a "common-law understanding of a woman's role within the family," harkening back to a time when "a woman had no legal existence separate from her husband, who was regarded as her head and representative in the social state" (ibid., 2830–31, quoting *Bradwell v. Illinois*, 16 Wall. 130, 141 [1873] [Bradley, J., concurring]). "These views," the Court observed, "are no longer consistent with our understanding of the family, the individual, or the Constitution" (ibid., 2831).

Justice Blackmun, who authored *Roe*, endorsed the gender-conscious reasoning of the *Casey* decision and drew upon it to advance the argument that restrictions on abortion offend constitutional guarantees of *equality* as well as privacy. In this equality argument, Justice Blackmun emphasized that abortion restrictions are gender-biased in impetus and impact. When the state restricts abortion, it exacts the work of motherhood from women without compensating their labor because it assumes that it is women's "natural" duty to perform such labor:

> The State does not compensate women for their services; instead, it assumes that they owe this duty as a matter of course. This assumption—that women can simply be forced to accept the "natural" status and incidents of motherhood—appears to rest upon a conception of women's role that has triggered the protection of the Equal Protection Clause.   (ibid., 2847; citations and footnote omitted)

Restrictions on abortion do not stem solely from a desire to protect the unborn; they reflect—and enforce—judgments about women's roles. While the abortion controversy is typically discussed as a conflict between an individual's freedom of choice and the community's interest in protecting unborn life, Justice Blackmun's opinion reframes the conflict. The community's decision to intervene in women's lives is no longer presumptively benign; its decision to compel motherhood is presumptively suspect, one more instance of the sex-role restrictions imposed on women throughout American history.

While Justice Blackmun has recently retired from the Court, Justice Ruth Bader Ginsburg, who has recently joined the Court, shares the view that restrictions on abortion may violate constitutional guarantees of sex equality (Ginsburg 1985:1992). The Court as a whole is by no means ready to embrace the view that restrictions on abortion violate guarantees of equal protection;[27] but its opinion in *Casey* makes clear, as *Roe* did not, that "[t]he ability of women to participate equally in the economic and social life of the Nation has been facilitated by their ability to control their reproductive lives" (*Casey*, 2809).

What the Equality Argument Illuminates: Advantages of Analyzing Abortion Restrictions as Caste- or Status-Enforcing State Action

There are several advantages to analyzing abortion restrictions as caste- or status-enforcing state action. First, as this paper illustrates, the framework creates a hermeneutic of suspicion: historical analysis can be combined with conventional methods of demonstrating discriminatory bias, to show that gender-, race-, and class-based judgments may animate or structure abortion restrictions—and so call into question the "benign" justifications conventionally offered for fetal-protective regulation. As *Casey* illustrates, the Court will oppose abortion restrictions when it believes they are gender biased in impetus or impact, even if the Court is not ready to adopt the equal protection clause as the constitutional basis for protecting the abortion right.

Second, the caste framework offers a basis for discriminating between subordinating and emancipating forms of state intervention in women's reproductive lives. Because the inquiry focuses attention on the normative premises of reproductive regulation and its practical impact on women's lives, it supplies a framework that reconciles feminist objections to state involvement in matters of reproduction with feminist demands for state involvement in matters of reproduction.

Third, the caste framework is useful because it shifts the focus of critical inquiry from the physical to the social relations of reproduction—from the maternal/fetal relation to the network of social relations in which women conceive, gestate, and raise children. In distinct but related ways, this paradigm shift is important for purposes of legal argumentation and political coalition-building. Focusing analysis on the social conditions of motherhood reveals how discriminatory bias can infect reproductive regulation; this exercise in turn demonstrates that this society's professed concern for the welfare of future generations is pervasively contradicted by the manner in which it treats children and the women who raise them. Thus, the very analysis that reveals discriminatory bias in abortion restrictions and other forms of fetal-protective regulation simultaneously advances an argument that this society needs to reform the social conditions of motherhood if it in fact intends to promote the welfare of future generations. In this way, objections to coercive interventions in women's reproductive lives lead to demands for supportive intervention in women's reproductive lives, so that legislative support for the Freedom of Choice Act,[28] adequate child care, the Family and Medical Leave Act,[29] and supplemental nutrition programs[30] are tied together, as they are not under a privacy analysis. When the abortion question is reconfigured in this fashion, it is possible to argue for abortion rights without seeming to oppose motherhood; the charge that women seeking abortions devalue children and the work of raising them can be turned on its head and aimed at the society that would regulate their conduct. The argument for abortion rights is thus transformed into a dare and a demand: that this society honor the commitments putatively expressed in fetal-protective regulation by supporting those who are struggling to raise children.

Finally, there is value in the act of translation itself. Becoming multilingual about rights discourse facilitates a certain self-consciousness about advocacy. In this case, examining equality arguments for the abortion right can help identify elements of pro-choice rhetoric that are dysfunctional artifacts of early second-wave feminism. For example, some arguments in defense of the abortion right have equated freedom of choice with freedom from motherhood, without demanding the social reforms that would enable women to choose motherhood freely, i.e., without status-linked consequences for their welfare or autonomy. Moreover, defenses of the abortion right rarely address the ways that racism has shaped reproductive policies in this nation—focusing on birth-compelling regulation without acknowledging the history of birth-deterring regulation directed at poor peoples of color. Analyzing the case for abortion rights in a caste or equality framework illuminates these antimaternalist and race-essentialist tendencies in pro-choice arguments, and so explains why such arguments may alienate many women and men who otherwise might support the abortion right. For this reason and others, developing equality arguments for the abortion right can in fact reinvigorate privacy discourse. The exercise in translation should encourage us to identify the peculiar strengths of privacy discourse and to articulate privacy-based claims in ways that complement, rather than contradict, equality-based arguments for the abortion right (cf. Cohen 1992; Gavison 1992).

NOTES

1. 410 U.S. 113 (1973).

2. For some briefs written from the sex equality perspective, see Brief for the National Coalition Against Domestic Violence as Amicus Curiae Supporting Appellees, *Webster v. Reproductive Health Services*, 492 U.S. 490 (1989); Brief of Seventy-Seven Organizations Committed to Women's Equality as Amici Curiae in Support of Appellees, *Webster v. Reproductive Health Services*, 492 U.S. 490 (1989); Brief of Canadian Women's Organizations, Amici Curiae in Support of Appellees, *Webster v. Reproductive Health Services*, 492 U.S. 490

(1989); Brief Amici Curiae on Behalf of the New Jersey Coalition for Battered Women et al., *Right to Choose v. Byrne*, 91 N.J. 287, 450 A.2d 925 (1982).

3. While the common law required a wife to obtain her husband's consent to engage in many transactions, it did not require wives to obtain spousal consent for an abortion, thus treating the law of abortion in terms entirely distinct from the law of marriage. See Means 1968:428–34.

4. For analysis of the ways in which the reform of marital status law diverged from and converged with the criminalization of birth control practices in the postwar era, see Siegel 1992:319–23.

5. 208 U.S. 412 (1908).

6. For example, in 1873, when the Court upheld Myra Bradwell's exclusion from the Illinois bar, Justice Bradley justified the State's decision to prohibit women from practicing law by citing the contractual disabilities imposed on wives by the common law. See *Bradwell v. Illinois*, 83 U.S. (16 Wall.) 130, 141 (1873) (Bradley, J., concurring).

7. *City of Akron v. Akron Center for Reproductive Health*, 462 U.S. 416, 461 (1983) (O'Connor, J., dissenting) ("[P]otential life is not less potential in the first weeks of pregnancy than it is at viability or afterward. . . . Accordingly, I believe that the State's interest in protecting potential human life exists throughout the pregnancy").

8. For an analysis of how gendered assumptions structure putatively gender-neutral justifications for abortion restrictions, see Siegel 1992:350 and n., 362, 361–68.

9. See infra, text accompanying nn. 11–15.

10. See Tussman and tenBroek 1949:344 ("The Constitution does not require that things different in fact be treated in law as though they were the same. But it does require, in its concern for equality, that those who are similarly situated be similarly treated").

11. See *Craig v. Boren*, 429 U.S. 190, 198 (1976); ibid., 198–99 (rejecting statutory schemes premised on "increasingly outdated misconceptions concerning the role of females in the home rather than in the 'marketplace and world of ideas' ") (quoting *Stanton v. Stanton*, 421 U.S. 7, 14–15 [1975]).

12. *Califano v. Webster*, 430 U.S. 313, 317 (1977).

13. *Stanton*, 421 U.S. 7, 14.

14. 417 U.S. 484 (1974).

15. *Michael M. v. Superior Court*, 450 U.S. 464, 469, 471 (1981) (plurality opinion); ibid., 478 (Stewart J., concurring).

16. 1429 U.S. 125 (1976).

17. 42 U.S.C. §§2000e to 2000h–6 (1989).

18. Pub. L. No. 95–555, §1, 92 Stat. 2076, 2076 (codified at 42 U.S.C. §2000e[k]) (1989) (amendment to federal employment discrimination law, providing that distinctions on the basis of pregnancy are distinctions on the basis of sex).

19. The comparable treatment standard defined equality formally, and so provided no basis for challenging "facially neutral" employment practices having an exclusionary impact on pregnant women. See Siegel 1985: 931–33.

20. A leading feminist proponent of the comparable treatment standard described its purpose in the following terms: "It sought to overcome the definition of the prototypical worker as male and to promote an integrated—and *androgynous*—prototype" (W. Williams 1984–85:363) (footnote omitted; emphasis added).

21. As Justice Brennan observed in *Plyler v. Doe*, 457 U.S. 202, 217 n. 14 (1982), "[l]egislation imposing special disabilities upon groups disfavored by virtue of circumstances beyond their control suggests the kind of 'class or caste' treatment that the Fourteenth Amendment was designed to abolish." See Strauss 1989:940–44 (equal protection jurisprudence concerned with issues of partiality, subordination, stigma, and second-class citizenship).

22. See Lawrence 1990:439 ("The holding in *Brown*—that racially segregated schools violate the equal protection clause—reflects the fact that segregation amounts to a demeaning, caste-creating practice").

23. See Fiss 1976:157 (condemning practices that inflict "status harm"); MacKinnon 1979:117 (condemning practices that "contribute to the maintenance of an underclass"); Tribe 1988:1520 (condemning practices that "perpetuate subordination [and] reflect a tradition of hostility toward an historically subjugated group").

24. See text accompanying nn. 11–13.

25. Recently, for example, in *UAW v. Johnson Controls*, 111 S.Ct. 1196 (1991), the Court held that a battery manufacturing plant could not protect the offspring of its employees by prohibiting fertile women from working in lead-exposed jobs; the Court ruled that such a policy, directed at fertile women, but not at fertile men, was a form of sex discrimination. While the *Johnson Controls* opinion rests in significant part on the text of the Pregnancy Discrimination Act, the opinion also reflects the Court's growing appreciation of the fact that fetal-protective regulation may reflect judgments about women's roles, and not simply their bodies. In *Johnson Controls*, the Court observed that "[c]oncern for a woman's existing or potential offspring historically has been the excuse for denying women equal employment opportunities" (1206) and cited *Muller v. Oregon* in support of this point.

26. 112 S.Ct. 2791 (1992).

27. It is noteworthy, for example, that in *Bray v. Alexandria Women's Health Clinic*, 113 S.Ct. 753 (1993), a case deciding whether federal civil rights laws apply to protesters at abortion clinics, Justice Scalia, writing for a majority of the Court, rejected the notion that "opposition to abortion can reasonably be presumed to reflect a sex-based intent" (761).

28. S. 25, 103d Cong., 1st sess. (1993); H.R. 25, 103d Cong., 1st sess. (1993); H.R. 1068, 103d Cong., 1st sess. (1993).

29. P. L. 103–03, 107 Stat. 6 (1993).

30. For example, the supplemental food program for needy women, infants, and children (commonly known by the acronym WIC), *Child Nutrition Act of 1966*, §17, U.S. Code, Vol. 42, §1786 (1989).

4 | The Legal Construction of "Mother"

M. M. SLAUGHTER

The role of primary caretaker for children usually brings with it a diminished earning capacity and, thus, a vulnerability to economic pressures. This has long been recognized as a situation that has acted to the disadvantage of women, traditionally the primary caretakers. Years of discussion and legal reform, however, have done little to better their economic situation. It remains the fact that married women with children are normally economically dependent on their husbands, while unmarried women with children are often dependent either on the state or on former partners. This paper argues that legal reforms have been ineffective largely because they have failed to address the multidimensional quality of such women's economic marginalization. Drawing on Foucault's theory of social power, which recognizes that multiple forces intersect to cause or construct social phenomena, I will present a more complex picture.

Before I proceed, a word about terminology. *Mother* is a term that refers to two functions—childbearing and childrearing. Since women are usually the primary childrearers as well as childbearers, the two functions are usually collapsed under this term. I separate them as a deliberate measure to illustrate my point that it is social relations that produce *female* Motherhood. In this article, I use the word *Mother* (with a capital M) to indicate the person who rears children, rather than the person who bears them. In this usage, there is nothing in nature that requires women to Mother, or prevents men from doing so.

Foucauldian analysis reveals that we inhabit all-encompassing, interlocking systems of power. These networks of power overlap to produce institutions, practices, norms, and discourses that are interwoven into webs of regulation that produce social subjects, such as, for example, "homosexuals." Power works similarly in multiple ways to produce compulsory Motherhood for women. Central to this production are the power relations that exist between the waged labor market and the nuclear family. As they currently exist, these are interrelated. Because of that, so are the roles of Breadwinner and Mother. One will change only if the other changes.

Women are socially constructed as Mothers or childrearers because of a system of power that keeps them from working to full capacity in the labor market. This is the result of two interrelated factors. First, waged labor is predicated on a division between the functional roles of Breadwinner and Mother, between an Ideal Worker free to devote all his time to his employer and a person at home providing domestic services (J. Williams 1991; Abrams 1990; Dowd 1989; Finley 1986; Law 1983). Second, because of the way the labor market operates in relation to the family, these specialized roles come to be gendered. Discrimination and labor market constraints on opportunity cause women to turn to Mothering.

To put this in more concrete terms, the Ideal Worker is a worker with no childrearing obligations. Workers who have these obligations—mainly women—are less valued and their opportunities constrained. As a result, childrearers develop tenuous ties to the labor market and are more associated with the domestic economy. This cycle is self-perpetuating. Women relinquish labor market ties in order to devote their energies to domesticity; because of their domestic ties women are devalued as workers and discriminated against in the labor market, which in turn forces them to turn more to domesticity. Thus, within the gendered division of labor, women can either be Ideal Workers but not Mothers; or Mothers but not Ideal Workers. Or they might be one during youth, the other in maturity. Alternatively, they might work the second shift and do both simultaneously but neither ideally. What the norm of the Ideal Worker and the gendered division of labor do not permit—for women and hence for men—is an equal distribution of work and childrearing.

It is, therefore, social forces that create the norm of female Motherhood and construct women as Mothers (as men are simultaneously constructed as Breadwinners). The grounds of that construction are then erased; the family and market generate an essentialist vision of women as having a natural connection to the role of Mother. The family and market construct the roles of Breadwinner and Mother as gendered. Since this construction is made to appear invisible, however, these gendered roles appear natural and thus change seems difficult, if not impossible.

The elements of this social system are mutually constitutive, and therefore any law or social policy that is premised on the norm of the Ideal Worker ties women to the role of Mothering. Anything that constructs or favors men as Breadwinners also constructs or favors women as Mothers. Anything that keeps or drives women from full status in waged labor constructs or maintains the traditional division of labor and gendered roles. The only way out of this cycle is change in the nature of waged labor, that is, change in both discriminatory practices *and* the norm of the Ideal Worker.

These two factors must be seen as interrelated. If labor market discrimination against women ended, the *functional* division of roles would still be left in place. We would simply have women who were permitted to become like men, i.e., Breadwinners who conform to the norm of the Ideal Worker. Just as women could become Breadwinners, men could become Mothers. All that does, however, is challenge the gendered nature of the specialized roles. To change relations of dependency it is necessary to end the norm of the Ideal Worker. This means that men and women must become *both* workers and parents at the same time.

Law is a discourse produced by social power that both constitutes and legitimates these social arrangements. It is part of a normalizing system that regulates and constructs subjects. In the second half of this paper I examine examples from sex discrimination law, social welfare law (Unemployment Insurance, Aid to Dependent Children, Social Security), as well as immigration, tax, divorce, and alimony law, to show how they are complicitous with the construction of female Motherhood. Because law is treated as an "objective" discourse free of power relations, it is not recognized as a mechanism that constructs and maintains the power relations inherent in the gendered division of labor and compulsory Motherhood for women.

Foucault and Social Construction Theory

For my purposes, the critical feature in Foucauldian theory is that it points to an all-encompassing, multidimensional network of social regulation with interdependent and mutually constitutive parts. Through this theory we can understand how Motherhood for women is made compulsory by regulative forces that operate throughout the entire social system. It is the interlocking and mutually constitutive nature of social institutions, practices, and discourses that makes the system so resistant to change.

In Foucault's theory, society is saturated with power; power, like air, is everywhere. It has "a capillary form of existence . . . [it] seeps into the very grain of individuals, reaches right into their bodies, permeates their gestures, their posture, what they say, how they learn to live and work with other people" (Sheridan 1980:217; Foucault 1980b:98). It is not localized at any one point or with the sovereign or state. Nor does it operate simply by punishing or repressing a priori subjects. Foucault objects to the repressive theory of power because it "adopts a purely juridical conception of such power, [one that] identifies power with a law which says no" (Foucault 1980b:119). For Foucault, the main function of power is to produce rather than repress subjects (Foucault 1980b:141). It is "a productive network which runs through the whole social body" (Foucault 1980b:119). Power is constantly exercised by regulation or "surveillance" to create a "society of normalization," i.e., a society that is organized so that there are multiple social pressures forcing people to conform to particular socially constructed norms (Foucault 1980b:107). This normalizing society is maintained through a number of regulative apparatuses that arise under "local conditions" coming from the bottom up, not from the top down. Law is one of these and operates not simply to punish but to normalize or produce (Foucault 1980a:144).

As power "fixes its gaze" on subjects, it constitutes, regulates, and disciplines them into oppositional relations. Power also essentializes these categories and makes them appear natural and necessary. Foucault, however, argues that individuals do not have a priori, essential natures (like masculine/feminine, homosexual/heterosexual, Mother/Breadwinner). Rather, identities are contingent and constructed; they are created by normalizing discourses, not nature. Thus in his most famous work Foucault shows the way in which homosexual identity was created in part through the power of the law in the eighteenth century. What had been an individual person who engaged in particular sexual acts came to be seen as kind of person, "a type of life," "a species" (Foucault 1980a:43–44; Dreyfus and Rabinow 1982:173). Homosexuals and heterosexuals were constructed as categories of being and represented as kinds of life (Foucault 1980b:125; 1980a:100–101). Homosexuality was produced or marked out as a prohibited category and compulsory heterosexuality simultaneously was produced as the norm. In the same way, because of the gendered division of labor, female Motherhood has been constructed as the essential form of childrearing.

Power constructs and normalizes through specialized knowledge and discourse, e.g., medicine, psychiatry, law, criminology, social science, economics, and so on, operating in conjunction with institutions (Foucault 1980b:159). Discourse or specialized knowledge (like law) purports to stand outside the system of power to declare what is right, objective, real, or true. Foucault argues, however, that we are never outside of power, and as a result, discourse precedes rather than represents the subject.[1] Women, for example, are treated as if they were naturally and essentially Mothers. For Foucault, however, there is no underlying, essential, foundational reality (such as female Motherhood) outside the system of power; discourse simply masks underlying relations of power. All discourse and knowledge comes from and is imbued with power. Thus:

> Power and knowledge directly imply one another. . . . There is no power relation without the correlative constitution of a field of knowledge, nor any knowledge that does not presuppose and constitute at the same time power relations. . . . It is not the subject of knowledge that produces a corpus of knowledge . . . but power/knowledge . . . that determines the forms and possible domains of knowledge. (Foucault 1979:27–28)

The point is not so much that everything is contingent or untrue or bad but that "everything is dangerous" (Dreyfus and Rabinow 1982:232).

Identity, like knowledge, is not essential; it is constructed and contingent and *because* of this it can change. In a Foucauldian world, therefore, roles are not entirely determined.[2] They are inevitably in tension and conflict. Power does not repress and leave the field to one eternal master. Rather, because it emanates from local conditions, power produces endless conflict in which contenders can maneuver and resist. There is continuous struggle between those who name and are named, who construct and are constructed. The forces of social power are always at war (Foucault 1980a:95; Sawicki 1988). The task is to resist and unmask the power behind the institutions and discourses that name. The practices of the market, for example, are in conflict with the practices of the family. Although this produces conflict for women, it is because of this conflict that there can be resistance—both to labor market discrimination and to the construction of compulsory family roles.

Power

The Labor Market System

To simplify immensely, in an agriculturally based economy like the one that existed prior to the nineteenth century, there was little separation between home and market and between work and childrearing. All family members, male and female alike, worked in the domestic economy and took part in childrearing. With the onset of industrialism, men began to work outside the home. This is not to say that women did not; Black women in particular were likely to work for wages. But most women, if they worked at all, did not develop as strong or as continuous ties to the labor market as men. They often went out to work before marriage, or at seasonal times during marriage, or as necessity dictated and their ability to care for their children allowed. Most important, whatever their actual participation in waged labor, an ideology of separate spheres developed that presented a picture of women as full-time homemakers and in control of the domestic sphere (Cott 1979; Bloch 1978; Olsen 1983).

Separate spheres ideology, and its attendant gendering of labor, was a social construction that covered up and contained complex power relations in economic and social spheres, particularly relations between men and women and family and market (Kerber 1988). In actual fact the household was a mixed economy rather than a self-enclosed entity. Domestic labor helped "produce" the household and had value parallel to the value of the paid worker. Yet in the course of the nineteenth century this value came to be ignored and unpaid domestic production appeared to be effortless and natural. Paid labor came to be more highly valued than unpaid housework and the gendered division of labor was established. Separate spheres ideology was, therefore, a rhetorical construction that justified and maintained this division (Boydston 1990).

The gendered division of labor was predicated on the norm of the Ideal Worker, which assumes that the worker has the time and ability to work to whatever level the employer demands. This assumes in turn that there is a homemaker who cares for the household and children. In exchange for his efforts, the Ideal Worker would earn a living wage that could support a family (Macnicol 1980). Even though the living wage was a myth for many working-class men, the gendered division of labor within the family was built around it. Given this assumption of a family wage and the realities of raising large families, women came to work in increasing numbers inside the home. Even though they might at times go out to work, or take work in, Mothers were by definition excluded from the status of the Ideal Worker.

Mothers now work outside the home in unprecedented numbers. In March 1991 close to 60 percent of Mothers were in the labor force. Nearly 40 percent worked full-time; 17 percent part-time. Of those working, 42 percent had children under the age of six; 41 percent between 7 and 14 years, and 17 percent between 15 and 18 years (Chira 1992:L1, L2; Richardson 1992:B1, B5). In 1989 the average wife increased her waged work by 268 hours and all the rise in the income of an average married couple ($3,450) was attributable to the work of the wife (Mollison 1992:H3). Nevertheless, although these Mothers are workers, they are still not Ideal Workers or Breadwinners in the sense defined by the gendered division of labor. No matter how much Mothers work, few can work to the full level of commitment required by the norm of the Ideal Worker. As a result, many Mothers are forced to drop out of the labor market entirely, or work part time or seasonally. Often Mothers work in the labor market discontinuously depending on family and children's circumstances.

Other ways in which Mothers attempt to accommodate work and family responsibilities include working full-time, but at jobs like school teaching that allow summer vacations, or jobs that provide regular nine to five hours or are located near a child's school or baby-sitter. Alternatively, a Mother might take a job that requires fewer hours than other positions, like permanent law associate rather than partner, or that is less stressful or demanding than she would take if she did not have children, like selling small-ticket items at Sears rather than big-ticket items. Also included here is the professional Mother who takes a job that does not require travel or, in the case of the attorney, litigating; or the Mother who does not publish as much as male or childless colleagues, or leaves her job an hour early because of the baby-sitter, or fails to submit a grant proposal, or misses a meeting, ad infinitum. At every point that a Mother directs her time or energy to childrearing rather than to the labor market, she departs from the norm of the Ideal Worker.[3] Accordingly, in what follows, I use the phrase "drop out" to refer to any degree of departure from the underlying norm of the Breadwinner as a person giving full commitment of time and energy to labor market work.

I take it as axiomatic that, barring discrimination, the more one invests in waged labor the more one will realize a return and progress. (Clearly discrimination affects this, and at the lower end of the market there is a diminishing return.) The person who works full-time will gain over the person who works part-time, whether in the form of salary, benefits, experience, seniority, eligibility for disability or Social Security, and so on. This is equally true for the person who has a strong, long-term, continuous attachment to waged labor as opposed to the person who drops in and out of the labor market as many Mothers do. With very few exceptions, the Mother who returns to the labor market after her children are established will rarely achieve the same professional level as her similarly placed colleagues who have worked at their careers continuously.[4] Clearly, women as a class do not reap as many gains as they would if they did not have to shoulder most of the child-rearing obligations.[5] Relative to the Ideal Worker, they lose.

This loss is seen, for example, in discrimination against pregnant workers. While pregnancy is protected by the Pregnancy Discrimination Act, it is treated as a disability and the Act provides only that if an employer gives disability leave to other employees, it must give similar leave to expectant mothers. If others do not get the leave neither do pregnant women. They have no affirmative protection.

This loss is also exemplified by inadequate family leave policies. Until recently, less than one half of workers had a right to parental leave. In 1988–89, in private businesses employing more than one hundred employees, it was available to 31 percent of full-time working women and 16 percent of men (Grossman 1992). In state and local government the figures were 50 percent and 33 percent respectively (Dedger 1992). The newly enacted Family and Medical Leave Act of 1993 covers businesses employing more than fifty workers and workers who have worked for at least 1,250 hours in one year (25 hours a week). It provides twelve weeks of unpaid leave in any twelve-month period upon the birth or adoption of a child or to care for a child with a serious health condition. The worker must be returned to his previous position or an equivalent one and health benefits must be maintained during the leave (Clymer 1993:A1). The Women's Legal Defense Fund estimates the Act covers 60 percent of American workers. This Act might be helpful to some childrearers, but since it does not pay salary benefits, it is not clear how much difference it will make, especially to low-income earners. More problematic, most women work for small businesses, which are exempt from the Act. Furthermore, the Act does not provide full protection: workers can still be dismissed for "poor performance" even in cases where the performance was related to a family member's illness as, for example, a child dying a lingering death from cancer (Barringer 1993:C1). Despite the Act many Mothers will still be forced to split their time and energy between workplace and family.

Another recognition, indeed institutionalization, of the loss suffered by childrearers are "mommy track" positions for professionals (Schwartz 1989; Lewin 1989:A18; Erlich 1989a:126). Typically, the Mommy gives up her chances for partnership or for promotion to top management in exchange for a less demanding or less time-consuming job, such as the position of permanent associate. The mommy track is a recognition of the fact that Mothers need time and energy to devote to their children, and that because of this they are unable to perform to the standard of the Ideal Worker.

Because the norm of the Ideal Worker assumes a total commitment to the employer, even when Mothers attempt to combine working and parenting their work efforts are devalued (Abrams 1989:1221). The mommy track, for example, is devalued rather than construed as an appropriate and respectable way to combine the dual obligations of work and family (Abrams 1989:1237 at n. 197). In addition, when parental leave is available, taking it is often considered an unwise career move (Erlich 1989a, 1989b:98). This devaluation stems from and reinforces the division between the family and work (Abrams 1989:1223) and disproportionately burdens working Mothers (Rhode 1991:1744).

Law has legitimized and reified this norm of the Ideal Worker and its consequent division of labor by acceding to employers' demands that any accommodation to workers be tempered by "business necessity" (Abrams 1989:1227–28). Similarly, employers and legislators have in many cases failed to take steps to alleviate this socially constructed dichotomy. Such steps include arrangements for flextime, part-time work with benefits, leave for child care, and so on (Abrams 1989:1237). Breaking down the socially constructed norm of total commitment to labor market work—and the gendered division between work and family—is necessary to enable both men and women to work and to Mother. One might argue that (some) women could achieve the status of Ideal Worker through child care—that Mothers might conceivably reach male norms by having others do their childrearing. This just shifts the problem to a different structural level. It still assumes and constructs women as Mothers. The providers of child care are overwhelmingly women whether they are hired or are family and, if their work is not free or bartered, it is typically low paying. In the case of relatives, it continues the tradition of treating childrearing as unpaid work. In the case of workers, it creates a class of paid Mothers who perform this task because they have few or limited options in other sectors of the labor market. Thus these women recapitulate the plight of all women who are constrained to take on childrearing because their other options are limited. Ultimately it simply places poor women in a position of Mothers relative to more endowed women who act as Breadwinners. It constructs poor women as compulsory Mothers.

Marriage and the Market

The discussion so far has recognized a complementary division between market and family and a concomitant division between the roles of Breadwinner and Mother. These roles are, but need not be, gendered. Women are not "given" as Mothers. Rather, mothering is constructed as a woman's role. To understand how this construction takes place, in addition to the norm of the Ideal Worker we must also look at the discriminatory nature of the waged labor market.

It is widely recognized that within the labor market there is explicit discrimination against, and job segregation of, women (Rhode 1989:162–64). Forty percent of women still work in the pink collar ghetto in secretarial work, retail sales, bookkeeping, domestic work, elementary school teaching, waitressing, and nursing (Pearce 1990:269). Women are also disproportionately represented in low paying, dead-end jobs. Furthermore, there are substantial disparities in income between men and women. Given the same amount of capital investment in work—in education, time, skill, and so forth—women do not advance as rapidly as men (Rhode 1991:1758), and despite recent gains women still make only 65 cents to the male dollar. This is partially because it is assumed that the male is the Breadwinner and needs to make a living wage, while women's jobs are considered to be supplementary to family income. The division of labor between Breadwinner and Mother within the nuclear family operates against this background of discrimination.[6]

To understand how discrimination interacts with domestic choices it is useful to look at Gary Becker's economic theory of the family (G. Becker 1991:31–79). This theory suggests that women turn to domesticity because of their limited options and rewards elsewhere. Becker argues first that specialization of roles is economically efficient and marital partners will seek this efficiency since it maximizes utility or gain. He then asserts that a person with a comparative advantage will invest in the market in which he or she has the advantage. The comparative advantage is different for each person depending on all the individual factors that have gone into his or her development.

Becker goes on to argue that there is an inverse relation between a worker's worth in the market and his domestic investment. If a worker's value in the labor market is low, the cost of investing in the domestic economy is low, and the worker will invest heavily in domesticity. In the nuclear family, this investment is relative and comparative. Assuming the couple will maximize total family income, the marital partner with the lowest value in waged labor (i.e., the one who commands the lowest pay) will be the one to make the heaviest investment in domesticity. When women make less than men—and they usually do—it is "rational" that they be the ones to cut back or drop out of the labor market (in the incremental sense defined earlier) to rear the children and to provide domestic services.[7] Until the benefits that the wife could gain from the labor market outweigh the benefits of domestic production, she will invest in the household economy by bearing and raising children and developing the husband's career. As long as the husband gains more than the wife loses, it is best for the family that the lower earning wife be the childrearer.

This is the origin of the cycle of dependency. Once they start devoting their energies to childrearing, Mothers fall behind in developing market skills and in maintaining their place in waged labor. This makes them the appropriate candidates for assuming the childrearing duties but at the same time it drives them further into economic marginalization and dependency on the Breadwinner. It also affects the dynamics of gender roles within the nuclear family. Women have less bargaining power because of men's superior position in the workplace. Since men usually have better work opportunities and higher salaries, they have the power to refuse to engage in domestic activities, which in turn helps them maintain their superiority in work (England and Farkas 1986:191–94; Furstenberg 1990:381; Gerson 1985:174). Because women become the Mothers, an all-embracing system is perpetuated and women are kept economically marginalized.

Becker has been read to assert that women have the comparative advantage in childrearing and choose Motherhood because of biology, i.e., that their specialization in Motherhood is biologically determined (Hochschild and Machung 1989:4; Rhode 1991:1757–58). Since their comparative advantage is in childbearing, they will rationally opt for domesticity. In the new edition to his *Treatise on the Family*, however, Becker explicitly disclaims this reading (G. Becker 1991:4). Rather he claims that his theory asserts only that one parent will specialize in Mothering and that, all other things being equal, that could be either the husband or the wife, depending on the particular individual's comparative advantage.

Becker goes on to point out, however, that there is discrimination against women in the labor market and that this is often what gives men a comparative advantage as Breadwinners. According to Becker, if there were no discrimination, either the husband or wife would Mother according to what their individual preferences, skills, or advantages dictated. It is because the market disadvantages them (through less opportunity and less money) that women rather than men become Mothers. Because they are constrained in the market, they choose Motherhood. Indeed this creates the norm of the nuclear family that assumes that wives/Mothers must be attached to husbands/Breadwinners. Martha Fineman points out that the disadvantaging of Mothers would not be a problem if there were state support for them. The system we have, however, is one that is driven by the policy of providing private, family support for childrearing (Fineman 1992:663–65; Fineman, this volume).

Becker's theory is both descriptive and normative. It clearly describes the economic choices made by many couples today. Whether it is fully adequate as an explanation of those choices is another question. Evidence indicates that family decisions are shaped, inter alia, by class, cultural background, marital relations, time, location, availability of child care, as well as perception of job opportunities, earning potential, opportunities for advancement, and family economics. Thus it is possible that the fact that women are lower earners interacts with other factors in influencing their decision to Mother.

More problematic is Becker's application of rational choice theory to women's "choice" to Mother instead of to work at waged labor. Theories such as Becker's suggest that women freely choose to Mother and in so doing they contribute to their own dependency and economic marginalization. They imply that women are either unaware of this contribution or that they are complicitous with it. They do not acknowledge that women are constrained by a number of social and economic forces to choose Mothering and that the choice here is clearly limited. The fact is that while women might contribute to their own marginalization, often it is because that is the best of the available options. It should not be assumed they do so, however, either because of their biological preferences for children or because they are unaware of the fact they are doing it. Often they are painfully aware. They know they cannot be

Ideal Workers and Mothers at the same time and that something has to give. They also know that they should develop attachments to the labor market because of the threat of divorce and its impoverishment. When they are forced to diminish labor market ties in favor of childrearing they know they dig themselves deeper into a hole of dependency and its attendant risks. But at the same time, they realize that they have to take care of their children because there is no one else who will do it. Gerson especially shows the tensions, negotiations, and compromises between Breadwinners and Mothers over the question of who will do the domestic work (Gerson 1985). All but the most traditional and endowed Mothers are in a constant state of conflict about where to invest and how to divide their energies. The most apt response to this situation is Joan Williams's: "if a rapist puts a knife to your throat and offers you a choice of rape or sodomy, you do not celebrate your 'choice'—you protest the range of choices offered as fundamentally unacceptable" (J. Williams 1991:1612).

The tensions women feel between the pull of the workplace and the pull of childrearing are created by conflicting norms and reveal the way in which Becker's theory is a normative discourse masking relations of social power. It is implicitly normative in its assumption that Mothers will rationally maximize benefits for their families by giving up work and specializing in domesticity. This is a covert ideology that implies that women should not have interests independent of, or in opposition to, their families' interests, however those may be defined. What it does not recognize is that women may have independent interests in career development—self-esteem and self-expression, for example—that they consider to be worth pursuing, even if they do not maximize family income (Okin 1991:147). In addition, given the reality of the increasing likelihood of future divorce, Mothers also have to look to their own interests as potentially the sole supporters of themselves and their children.

Thus the premise of Becker's theory—that families seek to maximize income—is essentially normative and, like all normative and power driven discourse, shapes individuals and their behavior. It erases any interests of women that are independent of their families and makes women's claims to self-development invisible. In doing so, it subordinates their interests to those of their families and children. It constructs them as Mothers and masks relations of power—the power, for example, that defines what is rational. This is a discourse that purports to assert a reality, i.e., that it is rational (read "right") to maximize family income. It makes this choice seem natural and inevitable. Becker's discourse, however, erases the real costs and conflicts, erases the relations of power it contains, and erases the wider contexts of choice, change, and resistance.

Knowledge: Legal Discourse

As we have seen, the norm of the Ideal Worker and the gendered division of labor are social constructions resulting from relations of power that are masked and made to appear natural. These constructions create a regulatory or disciplinary regime in which women are channeled into Motherhood because they are cut off from labor market opportunities and their efforts are devalued. There is no single marketplace factor that causes this marginalization and devaluation; rather, there are a myriad of regulative devices—small and large, social and legal—that directly and indirectly weave this web of social power. Multiple local conditions produce an entire regulatory system that constructs Mothers.

Law is a discourse that is complicitous with and legitimates this process. Law operates within the field of power to support the gendered division of labor and the institutions that create it. It either maintains the status quo with its built-in gender disparities or it is used to shape workplace and family policies based on a gendered division of labor. Law is, therefore, a discourse that masks power relations and strategic interests; it is not a source of truth, justice, or resistance.

Discrimination Law

One of the most illuminating examples of law that lets stand existing gender disparities is that relating to sex discrimination in the labor market. Rather than acting as an agent of change to correct the structural asymmetries between men and women, the law reflects and reinforces asymmetries that, it claims, exist prior to entry into the marketplace—i.e., differences found in men and women either because of nature or socialization. Thus despite the fact that the law claims it prohibits discrimination, it is often part of the system and the conditions that create it.

Courts have revealed a reluctance to scrutinize and hence change discriminatory conditions in the marketplace (Schultz 1990). One tactic has been to claim, for example, that women are marginalized through their own choices rather than through employers' discriminatory practices. These judicial decisions have relied on theories about the nature and interests of women, particularly their Mothering natures and interests. Given these, marketplace practices are irrelevant. Thus legal discourse assumes a position outside the phenomena it judges and in so doing asserts that it is dealing with a pre-given reality rather than creating one.

The most famous example of this is the *Sears* case (628 F.Supp. 1264, affd., 839 Fd. 302 [1988]) brought by female employees selling low-ticket items who had been denied commissioned jobs selling appliances and other big-ticket items. The court ruled for Sears, finding that the company had not kept women from these jobs; rather, women had shown little interest in them because they were more stressful and time-consuming. Women preferred to devote their energies to their families rather than invest them in more demanding jobs.

Vicki Schultz has shown that the law assumes that women enter the labor market with preformed and fixed interests in Mothering and that these are beyond the control and concern of the market and the law. She argues that, to the contrary, women's "interests" are highly elastic and are shaped by context and circumstance. They are socially constructed. Thus to the extent that women have no "interest" in nontraditional or challenging jobs, it is in large measure because they perceive long in advance that there is no opportunity for advancement (Schultz 1990:1828). Schultz concludes that if labor market opportunities and circumstances are altered, so too will women's "interests" and preferences and in turn their choices and behavior. If there is less job discrimination and more opportunity, women will be less "interested" in investing in childrearing. The law could act as an agent of that change. A different legal discourse would deconstruct women as Mothers (W. Williams 1991).

Social Welfare Law

A good example of the way in which the legal system devalues Mothering is found in the laws governing social welfare, including Unemployment Insurance, Aid to Families with Dependent Children, and Social Security pensions. Each is predicated on a norm of the Ideal Worker and a gendered division of labor within the family; each undermines the position of Mothers relative to ideal Breadwinners and thus perpetuates a status quo in which the weaker party is the one who is constructed as Mother. These schemes had their origin in the earlier part of the century in a deeply gendered division of labor between Breadwin-

ner and Mother and a labor market that afforded women little opportunity to earn a living wage.[8] The current legal regime of social benefits
continues to operate in terms of this two-track, gendered division and
in so doing, discriminates against Mothers in ways that were not originally contemplated. This can be seen most clearly in the contrast
between Unemployment Insurance and Aid to Families with Dependent Children.

Unemployment Insurance and Aid to Families with Dependent Children The law regulating Unemployment Insurance (UI) provides benefits only to workers with strong attachments to the labor force, i.e.,
those who have worked full-time for the relevant qualifying period or
have accumulated a specified amount of wages (U.S. Dept. of Labor
1991:3–3). Thus the program is based on the norm of the Ideal Worker,
most of whom are men. It should be stated at the outset that UI regulations vary widely from state to state and any given state may provide
an exception to this rule. Nevertheless, the general thrust of the law disfavors Mothers. It does not provide for many part-time and casual
workers, most of whom tend to be women. Seventeen percent of
women work part-time because they find this kind of work compatible
with childrearing (Chira 1992:L1). UI works on the assumption that
workers are only temporarily dislocated and will return to the labor
market quickly. It thus operates to affirm the recipients' identities as
(Ideal) Workers.

Mothers by contrast often work intermittently and leave the job
market for extended periods of time. When they do they are considered
to have severed their ties with the labor market entirely even though
many, if not most, eventually return to it. Thus their childrearing and
work patterns do not align with those of the Ideal Worker; as a result
they are squeezed out of the UI system. Because of their particular work
patterns, Mothers often fail to meet UI eligibility requirements. Diana
Pearce shows, for example, that in 1981 in Virginia, eligibility for UI
required earnings of $2,200 for two quarters. Thirty-three percent of
women workers could not meet these requirements compared to only
20 percent of men (Pearce 1985:451). In 1992 the Virginia wage
requirement for two quarters was $3,250 (U.S. Dept. of Labor
1992:3–28). Although they do in fact work—both in the household
and in waged labor—women's identities as workers during their periods
of domestic work are not recognized or rewarded.

Mothers are also disadvantaged by what is considered to be a legitimate reason for quitting. Although federal legislation prevents disqualification "solely on the basis of pregnancy," given the structure of some state eligibility schemes, a pregnant worker can nevertheless be disqualified.[9] Many states disqualify all workers who voluntarily quit without good cause and define pregnancy as being in that category. The Supreme Court has upheld such a disqualification for a pregnant worker on the grounds that they are not singled out. All that the federal law requires is that the disqualification be nondiscriminatory (*Wimberly v. Labor and Industrial Relations Comm. of Missouri*, 479 U.S. 511 [1987]). Moreover, there is no affirmative protection for pregnant workers. Quitting for domestic reasons (to marry, join a spouse, fulfill family obligations in the case of illness of a child, or perform the duties of homemaker) is often not covered (U.S. Dept. of Labor 1991:4–15, 4–50).[10] Furthermore, many Mothers cannot meet the requirement that their availability and willingness to work be unlimited. For example, a Mother may not be able to accept a job on the graveyard shift because she cannot find available child care.[11] The awards go to those who meet or approach the norm of the Ideal Worker with no or few domestic obligations, and many Mothers cannot meet that norm. Again, the regulatory system of UI provides little recognition of the fact that Mothers are workers and want to be workers. What controls the system is the way in which UI law defines the term *worker*.

Unemployment insurance is to be contrasted with various social welfare programs for Mothers with dependent children. Aid to Families with Dependent Children (AFDC) substitutes for the income of a Breadwinner; thus it operates like alimony or a widow's pension. It does not recognize or pay the Mother directly for childrearing as work in and of its own right as does UI. Rather it "gives" her money. This creates a social construction in which Mothering is placed outside the category of work. In so doing, it produces and reifies the division between Breadwinning and Mothering. A person raising her own children in her own home could receive AFDC (or child support) while the same person going next door to do the same job for someone else's child could later qualify for UI.

AFDC also focuses on the nurturing capacities of women rather than on their labor market capacities (Nelson 1990). It prohibits the Mother from earning more than a given amount in an implicit assumption that she is and should be a childrearer not a Breadwinner or both a Breadwinner and childrearer in equal parts. This in turn supports a division of labor between Breadwinners and Mothers. Thus while the programs for men increase or aid their attachment to paid labor, the programs for women reinforce their roles as caretakers. Mothers receiving welfare are placed in a position of dependency on the state similar to the one nonwelfare Mothers are in relative to their Breadwinning husbands.

The employee receiving UI is not similarly considered to be dependent. Unemployment Insurance is characterized as a "contributory" program. The employer pays directly into the insurance fund on the basis of the worker's earnings. This gives the worker an aura of legitimacy when he draws on the fund: it is money he has earned and taking it is as respectable as taking a deduction for homeowner's mortgage interest. He is not considered parasitic or the recipient of charity. By contrast, AFDC is characterized as "noncontributory" or unearned. This treats the Mother as giving "nothing" and receiving an unearned benefit. Collecting welfare is stigmatized in a way that receiving unemployment is not, despite the fact that recipients are working by raising children. In addition, most AFDC recipients have worked in waged labor in the past and will do so in the future, i.e., they have made contributions. This treatment of AFDC is again part of a regulative regime in which the childrearing contributions of women are treated as nonwork. It makes the socially useful labor provided by Mothers invisible and reifies the distinction between Mother and Breadwinner.

These distinctions between AFDC and UI are normative and need not be made. The period of childrearing, for example, could be treated as a time of unemployment for purposes of UI. Similarly, proportional benefits could be awarded to childrearers who work part-time, casually, or intermittently. This would send the message to both sexes that they would be treated equally in the time they spend away from waged labor in order to engage in childrearing.

Social Security Social Security is another regulative regime that constructs the division between worker and homemaker/Mother, and then penalizes the latter. It does this in two ways: first by failing to recognize homemaking as a job in its own right, and second by failing fully to reward those women who have both worked in waged labor and been homemakers. Full-time homemakers can only collect Social Security benefits indirectly through the benefits of their wage-earning husbands. They receive one half of his benefits during retirement and full benefits upon his death. Women who have worked can claim as a dependent and get half of their husband's retirement benefit if their own benefit is less than half of his.[12] A wife entitled to a retirement benefit in her own right that is equal to, or greater than, half of her husband's benefit will not be entitled to the homemaker's benefit.[13] Upon the death of her husband she is entitled to a survivor's benefit only if her own retirement benefit is less than half of his. If it is greater than half, she cannot claim on the basis of both her work and her years of domesticity.[14] Since dependents' benefits are often higher because husbands have greater earning power, two-thirds of the eligible homemakers who have worked collect retirement benefits on the basis of their dependent status (Fraser 1989:151). They forego their own direct contributions. Breadwinners, therefore, collect full benefits for the entirety of their work. Spouses who have been both waged workers and homemakers do not. Only their waged work or their domestic work is recognized. The system does not give full recognition to the two kinds of work they engage in. Furthermore, in the case of divorce the homemaker can claim dependent's benefits only if the marriage has lasted more then ten years. If she divorces before that time, she receives no dependent's benefits at all. None of her domestic work for the less-than-ten-year period is recognized. Finally, benefits terminate upon remarriage, in effect canceling out recognition of domestic work during the preceding marriage.[15] Presumably this is not work.

As Mary Becker concludes, "the system prefers those who have traditionally fulfilled men's traditional breadwinner roles over those who fulfilled women's traditional roles." In a labor market that prefers men and pays them higher wages, "it exerts pressures on homemakers to depend economically on men. . . . Indeed the system blatantly contributes to the subordination of women on an individual basis by linking old-age security for women (but not for men) to a continuation of the marriage bond until death" (M. Becker 1989:283).

Nancy Fraser builds on these observations about UI, AFDC, and Social Security and gives an acute analysis of the structure of social welfare benefits (Fraser 1989:144). She notes that UI and Social Security are oriented to paid labor and hence toward the individual. These laws, which mainly affect men, are not means tested and as a result construct their subjects as rights-bearing individuals. They place them in the paradigm of possessive individualism (Macpherson 1962) as contractors of labor and purchasers of benefits. AFDC, however, supplies or supplements the income of a Breadwinner and involves mainly women. In contrast to UI, AFDC is oriented toward households, not individuals. The benefits are based on family rather than individual income and are means tested. AFDC does not, therefore, treat its subjects as workers or individual, rights-bearing consumers but rather as clients receiving charity. By giving Mothers income conceived to be supplementary to that of the Breadwinner, AFDC fails to focus on the development of their capacities as waged workers (or for that matter their needs for day care, job training, and a family wage). It constructs them exclusively as Mothers (Fraser 1989:153). The same is true, although to a lesser extent and more indirectly, with Social Security.

Immigration Law and Child Care

The recent discussion of child care prompted by the withdrawal of Zoë Baird's nomination for Attorney General reveals the intricacies of the workings of law and power, and the way in which they constrain career opportunities for Mothers. I am not interested in her case per se but with what was revealed about day care and working mothers in the controversy that followed. What first became clear was that child care was thought to be a Mother's, not a father's, responsibility. As many pointed out, previously male appointees and officials had not been questioned about or disqualified because of their child care or domestic personnel. Judge Stephen Breyer's nomination for the Supreme Court is (almost) a case in point. Judge Breyer did not pay Social Security taxes to a part-time domestic worker who was past retirement age and already drawing social security benefits. Having been apprised of this, the Administration and Senate Judiciary Committee did nothing for several weeks to stop the vetting process. When the problem was revealed, several prominent lawmakers said they did not think it was a serious enough problem to prevent Judge Breyer from being nominated (Berke 1993:A11). He now sits on the Supreme Court.

The ensuing debate then revealed the way in which immigration and tax laws make child care a problem for working Mothers, particularly those without money (Rubenstein 1993:C1; Lewin 1991b:S4 18). It was openly recognized that there is a dearth of affordable child care in America (Cushman 1993:C8). Many working families cannot pay high wages and, because of the low pay, many Americans will not take child care jobs. Families are thus forced to turn to the black market in illegal aliens. This problem was recognized when Congress debated the Immigration Reform and Control Act of 1986, and it was proposed that there be an alien exemption for employers with less than three employees (Lewin 1993:B16). The proposal was defeated.

Under the current law, in order to hire an alien childminder, the employer must first advertise and if no suitable American is found, the employer, with documentation of his efforts in hand, can apply to the Immigration and Naturalization Service for a work permit. The certification can take from a few months to a couple of years (Lewin 1993:B16).[16] Upon receipt of the permit, the employer can legally hire the alien. Then a visa petition is submitted to the Immigration and Naturalization Service; approval usually takes a few months (Cushman 1993:C8). The worker must then obtain an immigrant visa in his home country, but visas can only be issued to those whose date of labor certification is before a cutoff date. In February 1993 the cutoff date was November 1987, and it was moving ahead one week per month. At that rate the alien worker might not qualify for sixteen years (Cushman 1993:C8). Between 1991 and 1993 only 10,000 unskilled laborers (the category into which childminders fall) were given green cards each year, and in 1993 there were over 80,000 in line (Cushman 1993:C8).

Even if there are no immigration problems, the tax laws are administratively complex and onerous. The employer must withhold federal and state income tax,[17] and a 6.2 percent federal unemployment tax on the first $7,000 of income.[18] In 1993 payment of Social Security tax was required for any employee who earned more than $50 a quarter. The tax is 12.4 percent of the worker's salary; half is to be paid by the worker and half by the employer (although many employers pay the total amount). The employer must also pay a 1.45 percent Medicare tax.[19] In one final twist, this regulatory scheme assumes that one can find workers who are willing to work when Social Security is paid. Many are not so willing, either because they do not report their incomes or because they do not plan to collect Social Security (as is the case with aliens who plan to return to their native countries before the qualifying period). The situation is even more difficult in the case of baby-sitters and house cleaners who are also subject to all the requirements. Anecdotal evidence, and there is a lot of it, suggests that it is almost impossible to find those who will agree to payment of Social Security even if it is added onto their usual base pay, probably for fear that it will subject them to income tax.

Assuming one can negotiate the hurdles of the Internal Revenue Service and the Social Security Administration and their multiple forms (Kelly 1993:A1), with payment of taxes the price of child care goes up, thus driving it out of the range of many women who would prefer to work. As a result, the working Mother who attempts to comply with the law has an even smaller pool of workers to choose from. If most families attempted to comply with the law the situation would reach crisis proportions. Immigration, tax, and welfare laws, in conjunction with government policy—all of which fail to recognize the childcare needs of Mothers—create a situation in which working Mothers are constrained in their job opportunities. This is little different than the situation of Mothers who are forced to cut back to part-time work or go into the mommy track.

Family Law

Traditionally the gendered division of labor was guaranteed by the perpetuation of sex roles and investment in marriage-specific behavior by women. Marital investment in turn was fostered by the norm of stability and the long-term contract of marriage that was protected by fault divorce law. This offered the wife a lifelong wage in exchange for the dependency created by her domestic labor and childrearing. Furthermore, it compensated her for the fact that her initial contribution to the marriage—the rearing of children—was made in its early years. Finally, long-term marriage also compensated the Mother for her transfer of human capital to her husband's career. She reaped the benefits of the life of his career and thus received a return for her investment. While fault divorce law protected marital stability, however, it reflected and reinforced the system of asymmetries between men and women in the labor market and consequently between these asymmetries and the family. It assumed and fostered the traditional division of labor between Breadwinner and Mother.

In a fault divorce regime, alimony substituted for the Breadwinner's support obligation after divorce and acted as a penalty to discourage him from abandoning his dependent family. In conjunction with fault divorce, alimony strengthened the long-term marriage contract and gave women an incentive to invest in the family (Landes 1978:48–49). Against the backdrop of a labor market that did not offer women a living wage, it encouraged gendered specialization in the family and thus reinforced compulsory Motherhood for women.

No-fault divorce has facilitated exit from marriage. This in theory destabilizes the family[20] and discourages investment in Motherhood. No-fault has also rendered the traditional concept of long-term alimony as the continuation of the support obligation meaningless. Because there is no obligation (and often no disposable income), there are few alimony awards, and what awards there are, are small and hard to collect (M. Becker 1989:282 at n. 97). Scholars have attempted to re-establish a rational basis for alimony that will encourage marital investment and discourage "self-insuring" (Ellman 1989; Carbone 1990; O'Connell 1988; Krauskopf 1985). The theory is that alimony awards that fully compensate for Mothering will encourage women to Mother rather than to enter the labor market. This should encourage specialization in domesticity by making childrearing costless. The most sophisticated theory notes that women make their greatest contribution in the early years of marriage (in childbearing and childrearing) when the Breadwinner is only getting started in the labor market; the Bread-winner makes his greatest contribution in later years through increased earning power. Thus the Breadwinner cannot compensate the Mother at the time of her contribution and goes into her debt. The amount of that debt is measured by the loss of human capital she suffers through domesticity. The loss is measured by what capital she would have developed had she not dropped out of the labor market. In effect it is delayed wages for Mothering (Ellman 1989). Alimony should, therefore, pay for past childrearing by substituting for the opportunity the Mother would have had outside the home.

Traditionally, fault divorce occurred in conjunction with alimony, making divorce both difficult and costly. No-fault divorce splits apart the relation between divorce and alimony. While alimony exists in theory, in reality it often does not. The law, therefore, presents two regimes: no-fault divorce with alimony and no-fault divorce without (or with inadequate) alimony. No-fault divorce with the promise of alimony continues to some extent to create incentives to invest in marriage rather than develop and maintain labor market ties (although these incentives are undercut by no-fault). Thus it perpetuates the construction of Motherhood.

A no-fault divorce regime without alimony is more complex. On the one hand, because their futures are unclear and because they have not maintained their position in the labor market, some women devote themselves to the marriages they have, or at least do not rock the boat. They do not invest too much in paid work or make too many demands on their partners to share in childrearing. This maintains an uneasy status quo. For other women, however, the fear of no-alimony discourages Mothering and increases incentives to develop work skills. Knowing that they might find themselves divorced, these women protect themselves by having fewer children while at the same time maintaining one foot in waged labor.

Liberal feminists argue that alimony should be eliminated (prospectively) because this will encourage women to develop labor market ties (Kay 1987a, 1987b). This argument, however, only works against two background assumptions. One is that men will take up the slack in childrearing, a dubious assumption given the unequal distribution of market power between men and women. The other is that women will participate in the market because opportunity is unlimited. Structural asymmetries in the market, however, put a brake on whatever shifts women may make from family to market. The combination is lethal: marital ties are destabilized by no-fault, leaving Mothers without the protection of lifelong marriage, but earning power is still constrained, leaving them without the means to support themselves and their children fully and adequately. The legal regime constructs women as Mothers but requires them to function as potential Breadwinners, which they cannot do because they are Mothers.

No-fault and alimony also point to the way in which legal discourse intersects with social institutions to create social roles. Because of the structure of waged labor, even though the elimination of alimony might create an incentive for women to work, it is still women who would do the lion's share of the childrearing. It leaves in place the gendered division of labor in which women, rather than either or both sexes, are constructed as childrearers. The gendered nature of the division of labor would be affected only if there were a change both in the alimony law *and* in the waged labor market.

If there were an equal and nondiscriminatory labor market, there would be two possibilities for alimony: one is to eliminate it, the other is to award it. If denying alimony creates an incentive to work rather than to rear children (assuming the market is equally as open to women as to men) in a no-alimony regime it would seem that both sexes would work rather than parent. Indeed, that is to some extent what we see with dual-career professionals who have no children or little time for the children they have. That is not necessarily a result to be desired. By contrast, if awarding alimony discourages working and encourages parenting by making divorce costly (assuming the market is equally open to men and women), in an alimony regime there would be no reason why men would not also have an incentive to Mother. Mothering would be attractive to either sex.

While this would be a good result in that it would encourage parenting and would change the gendered nature of the role specialization, it might not necessarily change the division of labor between Breadwinner and Mothers; they would just be male or female as the individual case might dictate. Although this might get women out of the problem of dependency, it does not get Mothers out of it. Whether male or female, the problems of Motherhood would remain. What is necessary to change the role specialization is an additional change, viz., a change in the norm of the Ideal Worker. That would entail recognition of the fact that workers with families are both workers and parents and would in fact mark the end of the Breadwinner/Mother construction. Workers cannot devote all of their time and effort to their employers because some of it has to go to their children. Ultimately the ideal would be to distribute the roles of working and parenting between partners. Each would develop their market skills so that in the event of parting they would be evenly placed; each would also be responsible for childrearing. It is often said that now that both spouses work, something has to give. More precisely, as we have seen throughout, a number of things have to give: the law, work opportunities for women, and the norm of the Ideal Worker.

This is by no means the end of the story of compulsory Motherhood. Indeed, one of the most powerful social movements today is the growing discourse of "family values" that acts as a new apparatus of regulation and construction. This discourse draws attention to the devastating condition of children in contemporary America due (depending on the political orientation) either to working moms and/or the feminization of poverty through divorce or single parenthood. It is accompanied by a booming industry in social and psychological studies of the effects of divorce on children. The study most cited is that of Judith Wallerstein, which unremittingly finds those effects to be long-term and negative (Wallerstein and Blakeslee 1989). There are also studies looking at the effects of "maternal deprivation" on children whose mothers go out to work and/or turn their children over to day-care centers. And volumes have been written about the effects of single Motherhood. The message in all these cases is clear and is saturated with ideology: any family shape other than the two-parent, intact family is to some degree detrimental to children, either economically or psychologically. According to the family values discourse, as a result of "broken" families we are raising a generation of unhappy and damaged, if not pathological, children. These studies purport to present an objective, scientific truth that simply reports the facts "out there." If we take Foucault's lessons to heart, however, we must analyze this as discourse that arises from a matrix of power. It constructs pathological children, fixes the blame on absent, working mothers, and calls for a return of women to Motherhood.

This discourse argues that women should not have interests (like developing work skills) independent of family interests. Rather, they should subordinate individual interests to the communal. This discourse works to channel women into marriage and Motherhood and keep them there. This vision of the family still promotes a fully gendered division of labor in which women bear the primary responsibility for childrearing and, as a result, bear the primary responsibility for sacrifice. In the family values scenario women are held hostage to their children (Etzioni 1992:32). Just as women have begun to resist the cycle of dependency, family values discourse has arisen to prevent their escape from compulsory Motherhood.

NOTES

I would like to thank David Gray Carlson, Eugene MacNamee, and Barbara Omolade for their helpful comments.

1. Legal discourse, for example, has devalued and constrained women's participation in the labor market, mainly by assuming their connection to children.

2. Feminists have questioned whether Foucault's theories themselves impose their own form of essentializing and foreclose opportunities for resistance and liberation discourse. See Alcoff 1988; Butler 1990; Frazer 1989; Diamond and Quinby 1988. On resistance, see Foucault 1980b:56; Dreyfus and Rabinow 1983:220–22.

3. It is not fortuitous that over 50 percent of working women but only 1 percent of working men have reported dropping out of the workforce at least once for family reasons (Rhode 1989:174).

4. A recent study of the salary histories of two thousand working women shows that even those who leave the workforce for only a year never catch up (Kantrowitz 1993:48). The Rand Corporation has estimated that a two- to four-year break in employment lowers lifetime income by 13 percent; a five-year break lowers it by 19 percent (Rhode 1989:213).

5. At age 27, a single woman earns almost 90 percent of the male wage; at age 35 with two children, working full-time, she earns 46 percent (Castro 1991:10). The presence of children often motivates Mothers, particularly single Mothers, to improve their education or position in the job market. Nevertheless, they would probably improve even more if they had more time to devote to these activities, i.e., if the effort of raising their children were shared more by others.

6. Although I address the dynamics of the work/family conflict in intact two-parent families, I do not mean to say that the husband-wife relationship is necessary to rearing children. I simply use the two-parent family to demonstrate that two hands or sets of resources are necessary, in the sense that there must be a source of support and there must be a caregiver. Many of my claims would remain true for single Mothers who are not working and whose welfare, alimony, and/or child support substitutes for a Breadwinner's wages. The case of single working Mothers who do not receive outside support is more complicated. They suffer in the labor market because they cannot meet the norm of the Ideal Worker on account of their childrearing obligations. They cannot, however, drop out of the labor market when the demands of Mothering become severe, because they need to support their families. While there is a solution to the need for two hands in the intact family—the father can parent equally—this solution is more difficult for the single parent. One possibility is public payment of these Mothers. But for the time being, within the current structure of family and market, the person who must occupy both roles of Breadwinner and Mother is in a very conflicted position.

7. This model obviously does not hold in cases where women make *more* than their husbands. This is significant in the African-American family where, in many cases, the wife's job opportunities are better relative to her husband's (although worse relative to white male workers).

8. The political interpretation of social welfare laws is complex, as is the question of whether they were originally "patriarchal" or "maternalist" policies, i.e., whether they addressed the needs of women and children by making provision via the Breadwinner or whether, like mothers' pensions, they provided for women and children directly. At issue is the question of whether protective laws are harmful or helpful to women (Skocpol 1993a).

9. See, for example, the Federal Unemployment Tax Act, 26 U.S.C.A. §3304 (a) (12) (1993).

10. Pearce discusses how this issue was dealt with by the House Committee on Labor. She refers to the statement of Juliet Stuart Poyntz as reflecting the view that UI was set up to benefit workers against unemployment that was not of their own doing and that domestic quits are often considered voluntary (Pearce 1985:452–53). Most workers who quit to accompany a spouse were women.

11. Federal law however requires that states not disqualify a worker "if the . . . hours . . . of the work offered are substantially less favorable to the individual than those prevailing for similar work in the locality" (U.S. Dept. of Labor 1992:4–9).

12. 42 U.S.C.A. 24 §402 (b) (1) (D) (1993).

13. See Social Security Ruling 64–52, Department of Health and Human Services, Social Security Administration Cumulative Bulletin of Social Security Rulings, 1964–3; see also 1 Unempl. Ins. Rep. (CCH) ¶12,309(.035).

14. 42 U.S.C.A. §402e (1) (C) (1992).

15. 42 U.S.C.A. §§402b (1) (C), 402b (3) (1993). Under the statute, a divorced woman's claim terminates with remarriage unless she marries someone entitled to retirement benefits in one of the following ways: as a divorced husband of a covered worker; as the widower of a covered worker; or as a father taking care of the children of a deceased covered worker and earning less than $6480 (in 1988) (see 1 Unempl. Ins. Rep. [CCH] ¶12,459 1265 [1988]); as the retired dependent parent of a deceased covered worker; or as someone originally entitled to benefits as the disabled child of a retired, deceased, or disabled covered worker (M. Becker 1989:283 at n. 99).

16. See 8 U.S.C.A. §1182(a) (5); 8 U.S.C.A. §1153(b) (1993).

17. 26 U.S.C.A. §§3401, 3402(a) (3) (1993).

18. 26 U.S.C.A. §§3301, 3306(b) (1993).

19. 26 U.S.C.A. §3121(a) (7) (B) (1993).

20. If the traditional family ethic and structure are grounded in and produced by a (discriminatory) waged labor market, the converse is also true. First of all, a person will enter marriage only if it appears that he will be relatively "better off" by doing so. Women with partners who cannot be "depended on" (for whatever reason, including adultery, abuse, indigence, and unemployment) might not enter marriage at all. Economic theories of marriage hold that if women gain in the market, they will become less dependent and have less incentive to form, invest in, or remain in families, or to Mother. It should be noted that this is based on a comparison as to whether or not they are in a better or worse position, relatively speaking, being married. They will stay married only as long as they are better off than being single, "better off" meaning emotionally, physically, etc., as well as financially. Where the disparity between their income and their husbands' income is not great (or alternatively, the disparity between welfare and their husbands' income is not great), they might leave the marriage. Their participation in the marketplace, therefore, could theoretically subvert the stability of a nuclear family based on the complementary roles of Breadwinner and Mother. The brake is that they are allowed only limited participation.

PART TWO

Nonconforming Mother

5 | Mother: The Legal Domestication of Lesbian Existence

RUTHANN ROBSON

Mother is a legal category. While mother is certainly a category in the nonlegal world, a category with biological, affectional, cultural, and religious implications, its legality is pervasive. As a legal category, it has the potential to domesticate lesbian existence and thus interfere with lesbian survival. I use the term *domestication* to indicate the law's potential hegemony over lesbian survival. Domestication is similar to other political processes that have been named "colonization" and "imperialism." However, while both imperialism and colonization describe concrete historical processes that have resulted in slavery, death, and destruction, domestication can be used to describe a less tangible, more naturalized form of containment and control.[1] Domestication is connotatively gendered. It denotes the relegation of women to the domestic sphere, a private place that can facilitate being dominated and inhibit collective action. It also signals that one's potential has been circumscribed to the service of another, as when animals are domesticated for human use. Most significant for my purposes, domestication can be used to describe what has occurred when the views of the dominant culture—in this case the legal culture—are so internalized that they are considered common sense. Domestication has occurred when we perceive the barbed wire enclosures (in this chapter the laws governing parenting) as existing for our protection rather than restriction.[2] We attempt to argue ourselves into—to make ourselves fit—existing legal categories so that we can be protected, not noticing how such categories restrict our lesbianism.

At the April 1991 National Lesbian Conference in Atlanta, I participated in a workshop discussing lesbian parenting. During a small
group discussion, lesbians—ever practical—began talking about what
our children should call us. The lesbians in the group did not know
each other. No one knew I was an attorney, and I was not thinking
about the law. My suggestion was that a child call both mothers simply
by their first names. This suggestion was vigorously objected to by
another lesbian, who said, "The law gives me twenty-four-hour-a-day
responsibility for that child. Me—and me only, not my lover and not
anyone else. I deserve to be called something special; something that no
one else calls me; something like 'mother.' " What surprised me was not
this lesbian's disagreement with my particular proposal but her appeal
to the law. Where I expected the pangs of biology, I got the legal rule of
parental responsibility. The other members of the small group took up
her point, agreeing not only with the special nature of the word *mother*
but appealing to its legal force.

When we talk about the legal rules as the basis for lesbian choices, I
believe we are domesticated. At stake is not whether the children who
live with us call us "Alice" or "Mama Alice" or "Mom"—the range of
choices is as wide as the range of lesbians. Rather, what is at stake is our
process. We can appeal to equality models in which no mother would
be "other": antihierarchichal models in which children are not deferential to adults, historical models in which children are property, and even
personal models based upon our own childhoods. Or we can simply
like the way something sounds. But when the reasoning for our lesbian
decisions is predicated upon an uncritical adoption of the rule of law, I
believe this is problematic. It marks lesbian domestication by law.

In seeking to move beyond our domestication by the rule of law, a
specifically lesbian legal theory is important. The first step in the formation of this lesbian legal theory is to examine the rules of law and
legal categories critically and assess them with regard to lesbian survival.
By "lesbian survival" I mean two things. First, I mean a daily individual survival that depends on food, shelter, and love—including, for
some of us, love relationships with children. Second, I mean an individual and collective survival that depends on some sort of identity as
lesbians. Thus I seek to center on lesbian concerns rather than legal
ones.

Legal decisions have real effects. The extent to which a lesbian is a
legally recognized mother determines the extent to which a lesbian's
relationship with a child might be protected. Yet even if this relation-

ship is legally defined as mother-child, this does not guarantee absolute protection. The law may determine that a particular lesbian is not within the category of mother as the law defines it. In such a case, the law denies the lesbian custody or visitation and places the child with another person or with the state. This chapter explores the state of the rule of law with regard to lesbian motherhood and examines particular cases in which the rules of law have served to domesticate individual lesbians. However, I also make the claim that the very category of mother domesticates our own thinking about our relationships with children.

The legal ramifications of lesbian motherhood have received much attention (Polikoff 1990:459; Sella 1991:135; Sheppard 1985:219),[3] although this attention has often focused on finding ways to manipulate the rules of law to achieve certain desired results and not on challenging the underlying premises of those laws. Many of the changes in the rule of law that have been the results of the work of legal reformers and scholars have benefited lesbians who seek to maintain relationships with children. It must be stressed at the outset, however, that any lesbian legal theory cannot assume that lesbian custody is the preferable outcome. As always, the emphasis must be on lesbian choice. By centering lesbians rather than law, a lesbian legal theory might be able to confront more directly the power of the rule of law to domesticate our lesbian lives.

Lesbian Mothers and Nonlesbian Challenges

Lesbians relationships with children are subject to legal interference by two general categories of nonlesbians. The first category is the other parent, the father. The relationship between mother, child, and father is a legal one. For lesbians who share parentage of a child with a man, regardless of whether they have been married or not, the law dictates that the man has parental rights. The rules of law determining men's parental rights have fluctuated throughout legal history. At one time the father had an absolute right to sole custody (of legitimate children), a consequence of the man's ownership of both the wife and the children. More recently, American rules of law employed a preference for the mother, especially if the child was of "tender years." This so-called tender years doctrine gave the mother a presumption of custody unless the father could prove that the mother was unfit. Under this standard, many lesbians were held to be unfit by virtue of their lesbianism.[4] The tender years doctrine changed as a result of recent feminist legal reform that led to the establishment of gender neutral laws. Present rule of law generally provides that in a custody litigation between the mother and the father, the court must determine the "best interests of the child." This gender neutral rule supposedly allows the parents to start off in equal positions. The court then looks at numerous factors in order to decide the relative merits of each parent. The factors applied vary from state to state but include economic, educational, social, and cultural considerations. Given women's disadvantage in these areas relative to men, it should not be surprising that current statistics reveal that fathers who litigate for custody have a high chance of prevailing (Chesler 1987:65–66, 78–79); it is often the case that what is considered to be in the "best interests of the child" is actually what is in the best interests of the state. For instance, judges often claim that it is in the best interests of the child to grow up in a conventional state-approved family.[5]

When lesbianism is raised in a case between a mother and a father, whether it is in an original custody case or in a suit seeking a change of custody because of the discovery of the mother's lesbianism, courts employ three different approaches. The first and most limiting approach is that living with a lesbian mother cannot be in the best interests of the child.[6] The second or middle-ground approach is that living with a (lesbian) mother can be in the best interests of a child as long as the mother is a mother and not a lesbian who flaunts her lesbianism, lives with a lesbian lover, or engages in lesbian politics.[7] The third and presumably most enlightened approach is the nexus approach.[8] Courts use what they call the "nexus test" to determine whether the mother's lesbianism actually harms the child. The application of this harm principle in practice often makes the nexus test indistinguishable from the first per se approach or the middle-ground, mother-first, lesbian-last approach. The types of harm that courts often consider under this nexus test include: the harm of molestation (although this is usually more likely in a gay father's case than in a lesbian mother's case); the harm of a potential gay or lesbian identity in the child; the harm of stigmatization of the child because of having a lesbian mother; and the harm of living in an immoral and illegal environment.

In a 1989 Missouri appellate court opinion, *T. C. H. v. K. M. H* (784 S.W.2d 281), the court specifically adopted the requirement that there must be "a nexus between harm to the child and the parent's homosexuality" but considered as evidence of harm that the mother "admitted on cross-examination that she had slept with friend while the children were in the house. She was also unable to 'say for certain' that she had not kissed her friend on the lips or touched her affectionately in front of the children" (284). The court also noted that even if the "mother remains discreet about her sexual preference, a number of experts at the trial testified and Missouri case law recognizes that a parent's homosexuality can never be kept secret enough to be a neutral factor in the development of a child's values and character" (285). The appellate court affirmed the trial court's award of custody to the father and his new wife, despite the fact that each child told the trial judge that he or she wished to remain with the mother.

Not all courts have applied the nexus test—or even the middle-ground approach—as homophobically as the Missouri court. Many courts, including appellate courts in New Jersey, Alaska, Massachusetts, South Carolina, and New York have specifically found that a mother's lesbianism did not constitute a harm to the child.[9] However, underlying even these relatively liberal opinions filled with fact-specific reasoning is the assumption that having a lesbian mother *could* be harmful to a child and can thus be considered to be not in the best interest of the child.

The second category of nonlesbians who can interfere with the relationship between a lesbian and her children are nonlesbians who are not parents to the child. These third parties can include interested relatives, foster parents, or the state. In these cases, the third party must generally prove the mother is unfit. The rule of law does not impose equality upon the mother and the nonparent. Third parties have to satisfy a higher burden than proving that it would be in the best interests of the child to remove the child from the lesbian mother. While courts do not generally consider lesbianism alone proof of unfitness, they do nevertheless consider it in making a determination, and many ultimately rely on it. For example, in a 1990 case from the Supreme Court of Mississippi, *White v. Thompson* (569 So.2d 1181), the court affirmed an award of custody to the paternal grandparents of the children of a lesbian mother, An White. Mississippi's highest court noted that even though the trial court "may have relied almost exclusively" on the mother's lesbian relationship, there was enough evidence in the record—including some conflicting testimony about the children being outside in cold weather without adequate clothing—to support the trial court's removing the children from An White's custody (1184). With respect to visitation the court ruled against allowing the children to visit with her in the presence of her lover. The mother in this case was not a middle-class model of respectability, but what is interesting is that she did not conform to that model when she was married either. In fact, her conditions had apparently improved since she had separated from her husband and begun living with her lover. No one claimed that the children's father should be awarded custody "given his financial situation and his drinking problem." Yet when An White became involved with a woman, her husband's parents decided that she should be denied custody. The courts of Mississippi agreed.

The per se rule of law that lesbian and mother are mutually exclusive legal categories is in disrepute. The enlightened view, subject to many permutations, is that lesbianism alone cannot satisfy the burden of proof of a mother being unfit should third parties attempt to gain custody. In the case where custody is sought by the father, the enlightened view is that lesbianism alone cannot be the factor in determining who best comports with the best interests of the child. This enlightened view has been forced upon the courts by many brave lesbian mothers who engaged in painful litigation with the advocacy of many hardworking and clever lesbian legal workers. It is certainly an advancement.

Nevertheless, this enlightenment can often be merely the patina of privilege. Like the specter of lesbian marriage, these liberal custody rules of law contribute to a division between bad and good lesbians and between bad and good children. Two examples are illustrative. First, there is Jane Doe, so good that she keeps her real name out of the court records. Jane does not have sole custody of her son, the eleven-year-old, "well-adjusted and above-average" Jack, but he visits her eight weeks in the summer and alternate Easter and Christmas vacations. Ann Smith Doe, the father's new wife, wants to adopt Jack and thus terminate Jane Doe's parental rights. A Virginia trial court agrees, terminates Jane's status as a mother, and allows the adoption. But when Jane appeals to the Supreme Court of Virginia, she prevails. The court's opinion in *Doe v. Doe* (284 S.E.2d 799) sounds like she is winning the contest for Miss Congeniality rather than a custody appeal:

> Although there was testimony that her relationship with the woman with whom she lives is unorthodox, the testimony is also that Jane Doe is an exceptionally well-educated, stable, responsible, and sensitive individual. Witnesses described Jane in various ways, but always in a highly complimentary manner. They referred to her as a conscientious and creative parent, friendly by nature, who instills in the boy a love for other people and for animals. It was testified that Jane's love for Jack was a nurturing love, and that she exercised a selfless wisdom in caring for him. Jane Doe has apparently earned the respect of her peers . . . because of

her civic work and active interest in the community and her relationship
with the people with whom she comes into contact.   (804)

I do not mean to belittle Jane Doe, or the accomplishment of her attorney for putting together such impressive evidence. But factors such as
being well-educated and engaging in civic work can be a bit daunting
to someone like An White, who lived in a trailer and worked in a con-
venience store. Also daunting are not only class considerations, but les-
bian-identity considerations. As the Supreme Court of Virginia specifically noted, it was not "approving, condoning, or sanctioning" Jane's
"unnatural lifestyle" (806), which was proper for the court to consider,
but found that it was outweighed in her particular circumstances, a resolution that the court warned might be temporary:

> Further, in determining her fitness as a mother and the future welfare of
> her son, we are not unmindful of her testimony that should it become nec-
> essary, for her son's sake, she would sever the relationship with the woman
> with whom she now lives. There may come a time when the welfare and
> best interest of her son require that she honor this commitment.   (806)

For women who are not willing to separate from their lesbian lovers,
courts are less lenient, particularly if the mother in question is less than
congenial and a little too dykey, and the child is less than perfect. In a
Pennsylvania case, *In re Breisch* (434 A.2d 815), the mother appealed
the state's taking away of her preschool son who had a speech problem.
The appellate court upheld the removal, writing an opinion containing
the following:

> [Joey] was exposed to a chaotic and harmful home life. The mother is a
> lesbian who effects a masculine appearance, wears men's clothing, and
> has a masculine-oriented mental status. At the time of the hearing, she
> lived with Nancy M. and two of her children in a two-bedroom apart-
> ment. . . .
>   [The caseworker] also found the mother to be uncooperative. The
> mother took notes throughout her meetings with the caseworker and
> responded in an adversarial manner that her attorney, J. D., "knows
> about this."   (817–18)

When the mother refused the condition that she not live with her lover,
the court found that this "revealed forcefully her true feelings and attitude's regarding Joey's [speech] therapy" (820). The appellate court
disingenuously rejected the mother's claim that the court was unneces-
sarily interfering in her lesbian relationship absent a causal connection

between the lesbianism and the harm. The court noted that the order to exclude the lover from their home was not meant to interfere with the lesbian relationship but only to establish order and foster the close relationship between the mother and son.

When conflicts over a child arise between a lesbian and a heterosexual man or state agency, our lesbian loyalties are undivided. Any lesbian legal theory must center the lesbian and privilege her position to choose custody. In most cases, a lesbian in a custody dispute has not chosen to be within the rules of law. There must be legal reform to afford lesbians who find themselves within that legal system their choices. A liberal nexus test that states that harm must be proven or else lesbianism will not be considered is not liberal enough: harm must not include a child being exposed to lesbian expression or a child's potential lesbianism or gayness. Exclusion of a lesbian's lover from her home is asking a lesbian to choose between her lover and her child. This is not the type of choice that any lesbian legal theory would seek to promote.

Yet a lesbian legal theory must stress lesbian choice rather than lesbian custody. An assumption that custody is what should be chosen by any lesbian is detrimental. A lesbian legal theory puts lesbians at the center, even to the exclusion of the children of lesbians. It is difficult to disagree with the legal standard of "best interests of the child," but a lesbian legal theory has a different focus. Its central focus is lesbian.

Lesbian Mothers and Gay/Lesbian Coparents

When conflicts arise over a child within our own communities, our lesbian loyalties can be divided. For instance, when two lesbians who are raising a child together separate, centering lesbians does not necessarily solve the problem. Before considering this scenario, I want to distinguish it from another scenario in which lesbian loyalties can be falsely divided and centering lesbians does reorient our perspectives. The scenario involves the gay sperm donor.

Under the rule of law, contribution of sperm gives rise to an entitlement to the benefits and burdens of fatherhood. Many states do have statutes that alleviate this rule somewhat, but importantly these statutes protect the rights of infertile fathers. They sever the sperm donor's paternity right when insemination is performed by a licensed physician on a married woman (see, for example, Uniform Parentage Act s5 [a], [b]). This severing is consistent with the rule of law's limitation of parentage: a child has one father and one mother, no more and no less (see, for example, Uniform Parentage Act sections 7000 et seq.). In the case of a woman married to an infertile man, the rule of law declares that the husband is the child's father and not the sperm donor (N.Y Dom. Rel. Law s73 [McKinney 1988; *Gursky v. Gursky*, 39 Misc.2d 1083, 242 N.Y.S.2d 406 (Sup. Ct. 1963)]). In the case of an unmarried woman, there is no husband to assume the role of father. A court, ever eager to promote fatherhood, bestows upon the sperm donor the appellation "father" and awards him visitation.

The California case of *Jhordan C. v. Mary K.* (179 Cal.App.3d 386, 224 Cal.Rptr.530 [1986]) is illustrative of this scenario. Although the court never tells us that Mary K. is a lesbian, the opinion does tell us that Mary decided to have a child by "artificial insemination" jointly with "Victoria, a close friend" (179 Cal.App.3d at 389, 224 Cal.Rptr. at 532). After making that decision, "Mary sought a semen donor by talking with friends and acquaintances. This led to three or four potential donors with whom Mary spoke directly. She and Victoria ultimately chose Jhordan after he had one personal interview with Mary and one dinner at Mary's home" (389). Without discussing Jhordan's sexuality, the court affirmed the award of Jhordan's visitation. The court also rejected Mary's constitutional challenges to the insemination statute, raised on her behalf by her attorney, Roberta Achtenberg of the Lesbian Rights Project.

The result in Mary K.'s case is troubling. While the court did not award Jhordan the joint custody he sought (which would have allowed him to participate in day-to-day decisions about the child), it did grant him father status and generous visitation. However, what I find particularly troubling is the response of the gay and lesbian community. Since the mid-1980s when Mary K. came before the California appellate court, I have heard of numerous cases of gay men who have been sperm donors now seeking court-ordered visitation of three-, four-, ten-, and thirteen-year-old children. The lesbians defending themselves against these lawsuits have often been denied representation and support from the organized gay/lesbian legal community. The gay/lesbian legal reform agenda is devoted to an expansion of the legal concept of family. This may include visitation for gay men who have been sperm donors and now decide to establish father-right. With the rule of law in their favor, gay men who have been sperm donors can most often win an award of visitation. It does not matter whether visitation is desired by the lesbians who have been caring for the child since birth. And it matters little whether visitation is desired by the child, for courts will presume and court-ordered psychologists will declare that a child should have contact with a "father."

If we center lesbians rather than gay/lesbian concerns, a different result is demanded. The rights of men, whether gay or not, should not be the focus of any lesbian legal theory. Just as marriage has a legal history of male dominance over women, so too does father-right. What needs to be preserved is lesbian choice, not father-right. Likewise, if we center lesbians rather than law—even law as expressed by the lesbian/gay legal reform movement—our loyalties are undivided. Again, what we must preserve is lesbian choice, not the legal category of family, however alternative or expansive.

The centering of lesbians is more difficult when the dispute is between two lesbians. In a situation in which two lesbians have a baby, the biological mother is the legal mother. The other lesbian is profoundly "other": she is a legal stranger to her child, just as she is a legal stranger to her lover. As in the case of lovers when no child is involved, it is necessary to distinguish between situations in which third parties are involved and situations involving only lesbians. The death or incapacitation of the biological/legal mother can interfere with the relationship between the "other" mother and the child. The biological mother can express her desires regarding guardianship of her child in a will or other document. However, although the law at times regards children as almost akin to property, wishes expressed in a will regarding guardianship are never determinative. A court can consider the biological mother's statement in the event of a custody dispute, where there is no apparent negative to such a statement. A document giving a person medical guardianship can name an adult entitled to make medical decisions for a child. In all these cases, however, the documents are outer-directed, intended to give the lesbian lover rights as against third parties who may claim an interest in the child. They are not intended to give lesbians rights as against each other.

How then are rights to be determined as between lesbians? As in relationships without children, many suggest the solution of contract law. While a contract cannot have as its subject the child (this would be baby-selling and considered illegal), a contract could give the adults rights against each other. However, as in a childless context, the danger of relying upon contract law is that lesbians will be forced to adopt the assumptions of contract law and that particular lesbians may be disempowered by the operation of those assumptions.[10]

The most often posed legal solution has been adoption. This is a recognized legal procedure that allows a nonbiological parent to become a legal parent. However, until very recently courts have been unanimous in their conclusion that parents are limited to a mother and a father. A child cannot have two mothers by adoption or otherwise, and a female parent must be a mother (Polikoff 1990:468–73). Lesbian legal reformers have argued against this view, impressively in both legal scholarship and the courts. A 1991 District of Columbia opinion, *In re Adoption of Minor T* (17 Fam.L.Rptr. 1523 [D.C. Super. Ct. 1991]), was the first to allow a lesbian to adopt the child born to her lover.[11] The court was troubled by provisions of the statute that terminated the rights of the biological mother on adoption. In order to overcome this problem the court decided to construe the statute's language as merely directive and found that the biological mother's rights did not have to be terminated. In this same case, the court also allowed a previously adopted child to be adopted by the other lesbian parent as well. In recent times there have been a few cases of two lesbians simultaneously adopting one child (Cullum 1993).

Absent an adoption, there are legal theories that might support a lesbian parent being awarded custody of a child should the biological parent die or become incapacitated. Such theories include de facto parenthood (also called psychological parenthood), equitable parenthood, and in loco parentis. In all these theories, the court looks at the actions of the adult to determine whether they emulate parenthood and on that basis decides whether or not the adult should be legally deemed a parent. In many of these cases, the adult's actions are judged not only as against an ideal parent but also as against any other parentlike adults in the child's life. At times, formal legal rights would be in direct conflict with these creative theories. For example, should a biological mother die, custody of the child might be awarded on the basis of the recognized father status of a sperm donor rather than the less formal psychological parent status of the lesbian parent. If the parents of the deceased lesbian seek custody of the child from the surviving lesbian parent, their grandparent status is entitled to some weight but is less compelling than father status.[12]

All these theories, including adoption, can be used like tools to forestall the effect of the rules of law that would otherwise be operative. In that capacity, I think they can be useful. Using these theories as tools to dissuade third parties from seeking custody of a child is also extremely useful. However, when these theories are the basis of a contest between lesbians waged in the legal arena, we tend to turn the tools and rules of law upon each other.

If two lesbians decide to have a child together, do so, and then decide to separate, the child's future becomes uncertain. In the best of all possible lesbian utopias, the two lesbians would exercise their lesbian choices in a way that honored themselves, each other, and the child. There would be no need to resort to the rules of law. But one lesbian can decide that she is the true and only mother, and if she is the biological mother (and there is no adoption), the rule of law will enforce her decision. The other lesbian can sue her ex-lover for visitation of the child, utilizing theories to persuade the court that she should be accorded at least some parental rights. She will be represented by gay/lesbian legal reform organizations, arguing for recognition of the lesbian family as analogous to the nuclear family. Other gay/lesbian rights organizations will file briefs as interested parties urging the court to expand the legal category of family to include both lesbian parents (and perhaps even the gay male sperm donor). In the courts that have considered this scenario, the nonbiological lesbian parent will lose. Despite the courts' opinions, there is a groundswell of liberal popular support for expanding legal concepts of parenthood and family to include the nonbiological lesbian parent.

The case of *Alison D. v. Virginia M.* (77 N.Y.2d 651) is an example. Decided in 1991 by New York's highest court, the decision rejects a claim for visitation from a lesbian nonbiological mother, deciding that she is not a "parent" within the meaning of the statute. Represented by Paula Ettlebrick of Lambda Legal Defense and Education Fund, and supported by briefs from the NOW Legal Defense Fund, the ACLU, and the Gay and Lesbian Parents Coalition, Alison D. argued that she was a de facto parent entitled to visitation (77 N.Y.2d at 656; 77 N.Y.2d at 588). Although the same court had the year before given an expansive reading to the term *family* in a rent stabilization case involving a surviving male lover, the court here declined to give a similar expansive reading to the term *parent.* Judge Judith Kaye, the only judge on New York's highest court who could even remotely be called a feminist, was the only dissenting judge.

Judge Kaye's dissent and many reactions to the case from heterosexual feminists and liberal nonlesbians are telling. Although a few feminists worried about the risk of exposing women to violence should de facto parent visitation include an abusive boyfriend of a battered woman, most sought to bring lesbians within pre-established legal definitions. Liberals extended their sympathies that lesbians were once again excluded.

Because Alison D. and Virginia M. are in conflict, it is difficult to center the concerns of both lesbians and not be inconsistent. Yet this inconsistency—and the dispute itself—is constructed by the rule of law. To the extent that the biological mother, Virginia M., supported her denial of visitation to her ex-lover with her superior position within the rules of law, she is domesticated by the legal regime. To the extent that the nonbiological mother, Alison D., believes she is entitled to visitation because she can fit herself into legal theories such as in loco parentis, she is also domesticated by the legal regime. Finally, to the extent that both lesbians appeal to the legalism inherent in categories such as "parent" and "family" as they attempt to settle their problem, they import the law into their lesbianism. In this way lesbianism is limited by legalism.

I am less concerned with the legal positions of Alison D. and Virginia M. than with how they came to make their claims in courts of law. This is not squeamishness about the public revelation of lesbians disagreeing but concern that we are being used by the law rather than using it. My concern is the same whether Alison D. wins or loses. My concern is even more pronounced if Virginia M. merely appeals to her superior legal status to resolve disagreements with the woman she once loved. When we use the law against each other, we are ultimately being used by the law: to sustain its own (nonlesbian) power. We sustain the law's power when we appeal to its categories rather than empowering our lesbian selves by appealing to lesbian categories.

We must decide whether or not mother (or parent) is a category that can be lesbian as well as legal. Just as I do not find convincing the argument that as lesbians we can enter the state-created marriage contract and transform it by our very existence, I do not think that as lesbians (either singly or in pairs) we can enter the state-defined parent role and transform it. Perhaps I am not optimistic enough. Or perhaps I am too intimidated by the rules of law that operate to give parents virtual ownership rights over their children unless the parents are not model state citizens. I am intimidated by the class and antilesbian model of the well-educated and well-liked Jane Doe and her summers with her well-adjusted and above-average son. And I am intimidated by judicial disapproval, profound enough to take a child away if a mother does not dress her children correctly in the Mississippi cold or does not dress herself correctly in feminine attire. Even absent a lesbian mother, the legal category of mother operates restrictively and punitively.

Ultimately, I think that the legal category of mother (or even parent or family) is too stifling for our lesbian imaginations and relationships.

The category of mother domesticates us. We have difficulty thinking in other than its terms. While I am not abandoning its strategic use, I am suggesting we recognize strategic uses of the legal category of mother in litigation, even as we attempt to develop lesbian categories for the complex relationships between lesbians and children. If we are ever to move beyond our domestication and insure lesbian survival on lesbian terms, we must theorize against the dominant discourse of the legal regime, including the legal regime that codifies the category "mother."

NOTES

This chapter is based on an article that originally appeared in *Hypatia: A Journal of Feminist Philosophy* 7, no. 4 (1992): 172–85. Portions of this work appear in *Lesbian (Out)law: Survival Under the Rule of Law* (Ithaca, N.Y.: Firebrand Books, 1992). I have benefited from the research assistance of Rebecca Baehr and Leslie Thrope, as well as the editorial assistance of Claudia Card and Isabel Karpin.

1. The term *colonization*, however, has been used metaphorically to describe a process of overlegalization. For an extended discussion of the concept of the "colonization of the life-world," see Habermas 1984 and 1985. I have employed the term *colonization* in an earlier form of theorizing about this process (Robson and Valentine 1990:511).

2. Domestication also has within it the idea of its opposite. To have been domesticated, one must have once existed wild, and there is the possibility of a feral future. To be feral is to have survived domestication and be transformed into an untamed state. Postdomestication lesbian existence is one purpose of a lesbian legal theory: if we can confront the ways in which we are domesticated, we can begin to challenge our domestication.

Despite my use of the domestication metaphor, I am not conceptualizing lesbians as women who have been trapped in little houses on the prairie by mean men, or as wild animals who have been harnessed to plow the soybean fields. While these are tempting images that foster an idealized version of our innocence and victimization, such images conflict with my experience. To use the postmodern phrase, we are "always already" domesticated. We are born and socialized with reference to the dominant culture. However, I do not believe that we are necessarily so constricted.

3. See also Dooley 1990:395; Pollack and Vaughn 1987; and Allen 1986.

4. See, for example, *Thigpen v. Carpenter*, 21 Ark.App. 195, 730 S.W.2d 510 (1987) ("it is not necessary to prove that illicit sexual conduct is detrimental [to the children]; it is presumed so"); *In re Marriage of Diehl*, 221 Ill.App.3d 410, 582 N.E.2d 281 (1991) ("Because of Jennifer's tender years

. . . it is in her best interest not to be exposed to a lesbian relationship"); *T. C. H. v. K. M. H.*, 784 S.W.2d (Mo.Ct.App. 1989) ("Even if mother remains discreet about her sexual preference, a number of experts at the trial testified, and Missouri case law recognizes, that a parent's homosexuality can never be kept private enough to be a neutral factor in the development of a child's values and character").

5. See, for example, *S. E. G. v. R. A. G.*, 735 S.W.2d 164 (Mo.Ct.App. 1987) (holding that the placing of four children with their lesbian mother was not in their best interest because it would affect their moral growth and cause them to be ostracized in their small conservative community).

6. See, for example, *In re Marriage of Williams*, 205 Ill.App.3d 613, 563 N.E.2d 1195 (1990) (holding that the "best interest of the child" was to be in physical custody of the father due to evidence showing the mother had a "gross character defect" of lesbianism).

7. See *Lundin v. Lundin*, 563 So.2d 1273 (La.Ct.App. 1990) (court awarded custody to lesbian mother, on the grounds that she did not live with her lover and was sincere in her resolve to shield he son from overt displays of affection and sexual activity); *Chicoine v. Chicoine*, 479 N.W.2d 891 (S.D. 1992) (trial court awarded lesbian mother restricted visitation on the condition that no unrelated female or homosexual male be present; on appeal by the father the South Dakota Supreme Court remanded the case to reconsider awarding such "liberal visitation rights" given the mother's character).

8. See *S. N. E. v. R. L. B.*, 699 P.2d 875 (Alaska 1985) (the standard to apply is whether the lesbian mother's conduct had or reasonably could have an adverse impact on the child's best interest. On appeal the court rejected the notion that an imagined or real social stigma attached to the mother's status as a lesbian be considered in the determination). See also *In re Marriage of Birdsall*, 197 Cal.App.3d 1024 (1988) (custody cannot be determined on the basis of sexual preference alone, and that parent is not unfit as a matter of law merely because s/he is a homosexual, but that a court may consider a parent's homosexuality as a factor along with the other evidence presented).

9. *S. N. E. v. R. L. B.*, 699 P.2d 875 (Alaska 1985); *Doe v. Doe*, 452 N.E.2d 293 (Ma. 1983); *M. P. v. S. P.*, 404 A.2d 1256 (N.J. 1979); *Guinan v. Guinan*, 102 A.D.2d 963, 477 N.Y.S.2d 830 (3d Dept 1984); *Stronman v. Williams*, 353 S.E.2d 704 (S.C. 1987).

10. The assumptions of contract include equality expressed in terms of bargaining power. Historical, cultural, and personal feelings of entitlement to bargain or lack of entitlement are not considered relevant to determining contracts. For a further discussion, see Robson and Valentine 1990:511.

11. D.C. Sup. Ct. Fam. Div. Nos. A-269–90 and A-270–90 (August 30, 1991).

12. See, for example, *In re Pearlman*, Florida Circuit Court Broward County, No. 87–24926 (March 31, 1989) 15 Fam.L.Rptr. 1355 (1989).

6 Complicating the Ideology of Motherhood: Child Welfare Law and First Nation Women

MARLEE KLINE

The damage wrought by child welfare systems on First Nation people and communities is well known and documented (Hawthorn 1966; Hepworth 1980; Johnston 1983; Hudson and McKenzie 1983; Indian Association of Alberta 1987; Armitage 1993). A number of studies have suggested this damage is explained in part by the way child welfare law is implicated in and informed by racist processes (Carasco 1986; Monture 1989; Kline 1992, 1994:451–76). I have argued, for example, that the ideological form and substance of child welfare law establishes a discursive framework that naturalizes the removal of First Nation children from their extended families, communities, and nations (Kline 1992, 1994:451–76). Racism is central to the relationship between law and ideology in this context. Racism does not, however, exist in a vacuum: rather, it operates in complex interaction with gender and class and other social relations. This is particularly important for understanding child welfare law, in which the spotlight of judicial scrutiny is on First Nation women often living in poverty. While consideration of the intersection of race, gender, and class informs the analyses of particular cases in earlier work on the application of child welfare law to First Nations (Monture 1989; Kline 1992), there has not yet been an attempt to construct a theoretical framework for understanding this intersection more generally. My aim here is to develop such a framework.[1]

I want to argue that a key to understanding the effects of child welfare law on First Nations lies in the way courts assess the mothering capabilities of First Nation women. Most courts tend to construct First

Nation women as "bad mothers," in the process of justifying the removal of their children and their subsequent placement in state care. The construction of First Nation women as bad mothers is mediated by the dominant ideology of motherhood.[2] Understanding the race, gender, and class specificity of this ideology therefore provides some insight into the complex relations of oppression and power that inform the material and discursive dimensions of child welfare law.[3] First Nation women are particularly vulnerable to being constructed by courts as bad mothers because, as a consequence of colonialist oppression and different cultural norms, they do not always meet the dominant cultural and middle-class expectations that constitute the ideology of motherhood. The following analysis of this dynamic begins with an overview of the present contours of the dominant ideology of motherhood and its historical specificity. I then illustrate how this ideology informs judicial decision-making in child welfare cases involving First Nation women, and conclude by drawing out some of the theoretical and strategic implications of the analysis.[4]

The Dominant Ideology of Motherhood

By the dominant ideology of motherhood, I mean the constellation of ideas and images in Western capitalist societies that constitute the dominant ideals of motherhood against which women's lives are judged. The expectations established by these ideals limit and shape the choices women make in their lives, and construct the dominant criteria of "good" and "bad" mothering. They exist within a framework of dominant ideologies of womanhood, which, in turn, intersect with dominant ideologies of family.

There are several core expectations that constitute the dominant ideology of motherhood. First, motherhood is understood as "the natural, desired and ultimate goal of all 'normal' women" (Stanworth 1987:14); in other words, a woman must be a mother before she will be considered "a mature, balanced, fulfilled adult" (Wearing 1984:72). This dictate of compulsory motherhood applies not only to pregnancy and birth but also to the matrix of behaviors deemed to constitute good mothering (Smart 1992:38), namely:

> A "good" mother is always available to her children, she spends time with them, guides, supports, encourages and corrects as well as loving and caring for them physically. She is also responsible for the cleanliness of their home environment.

> A "good" mother is unselfish, she puts her children's needs before her
> own.   (Wearing 1984:72)

A further expectation is that "[t]he individual mother should have total responsibility for her own children at all times" (Wearing 1984:72). I will refer to this expectation as the "primary care requirement." Finally, a mother is expected to operate within the context of the ideologically dominant family, one that is "heterosexual and nuclear in form, patriarchal in content," and based on "assumptions of privatized female dependence and domesticity" (Gavigan 1993). The latter assumptions have limited women's ability to participate in the workforce on equal terms with men and contributed to the devaluation of women's paid work, child care, and domestic labor (Molloy 1992). Perhaps to counter the lack of status and financial rewards accorded to motherhood, the role of "mother" has been idealized as "important, worthwhile and intrinsically rewarding" (Wearing 1984:72).

The dominant ideology of motherhood is an historically and culturally specific phenomenon, consolidated in the late nineteenth century in Western capitalist nations (Blackhouse 1981; Strong-Boag 1988; Boyd 1989b). It has undergone a number of shifts from that time, some of which correspond to changes in the political economy of capitalism. Since the 1960s and 1970s, for example, with rising numbers of women in the paid workforce, the ideology has increasingly countenanced some forms of "working mother," rather than dictating full-time, stay-at-home motherhood (Boyd 1989b). As well, in the last ten years or so, fathers have come to be constructed as also having a vital role to play in raising children, additional to, though different from, the role of mothers (Fineman 1992b; Smart 1991). Though changes such as these have had effects on the ideology of motherhood, they have not weakened its considerable power in disciplining women. Mothers who deviate from the ideals of motherhood are constructed as bad mothers, thereby justifying their social and legal regulation, including regulation by child welfare law.

It is not just mothers *as anomalous individuals* who are judged harshly against the ideals of motherhood. Motherhood has been ideologically constructed as compulsory only for those women considered "fit," and women have often been judged "unfit" on the basis of their social location. This has been the case (at various times during the last century and in different places) for disabled women, Black women, First Nation women, immigrant women, Jewish women, lesbian women, sole-support women, poor women, unmarried women, young women, and others (Asch and Fine 1988; Bock 1984; Collins 1990; Roberts, this volume). For these women, procreation has often been devalued and discouraged. The ideology of motherhood, therefore, speaks not only to gender roles and behavior. It also constructs some locations within social relations of race, class, sexuality, ability, and so on as more appropriate for motherhood than others. Thus, motherhood is better conceptualized as a privilege than as a right (Molloy 1992:301), a privilege that can be withheld, both ideologically and in more material ways, from women who are not members of the dominant groups in society or who are otherwise considered unfit.

Within this framework, so-called unfit women who want to have children are often confronted with serious barriers and difficulties. Single heterosexual women, lesbians, and/or disabled women, for example, are "expected to forgo mothering 'in the interest of the child' "(Stanworth 1987:15), and lesbians in particular find it difficult to gain access to safe alternative insemination processes (Coffey 1986; Cooper and Herman 1991; Harrison, this volume; Wigod 1993:A1). Moreover, though there is variation along lines of race and class, young women who become pregnant and who choose to carry their fetuses to term are often pressured, both externally and through the internalization of motherhood ideology, to give up their babies for adoption (Solinger 1992a, 1992b). When women considered unfit do have and raise children, it is difficult, if not impossible, for them to meet the societal image of the good mother.[5]

Historical analyses of motherhood discourses provide insight into the development of the race, class, and gender specificity of contemporary meanings of motherhood. Dorothy Roberts, for example, has examined the ideological devaluation of Black motherhood and the corresponding valuation of white motherhood during the period of slavery in the United States (Roberts, this volume). Dawn Currie argues that contemporary meanings of motherhood have some roots in late-nineteenth- and early-twentieth-century North American eugenics-derived birth control discourses that expressed concerns about "control[ling] both the growth of potentially unruly populations and the racial quality of future generations" (Currie 1992:4). In contemporary discourses of motherhood, however, the origins and operation of motherhood ideology within social relations of oppression, including intersecting relations of race, gender, and class, are submerged. Instead, the expectations of good mothering are presented as natural, necessary, and universal. The bad mother, by corollary, is constructed as the "photographic negative" of the good mother (Swigart 1991:8), again with the operation of racism and other such factors rendered invisible. Moreover, the realities of poverty, racism, heterosexism, and violence that often define the lives of mothers who do not conform to the ideology are effectively erased. As Marie Ashe has stated:

> Consideration of the material conditions of women's lives is made irrelevant through construction of the "bad mother" as a pure and essentialistic figure. She is defined as a woman whose acts or omissions constitute "bad mothering" whatever her class or race or household relationships.   (Ashe, Feminism and Legal Theory Workshop)

Thus, the construct of bad mother, though historically embedded in oppressive social relations, is presented as universal and thus innocent of its origins and effects.[6] This dynamic then helps to naturalize and legitimate intersecting oppressive relations of race, gender, and class in particular contexts, such as that of child welfare law.

The Ideology of Motherhood, Child Welfare Law, and First Nation Women

The imposition of child welfare law on First Nations in Canada vividly illustrates the intersection of multiple axes of power within the ideology of motherhood. Understanding this dynamic, I want to suggest, helps explain why the child welfare system has had such destructive effects on First Nations and, most directly, on First Nation women and children. Before illustrating this point by analyzing recent child welfare cases, I would like to make some preliminary observations.

First, while First Nation women are often victims of the child welfare system, they are not *passive* victims. Rather, they actively resist and negotiate within the system, and even rely on it when necessary. Second, I focus here on Canadian judicial decisions because courts play a critical role in First Nation child welfare matters: First Nation children are more likely to be removed from their homes statutorily (and thus through judicial order) than placed "voluntarily" into state care (Canada Child and Family Services Task Force 1987:8–9).[7] Though most First Nation child welfare decisions are unreported, those that can be obtained provide insight into the kind of reasoning and underlying "common-sense" assumptions that inform judicial decision making in this context. Finally, while it is possible that some important differences exist between the interests of First Nation children and the interests of their female First Nation caregivers, a fundamental premise of this paper is that the circumstances and treatment of First Nation women and the well-being of their children are connected in important ways. I am not suggesting, however, that First Nation children are never at risk of harm or neglect, nor in need of state protection and care. That they sometimes are is attested to by the fact that First Nation mothers—or extended family members, or Band social workers—often themselves involve child welfare authorities in the first place.[8] It is important to note, however, that judicial interpretations of events in relation to First Nation child welfare are often distorted and constrained by the dominant ideology of motherhood, leading to problematic and often short-sighted solutions.

At both the initial stage of child welfare proceedings, when it is determined whether a child is in need of protection, and at the dispositional stage, when support services and/or alternative care placements are ordered, courts draw on ideological conceptions of motherhood that form part of the common-sense knowledge of judges. This happens in two interconnected ways. First, judges focus on and blame *individual* First Nation mothers for the difficulties they face, without recognizing the roots of those difficulties in the history and current structures of colonialism and racial oppression. Second, the dominant ideology of motherhood operates to impose dominant cultural values and practices in relation to child raising on First Nations, and correspondingly to devalue concerns and practices of First Nations in this context. These two tendencies operate in conjunction with one other and with other processes to shape the final results arrived at by courts.

The following discussion attempts to reveal the racial, cultural, and class specificity of the ideology of motherhood by analyzing the effects of these two tendencies on First Nation women in child protection cases. It is based on my reading of about 240 reported and unreported Canadian child welfare cases. Most were decided within the last ten to twelve years and many within the last three or four years. The First Nation women who appear in these cases include mothers as well as extended family members such as grandmothers and aunts. Fathers are almost always noted by judges as absent or uninterested in the proceedings, and very few appear as parties.

While I am not suggesting that the tendencies I identify in these cases are statistically significant, they do reveal some of the complex and subtle ways that race, gender, and class processes interact within legal thought. The examples I draw on here illustrate these tendencies most explicitly.[9] My argument, however, is that the kind of thinking about motherhood these examples represent informs judicial decision making even when not explicit. The cases also reveal that the ideology of motherhood is not necessarily smoothly and unproblematically reproduced and reinforced. At times, some judicial sensitivity to the particular contexts of First Nation women is reflected in cases, and reasons are provided that challenge aspects of the ideology of motherhood that serve to oppress these women. Such cases remain the exception, but they do illustrate the dynamic nature of ideology: that it need not always be rigidly enforced to maintain its authority and power, and that it is continually constructed and reconstructed in the face of challenges by contradictory ideas and oppositional ideologies (Macdonell 1986:33; Hunt 1991:115; Eagleton 1991:45).

Individuation, Obfuscation, and Mother-Blaming

An important feature of the ideology of motherhood is the way it individuates mothers and the practice of mothering. This can be understood as related to the primacy of the individual in liberal ideology more generally. The individualistic focus of the dominant ideology of motherhood, and the related expectation that individual mothers will take full responsibility for their children, mean that when there is a problem with a child, the individual mother's mothering practices are subjected to critical scrutiny (Griffith and Smith 1987:97). The implication is that mothers are to blame for child neglect. In the child welfare context, judges and child protection workers focus almost exclusively on the caregiving capabilities and deficiencies of individual mothers and, in particular, on so-called questionable behaviors (Swift 1991:249). Even where there is no tangible evidence of neglect, children will still be considered at risk if their mothers are exhibiting behaviors thought to be risk factors for neglect (Marshall 1993:186).

This pattern of mother-blaming is partly facilitated by the framework of child protection legislation existing in each province. Child protection workers are directed to identify and design treatment for the problematic behaviors of *individual* caregivers (Swift 1991), not to document and develop responses to problems of poverty, racism, and violence, and the way these affect women's lives (Hooper 1992). Not surprisingly, then, child protection discourse tends to blame individual mothers for child neglect (Swift 1991; Marshall 1993:186). It is filtered into the judicial process through child protection workers, who play an important role in constructing cases and in providing evidence of child neglect in court proceedings. It is of course also likely that this professional discourse has particularly persuasive value with judges because it tends to reinforce mother-blaming aspects of the dominant ideology of motherhood.

The application of mother-blaming to First Nation women high-lights its racial and cultural specificity. In particular, mother-blaming obscures the wider context of racism, poverty, ill-health, and violence within which many First Nation women who appear in these cases are struggling to survive. It obscures the roots of these conditions in historical and continuing practices of colonialism and racial oppression, including land dispossession, the destruction of the traditional economies of First Nations, the transgenerational effects of residential schools, and the child welfare system itself.

The focus on individual bad mothers as the source of difficulties in First Nation child welfare cases effectively blames First Nation women for the effects of social ills that are largely the consequence of historical and continuing oppression. Vivid illustrations of this focus on individualized mother-blaming can be found in child protection cases involving First Nation women who are dependent on drugs or alcohol, or involved in a relationship with a violent man. In such cases, judges often refer to the alcohol and drug dependencies of First Nation women as their "personal lifestyle" problems, implying they deserve what comes (the removal of their children) if they do not rehabilitate themselves within a "reasonable" time. In *Director of Child Welfare of Manitoba v. B.* (1979) (4 C.N.L.R. 62 [1981] [Man.Prov.Ct.Fam.Div.]), for example, the Court referred to substantial alcohol abuse by the mother as an aspect of her "lifestyle" (64), stating that it included "personal traits and problems that severely limit her parenting abilities" (64).

Even more disturbing is the tendency to characterize the subjection of First Nation women to violence by male partners as simply a "personal problem" or a problem of lifestyle. In *Child and Family Services of Western Manitoba v. J. H. B.* (1990) (67 Man.R.2d 161 [Man.Q.B.]), a First Nation mother was characterized as beset by a "chaotic lifestyle" (161) resulting from an abusive relationship and alcoholism. The Court concluded that her children were "entitled to be free of the detrimental consequences which flow from care being provided by someone whose life is consumed and subsumed by *personal problems* [emphasis added]" (164). In *Children's Aid Society of Halifax v. C. F.* (1990) (96 N.S.R.2d 104 [N.S.Fam.Ct.]), the emotional involvement of a First Nation woman with an abusive man was referred to as one of her "addictions"

(106), along with alcoholism and drug use. In the view of the Court, "the three addictions [were] intertwined and tend[ed] to feed on each other" (107). In *K. B. v. Alberta (Director, Child Welfare)* (A.J.No. 840 [1992] [Q.L.]), a First Nation mother was admonished to overcome "*her* problem with . . . relationships with abusive men [emphasis added]" (14).[10] Similar characterizations of involvement in "volatile relationships" as an aspect of a woman's lifestyle have been observed in the files of child protection workers (Marshall 1993:138–39). Altogether, the characterization of battering and alcohol and drug dependency as personal problems reinforces the placing of blame for child neglect on the deficiencies of individual mothers.

This mother-blaming dynamic is also at work in the way the ideological expectation that mothers be unselfish and self-sacrificing is applied to First Nation women. The presumption underlying the expectation that it is possible to separate the needs of mothers from those of their children is particularly onerous for many First Nation women who, because of poverty and other difficulties, struggle to survive on a day-to-day basis. In *Re J. H and N. H.* (3 Y.R. 282 [1988] [Yuk.Ter.]), for example, a battered First Nation woman without employment or appropriate housing, who often required assistance from social welfare authorities to provide her children with basic necessities, was characterized by the Yukon Territorial Court as, at bottom, "preoccupied with her own needs" (287). The Court was not persuaded by her argument that "the achievement of those needs" was necessary to her being able to care properly for her children, and held, in any event, that her problems were "insurmountable" (291). The children were thus determined to be better off in the permanent care and custody of the Director of Family and Children's Services. The characterization of alcohol and drug dependency and involvement in battering relationships as "personal problems" has bearing here as well: the implication is that mothers who continue to be involved with such personal problems are acting selfishly, thereby enhancing the perception of them as bad mothers.

Illustrations of mother-blaming can also be found in cases that draw upon ideological constructions of the physical home environment "proper" for raising children. Women whose living situations do not meet these standards are judged as inadequate mothers. A mother is presumed not to be a good mother if, for example, she moves from place to place, or if the place where she lives is not clean and tidy. Such behavior is taken as evidence of the quality of a mother's care, regardless of whether there is actual neglect or inadequate care of the children.

Failure to meet the expectations of the proper home environment provides a ground in itself to deem the mother deficient (Swift 1991:257). This poses particular difficulties for First Nation women in child protection cases. Once again, the specificity of the application of the "proper" home requirement to First Nation women takes a mother-blaming form. The difficult life circumstances of many First Nation women are regarded by judges as indicators of, and risk factors for, inadequate mothering. This is particularly apparent in cases that manifest ideological expectations that a home be an established if not permanent one, and that it be clean and tidy.

With respect to permanency, First Nation women are sometimes characterized by judges as not meeting the ideological requirement of having a "proper" home environment on the ground they live "nomadic" or "transient" lives.[11] In *Kenora-Patricia Child and Family Services v. L. (P.)* (O.J.No. 1858 [1987] [Q.L.]), for example, a First Nation woman, whose three children had been apprehended from her, lived first with the father of her children, then off and on with her sister in Manitoba, and then with "another boyfriend" (3). The judge was concerned that even when the two parents were together, they had "no fixed home" (5). He considered the woman's situation to be "more than a 'nomadic life.' It indicates instability, insecurity, a lack of permanency—all of which are not positive factors for any family, and are more devastating for a young child" (5–6). The lack of an established home, in other words, was for the Court *ipso facto* a risk factor. Moreover, the Court was apparently uninterested in the fact that the mother had left her home on a number of occasions to escape beatings by her partner, and did not consider whether other moves were due to her lack of financial resources or other reasons beyond her control. Rather, the focus of the Court was on the mother's alleged deficiencies. She was, in the view of the Court, unprepared to assume "the responsibilities of parenthood" (15) and permanent custody of her three children was therefore granted to the provincial Crown (10).

In *New Brunswick (Minister of Health and Community Services) v. L. M. and F. G.* (93 N.B.R.2d 261 [1989] [Q.B.Fam.Div.]) all parental rights and responsibilities in relation to three First Nation children were transferred from a mother (and uninterested father) to the New Brunswick Minister of Health and Community Services. This was done, in part, because the mother "ha[d] been moving from one place to another and [was] simply not in a position to receive custody of her children" (265). Concern with the mother's "transient" lifestyle figured quite prominently in the reasons of the Court, and, yet again, there was no inquiry into whether she was forced to move as a result of housing short-age, poverty, violence, racism, or other factors. Similarly, in *Re A. B., C. B., and M. B.* (100 A.R. 150 [1989] [AHa.Prov.Ct]), the Court was concerned that the First Nation mother in question continued to live a "transient lifestyle" (153) after apprehension of her children. This was taken as an indication that she was not yet ready to regain custody of her children. Evidence in the case suggested, however, that her tendency to move from place to place resulted from depression, which was due in part to her being denied access to her children, and to her need to avoid phys-ical abuse by the children's father.

Like the "permanent home" requirement, dominant middle-class ideals of cleanliness and tidiness are central to ideological constructions of good motherhood, and have particularly oppressive effects for many First Nation women confronted by child welfare law. A vivid example can be found in *L. O. and S. O. v. Superintendent of Child Welfare* (N.W.T.R. 295 [1984] [Nwt.S.C.]). A nineteen-month-old Inuit girl suffering from serious skin rashes was apprehended from the Inuit couple who had taken her in when she had been abandoned as a baby because, according to the Court, their house "was just not tidy enough for such a tender-skinned little girl" (298). Interestingly, at this point the judge speaks of "parents" in the plural, but then goes on to attribute responsibility for "housekeep-ing" specifically to the Inuit woman, with the implication that she is more to blame for the situation. Though nurses had "tried to teach the parents basic hygiene," the house remained "a rough and ready one, with no sheets, no linen, with dishes never washed and generally very untidy" (298). The Inuit community, unlike the Court and medical profession-als, apparently did not view this as sufficient reason to remove the child. According to the Court, the parents were "respected and well-liked" within the Inuit community and their home was regarded as the child's "proper home" (298). The Court underlined this point by acknowledg-ing that, had the child been placed in foster care with another Inuit fam-ily in the community, she would have been "promptly returned" by that family to the home of her customary adoptive parents (298). Despite all of this, the apprehension of the child, and her placement with one of the only white families in the town, was sanctioned by the Court.

Though cleanliness and tidiness were constructed as essential to ade-quate mothering in *Re H. (A. M.)* (B.C.J.No. 2429 [1989] [Q.L.]), as well, the views of the First Nation community in question were held in the end to carry more weight. In this case, a mother who lived on the

Tsawassen reserve was characterized by the Court as having, among other things, a "neglectful and disorderly lifestyle" (2), including "concepts of housekeeping and hygiene . . . totally different from those of Social Workers" (10), teachers at her children's school, and various support service providers. However, because the Chief and Band social worker were "not as upset by [her] hygiene standards as the off-reserve people were" (11), the Court held the Band had a "right to go on . . . raising their young according to their own lights" (85), and the children were returned to their mother's care. This is a laudable result, and the judge should be commended for refusing to subject the woman to dominant constructions of cleanliness. At the same time, however, there is an unfortunate implication in the judgment that standards of hygiene in First Nation communities are the result of cultural difference, rather than a material consequence of poverty—overcrowded and substandard housing related to histories of colonialism and racial oppression (Monture 1989:14).

A final example of mother-blaming and the individualist focus of the ideology of motherhood can be found in the expectation that mothers assume primary care of their children, regardless of their circumstances. A mother must be self-reliant and care for her children with minimal or no assistance (Swift 1991:257). Again, the individualistic focus of this requirement ignores and obscures the colonialist roots of the problems faced by many First Nation women. Poverty is often responsible for the difficulties mothers, and in particular lone mothers, have in providing primary care to their children (National Council of Welfare 1990). This has specific implications for First Nation mothers who disproportionately live in poverty (Department of Indian and Northern Development 1990:55–57) largely as a result of colonialist practices and policies. In *Re J. H. and N. H.* (1988), for example, children were committed permanently to the care of the Director of Family and Children's Services because their thirty-two-year-old First Nation mother in the Yukon was unable to "provide *primary care* for herself and her children" (emphasis added) (287). The many times she had approached child welfare authorities or relied on relatives for caregiving assistance in crisis situations were taken by the Court to indicate "little improvement on *her* part in dealing with *her* problems *on her own*" (emphasis added) (288). Yet, part of what created her need for assistance in the first place was her lack of suitable housing and her inability to supply her children with basic necessities because of her poverty.

The individualizing and obfuscating effects of the ideology of motherhood do not always take the form of mother-blaming. They also submerge contradictions between the liberal framework of "choice" and the coercive and ideological forces in women's lives that make "options," such as giving one's child up for adoption, appear viable. An aspect of such processes in the lives of First Nation women—which operates in addition to economic and other material constraints—is racism and its expression through the dominant ideology of motherhood. As I have already noted, within the terms of that ideology, racism operates to deem racialized groups of women unfit to be mothers. One might ask to what extent does this contribute to the ideological pressure experienced by First Nation women (particularly those who are young) to give up their children for adoption? Not surprisingly, courts have not been concerned with such matters, but have instead taken at face value the "choice" of First Nation women to give up their children to foster care or adoption.

In *N. (M. L.) v. British Columbia (Superintendent of Family and Child Services)* (B.C.J.No. 1652 [1990] [Q.L.]), for example, a twenty-one-year-old Squamish woman sought to revoke, two years after the fact, her consent to the adoption of her then six-month-old daughter by a non-First Nation couple. This was denied by the B.C. Supreme Court, which held that the child was well-settled and thriving and should not be moved. The mother argued that, though the pregnancy was planned, she had been pressured into placing her child for adoption (most strongly by her mother and doctor) and had not understood the legal implications of adoption. The Court acknowledged that she had been distressed, depressed, alone, and unemployed during her pregnancy, and that she had "sincere misgivings and remorse over giving up her child" (21), but held nonetheless that the consent was a matter of personal choice and had been "given freely and voluntarily" (19) with full awareness of its effects. The woman in this case was thus held accountable for the consequences of her decision, and was even implicitly reprimanded for seeking to regain custody of her daughter: "A consent to an adoption cannot be taken lightly. Children are not chattels. They cannot be moved back and forth from their birth parents to their adoptive parents in their formative years while their parents straighten out their lives" (22). Absent from these reasons is any consideration by the Court of whether and how the decision of this young First Nation woman to give up her child might have resulted, at least in part, from the racialized operation of the ideology of motherhood in the minds of those advising her, and even in her own mind. Rather, the individualistic focus of the ideology of motherhood allowed the issue of choice to be presented in abstract and simplified terms, thereby submerging the issue of how racism intersects with dominant ideological constructions of motherhood, and how this might have affected the woman's decision.

These concerns apply as well to a similar case involving a white woman. In *King v. Low* (3 W.W.R. 1 [1985] [S.C.C.]), a white mother gave up her newborn baby, who was part First Nation, for adoption by a First Nation couple. Though she sought to revoke her consent only three months after it took effect, the Supreme Court of Canada declined to grant her request. The mother had experienced a very strict and traditional upbringing, and had initially sought the adoption out of fear of parental disapproval for having given birth to a child outside of marriage. But the Court constructed her decision only as a selfish act, as one aimed at solving "her own personal problems" (13). Rather than acting as a good, self-sacrificing mother, she was regarded as having been motivated only by the consideration of her own interests and was, thus, "unmindful of her parental duties" (13). On one level this case is similar to *N. (M. L.)*, since the Court made no attempt to situate the mother's choice within its ideological and material context. This context must be recognized as different for the women in the two cases, however; whereas the First Nation woman was subject to external and internal pressure not to mother her own child because of her race, age, and economic circumstances, the white woman was subject to pressure not to mother her own child because of her marital status—due to the patriarchal (and perhaps racist) structure of her own family. There was also an added factor in the case involving the white woman—namely, recognition by the Court of the First Nation heritage shared between her child and the adoptive parents.

Imposition of Dominant Cultural Norms and Devaluation of First Nation Norms

The ideology of motherhood not only individuates evaluations of mothers and mothering and obscures underlying social relations of colonialism and racial oppression, it serves as well to impose dominant cultural values and practices relating to child care upon First Nations. Correspondingly, it devalues First Nation child care ethics and practices, as well as First Nation communities as places to raise children. The requirement of primary care, for example, considered in the previous section in relation to mother-blaming, can also be understood as an imposition of dominant cultural norms upon First Nations. Mary Ellen

Turpel, and other First Nation legal scholars, have contrasted the col-lectivist norms of First Nations with the liberal individualism of the dominant order (Turpel 1989–90; Little Bear 1986; Monture 1989). Consistent with this, there tends to be greater expectation of, and reliance on, the participation of extended family members in the care of children in First Nation communities. According to an elder in Alberta:

> The Indian philosophy is that . . . in the family home, if things didn't work out well for [a] young couple, supposing . . . there was sickness in that family, or the mother died or the father died, it is the practice and cultured belief of our native people that automatically an uncle, an aunt or grandmother, grandfather or a cousin or even a good friend of those people would take over the responsibility for raising that child and this was expected of society in those days.
>
> (Indian Association of Alberta 1987:50–51)

In child protection cases, however, the involvement and commitment of extended family members to caregiving is often insufficiently recog-nized by courts. In *K. (C. J.) v. Children's Aid Society of Metropolitan Toronto* (4 C.N.L.R. 75 [1988] [Ont.Prov.Ct.Fam.Div.]), for example, a First Nation grandmother who had taken over primary care of three children from her daughter was characterized as only a "well-inten-tioned surrogate" (78).[12]

Even when a First Nation mother is receiving ongoing help from extended family members, that contribution is often ignored or regarded negatively. In such cases, the mother's individual skills and capabilities remain the primary subject of judicial scrutiny with little, if any, consideration of the role and contributions of extended family members. In *Mooswa v. Minister of Social Services for Saskatchewan* (1976) (30 R.F.L. 101 [Sask.Q.B.]), for example, the Saskatchewan Queen's Bench considered whether an apprehended child should be returned to her First Nation mother who had recently overcome an alcohol dependency. Though the mother had "established another home and . . . started a new life" (101) with her own mother, and had since given birth to another daughter who appeared adequately cared for, the Court still focused on her individual "capabilities as a mother" (102) and failed to consider seriously the clear evidence that the grand-mother would also be involved in the care of the older child (102). Sim-ilarly, in *Re D. L. C.* (4 C.N.L.R. 68 [1986] [Alta.Q.B.]), the issue was whether a two-and-a-half-year-old child was in need of protection from his alcoholic mother. Again, though there was evidence that three older children were well cared for, in part due to the involvement of extended family members, the Court still focused only on the mother's "own shortcomings" (70).

In a few cases courts have gone some way toward recognizing the role of extended family members in the care of First Nation children. In *Re E. J. C.* (79 A.R. 125 [1987] [Alta.Prov.Ct.]), the main issue was whether a two-and-a-half-year-old child in need of protection would be placed with his maternal grandmother in accordance with the wishes of his mother, or with his white foster parents who had cared for him for a year and wished to adopt him. The Court rejected the contention of the Crown that the grandmother had no legal status in the proceedings, acknowledging "the cultural practices in the Cree community of grandparents raising grandchildren, [and] the responsibility and willingness the grandmother ha[d] shown in the past to care for the child" (128). Nonetheless, the Court held that placement in the grandmother's home was "relatively equal" to permanent placement with the foster parents (130). Because the child protection workers who constructed the case had focused on the individual caregiving skills of the mother, largely ignoring the role of the grandmother, the Court determined it had insufficient knowledge of "the grandmother's capability, willingness, and commitment to provide care for [the] child" (130). To allow for the collection of new information, the child was left in the custody of the foster parents for another four months. In addition to demonstrating some judicial acknowledgment of the role of extended family members in the care of First Nation children, this case provides a good illustration of how the ideology of motherhood shapes the construction of child welfare cases by child protection workers before these cases even get to court.

Re H. (A.M.) (1989) goes a bit further in its recognition of the important role played by extended family members in the care of children in First Nation communities. In this case, as I have already noted, the Court concluded that the alcohol dependency of a Tsawassen mother, and her "neglectful and disorderly lifestyle" (2), would likely prevent her from providing the effective and consistent caregiving her children required. The Court was prepared, however, to accept the approach of members of the Tsawassen Band, which was "not so insistent on putting [a mother's] individual skills under the microscope" (17). Because the Court felt assured there would be "a degree of help inside the band and a fair amount of 'muddling through' to cope with emergencies" (16), the children were returned to the care of their mother, who lived on the reserve. In its recognition of the importance of not always enforcing the primary care requirement for First Nation mothers on reserves, this case

is somewhat encouraging. The approach of the Court is limited, however, by its application only to First Nation women on *reserves*. Effectively, it carves out an exception to the norm of primary care for those
women while reinforcing, or at least not challenging, the general validity of that norm. The Court states that First Nation women living in the
"wider community" (14) outside of "defined separate communities with
a distinct way of life, like the Indian Bands" (19), will be judged by the
standards of the wider community, including, by implication, the primary care requirement. Consistent with this approach, in *Re C. J. W. S.*
(1 C.N.L.R. 51 [1987] [Alta.Q.B.]), the Court rejected a family's plan
for a boy to leave foster care and live with his paternal Cree grandmother
and her four children in Edmonton, and be cared for during the day by
his Metis mother, who lived across the street. In reaching this conclusion, the Court appeared to have difficulty with the notion that traditional ways (including, presumably, the involvement of extended family
in child raising) could continue to be preserved and practiced within
urban environments, outside of Band and reserve communities.

The operation of familial ideology in First Nation child welfare
cases, in particular the norm of the nuclear, heterosexual, patriarchal,
middle-class, dominant-culture family, can, like that of the primary
care requirement, be understood in culturally specific terms. In *Re C. J.
W. S.*, for example, the Court's concerns that the relevant caregivers
were extended family members living in different houses, and that the
mother had no plans to live with the father at the end of his prison
term, can be understood as an imposition of a nuclear family norm.
The ideal of conformity to the ideologically dominant family form also
has implications for the evaluation of potential foster or adoptive families. In *V. S. and J. S. v. M. M. and C. M.* (N.W.T.R. 169 [1989]
[Nwt.S.C.]), for example, a couple in Nova Scotia were granted inter-
vener status in child welfare proceedings that involved an eleven-year-
old Chipewyan girl of the Dene Nation whom they had met while in
the Northwest Territories visiting relatives. The intervention was
granted over the objections of the child's mother and grandmother, and
even the Department of Social Services, all of whom were concerned
that the child remain "in her homeland and culture" (172). Nonetheless, the Court allowed the couple to intervene because then "the possibility of her finding a *congenial* and *suitable* permanent *family* environment [would] at least [be] given a chance of realization" [emphasis
added] (177). The Nova Scotia couple met the ideal of the ideologically
dominant family form, and this effectively facilitated and legitimated

the possibility that this child might be removed from her culture and heritage and placed within the dominant society.

That the dominant family form is racially, culturally, and class specific, with particular implications for First Nations, is further highlighted by *L. O. and S. O.* (1984). In that case, two families in the Northwest Territories, each of whom met the nuclear family norm, applied for custody of an Inuit child. The first family, an Inuit couple in their late fifties with six older children of their own, had taken the child in when she had been abandoned as a baby. The family lived, as described by the judge, in a small, four-room house that was "kept a mess" (297), and both parents worked outside the home. The second family, a white couple who fostered the child when she developed serious skin rashes, were in their mid-thirties. The man was a Royal Canadian Mounted Police officer, and the woman had done no waged work outside the home since she took over the care of the child. They lived in a "new and modern bungalow" (301) in the same town. Not surprisingly, the white couple were granted custody of the child. Such a result ensured, according to the Court, this "little girl's passage from sad and humble beginnings to a new future replete with hope and promise" (296). Even though the Inuit family met the formal expectations of familial ideology, the white couple clearly provided a better fit with its racial, cultural, and class expectations.

Finally, a further effect of the ideologically dominant family form in First Nation child welfare cases is illustrated by the way some courts have characterized First Nation mothers who struggle to regain custody of their children from foster care situations that meet the ideologically dominant family form. In such situations, courts have implied that the mark of a good mother is to leave the child in his/her dominant cultural and middle-class foster home, and not make a fuss about it. As Madame Justice Bertha Wilson said in *Racine v. Woods* (1 C.N.L.R. 161 [1984] [S.C.C.]), a leading Supreme Court of Canada decision on child welfare involving a First Nation mother, "It takes a very high degree of selflessness and maturity . . . for a parent to acknowledge that it might be better for his or her child to be brought up by someone else" (169). The Ojibway mother in that case was constructed as selfish and immature for struggling, over several years, to regain custody of her child from foster care. Her use of the media, and general politicization of the case, were also regarded as self-serving and contrary to the interests of her child. For example, Madame Justice Wilson questioned "whether [the mother's] concern was for her child as a person or a political issue?" (179). Rather than viewing her as a committed mother, one who resisted and challenged the child welfare system for, in her view, the good of both her child and herself, she was implicitly constructed as a bad mother, further justifying, in the eyes of the Court, the continuing custody and eventual adoption of the child by the foster parents (Kline 1992:407–10).

By corollary, one might expect First Nation mothers who cooperate in having their children raised in the dominant society to be constructed as self-sacrificing good mothers. For example, in *Simeonoff v. J. A.* (B.C.J.No. 279 [1992] [Q.L.]) the B.C. Court of Appeal supported a decision by a young Aleut sole-support mother residing in California to have her newborn daughter remain in the custody of non-First Nation potential adoptive parents in Vancouver, rather than go to members of the mother's birth tribe in Alaska, who were also seeking custody. For this decision, the mother was implicitly constructed by the Court as a good mother. This was, in part, because she wanted to keep her daughter away from the village, and consequently away from Aleut heritage and culture. This case was essentially a "fall-out" case, an illustration of the long-term consequences of the removal of First Nation children from their communities and cultures through the child welfare system. The young woman had herself been apprehended from her parents at an early age, and adopted by a non-First Nation family who moved eventually to California. As a result, she may have internalized dominant ideological constructions of the village of her birth that, possibly, affected her decision. The failure of the Court to take account of this context, and to interrogate in light of it the mother's desire to have her daughter remain with the potential adoptive parents, might be explained, at least in part, by the operation of racist and devaluative presumptions about the suitability of many First Nation communities, compared to the dominant society, for raising children. While I am not suggesting that the result in the case necessarily should have been otherwise, by failing to challenge the implication that the Aleut village was an unsuitable place for the raising of children, the Court effectively reinforced devaluative representations of First Nation communities. The Court's implicit construction of this woman as a good self-sacrificing mother, struggling to ensure that her child received the benefits of adoption by a dominant-culture middle-class family, served implicitly to devalue First Nation communities and culture, not to mention the struggles of First Nations to survive the effects of child welfare systems.

My goal in this essay has been twofold: first, as part of the ongoing discussion about intersectionality in feminist legal theory (Crenshaw 1989;

Harris 1990; Duclos 1993), to highlight the complexity of the dominant ideology of motherhood, in particular the race and class (in addition to gender) specificity of its form, content, operation, and effects; and second, to advance understanding of the oppressive and devastating operation of child welfare systems on First Nation women and their children and communities. As I have shown, these two goals are interrelated. Knowledge of the specificity and complexity of intersecting relations of race, gender, and class must be grounded in concrete analyses of particular ideological formations and their historical context of material conditions and power relations. The day-to-day practices of mothering always occur within social relations of race, class, gender, sexual orientation, ability, and so on (Spelman 1988), and the dominant ideological expectations against which mothering practices are measured and judged are inevitably constructed by, and given effect within, these relations. I have sought to illustrate this dynamic through an analysis of the judicial construction of First Nation women in child welfare law. The combined effect in First Nation child welfare cases of the individuation/obfuscation and imposition/devaluation processes rooted in the ideology of motherhood is to leave First Nation women particularly vulnerable to being constructed by courts as bad mothers in child protection proceedings, and to having their children taken away as a result of this construction.

An important theoretical and strategic question raised by this analysis is whether and how oppressive aspects of dominant ideology, in particular those reinforced by law, can be shifted and/or displaced, and what beneficial and/or transformative effects this might have. On one level, the more reflective judgments I identify in my discussion of cases may provide some cause for optimism in the First Nation child welfare context. They indicate that judges do not always unquestioningly accept and reproduce the expectations of dominant ideologies, and that judicial education may therefore hold out some promise for bringing about change. At a deeper level, however, I do not believe substantial modification of the dominant ideology of motherhood will occur without a more fundamental shift in the social relations of race, gender, class, sexual orientation, and ability underlying it. In the First Nations context, moreover, such concerns are further complicated by the role of child welfare systems in the colonialist oppression of First Nations in Canada (Hudson and McKenzie 1983; Monture 1989; Kline 1992, 1994). Simply challenging the ideological assumptions informing the present system will leave undisturbed, and possibly even reinforce, the power now accorded to institutions of the dominant society to impose destructive child welfare regimes on First Nations.

In the final analysis, the material relations of colonialism and racial oppression within the child welfare system and more generally within society must be directly challenged and replaced. This is the struggle First Nations have been pursuing through a variety of self-government strategies, in the context of which different communities have been working toward developing their own child welfare services, some outside the framework of existing provincial legislative schemes.[13] This is not to say there are no debates within First Nations communities as to the shape and institutional structure of such services, nor has the provision of services by First Nations been without problems of implementation (Giesbrecht 1992; Armitage 1993:168–69). The only way to stop the problematic application of dominant legal and ideological processes, however, is to support First Nation communities in working through these difficulties. This means First Nation communities—both urban and reserve-based—should be provided full financial, institutional, and legislative support to facilitate meeting this challenge.

In the meantime, however, First Nation mothers will continue to confront dominant legal and ideological processes in the child welfare context. The possibilities and limits of challenging and changing the legal and ideological framework within which judges operate therefore remains an important site of political struggle. My hope is that greater knowledge of the complexity of processes responsible for the present destructive impact of child welfare law on First Nations will contribute to the development of effective strategies both for moving forward within the current system while it continues to apply to First Nation people and, more importantly, for moving beyond it.

NOTES

I would like to thank Joel Bakan, Susan Boyd, Didi Herman, Nitya Iyer, Hester Lessard, Judy Mosoff, J. C. Smith, Veronica Strong-Boag, Laurel Wellman, Claire Young, and Margot Young for reading and/or commenting on earlier versions of this paper, and Barbara Brown for her excellent research assistance and helpful suggestions. I am grateful as well for the provocative questions and comments that followed presentations of earlier and related versions of this paper at the Workshop on Motherhood, Feminism, and Legal Theory Project, Columbia Law School, December 1992; Center for Research on Women's Studies and Gender Relations Colloquia

Series, University of British Columbia, March 1993; Faculty Seminar, Faculty of Law, University of Victoria, April 1993; and the Law and Society Association Meeting, Learned Societies Meetings, Ottawa, June 1993. The financial support of a University of British Columbia Humanities and Social Sciences Large Research Grant is also gratefully acknowledged. This paper was originally published in the Queen's Law Journal *18, no. 2 (1993) and is reprinted here with the permission of that Journal.*

1. Sexual orientation and disability are also implicated in the application of child welfare law to First Nations. Because the available cases do not consider these dimensions, however, this paper will focus on relations of race, gender, and class.

2. The concept of ideology I rely on comes out of a socialist feminist tradition (Gavigan 1993). I recognize the beliefs, images, explanations, and evaluations that constitute ideology as constructed historically in conjunction with, and in relation to, material and cultural conditions and power relations, which are then represented as natural, inevitable, and necessary—as simply part of common sense—in the current social order.

3. In complicating how we understand the ideology of motherhood, I am building on some of the ground-breaking feminist work in this area (Boyd 1989a, 1989b, 1991, 1993; Arnup 1989; Currie 1993; Roberts, this volume; Fineman, this volume; Davidoff 1992).

4. Given that I am a non-First Nation woman, the purpose of this paper is not to consider how First Nation women experience the destructive impact of child welfare law, nor how ideologies of motherhood or other processes within First Nation communities might challenge destructive aspects of child welfare law, including the operation of the dominant ideology of motherhood. Rather, my goal is to analyze some of the more subtle means by which *dominant institutions*, such as that of child welfare law, come to have specific destructive effects on First Nation women.

5. This is not to say, however, that white middle-class women find it easy to meet the ideals of motherhood or necessarily experience motherhood as fulfilling and rewarding (Rich 1976). For reasons inherent in the ideology of motherhood, however, it is more difficult for women who are poor or working class, and/or First Nation, and/or Black, and/or lesbian, and so on to meet the dominant expectations of motherhood (Boyd 1991; Gavigan 1993). This complicates and provides insight into the further link drawn by some between the failure of women to conform to ideal patterns of mothering, violence, poverty, and social disarray.

6. This point is analogous to Peter Fitzpatrick's discussion of how law's claim of innocence obfuscates its role in reproducing and reinforcing racism (Fitzpatrick 1987:119).

7. I have qualified the term *voluntarily* to indicate that when mothers

"choose" to place their children into state care, they are likely to feel that they have "no choice" and do so as a result of their circumstances and/or pressure exerted by child protection workers.

8. See *Re H. (A. M.)* (1989) B.C.J. No. 2429 (QL): Chief and Band Social Worker initiated the apprehension but then contested permanent removal of two children from their mother; *Northwest Child and Family Services Agency (Man.) v. L. A. C. and A. S. C.* (1988), 53 Man.R.2d 146: apprehension initiated by an aunt; *Re J. H. and N. H.* (1988), 3 Y.R. 282 (Yuk. Terr. Ct.): mother requested assistance from child welfare agency in crisis situations; *Re Cherie* (1983), 53 A.R. 48: voluntary placement of child into care by mother; *Racine v. Woods* (1 C.N.L.R. 161 [1984] [S.C.C.]): initial placement of child into care by mother voluntary.

9. I found explicit examples of one or both of the tendencies I have identified as flowing from the ideology of motherhood in almost a quarter (51) of the 240 cases. Susan Boyd (1989b, 1993) has taken a similar approach to ideological analysis in judicial decision making.

10. The latter decisions involving women battered by their male partners indicate little understanding of cycles of battering and the difficulties faced by women attempting to break free of abusive relationships. There is also little recognition of the difficulties involved in trying to provide consistent care for children within abusive contexts.

11. Mobility is a useful indicator of socioeconomic conditions, as well as the availability of goods and services and employment and educational opportunities (Lithwick, Schiff, and Vernon 1986:46). This 1986 study (based on 1981 data) found that the mobility rates of off-reserve Indians—in particular, off-reserve Indian women—were higher than those of the general reference population. In addition, more off-reserve Indians surveyed had moved residence and locale in the preceding five years than on-reserve Indians. A more recent study in Vancouver found that: 11.5 percent of the First Nation people surveyed had lived in only one residence in the preceding five years; 23.9 percent had lived in two different residences; 38 percent had lived in three to five different residences; and the rest had lived in six to twenty-five different residences. With respect to movement between locales, the same study found that over one-third (37.7 percent) had lived in only one locale in the preceding five years, another third had lived in two locales, 14.7 percent had lived in three different locales, and the rest had lived in four to fifteen different locales (Rowe and Associates 1989).

12. The grandmother had recovered from various health problems and was applying for the return of her grandchildren from foster care. Given the construction of her role as only that of a "well-intentioned surrogate," it is not surprising that the Court determined they should remain in their non-First Nation homes.

13. For a sense of the extent of such development, consider that by 1990–91, the following First Nation Child Welfare Agencies were operating in

Canada: two agencies representing nineteen Bands in British Columbia; three agencies representing fifteen Bands in Alberta; seven agencies representing sixty Bands in Manitoba; seven agencies representing eighty-four Bands in Ontario; seven agencies representing fifteen Bands in Quebec; eleven agencies representing twenty Bands in the Atlantic Region; and one agency representing one Band in the Yukon (Armitage 1993:155). For illustrations of the approaches of some First Nation communities to the development of autonomous child welfare services, see Esse Networks 1990; British Columbia 1992. More comprehensive surveys of the range of First Nation child welfare initiatives can be found in Pellatt 1991:5–30; Wharf 1989; Armitage 1993; Ratner 1990.

7 | Postmodernism, Legal Ethics, and Representation of "Bad Mothers"

MARIE ASHE

Postmodernist theorists frequently express the nature of their project as the "throwing into question" of foundational concepts of Western liberal humanism. The notions of "the State" and of "Man," going the way of the Nietzschean "God," have been disturbed and de-centered by postmodernist deconstructions. The notion of "Woman," too, has begun to be interrogated by postmodernist feminisms. To recognize the significance of the postmodernist current it is essential to appreciate that its consequence is a state of "question" marked by spiritual as well as intellectual distress. This apparent consequence of theory and its contribution to deepening skepticism in an already uncertain time have assured that the problematizings to which postmodernists are inclined will present matters of no mere academic interest.

It has become almost a commonplace to observe that postmodernity is a time of crisis. Postmodernist theorists heighten our uncertainties about the continuation of social institutions seemingly founded on concepts currently threatened by deconstructionist siege. The more pressing reality, one frequently given greater emphasis by critics than by exponents of postmodernism, is that we live in a time of profound uncertainty about the very possibility of human survival. To address issues of legal ethics, then, must certainly be a problematic undertaking. Clearly, notions of law and of ethics have been as disturbed as any by deconstructionist currents. We think about legal ethics in a time in which uncertainty abounds concerning the possibilities of knowing (let alone approaching) either a justice that would support the legal or a good that would support the ethical.

This essay undertakes an examination of certain problems of legal ethics that arise for lawyers who represent and advocate for people who seriously injure their own children; that is, for people who—in a world in which much is indeed in question—continue to be generally perceived as "bad." Much of my work of the last several years, in practice and in clinical teaching, has been engaged with such clients. These are people whom many practitioners and law students experience as morally problematic. Most of these people whom I have encountered as my clients have been women. I thus attempt an interrogation of what it may mean to be good lawyers for "bad mothers."

That we live in postmodernity does not mean that we cannot speak of "the good." Indeed, that we live in postmodernity *requires* that we do so, and requires that we do so differently.

"What's all this *postmodernism*, anyway?" The voice is my son's. We are in my study. It is afternoon, and I have been packing all day. David and his friend look at the titles of books remaining on my shelves. I stand surrounded by books that cover desks and trunks, that balance on windowsills. Brown boxes are stacked along one wall, labeled and taped. Others hold their flaps open to receive appropriate contents. I'm not sure how to fill them.

I seem to have lost the skill, which I've exercised all day, of making distinctions. Of each of the books remaining unpacked, I ask myself: Is this philosophy? theology? critical theory? poetry? sociology? history? women's studies? psychoanalytic theory? fiction?? Each book, within its bindings, resists me. They threaten my orderings. They defy definition. In a kind of wild exogamy, their texts reject my categories. They refuse containment. Where to put Roland Barthes? Or Julia Kristeva? Audre Lourde? Adrienne Rich? bell hooks? Susan Griffin? Where Patricia Williams??

I am often uncertain (in general) whether my son's remarks are meant as comment or question. But David's friend, Eli, says, "Yeah, what is it exactly—postmodernism? People refer to it all the time but no one ever defines it."

I'm glad to sit down. To abandon the classification dilemma. I start to talk to them about modernism and existentialism and poststructuralism. I like my chronological approach. They listen politely. But I have to stop short and laugh, at myself. I hear myself trying—presuming—to define to them the world in which they have grown and in which they now live. A world that they know more intimately and more exclusively than I know it. A world that seems much more nearly to them, I imagine, than it has to me—a *native* home. I think of the music my son plays most often. Of how for years I have been hearing its insistent invasions or distant emanations from his room. It is music Blakean in its imagery, nearly nihilistic in its theme, with a beat sounding the cruelty of beatings more than any beatitude. In it the sound of critique pulses

from a woundedness hardly short of despair: "**So you think you can tell
heaven from hell, blue sky from pain. Can you tell a green field from a cold
steel rail? A smile from a veil?**"[1]

The world inhabited by my children is one in which it seems more meaningful to speak of cold comfort than to speak of hope. In which the notions of
"faith" and of "love" have become so problematic that they have virtually disappeared from public discourse. A world that is both post-Holocaust and
apparently inevitably pre-Holocaust.

It seems to me evident that to conduct self-inquiry or any moral inquiry
at the present time is necessarily to engage in an inquiry that is postmodernist. When I say this, I do not mean that we necessarily draw
from our bookshelves the texts of Derrida or Foucault, of Barthes or
Kristeva—though some of us may do so—as we commence that
inquiry. I do mean that we live within and inhabit a culture that bears
the marks of postmodernism. I mean that "postmodernism" is not (or
not only) the name of an intellectual weather but is the name of a moral
climate, a climate within which human eyes and ears and souls are continuously assaulted and impressed by realities of violent disorder. In this
culture, the reality of fragmentation has become so pervasive that the
very notion of the human self has been called into question in singular
fashion. Such calling into question does not occur only within written
texts that themselves challenge boundaries and definitions. It erupts
from cinemas and video screens, in our fashions as in our music.

I am struck that some trace of the breaking of familiar structures, the
fragmentation that I hear in the music, is expressed in the seeming
impossibility of packing my books. The books that defy my simple clas-
sifications and orderings have themselves, in their texts, effected massive deconstructions of boundaries. On the slippery ground of
antifoundationalism they've expanded in radical multidisciplinarities
that surface where old foundations have apparently melted in air.

I hear among the themes in my son's music the experience of orphan-
ness, the loss of fathers, the inadequacy of mothers, and a history and
an apparent inevitability of massive self-destruction. When I try to
explore the specific question of the moral meaning of the representation
of bad mothers by good lawyers, I have to ask myself whether my activity contributes to the figurings and broadcasts of those themes, to a proliferation of pain and injury. My project involves an examination of
lawyering activity that typically takes as its end the perpetuation of certain family—generally parent-child and mother-child—relationships
in situations in which the parent engages in what, in American law, is

referred to as the "abuse or neglect" of children. I thus explore the work of lawyers who advocate for people who are powerful relative to their children and who seem to make use of their power in destructive ways.

When I attempt now to examine "who I am" and "the meaning of what I do," my examination will take as given the ordinariness of the experience of postmodernism. When I think about legal ethics and its relationship to a broad ethic, I have to ask myself whether my tentative formulations express any solid footing or even any firm toehold against the antifoundationalism expressed not only in critical theory but in pervasive cultural structures. And I have to ask myself whether my formulations can mean anything to my children, who listen to Pink Floyd. Or Velvet Underground. Or Jane's Addiction. Or to my students, who listen to music that I cannot even identify.

I suspect that there are certain features of any formulations that will reliably elicit their dismissal by my children and by my students. There are certain features of a moral account that will never withstand the critical perspectives that seem to come naturally to my children and my students. Those are features that seem unattached to *lived experience*, to the practices of daily life, including the practices in which we engage in our work. The dissatisfaction of my children and my students will necessarily become my dissatisfactions. I will experience their restlessness or irritation as a prod, a spur, a twinge, an incentive to keep moving, to persist in trying to say something further, something of meaning.

When I seek to understand my own activity, when I attempt to construct the meaning of my work, I am in need of interpretation that will take account of my recognition of the power of horror and the pervasiveness of destruction. An ethic able to assert itself against the near-nihilism that flashes and echoes through the fragments, the flashings, and the sound waves of my children's lives and my students' lives.

So, it seems to me, a sustaining ethic will be one able to do justice to the common postmodern experience of feeling even the reality of my subjectivity under attack. Such an ethic must give some account of life within this period in which I feel daily the fragility of human life on a planet marked by massive cruelties, stricken by what often seems limitless pain.

Representing Bad Mothers

"It bothers me a lot," my student says, in the third week of our clinical seminar, "to be assigned to represent a mother whose daughter has been taken away from her because of abuse. I think I know something about what children need. It bothers me a lot to think that I may be helping to return a child to a mother who will not take care of her."

The other students in our group nod, understandingly. I listen to their reservations.

My students tell me that they welcome opportunities for representation in the best interests of children. They tell me, often, that they are inclined, in their work, to define certain categories of clients whom they will *always* decline to represent on moral grounds. Some tell me they could find moral certitude in the decision: "I will never represent a rapist." Others say, "I would never represent landlords." *Many* say: "I would not represent abusers."

Limits of Traditional Justifications

In my practice and my clinical teaching, I have represented clients, children or their parents, in hundreds of cases in which the custody of children and the relationship of children and parents have been at issue. I realize that to some extent my students' belief that it would be "easy" to represent the children who are the subjects of abuse and neglect proceedings reflects their inexperience of the demands and difficulties of parenting and their failure to appreciate the complex and often seemingly contradictory needs of children. I see their readiness to assume that representing children would be easier as expressing a loss of faith in the possibility of knowing—and on that basis representing—mothers. I see it also as expressing a sympathy with the pain of children that, while commendable, risks becoming self-indulgently limited to the degree that it avoids engagement with the complex realities of the families and the culture within which some children thrive while others suffer.

There are many justifications that can be summoned up in support of the role adopted by the lawyer representing a parent charged with child abuse. Many of these may not be immediately apparent to people who observe the "child dependency" legal system from a distance, but they are readily apparent to the public defenders, the Legal Aid lawyers, and the court-appointed counsel commonly assigned roles of defense. These are the same kinds of justifications that tend to support the daily work of criminal defense lawyers. These justifications are sometimes expressed in terms of the lawyer's playing an essential role in a somewhat imperfect but basically good system (Freedman 1975). More typically, I think, they come out of the defense lawyer's fairly firm conviction that she does something positively good by resisting the operation of a system that is itself perverse or skewed in its unjust operation against the accused.

Lawyers who represent parents charged with child abuse frequently point to the unfairness of a system that, in the name of child-saving, defines and imposes standards of child care more related to the utopian visions of white, middle-class social workers and social scientists than to the realities of the lives of "different" people.

Lawyers representing parents charged with child abuse are positioned to be keenly aware of the particularly gendered focus of child dependency law. The parents from whom children are judicially removed are typically mothers and it is typically a bad mother who is charged with abuse and neglect (Ashe and Cahn 1993:76, 79). The male parents of such children are generally so absent that if they are identifiable at all, they are often in whereabouts unreachable by summons or subpoena. They have almost always already escaped or evaded the jurisdiction of the court as they have escaped or evaded the family and, in particular, any bond to the adult female from whom the child stands about to be rescued (Ashe and Cahn 1993:76, 79). In making their escapes male adults avoid both the onus of caregiving responsibility and the stigma of badness that attaches to women who prove inadequate in meeting that responsibility. Lawyers representing such mothers are challenged to construct defense narratives that explain or even excuse the alleged maternal behaviors. In performing this task defense lawyers participate in the larger cultural project of subjectifying motherhood that has recently been identifiable in a wide range of feminist works (Ashe 1992:1029–36).

Subjectifying motherhood can be understood as an expression of the broad range of subjectifyings accomplished by and through postmodernism. Critiquing liberal notions of individualism, postmodernist theorists typically displace the liberal construction of the autonomous individual to allow the emergence of subjects whose reality and experience have been erased through that construction. Indeed, whatever emancipatory potential attaches to postmodernist thought has been located in its enabling such processes of displacement and rearrangement.

The processes through which formerly invisible subjects become recognized typically take shape through the production of texts, in particular through the elaboration of narratives that are particularizing and contextualizing. This understanding of subjectifying can be expressed as the beginning to speak of the formerly objectified, the emergence of new speaking subjects.

Postmodernist theory can be characterized as committed to a process of exploration of Woman whenever it addresses Otherness. Alice Jar-

dine has examined a range of writings that take as their point of departure a recognition that "the *Other* is always female," that "the space of
altereity to be explored always already must connote the female" (Jardine 1985:114). Many writers producing such gyn-etic work would
strongly resist definition as feminist because their work does not focus
directly on women in their culturally and historically embedded female
lives. Other writers, even when in fact so focusing, resist confinement
to the ideological constraints implicated in feminism as in other "isms"
(Kristeva 1992:208).

The interactions, tensions, and boundary lines between feminisms
and postmodernisms are complex, variant, and contested (Ashe 1987,
1990). There has, however, developed a range of work that has come to
be identified, however problematically, as postmodernist feminism,
which has directly addressed the experiences of women in culture and
in history. This work could be characterized as expressing a variant of
the postmodernist formulation that "the Other is always female," and a
specifically feminist reconfiguration of that notion in the form of a
recognition that "the female is always (in some sense) Other." Such
work, while recognizing that it is always Otherness that is at issue, and
that this Otherness will not attach exclusively to female-gendered subjects, focuses on the ways in which it is in fact so projected. This work
has begun to examine the social, cultural, and legal processes through
which the equation of Otherness with female-ness is produced and perpetuated (Frug 1992).

In their treatment of the institution of motherhood, postmodernist
feminisms have begun to explore the construction of mothers by law
and other cultural forces and have resisted the extraordinary simplifica-
tion of women so constructed. Perhaps the most well-known American
precursor of this genre is Adrienne Rich, in her classic study, *Of Woman
Born* (Rich 1976). In this effort, Rich essayed a subjectifying that resists
two forms of essentializing. The first of these is the essentializing
accomplished by a cultural institution, motherhood, that equates
women with mothers. The second is an essentializing that would erase
the differences among women who are mothers. By faithfulness to a
first-person narrative form, Rich expresses what she is able to say about
her experience without claiming that her account includes the experiences of *all* women or of *all mothers*. This voice and method assure an
avoidance of the grand narrative eschewed by postmodernism. They
assure a rejection of any claim to provide full explication or full interpretation of the human experiences out of which they emerge. They

operate to invite still other contributions to the something more that always remains to be said. The still relatively few but increasingly numerous writers who have begun to explore the regulation of motherhood by law have contributed further to this project, which expresses the variations of woman and mothers as well as the possible and problematized meanings of representation (Ashe 1992:1029–37). Lawyers engaged in representation of bad mothers can be seen as participating in the effort to open up spaces within which the specific subjectifyings of particular women may begin to emerge.

Sometimes the lawyer's investigation will disclose that the facts alleged in a complaint filed against a parent are quite erroneous. Or the lawyer—particularly if she has herself had some opportunity to experience the responsibility entailed in the day-to-day care of children—will be persuaded that the facts alleged, if true, would amount to a showing of relatively inadvertent neglect rather than parental abuse. She may be persuaded that court intervention is entirely unwarranted. In such circumstances, the lawyer for the bad mother resembles the criminal defense lawyer persuaded that the criminal defendant-client has been overcharged. In those circumstances the lawyering activities of defense and resistance can seem well justified.

Lawyers representing abusive parents may also come to believe that they perform a useful function in resisting laws that are facially unjust as well as unjust in application. Thus, even when defense lawyers recognize the necessity of removing a child from the home of his or her parents, they may still believe that the law of termination of parental rights is excessively harsh and brutal, that it disserves children as well as parents, and that maximal resistance to it is therefore justified.

Lawyers who devote their energies to the work of representing allegedly abusive parents may find themselves in these circumstances— in which self-justification is not difficult—in an overwhelming majority of cases. Their acquaintance with their clients and their engagement in the work of subjectifying motherhood give them access to a multiplicity of stories, different experiences, and understandings of the demands of motherhood. This understanding impresses defense lawyers with the various ways in which the institution of motherhood is differently experienced by different women in diverse social situations. This work reminds us that while caring for children is never easy, being poor makes it harder; experiencing racism makes it harder; experiencing homophobia makes it harder; and experiencing the fear of violence within one's own household makes it harder still. Lawyers

engaged in the project of subjectifying motherhood are supported by
emerging social scientific data that demonstrate linkages and correla-
tions between and among the particular conditions of the lives of bad
mothers and what the law defines as child abuse. Particularly striking
findings include data correlating mothers' violence toward children
with their own experiences as current or past victims of household or
family violence (Ashe and Cahn 1993:86–90). These data suggest that
the mysterious behaviors of women who are often unhelpfully diagnosed as borderline personalities may be traceable to the particular
kinds of sexual injuries they sustained in their own childhoods (Herman 1992:125–26).[2]

Through their involvement with such work, defense lawyers express
in practical ways the resistance to essentialism that has been a prominent feature of much recent critical theory. Anti-essentialist effort
strongly resists the reduction of different women's experiences to either
"*woman's*" experience or the "experience of *all* women" (Harris 1990;
Spelman 1988).

In defining or naming "bad mothers," law operates to erase realities
of class, of race, of inequality, and of danger that variously define the
lives of different bad mothers. This process occurs whenever judges and
lawyers (including lawyers purporting to represent such women) initi-
ate or accede to the rightness or necessity of prosecutions of child
neglect or abuse without fully recognizing and representing the conditions of the women alleged to have perpetrated the abuse. Feminist theorists have pointed out the ways in which the essentialist construct,
Woman, has political implications for all women and for all human culture (Ashe 1990). Defense lawyers do battle on a daily basis against the
erasures that continue to construct and re-construct the "bad mother"
as a particular essentialistic figure.

There are circumstances, however, in which defense lawyers find
themselves at a loss to interpret their "bad mother" clients by reference
to the variables I have mentioned here. They become unable to understand their clients' behaviors toward their children; the clients' repeated
injurious or unthinking acts; the clients' refusals to participate in the
parenting programs proposed by the child protective services depart-
ments; the clients' refusals to cooperate in various ways with social
workers; the clients' refusals or failures to visit with children who have
been placed out of the home into foster care or institutions; the clients'
failures to send children to school; the clients' failures or refusals to provide medical care; their failures to protect children from injury com-

mitted by others. In these circumstances, defense lawyers, in frustration and exasperation—and with some concern for the children affected—often feel ready to accede in their hearts that the client is indeed a "bad mother." Seeing no readily available possibilities for further subjectifying, they become content to refrain from further inquiry. How do we justify our work when we reach precisely such points? How do we support our continued participation in a system in which our role is to advocate for return of a child to the care of a woman clearly unwilling or unable to provide what the child seems to require for minimal well-being?

I want to suggest that it is precisely at the point at which the mother-client appears to her lawyer truly "bad" that the lawyer needs to re-turn to an ethic based on notions of resistance, needs to re-turn to a faith that *every* essentialist casting of women as essentially "bad" is suspect. It is at this point that lawyers need to remind ourselves that *every* construction of the "bad mother" as a pure and essentialistic figure operates to arrest our inquiries into the material and spiritual conditions of women's lives, making those conditions irrelevant to the law.

In justifying their exercise of the discretion to prosecute child abuse and neglect matters, prosecutors often assert that the conditions of constraint relating to class, to race, and to domestic violence are either intrinsically or ultimately irrelevant to their determination to prosecute. They resist suggestions that they have acted with impropriety or with bias in determining to file an abuse or neglect complaint against a particular woman. They may do this by proposing that their determination has been made with blindness to class, to race, and to conditions of danger in women's lives. More persuasively, they may propose that those conditions have been made to be irrelevant precisely through the discretionary process itself—that is, they will comfort themselves, the judges, and often the defense attorneys and the bad mother as well, with the assurance that they have controlled for the factors of poverty, racial discrimination, and violence—that they have both considered and allowed for those variables and have made the decision to proceed with prosecution only because the bad mother in question is a woman whose behavior cannot be fully interpreted by reference to those variables.

The prosecutor's assurance will often take the form of an assertion that any woman who behaved as the bad mother is alleged to have done should be prosecuted. That assertion is typically accepted uncritically by judges and, I have suggested, in some situations and at some level, by defense attorneys. The law compounds the insidiousness of this discursive process by constructing in opposition to the bad mother her precise other in the figure of her extremely sympathetic, vulnerable, injured or needy, tender, and—above all—innocent child. Each of these constructs—the essentially bad mother and the innocent child—poses problems for the defense lawyer's interpretation of his or her role.

"Subjectifying" Mothers and Resisting New Essentialisms

In their contribution to the project of subjectifying motherhood, lawyers representing bad mothers undertake what may be the most difficult aspect of that task: they attempt to represent the most unsympathetic of women. While the task is one of enormous difficulty, it is one of commensurate urgency. To the degree that lawyers fail to access and represent the subjectivities of neglectful or abusive mothers we participate in sustaining the legal structures of class division, of racial injustice, and of domestic violence that denigrate and oppress all women and that absolutely assure the reproduction and perpetuation of child abuse as a prevalent cultural reality. I have already suggested some of the difficulties involved in the task of resisting the unified figure of "bad mother." This work requires exposures of the limitations imposed by racism, by poverty and classism, by sexism in general, and specifically by patriarchally determined household arrangements (including heterosexual marriage and other structures that mirror that model), all of which operate to impair effective caregiving and contribute to the neglect and abuse of children.

But the difficulty of the subjectifying task is greatly compounded by an additional reality, namely the reality that the figure of the bad mother is located not only in visible social structures but, as psychoanalytic theory and anthropological data have discerned, in the deepest reaches of human consciousness (Kristeva 1980; Douglas 1966). Within the psychic selves of representing attorneys, as well as in more visible cultural structures, women are designated "caregivers" and their caring is never sufficient (Chodorow and Contratto 1988:80–84; Doane and Hodges 1992). Lawyers representing bad mothers, like all of us in the larger culture, experience ambivalence and anxiety in confronting these clients (Chodorow and Contratto 1989:88–92; Doane and Hodges 1992). We find in our clients women who seem to say (evoking our pity) that they cannot—or to say (evoking our terror) that they will not—care. The conflicted feelings and ambivalences we experience can lead us to suspend our critical perspectives in the face of lulling assurances that what is involved in the prosecution of child dependency matters is indeed a process that has truly controlled for variables of class, race, and gender, among others. We are called upon to accept the process as neutral and objective, treating bad mothers justly. We are encouraged to believe it is the best alternative available to us.

Recent writing has begun to address the tendency to justify prevailing judicial practices relating to child dependency by falsely denying their implication in processes of sexism, racism, and classism. Thus, for example, Dorothy Roberts has written powerfully about the construction of the young, single, African-American, drug-using, and welfare-dependent mother as the current prototype of "bad mothering" (Roberts 1991). Roberts probes the operations of racism veiled by what might appear to the uncritical observer an irreproachable prosecutorial and judicial determination to save children from crack-addicted mothers. Roberts's effort, I think, exposes the ways in which ambivalence surrounding the seemingly neutral notion of mother will express itself variously as it intersects with realities of class, race, and susceptibility to violence.[3]

The ambivalences of defense attorneys thus continue to be in need of exploration in face of the urgency of subjectifying bad mothers. That urgency attaches to the realities of legal outcomes for specific clients and their children. And it attaches also to the threat to survival posed by continuation of class and racial tensions and by destruction of women's and children's lives through violence and other abuses. The measure of the advocate's zeal in the representational task will have to be seen as identical to the degree of his or her commitment to development of a defense narrative that exposes all the specificities of women's lives. That narrative should expose the differences among women that unjustly favor some women's children over others, and should persistently resist newly emerging models of essentialized "bad mothering."

Sometimes the underlying realities of mothers' lives remain so private that their nature is not readily suggested by references to race or to class. And sometimes hidden wounds are not fully recognized as related to gender either. In such circumstances, the defense attorney may find herself profoundly troubled about the implications of her work. She will find herself unable to construct a defense narrative that will persuade her or others of the non-badness of the mother. When this experience is compounded by a perception of very significant injury to a child, the task of moral interpretation becomes daunting indeed. While such challenges arise fairly rarely, they are profoundly affecting.

In the course of my practice I once represented a woman whose very young child was alleged to have incurred broken bones and severe burns at the hands of the mother's housemate and sexual partner. Representing the woman at the early stages of a detention hearing at which she contested the infant's having been temporarily removed from her custody, I was successful in having the child returned to her. Several weeks later I was called to represent the mother again when the child was returned to the hospital with evidence of further fracturing of arm and leg bones and with a fractured skull. The prosecutor presented me pictures of the small child lying in a tiny hospital bed, his face having lost all traces of symmetry as a consequence of the neurological damage caused by the skull fracture. I have remembered that case for many years. I expect to forget neither the child nor the mother.

At the time of my representation of that "bad mother" client, I was unable to discern what had so injured her that she permitted the perpetration of such extreme harms to her child. Her wounds, whatever they were, were not visibly listed under the headings that we now recite readily as gender, class, and race. They remained invisible because they were unnamed. Without my own words to name her and without any words of hers to assist me,[4] I felt or performed sometimes the kind of abjection of which Julia Kristeva has written (Kristeva 1992; Spivak 1988; Jack 1991). At the same time, I experienced her life and behavior as a compelling and demanding mystery.

Lawyers called upon to represent bad mothers feel hesitancy not only because of the ambivalences regarding motherhood that afflict us all but also because of unwillingness to participate in processes that truly injure or destroy the bodies and spirits of our children.

"Bad Mothers" and Their Lawyers: Certain Contexts

It is half past eight on a March morning. I am on my way to work. I stop at my children's elementary school to take my youngest child, Devin, into his kindergarten class. Approaching the front door of the school I watch a woman, her small son in tow, climbing the steps to the doorway. She is wearing a tweed suit, a pair of Reeboks, tailored jewelry. She might be a lawyer. Her son is resisting climbing the stairs and she tugs him along. They enter through the door before we reach the stairs and she emerges alone a few seconds later. She hurries past us down the steps.

I am in a hurry too. I have to meet my students to go to court. I open the right-hand side of the double-doored school building and find, pressed against the inside of the left-hand door, the child just left there by his mother. He has made small fists and is beating them against the door. But his effort makes no sound that I can hear in the bustle of the early morning corridors. He has drawn in his cheeks and there are tears in his eyes.

I am not sure what to do.

I am in a hurry. I have my own child to attend to.

I will have to rush through my own kindergarten good-byes. I have entered the school with a guilty hope that Devin will not ask me to delay—to see how the chicks have grown since yesterday or to visit the guinea pig.

I decide to move on with my child to his class, saying nothing to the boy at the door.

I say my good-byes to my son and retrace my steps. The child has removed himself from the entryway and begun to walk through the corridor. I am relieved that he is on his way to his class. His face is still damp and his jaw is set. He looks both determined and furious.

I leave the building with a feeling of dread. I trace, toward my car, the path along which his mother has just passed.

I hurry to meet my students and our "bad mother" client.

It is their perception of a reality or a likelihood of harm to children that troubles my students more than anything else about the prospect of working for bad mothers. They imagine that representing the bad mother amounts to collusion with evil. They read horrifying accounts of the physical and sexual and emotional abuse of children. Sometimes they recall experiences of their own.

When they try to imagine themselves as zealous advocates for bad mothers, my students find that the referential paradigm fails them. They fear that they could indirectly cause serious harm to a child. They could not forgive themselves if they occasioned such harm, they tell me.

I am readily able to tell my students the *how* of zealous advocacy. Courts and disciplinary committees of the bar have defined with some specificity the minimal *standards* of advocacy that a lawyer should exercise in representing parents in dependency cases. And publications addressed to practitioners contribute to an increasingly sophisticated literature elaborating strategies for zealous advocates. None of these, however, answers for me or for my students the deeper, more troubled and more troubling questions through which lawyers self-interrogate: What am I doing when I do this work? What does this work have to do with who I am? What is best for my client? What is best for her children? What is right for me? My students will not attend to the *how* unless they are able to tell themselves *why*. Why should we represent "those people"?

And when they perceive the injuries alleged in dependency complaints, ranging from the harms experienced by the child whose mother keeps him home from school too often to the massive bodily injuries caused by brutal treatment at the hands of a mother or a mother's companion, they are often unwilling to proceed further.

Perhaps what most immediately strikes lawyers in the work of representing bad mothers is the great pain their clients suffer. Sometimes the sources of that pain will not be evident. Within the dailiness of trial practice and the occasionality of appellate work, lawyers contribute to the shaping of a prevailing legal discourse. The lawyer for the bad mother will find her client generally swallowed up in that discourse. Within the adversarial or quasi-adversarial positioning of best interests of children against parental rights, the reality of a bad mother's pain will appear utterly irrelevant. And, as already suggested, in a weighing of the pain of the innocent child against that of the noninnocent mother (and, as dominant themes of our culture have perhaps always insisted, mothers are *never* innocent) (Chodorow and Contratto 1988:89–92), the latter will always be relatively devalued.

In recent years there has been a tremendous increase in the public conversation concerning child abuse (Ashe and Cahn 1993:75–77, 83–90). This development is not unprecedented. Linda Gordon has documented that the discourse about child abuse and other family violence has waxed and waned with changing times (Gordon 1988: 168–203). What is striking about the present conversation, however, is that it has begun to identify the phenomenon of child abuse as occurring in every social class and in every kind of traditional and nontraditional family configuration. Attention to the incidence of child abuse and to its continuing harms has been very visible in the proliferation of self-help groups and other organizations that focus intensively on encouraging adults to explore their own inner child-selves through processes that involve revisiting and even reexperiencing injuries from childhood.

I have written elsewhere of the work of Alice Miller, the Swiss psychologist who has delivered perhaps the most powerful currently circulating messages about the everywhere-ness of child abuse (Ashe and Cahn 1993:93–97). Miller details the experiences of pain and humiliation that children suffer daily through the misuse of adult power (Miller 1984:192–95). Her definition of abusive behavior toward children is by no means limited to what the law would recognize as such. She carefully traces the injuries perpetrated by indifferent neglect, by angry words, by care-less insults, by adults' refusals to accommodate the timings, rhythms, and other needs of children. And Miller tracks the consequences of these injuries, defining them as "the greatest crime that one human being can commit against another—causing psychological deformation in the next generation" (Miller 1991:51).

Certainly, when we read Alice Miller we become unable to minimize the importance of the suffering attached to painful partings that occur each morning at the doors of children's houses or day-care centers or schools. We become unable to minimize the importance of the neglects and abuses that occur in most of our homes every week, when the demands of child care exceed the resources of caregivers. Miller requires that we acknowledge the significance of our children's unhappiness, something we are often inclined to deny when we see no ways to prevent it. In her accounts of children's experiences Miller revives her readers' recollections of their own childhood experiences of injustice, humiliation, and other hurts. Those recognitions make it particularly difficult to deny the truth of what she writes.

Miller urges that to the degree that we accept injuries to children as necessary and unavoidable, minimizing their consequences, and comforting ourselves with reassurances that our inadequate care will ultimately be in their best interests, we resign ourselves to the inevitability of reproducing and magnifying those injuries in our own children and in our world (Miller 1991:vii–ix).

It seems to me that what Miller writes is something that most of us, at some level, recognize as true. It is painful for parents to read Alice Miller because her work tends to leave us with feelings of guilt and frustration as we recognize our own participation in patterns injurious to our children.

Miller's work is paralleled by the increasingly well known and still emerging body of work by writers who expose and detail the effects upon adult women of childhood sexual abuse (Fraser 1987; Herman 1981; Rush 1980). These writings provide powerful accounts of the long-term and continuing impact of such injuries. All of these developments support the profound misgivings experienced by lawyers assigned to work for bad mothers.

Judith Herman's recent writing takes up some of the themes that preoccupy Alice Miller. In her study of childhood victims of incest, Vietnam veterans, and Holocaust survivors, Herman identifies the commonality of experiences of people who have been powerfully injured, whose injuries have been overlooked or denied by their communities, and whose injuries have been ignored through the silence of collusion that discourages public tellings of painful experiences (Herman 1992). Herman lends her voice to the increasing chorus that includes Miller and a large public that insists on *naming* the horrors of injury.

The force of writings like Miller's and Herman's resides in the response that readers give to it. And readers have responded because they recognize what is being said as true. We all know at very deep levels the ways in which family patterns of relationship reproduce themselves, and we know the consequences of injurious treatment of children by parents. We come to know, increasingly, the ways in which familial patterns reflect and reproduce larger patterns of power throughout the culture.

So it seems to me that when my students express reluctance to engage in work aimed at perpetuating destructive relationships, they may speak from a very sound desire to avoid doing evil. What reply could an ethic of resistance raise against precisely the kinds of injury that we want to call unequivocally evil? I would urge that reply must take shape in the form of a recommitment to struggle against the larger structures that present us with the unacceptable alternatives of seeming to save children or seeming to collude with bad mothers.

The limitations and failures of the child welfare system in the United States have been extensively reported in recent years. We have become increasingly aware of the problems experienced by children "saved" by the welfare system by removal from bad mothers. In light of this information there is urgent need to reassess the ongoing escalation of judicially or informally arranged placements of children out of their homes into other sites of care.

In the course of an engrossing and very paining account of a New York family's experience of the child welfare system through three generations, Susan Sheehan has recently reported that in 1984 there were 16,240 children in foster care in New York City and 27,187 in care in the state of New York; that in 1989, there were 45,931 children in foster care in New York City and 58,540 in the state; and that by 1991, the numbers were 50,518 and 64,584 (Sheehan 1993a:60). She thus indicates that the number of wards in foster care in New York City has *nearly tripled* in the past ten years (Sheehan 1993b:79).

Sheehan details life histories that support a belief I have come to hold during my years of practice. I believe that the injuries inflicted upon children are *directly* related to injuries suffered by their mothers (and fathers) in their lives. I hold this belief because everything I have seen in my practice has supported it and nothing has contradicted it.

In closing her account of the painful history of the family about whom she writes, Sheehan herself states what has become a prevailing attitude reflecting unhappiness, regret, and lack of hope or vision. She observes:

> The simple remedy one hears proposed most often is that the money spent on foster care . . . would be better spent trying to solve its root causes: poverty, drug addictions and homelessness. Yet experience has shown that these social problems are amenable only to slow, expensive and hard-thought-out measures. In the meantime, something has to be done to take care of the children.   (Sheehan 1993b:79)

This resigned suggestion that the problems of lost childhood and lost motherhood exceed our resources must be resisted no matter how difficult it may be to alter the underlying factors that contribute to the misery that Sheehan reports. The process by which Sheehan exhaustedly (and understandably so) invites us to adopt an attitude of resignation for some time—temporarily and in the meantime—seems to me to parallel that of the prosecutor and the social scientist who re-construct bad mothers and direct us to cease our inquiries into their cultural contexts. Both Sheehan and those others commit the fallacy frequently identified by postmodernism—that of mistaking the story that has been told for the whole story, that of failing to imagine that there is more to be said.

The error of resting where we are is not a minimal one, for to the degree that we rest comfortably, or even in uncomfortable resignation, on self-assurances that we are doing what we can to address issues of child dependency, we permit the waste of human hopes and human lives. Indeed, the urgency of the issue could not be more strongly expressed than by Sheehan's report on the virtual *tripling* of foster care placements in New York City in the past decade.

What, then, is to be said? Certainly a departure point will be the recognition that ineffective attempts to save children from their bad mothers are and continue to be expressions of a blindness—and what must at this point be called a willful blindness—to the abuses of power that themselves construct both bad mothers and children in need of rescue. Lawyers committed to subjectifying bad mothers will contribute to the effort of investigating and exploring the still-hidden and the visible-but-as-yet-unattended injuries of mothers and fathers that profoundly injure our children.

In child dependency practice, lawyers for bad mothers find ourselves participating in an area in which the discourse of rights has already visibly given way to other assertions of need or entitlement. We work in a place in which the truly relational nature of adjudication is exposed. At this point, we must resist a premature erosion or collapse of rights discourse that threatens to swallow up protections of due process guaranteed to parents in theory if not always in practice. We are challenged to recognize and to support the acknowledgment of certain realities of parent-child relationships that have been properly, if crudely, embodied in notions of parents' rights.

Mysteries of Representation

I am having dinner with my son, David. He has been reading Stanley Fish. He is talking about antifoundationalism. And he is telling me about his Wittgenstein seminar. I am remembering studying Wittgenstein myself, more than twenty years ago. I am remembering that after he wrote his *Tractatus* Wittgenstein left England for several years and spent that time teaching children in an elementary school in Bavaria, before returning to write *Philosophical Investigations.*

David says to me: "Some things he writes are really moving." That word is quickening for me.

"What's moving?" I ask him.

"Oh," he says, "there's a place where Wittgenstein has gone on and on through the most detailed, exhausting arguments, and then he says something like: 'If I have exhausted the justifications, I have reached bedrock, and my spade is turned. Then I am inclined to say: "This is simply what I do."' "

Is that the most fully developed ethic I can articulate—that my practice of law is "simply what I do." It seems sometimes that indeed there is nothing else to say.

It seems sometimes that the implications of postmodernism may leave nothing else to say. It is interesting, however, to consider the ways in which the work of major figures of postmodernism may relate to realities of violence directed against children such as those considered here. It is interesting to speculate, following the lead of Alice Miller (Miller 1990), about the ways in which the experience of suffering or the perpetration of violence may mark the thought of postmodernist theorists—such as Wittgenstein or Foucault, for example—who have been among the major intellectual figures of the century.

It is interesting and distressing to read of Wittgenstein's work as an elementary school teacher in an impoverished Austrian village during 1925–26 (Monk 1990:192–233). His biographer records Wittgenstein's departure from the educational reform movement, which was otherwise attractive to him, by a reliance on corporal punishment. Indeed he notes that "the reminiscences of [Wittgenstein's] former pupils abound with stories of the *Ohrfeige* (ear-boxing) and *Haareziehen* (hair-pulling) they received at his hands" (Monk 1990:196). He reports that Wittgenstein once hit one of his pupils, Hermine Piribauer, so hard that she bled behind the ears (Monk 1990:233). And he reports that in April 1926, Wittgenstein struck a frail and sickly eleven-year-old school-boy, Josef Haidbauer, "two or three times on the head, causing the boy to collapse" (Monk 1990:232). Of this incident, one of the child's fellow pupils commented, not reassuringly: "It cannot be said that Wittgenstein ill-treated the child. If Haidbauer's punishment was ill-treatment, then 80 percent of Wittgenstein's punishments were ill-treatments" (Monk 1990:232).

The injuries to the Haidbauer child led to one of the villager's charging to Wittgenstein that he "wasn't a teacher, he was an animal-trainer! And that I was going to fetch the police right away!"(Monk 1990:233). Immediately following this encounter Wittgenstein abruptly disappeared from the village during the night (Monk 1990:233).

A commentator such as Alice Miller might be persuaded that Wittgenstein's abusive acts clearly reproduced experience that he had himself sustained in childhood (Miller 1990:137–70). Without knowing of his childhood experience, we may be struck by the import of what Wittgenstein's sister, Hermine, wrote of him during this teaching experiment, which many observers saw as evidence of Wittgenstein's "saintliness." Hermine noted that she "would (often) rather have a happy *person* for a brother than an unhappy *saint*" (Monk 1990:198).

Like Wittgenstein's work, that of Foucault, which is perhaps the other best-known instance of the changed shape of philosophy of the twentieth century, offers no well-developed ethic. And it is interesting to think about the experiences of violence recorded in a recent account of Foucault's life and work (James Miller 1992:365–67),[5] which strongly suggests his father's abusive exposure of Foucault, during his childhood, to violence and to horror. This suggestion has its basis in a short story written by Hervé Guibert on the day after Foucault's burial, one of whose characters appears strongly modeled on Foucault (James Miller 1992:365–67).

Guibert visited with Foucault frequently during the weeks of his hospitalization immediately prior to his death, and Guibert's story includes accounts that Foucault may have shared with him on his deathbed. Among these, according to Guibert, is Foucault's recollection of himself as a "philosopher-child, led by his father, who was a surgeon, into an operating room in the hospital at Poitiers, to witness the amputation of a man's leg—this was to steel the boy's virility" (James Miller 1992:366, quoting Hervé Guibert). In his literary biography of Foucault, James Miller summarizes the content of this recollection: "the sadistic father, the impotent child, the knife slicing into flesh, the body cut to the bone, the demand to acknowledge the sovereign power of the patriarch and the inexpressible humiliation of the son, having his manliness put to the test" (1992:366).

We would not need to be fully persuaded by Alice Miller's positing a strictly causal connection between violence committed and violence experienced in order to find persuasive James Miller's suggestion that "fragments of this scene keep bobbing up throughout Foucault's life and work" (1992:367).

The experiences of violence in the lives of Wittgenstein and Foucault were not matters that either man directly addressed in the published work by which he is widely known. They are in some sense secrets. That either or both these men may have experienced or perpetrated violence in no way diminishes the relevance or enormous significance of their work. Indeed, those very realities surely might account to some significant degree for the particular and profound resonance that their work has carried in a century in which violence and torture have been common, if not universal, underlays to human experiences and imaginings.

My suggestions here about the value of exploring linkages between the private life and the public works—with their ethical implications—of major postmodernist theorists should not be construed as intended in any way to impugn that work, to reduce it to the particularity of a single human experience, or to provide any other basis for dismissing it, summing it up, or regarding it as irrelevant. On the contrary, I want to suggest that perhaps the life that such work has had in the imaginations of twentieth-century intellectuals can be better understood by our exploring the private as well as the public contexts from which it has emerged. That kind of exploration might shed additional light on the connections between high and low cultural expressions of postmodernity. With regard to Wittgenstein and Foucault in particular, such an approach might work as a deconstruction of their deconstructions, exposing something absent from—in postmodernist terminology, "under erasure"—in their work and something of great relevance to those struggling to articulate new understandings of our own efforts to live and to work in postmodernist times. It might expose their refusals or failures to engage explicitly with a working through of personal and individual suffering, its individual and social meanings and consequences.

If work accomplished upon forgettings or upon only secret recollections of experiences of violence may give rise to such stark, compelling, and relatively bleak commentaries as those of Wittgenstein and Foucault, writings that hardly provide well-developed accounts of the avenues to more promising or hopeful locations, it becomes important to consider whether perhaps writings in which that struggle with suffering *is* more explicitly explored may have immediate relevance to the ethical undertakings of a postmodernist time. We may wonder whether work in which individual experiences of violence are directly confronted and contemplated might carry implications more promising, might carry the kind of power able to sustain hope in uncertain times.

Like my son, I am moved by Wittgenstein's words: "This is simply what I do." And I look for other words able to sustain me. Sometimes I find them. Feminist writers of fiction giving accounts of the complexities and darknesses of the relationships between mothers and children have engaged profoundly, openly, and persistently with the meanings and implications of cruelty perpetrated against children. They have, I believe, produced work that reflects the same resistance to essentialisms that I find in Wittgenstein and Foucault. And they also state a sustaining vision and hope difficult to discern in many deconstructionists.

Alice Walker is one of the writers of fiction who has worked most concentratedly and persistently with themes of mothering and of injury to children. In these postmodern times, Alice Walker has written:

> [T]here could be no happy community in which there was one unhappy child. Not one!   (Walker 1992:7)

Walker has written, in a time of anti-foundationalism:

> What is the fundamental question one must ask of the world? I would think of and posit many things, but the answer was always the same: Why is the child crying?   (161)

And in a time of uncertainty, Walker has written:

RESISTANCE IS THE SECRET OF JOY!   (279)

Walker is not alone in exploring these themes or in producing the feminist fiction (Ashe 1992:1029–37) that tells me about mothers who fail their most dearly beloved, who—like me and my clients and my neighbor at the schoolhouse door—sometimes injure what they believe to be their best things—their children (Morrison 1987:273). I read these works for what they tell me of myself and of my clients. I read them for what they say of how we are, each of us, haunted by strange familiars. I read them because they imagine some possibility of deliverance from personal and familial and cultural disintegrations. I read them for what they say of the possibilities of reintegration. I read them because the starkness of their telling compels me. And I read them because they uncover what I think is the only basis of hope, the healing imagination of women and men who have survived great oppression and wounding. I read them because they remind me that new possibilities can arise in communities of real and limited people—among people variously scarred and disfigured, like all of us, by deprivations. I read them because in a time of fragmentation and almost-hopelessness, except for them and for writings like them, there appears to be nothing else left to read. I read them because they are dedicated to me and you and our children:

> I know you are reading this poem listening for something, torn between
>   bitterness and hope
> turning back once again to the task you cannot refuse.
> I know you are reading this poem because there is nothing else left to read
> there where you have landed, stripped as you are.   (Rich 1991:25)

When I try to define why I return, as I always do, to representing bad mothers—although sometimes those cases exhaust me, wear me down, make me depressed, make me angry, leave me spiritually depleted, and therefore make me ask: Why am I doing this?—I find that notion—a task that you cannot refuse—as meaningful as any. The reasons for doing it are not rational ones. The work is something I cannot refuse for two reasons: I cannot refuse because I believe it needs to be done; and I cannot refuse because I want and need to do it. My wanting and needing to do it, I think, are for me as much as—or more than—for my clients.

In feminist critical theorizings—as those have taken novel forms in recent years—I find expressions of relationship that help me to imagine new understandings of friendship. And I find in them tracings of a spirituality that does not exclude me. Such works seem both faithful to postmodernist recognitions and supportive of hope. Joyce Treblicott has proposed as a formal statement of the nature of feminist narrative and theory: "Feminism reconstructs the concept of theory as an account of reality that does not move either inductively or deductively between the general and the particular but, rather, sites the general in the particular" (Treblicott 1991:49). In such kinds of theorizing I find support for a practice of law within which I move back and forth from the immediacy of the pain of my single client to a recognition that her experience both reflects and holds up a mirror to our cultural possibilities and disfigurings.

I have recently finished reading a biography of Anne Sexton (Middlebrook 1991). I have been reading her poetry for thirty years. I began to read it, when I did, for the reasons I read Toni Morrison now. I have always been profoundly moved by what Sexton has told us of herself, her mother, and her children. I read in her biography that Anne Sexton hurled her two-year-old daughter across the room in anger (Middlebrook 1991:33). I read further and remember her words to that child: "I made you to find me" (Sexton 1981). I read further and find catharsis and resignation in the aftermath of her suicide (Middlebrook 1991:96). But I cannot accept the resignation, the tragic vision, myself, because I believe that what sometimes seems the inevitability of destruction is in fact a false necessity. And because I believe that Anne Sexton's practices of self-destruction, or yours or mine or my clients', while utterly comprehensible, are not necessary.

I represent bad mothers because I need the truths they tell me concerning our common culture. They tell truths by exposing to me our likeness and our differences. I see myself reflected in them sometimes, recognizing in their gestures and their attitudes variations of ones familiar to me because they are my own. Beyond that, though, in their *difference* they tell me truths. They tell me truths when they refuse to let me see who they are, when they hold up a mirror facing me, between themselves and me, so that I confront that mirror as a barrier. It tells me of my situatedness in our culture. It reminds me of realities of class and of race, for example, that impede my understanding of my client and hers of me, that impede our working together and my adequately representing her. It reminds me that however much I know and care for her, there are ways in which I do not understand her. The ways in which I do not understand her are precisely proportionate to, and congruent with, the ways I do not understand myself. The "bad mother." She is familiar to me in myself and she is a mystery—which is why I want to know her.

NOTES

This essay appeared in earlier and different form in Georgetown Law Journal *81, no. 7 (August 1993):2533–66, under the title " 'Bad Mothers,' 'Good Lawyers,' and 'Legal Ethics.' " I have been enormously assisted by the support and encouragement of Martha Fineman and Isabel Karpin. My thanks to both of them.*

1. Pink Floyd, "Wish You Were Here," *Wish You Were Here*, CBS Records.

2. The client who, it turns out, has been "diagnosed" as a "borderline personality" often proves particularly problematic for lawyers. Apparently the diagnosing psychological professionals find her as troubling and frustrating as do her lawyers. It is instructive to see the clues to underlying mysteries emerging in Judith Herman's work. See, particularly, Herman (1992), suggesting that severe childhood trauma is a common factor in a substantial percentage of "borderline personality disorder" cases (125–26).

3. Other important work exploring the intersections of female gender, class, race, and susceptibility to violence, and the experiences of mothers at those intersections includes Fineman 1995 ("Poverty Law Discourse," this volume), 1994; J. White 1993; Cahn 1991; and Mahoney 1991.

4. For a treatment of the issue of presuming to speak for the "other," and an analysis of the conflicts, complexities, and erasures involved in representation of oppressed individuals and groups, see Spivak 1988:271–313. For discussion of a particular instance of some women's inability to articulate their own suffering and the impediments to such articulation, see Jack 1991, where the author examines the ways in which clinical constructions of depression dominate our understandings of that experience.

5. See also, for powerful critique of James Miller's work, Wendy Brown reviewing James Miller, *The Passion of Michel Foucault*, in "Jim Miller's Passions," *differences: A Journal of Feminist Studies* 5, no. 2:140–49.

8 Fresh or Frozen: Lesbian Mothers, Sperm Donors, and Limited Fathers

KATE HARRISON

Since the first "test-tube baby" was born the rapid developments in reproductive medicine, in combination with the extensive publicity given to the new technologies, have fundamentally changed our way of thinking about the process of reproduction. Conception was once inherently connected to the act of heterosexual intercourse, but just as the widespread use of reliable birth control created a disjuncture between sexual practice and conception, new reproductive technologies have created a second disjuncture, allowing for conception without sex. Since the focus on fertility is overwhelmingly oriented toward the infertile male/female couple who seek medical assistance to enable them to conceive, in the usual construction of the reproductive technology process, the sexual act is replaced by the intervention of the medical professional. Significantly, however, the resultant family structure remains the same nuclear triad.

Beyond the paradigm of the infertile heterosexual couple, however, the separation of sex and conception has a more profoundly transformative potential for women. Insemination, a very effective reproductive development at the low-technology end of the scientific spectrum, is being used by more and more women who are choosing to conceive on their own—often lesbians or unmarried women (U.S. Congress, Office of Technology Assessment 1988). Home-based, low-tech, and easily carried out without the involvement of medical professionals, self-insemination opens new options for women who want to become mothers outside the traditional sexual partner/dual parent paradigm (Wikler and Wikler 1991). The growing use of insemination by women is a significant development, as women are increasingly exercising individual control over their reproductive capacities. As such, the process has the potential to change not only the way we think about conception but also the way we think about families, about motherhood, about parenting, and about fatherhood.

The radical potential of insemination lies in the fact that it alters the basic reproductive unit, destroying the centrality of the (hetero)sexed couple, and re-centering the woman. Its enabling capacities equalize women without men—both heterosexual women who are not in relationships with men and lesbian women—in an area that is critical to many women—their reproductive potential and their desire to bear a child. Despite its widespread use, in popular writing on reproductive technologies insemination is little discussed. Dewar comments, "[I]t is precisely the opportunities offered to women through AID that have led to its being assigned a relatively low status in the hierarchy of reproductive technologies, and thus largely ignored" (Dewar 1989:116–17).

Among the women taking advantage of the increasing availability of insemination are many lesbians. While there are no reliable statistics measuring lesbian pregnancies, it has been estimated that 10,000 lesbians and gay men have had or adopted children in the last fifteen years (Curry, Clifford, and Leonard 1993:3–4). Lesbian parenting support groups have been operating for over a decade now, and the children born to lesbians and to gay men are now a well-established part of the organized gay community. Parenting is not booming only among lesbians. Gay men are also seeking out women (often lesbians) who want to have a child, or are adopting children. It has been suggested that the sense of regeneration in parenting has particular significance in a community that has been so devastated by AIDS, and in which the sense of loss and death has become so pervasive.

One of the most controversial issues in insemination has been whether restrictions should be imposed on access to sperm, such as limiting access to married women or refusing access to lesbians. Outside the United States, where women can order semen directly from sperm banks, access remains difficult. In Canada, for example, nineteen of thirty-three clinics refuse lesbians access to sperm (Canadian Royal Commission 1993:429). Perhaps in response, or perhaps simply in a desire to avoid involving any medical professionals, in some places an entirely separate subculture of self-insemination has been created, with women obtaining sperm and inseminating without the involvement of doctors.

The initial question facing every woman who wants to conceive through insemination outside a heterosexual relationship is whether to choose an unknown or known sperm donor. Opting for an unknown donor is effectively a decision that the woman does not want the donor to be known to the child or involved in the child's life. Using semen from an unidentified donor, obtained through a doctor or from a sperm bank, ensures this result. Semen obtained from a doctor or a sperm bank should be frozen.[1]

Alternatively, semen from an unknown donor can be obtained through lesbian insemination networks, delivered to the woman through a third party to maintain the anonymity of the donor. In this case, it is likely that the semen would be fresh rather than frozen. In both cases, however, the donor remains unknown, and the exchange implies that there will be no future contact between the donor and the child.

Some sperm banks offer a variation on unknown donor semen, giving clients the option of selecting an unknown donor who is willing to become known to any children conceived when they turn eighteen years old. This type of donor can be described as a "suspended identity" donor. Since his identity cannot be ascertained until the child reaches majority, he will have no involvement in the child's early life, and no involvement at all unless the child at age eighteen decides to identify and contact him.

If the woman decides to have a known donor, then a series of other decisions must be made. She must decide whether he will be identified to the child or be named on the birth certificate; whether she will give him information about the child and if so how much; and, most significantly, whether he will meet the child and have an ongoing involvement in the child's life. If he is to be involved, then the nature of his role and his relationship with the child need to be determined.

Thus two further types of donors arise to complement the categories of "unknown" and "suspended identity" donors—the "identified but uninvolved" donor, who has no ongoing relationship with the child, and the "involved" donor. The category of involved donor in turn encompasses a wide range of possible relationships between the donor and the child. The term would include situations ranging from equal coparenting, to situations in which the donor agreed to give up his legal parental rights and adopt a role more akin to that of a noncustodial relative, asserting no decision-making authority with respect to the child and having only minimal visitation.

Some women see less need for an involved donor if a lesbian couple are planning to coparent the child, but whether or not they have a partner coparenting many lesbian mothers want the donor to have some level of involvement with the child. For most, however, equal coparenting between the mother and the donor is not the proposed model. Rather, many women are seeking to agree in advance with the donor on a model for his involvement that fosters a limited relationship between the child and the donor. He may be publicly recognized as the child's biological father, but the agreement may seek to limit his rights with respect to the child. With more and more lesbian mothers entering into agreements with donors that circumscribe the nature and extent of the donor's involvement with the child, and attempt to restrict his legal rights, the lesbian community is effectively generating a blueprint for a new concept in parenting, the "limited father"—a concept not, of course, recognized in law.

As increasing numbers of lesbians have children and establish families, the failure of the law to recognize different sorts of parenting roles and respect the new types of family structures that are being created will become more stark. The move toward greater individual control by women over their reproductive capacities has not been matched by a parallel recognition of any right to control the legal aspects of parenthood. For lesbians in particular the attempt to re-define the parenting status of an involved donor has given rise to considerable legal uncertainty.

The legal status of an "involved donor" remains uncertain. For lesbian couples who are coparenting, the position of the biological mother's partner (who I will hereafter refer to as the co-mother) is also legally tenuous. For all the planning the parties may put into deciding the level of donor involvement, the law still lacks any considered basis on which to interpret the position of a biological parent who agreed to relinquish parental rights prior to conception. While the parties involved may clearly understand the different roles and responsibilities of the various adults who will have relationships with the child, the law generally continues to see only parents and nonparents. A person either is "a parent," with all the legal rights and obligations that entails, or is not, which in most cases will lead to the result that they will have no legally recognized relationship to the child at all.

Lesbians, Gay Men, and Families

As Weston notes in her thoughtful analysis of lesbian and gay kinship, gay families contradict the well-entrenched distinction between the image of the (deviant) homosexual and the image of the (normal) traditional family (Weston 1991). Both stereotyped images of lesbians and gay men, and their perceived inability to reproduce, fed the perception that lesbians and gay men somehow threatened the family unit. The fact that many lesbians and gay men are now actively involved in building families themselves, holding commitment ceremonies, registering as domestic partners, celebrating long-term relationships, and having children, has the potential to disrupt those elements of heterosexual prejudice which center around issues of family.

At the same time, however, there is a political price as part of the gay community moves toward a more family-identified basis for personal relationships. Homosexuality does indeed threaten the traditional family, although not quite in the manner those presenting such charges usually mean. Historically and politically, lesbian and gay relationships have challenged the dominant structure and concept of the traditional family unit. For many lesbians, the dominance of feminism as an ideology connected to lesbian practice in the 1970s spelled out an overt critique of the family that won widespread adherence. For gay men, in the pre-AIDS era of sometimes numerous sexual encounters, possibly within the context of a long-term primary relationship, the gay sexual experience presented the strongest possible challenge to the concept of a stable, monogamous sexual couple, central to the traditional notion of the family.

In the move to embrace family rather than challenging it and creating new and more radical forms of relationships, the gay community could be seen as mimicking the heterosexual family. Indeed the presence of a child itself bestows a new legitimacy on the lesbian who becomes a mother—she will be perceived to be heterosexual, purely as a result of the fact that she is a mother (Weston 1991:25). Arguably, gay men and lesbians have been co-opted by the very social structures and institutions that were once under challenge, and the move toward the family reflects the strength of the desire to be included, to move from the position of an outsider to that of an insider, to be assimilated back into mainstream lifestyles (Fuss 1991). Such a shift both reduces the potentially productive political tension between lesbian and gay rights and the family and reinforces the cultural centrality of notions of the family at the expense of alternative forms of relationships and social structures.

It can still be persuasively argued, however, that even with a monogamous, long-term couple raising a child or children together, a lesbian or gay family remains intrinsically different from the traditional family.

Despite its parallel structure to the straight family, the gay family unit still embodies a subversive capacity. This is particularly the case for lesbians choosing to give birth to children and having to make decisions about the sort of family structures they wish to create.

The fresh or frozen decision is fundamentally a decision about the structure of the family unit. In deciding whether to have a known or unknown donor, women are effectively choosing whether to include a biological father in some capacity in their family. Choosing a known donor and integrating him into the child's life creates a new type of family structure. Although there are some similarities to the position of the noncustodial father, the critical difference is that the donor did not participate in the attempt to conceive anticipating that he would play the role of a live-in, full-time parent.

If women choose to have an unknown donor, then the choice is generally for a family designed without a traditional "father." Instead, the family design may include two mothers of equal status. The concept of a child having two women of equal parenting status as parents appears to be difficult for people to accept. The atypical nature of the lesbian family is reflected in the problems in the use of language describing lesbian co-mothering. The coupled words "mommy and daddy" linguistically reinforce the perceived centrality of the two-sexed adult pair in child raising. With lesbian mothers, there is no word in the language that accurately describes the role of the woman who does not give birth to the child—other than the word *mother*, which is seen both legally and socially as applying exclusively to a birth or adoptive mother. Indeed the issue of nomenclature attracts inordinate concern, as if the key issue in lesbian parenting were the terminology of address (Weston 1991). In fact, the language of maternal address clashes with the reality that the child of a lesbian couple can have two mothers, since the language reinforces the notion that the role of the nonbiological mother is inherently different from that of the biological mother, and inevitably secondary. Without a recognized word to describe the position of the nonbiological mother, her position lacks clarity and certainty, even rendering her role invisible.

Fresh or Frozen—The Practicalities and the Legal Implications

For lesbians seeking pregnancy, obtaining sperm can present a major problem. A woman who is trying to become pregnant should ideally inseminate three times each month on three successive days to maximize her chances of pregnancy. Since it takes an average of three to four months to become pregnant, in most cases the woman needs access to an ongoing supply of sperm.

Frozen sperm has many practical advantages over fresh. Sperm banks are available in most large cities, and many will air freight semen to anywhere in the United States. Although some banks supply directly to women for self-insemination, many will only supply sperm to doctors, although they generally place no restrictions on the status of the doctor's clients for whom the sperm is being ordered. The banks generally say that their sperm is obtained from students, or "young professionals," and will supply sperm in response to specified characteristics, such as race, height, weight, hair color, eye color, and the nonbiological characteristic of education. An important advantage of frozen sperm obtained through a sperm bank is that it should be subject to HIV controls and testing.

A major drawback of selecting frozen sperm is the cost. Although the price varies from bank to bank, around $100 per unit (a small vial) seems to be standard. If three units are used each month, with another $100 for air freight costs, the total of $400 per month puts the frozen sperm option beyond the reach of many women. A further disadvantage of frozen sperm for some women is that it is thought to produce disproportionately more boys than girls, a factor that is important for some lesbians who have a preference for female children. The evidence on this issue, however, appears uncertain, and the banks claim that there is no difference between fresh and frozen sperm in this regard.

Selecting the option of frozen sperm usually means complete anonymity. The banks may require release forms to be signed that state that the person using the sperm agrees not to try to determine the identity of the donor.

The alternative option of fresh sperm can be far more problematic in practical terms. One option, even for lesbians, is simply to have sex with a man at the optimum time of the month. The advantage of this approach over simply asking the man to donate sperm is that it allows the woman to attempt to become pregnant without informing the man of her intention. If the man is a stranger, then he may never find out about the pregnancy, and hence will never seek to enforce any of the parental rights he would have. In the age of safe sex, however, the option of simply finding a partner for unprotected sex is a risky practice. Moreover the fact that three inseminations per month may be required for at least three or four months creates further difficulties for this approach. Most lesbians choosing fresh sperm probably rely on alternative ways of obtaining it, using a variety of approaches (K. Hill 1987:111). If the woman has chosen to have a known donor, the donor and the woman can simply arrange a time to get together so that he can ejaculate and she can immediately inseminate.

Women have also organized very effective networks for obtaining fresh sperm from unknown donors. Women's health centers, lesbian parenting support groups, or simply helpful friends perform the role of intermediary—arranging for the donor or donors to produce the sperm, and immediately collecting it and delivering it to the woman for insemination. The mask of anonymity in such situations, however, is thin indeed. The intermediary knows the person or people who provided the sperm, and would be in a position to reveal the information later if pressed by the mother, or later by the child. Moreover the man or men involved know the intermediary and could also find it easy to trace the woman if they chose to press a paternity claim.

Given the array of options open to women to try to become pregnant, for women the key distinction, partially reflected in the fresh/frozen dichotomy, is whether the donor is known or unknown. In most states, however, the law relating to paternity after insemination reflects a distinction not between known and unknown donors, but between insemination performed with the assistance of a doctor, and insemination performed without medical assistance. A second distinguishing factor in many states is that the legal position of the donor is dependent on the woman's marital status (Tate 1992).

In most states, if a woman is married, and she inseminates with the consent of her husband, then the husband is the legal father of the child and any rights or responsibilities the donor may have had (such as child support) are eliminated. The 1973 Uniform Parentage Act, for example, provides that a sperm donor will not be treated as the natural father of the child where a married woman was inseminated under the supervision of a licensed physician with sperm donated by a man other than her husband.

The position of the single woman is considerably less clear—the biological nexus is not broken by the presence of an alternative "father" and the donor could seek a declaration of his paternity (Robson 1992:135). In many states, while the statutes governing paternity and insemination carefully spell out the legal status of the donor for the married woman, in a fascinating denial of the potential of insemination, they completely ignore the position of the woman who is not married, simply failing to specify in the statute whether the donor has paternity rights with respect to a child born to an unmarried woman.

In states where statutes fail to address the situation of the unmarried woman, or where there are no relevant statutes, it remains a matter for the courts to decide whether or not the donor can assert rights with respect to the child. In *C. M. v. C. C.* (1977), a New Jersey court con-sidered a visitation claim by a known donor whose sperm had been used by an unmarried woman. The court rejected the woman's testimony that the donor had agreed to waive his parental rights, found that the donor in that case had intended to assume "the responsibilities of parenthood," and granted visitation. In that case, the court also appeared to apply a "best interest" analysis, noting that it was in the child's best interest to have two parents.

Indeed, even where a state statute does address the position of an unmarried woman, and does on its face eliminate the donor's parental rights, it may not necessarily protect the woman from a paternity claim. In *Jhordan C. v. Mary K.* (1986) the California court held that even though the statute did extinguish the rights of donors providing semen through doctors to unmarried women, the donor's parental rights were not extinguished because no doctor was used. The case concerned two women who decided to coparent a child, and arranged insemination with sperm from a donor selected after discussions with three or four potential donors. The testimony of the biological parents conflicted as to the agreed role of the donor after the birth, and there was no written agreement. The fact that the biological mother had maintained social contact with the donor during the pregnancy was seen by the court as reflecting the fact that there was no clear understanding that the donor would have no parental rights. Hence the Court of Appeal affirmed the Superior Court decision that the donor was the legal father of the child. The court formalistically applied the statutory provisions that link paternity in insemination cases to whether the sperm was "provided" to a physician. The court said that the women (although unaware of the law) had the option of choosing a method of insemination that would not give rise to paternity rights, even if they wanted to inseminate themselves with the sperm of a known donor because they could "obtain" the sperm through the physician.

In a 1989 case, *In the Interest of R. C.*, the Colorado Supreme court found that the statute that quite clearly extinguished the parental rights of donors supplying the sperm to unmarried as well as married women, through a doctor, did not cut off those rights if the donor and recipient had agreed that the donor would be treated as the child's parent. In that case the court rejected the mother's account of the facts. She had stated that it was never intended that the donor would be involved with the child, and the court instead accepted the donor's claim that he was always going to be treated as the child's father. The court found that where there was an agreement at the time of the insemination that the donor would be treated as the "natural father" of the child, both the agreement and subsequent conduct are relevant to preserving the donor's rights despite the statute.

Whether courts choose to adhere to the letter of the statutes or find ways to move around them, any ongoing significance of the involvement of a doctor in the analysis of paternal rights is inappropriately deferential to a medical model of insemination. Reasons that have been advanced for limiting the protection against paternity claims to cases where the insemination was done by a physician include the public health interest in having a physician screen the donor and obtain a medical history, and the creation of a formally documented structure for the donor-recipient relationship (*Jhordan C. v. Mary K.*). In some states it is illegal for a person other than a physician to perform artificial insemination.[2]

The legal emphasis on the role of the doctor in symbolically breaking the nexus between the sperm donor and the child has no basis in the reality of women's choices—choices as to whether they want a known or unknown donor and choices about whether they choose to inseminate themselves or be inseminated by a physician. A woman can be inseminated by a doctor with sperm from a known donor, or inseminate herself with sperm from an unknown donor.

The law's recourse to the role the doctor plays in defining the potential rights of the donor displays both an incorrect understanding of the available options, and a traditional appeal to the dominant place of the medical expert over the intentions of the woman or women involved. The law in this area needs to come to terms with the variety of possible methods of achieving pregnancy, and begin to recognize that the presence or absence of a doctor bears no relation to the choices, intentions, or understandings of the parties involved.

The courts that have considered claims by donors have all looked at the intentions of the parties as to the role the donor would play in the life of the child and whether it was agreed that he would be recognized as the child's father. While one might well disagree with the court's analysis of the facts in each of the cases presenting donor claims, the centrality of intention in the court's approach is appropriate as a means of recognizing an individual's parenting choices—even if those choices circumvent the strict terms of the statute. At the same time, however, the language and approach of the courts appears to be grounded in a strong judicial interest in the recognition and inclusion of a father for the child. Once the donor is known, the spectre of his being granted full parental rights is raised, and the mother's evidence of any agreement that his rights be waived or limited may not be accepted.

Known Donors and Limited Fathers

For lesbians, particularly lesbian couples, the choice between having a known or unknown donor involves a complex balancing of concerns about the sorts of familial relationships they want their child to have, and the risks of the personal and legal ramifications that inevitably accompany the choice of an involved donor.

There are a variety of reasons why lesbians would choose to have an involved donor. Just as people who are adopted often want to locate their biological parents for reasons connected with their own parentage and sense of identity, or to obtain information such as a family medical history, lesbian mothers may see it as important to allow a child to know her biological father's identity; they may consider that this knowledge will provide the sense of family and heritage that appears to be psychologically important for some people to establish (Bartlett 1984).

A desire to provide a paternal role model is another reason for choosing an involved donor. Providing an opportunity for a child to develop an intimate and ongoing relationship with a man as well as with women may be seen as an important aspect of raising a child in a two-sexed world. While theoretically any man could play the role of "father" in a child's life, the mother(s) may believe that a man who is biologically connected to the child will be more likely to sustain his involvement. While all children need some role models of both sexes, for some women concern about the absence of a father may be more pronounced if the child is a boy, leaving the child with no male role models inhabiting his domestic world. Such arguments based on role models are strongly rejected by other women, who take the view that the society at large provides sufficient male role models, and that it is not necessary to have a male father figure within the child's domestic world—for children of either sex. With the increasing numbers of children being raised in families without a father, the absence of a father figure in the home is no longer unusual for children.

Another reason for choosing an involved donor is to try to "normalize" the child's situation as far as possible. The rationale presented is that any child with two lesbian mothers is located in an atypical family living situation. The addition of a father shifts the family structure back toward that of most other children, who are able to identify both female and male parents even if they do not live with them. Other reasons for opting for a known father include a desire to involve another willing adult from outside the home in an integral way in the child's life, or a concern that the child might idealize an unknown father, or blame the mother(s) for his absence.

The reasoning underlying the decision to have a known donor intersects with the nature of the role that is negotiated for the involved donor. If a known donor is selected so that the child will be able to identify her biological father, then the donor need not necessarily have an ongoing involvement with the child. Such a donor could be known but not involved. However if the reasoning underlying the choice focuses on the perceived need for a male role model, then clearly the intention is that the donor will be involved in the child's life in an ongoing way. Lesbians choosing an involved donor would look for agreement with the donor on the basis of a "fit" between the type of parenting role the donor is looking for, and the nature of the father role that the mother(s) are seeking. The agreements are often reached after lengthy discussions, and sometimes reduced to writing. Such parenting negotiations, in which a donor enters into a preconception agreement limiting his parental rights and his future involvement with the child conceived, have created the new, quasi-parental status of a "limited father."

A number of issues need to be addressed by the donor and the mother(s) prior to deciding that they will proceed with insemination using an involved donor who will act as a limited father. First, the level of contact with the child is negotiated and spelled out. The donor may act as a noncustodial but very involved parent, spending regular time with the child on a frequent basis and developing a close emotional bond to the child; on the other hand, he could be more removed from the child's day-to-day life, seeing the child occasionally but maintaining a more distant presence, well removed from the intimate family unit, and less emotionally connected to the child.

Second, the issue of decision-making authority with respect to the child should be determined. Even for involved donors acting as limited fathers, many women will allow considerable access but require that the donor agrees that he will not have any such decision-making authority. The mother(s) have an understandable interest in protecting their authority to make decisions such as where the child attends school, or what religious instruction or medical treatment the child receives, without interference from the limited father. Decisions about the child's life are made within the primary family circle of the mother(s) and the child, not collaboratively between the mother and the limited father (Pollack 1987:123).

A third issue is the allocation of financial responsibilities for the child. The mother(s) may expect some contribution from the limited father toward the child's upkeep, or may alternatively take the view that not expecting the donor to take any financial responsibility for the child further evidences their intention that his role is not intended to be that of an "equal" parent.

The most critical issue that needs to be addressed is what the parties are intending their respective legal rights to be. The essence of the position of the "limited father" is that it is an attempt to allow for some participation by an involved donor in the child's life, which stops short of granting or imposing on the donor the rights and responsibilities that normally attach to biological parents. A written agreement may state that the donor has no parental rights whatsoever with respect to the child, regardless of any contact he has with the child (Martin 1993:Appendix I). More commonly, such agreements are not reduced to writing.

In fact, of course, many heterosexual fathers in traditional family situations fit the description of a "limited father" as described in this paper, as do many noncustodial fathers. They spend very limited amounts of time with their children, and the mother makes all the important decisions with regard to the children. The fathers may or may not carry the financial burden of maintaining the household and children. The difference is that in the case of lesbian mothers, the role of limited father is devised as such, is determined before the act of insemination, is articulated openly and understood as such by both parties, and is a predicate for the act of insemination to occur. Only if the woman or women and the man agree on the nature of his position will the pregnancy occur. Further, both the man and the woman enter into parenting with a clear agreement that the mother is the primary parent, who will have custody and complete control of the child, and that the father will have a very different and specifically secondary level of involvement with the child. Finally, limited fathering agreements differ from traditional fatherhood in that there is a deliberate attempt to enshrine the understanding of differing parenting involvements in a negotiated agreement, by overriding any parental rights that would otherwise attach to the donor.

On a broader ideological basis, the concept of the "limited father" should be seen as a newly emerging parenting status, emanating from women's increased control over reproduction and devised by lesbians because the existing legal and social framework of parental positions cannot accommodate the types of family and interpersonal structures our community is establishing. Although the idea has been formulated specifically to remedy perceived shortcomings in the law it is not unexpected that to date the concept has not been recognized by the law.

The phenomenon of lesbian mothers attempting to create new parenting rules outside those imposed by the legal system is evidence of the inability of the law to cope with the increasing variability of existing family structures. Traditional family law rules simply do not fit the reality of many parenting arrangements, and leave little if any space for flexibility in their application. The attempt by the lesbian community to establish new norms and rules outside the established legal system also reflects the fact that lesbian and gay relationships are not legally recognized and hence have been forced to exist outside the law.

The law currently lacks the flexibility that would enable legal recognition of the concept of a "limited father." If paternity is acknowledged or ordered, full parental rights follow, creating significant legal problems if the agreement between the parties that specified more limited and delineated roles breaks down. The law sees parental rights as an all-or-nothing phenomenon—once parental status is established, full parental rights and responsibilities automatically follow.

The law's traditional adherence to freedom of contract does not apply in family law, where public policy plays a role and statutes govern the parental rights and duties of the parties, to date allowing no scope for any contractual alteration of the statutory scheme. The judicial rejection of contractual principles as a basis for determining disputes arising from surrogacy contracts reflects the courts' disquiet with allowing contractual resolutions of issues concerning children. To date, the law refuses to enforce preconception contracts that trade away parental rights for payment in surrogacy arrangements.

The implications of the law's refusal to recognize the limited father concept for lesbians choosing to have children with an involved donor can be devastating for lesbian families. Women can take meticulous care to find a donor who fits their requirements and who wants the type of limited fatherhood that they want, negotiate all the details, draw up a contract that expresses the agreed views of all the parties—only to find that if he later changes his mind and wants more control over or access to the child, he may not be constrained by the contract but can approach the courts to press his claim for "full" parental rights at any time.

Whatever the agreement between the parties, a court's refusal to enforce an agreement may mean that the donor can seek custody or visitation. If the biological mother were to die, regardless of any agreement that the co-mother keep custody of the child, the donor/father could seek custody, a claim that in some states could not even be challenged by the co-mother (Bartlett 1984:900).

While the law does not recognize a "limited father" created by agreement before the insemination, the concept has obvious parallels in the position of noncustodial parents after divorce. In some cases where courts have imposed very structured visitation limitations on fathers after divorce, the role of the father is effectively narrowed by the court into that of a legally confined "limited father." The courts feel little hesitation in circumscribing the position of the noncustodial father by imposing restrictions as to the amount of time he can spend with his children, or the nature of the decisions he can be involved in with regard to his children. The parties themselves, however, have no recognized right to create this family structure in advance, outside postmarital separation.

Judicial Treatment of Lesbian Co-Mothers

The law's inability to acknowledge the diminished parental status of sperm donor limited fathers is paralleled by its failure to recognize any parental status for the lesbian co-mother. Just as the law sees only one type of father, with complete parental rights regardless of the level of involvement in conception or parenting, so the law has traditionally recognized only one type of mother—the person who either gave birth to or adopted the child. If two women coparent a child with an involved donor acting as a limited father, the existence of three people acting in a variety of parenting relationships to the child presents the courts with an unrecognizable family structure. In response, the law has yet to find the degree of flexibility needed to embrace the different family structures adopted by lesbians and gay men.

Perhaps some perspective on how a dispute involving a lesbian couple and a "limited father" might be treated can be gained from the way the courts have generally approached gay and lesbian cases. The courts have traditionally been hostile to claims for legal protection for gay men and lesbians, especially where children are involved. In New Hampshire, for example, gay men and lesbians are statutorily prohibited from adopting or fostering children.[3]

In more progressive states, however, there are signs that the law is beginning to recognize gay families. In the 1992 New York Surrogates Court decision *In the Matter of Evan*, a lesbian was permitted to adopt the biological child of her partner. The couple, who had been together for fourteen years, were jointly parenting a six-year-old child one of them had conceived through insemination with a friend's sperm. The donor had relinquished all claim to the child. Judge Eve Preminger approved the adoption as being in the best interests of the child, resolving future legal problems of succession, social security, and child support, and providing the child's relationship with the nonbiological mother with some formal recognition. Despite statutory requirements that after an adoption the biological mother would lose her parental rights, the court exercised its equitable power not to discontinue her rights.[4] In fact, however, this resolution was not contested. All the parties involved—the two women and the donor—supported the adoption, and the court's role was not to intervene to resolve a dispute but simply to allow the intended and agreed restructuring of the legal relationships between the parties.

Quite a different picture of judicial treatment of gay parenting relationships emerges when the parties do not agree and the law is trying to resolve a dispute involving gay parents. Four recent decisions involving judicial resolution of parenting disputes between former lesbian partners who had been jointly raising children illustrate the approach the courts have taken toward lesbian parents.

Of the four cases, from Wisconsin, California, New York, and New Mexico, only the New Mexico court showed any willingness to consider that the co-mother should be granted a parental or quasi-parental status.[5] The remaining cases, by categorizing the co-mother as a nonparent rather than a coparent, effectively relegate her to a lesser legal status, increase the legal burden on her, and render a successful visitation action virtually impossible. The courts apply the "parental preference" standard in custody disputes, without acknowledging a partner's claim that she is also a "parent." Rather, the courts describe the partner's relationship with the child as "parent-like," without any discussion of what distinguishes a "parent" relationship from a "parent-like" relationship.

Analysis of the majority opinion in a case addressed by the Wisconsin Supreme Court in 1991, *In Re the Interest of Z. J. H.*, illustrates the problems of categorized analysis that arise in resolving these disputes. The case concerned a lesbian couple who had separated after one of them had adopted a child during the course of their eight-year relationship. The court cast the partner who did not adopt the child in the role of a stranger, refusing to discuss or acknowledge her role in the adoption or mothering of the child. Her role as parent and mother is rendered invisible in the judgment, replaced with a role devised for her by the court—as merely a third party who provided care for the child.

The status of the co-mother was further reduced by the court when it considered the public policy considerations in limiting the number of individuals in the child's life to promote stability and avoid situations where the child "is subject to multiple custody and visitation arrangements." The court stated:

> Were we to permit individuals standing in *loco parentis* to obtain custody
> . . . we would open the doors to multiple parties claiming custody of
> children by virtue of their in *loco parentis* status.   (208)

This remark completes the re-insertion of the partner into the picture as merely one of many people with a role in the child's life. In the court's eyes only two categories exist—"legal parent" and "others." Hence a coparenting lesbian partner is placed in the same "other" category for custody considerations as, in the court's own words, housekeepers, prior companions, day-care providers, and others. The court also refused to enforce an agreement between the women that did allow visitation, saying that rights to custody and visitation could not be contracted away. The agreement was contrary to the statute and therefore void.

In the 1991 California case *Nancy S. v. Michele D.*, the court rejected several different bases on which the nonbiological mother argued that she was legally a "parent." The argument that she was a "de facto" parent, someone assuming the daily role of a parent, attempted to introduce into custody cases a concept that was used to allow foster parents to intervene in dependency proceedings. The court rejected this claim on the basis that even a de facto parent would need to show detriment before obtaining custody over a parent. The second basis for the claim of parental status rested on the tortious "in loco parentis" concept.

Again the court refused to extend the concept beyond its use in tort cases to custody cases.

Equitable concepts of parenthood were also relied on. The court rejected the argument of "parenthood by equitable estoppel," which has been used in child support cases to stop men denying the paternity of children they have been fathering, again saying that it should not be extended into custody or visitation. The "equitable parent" concept, related to the statutory recognition of equitable adoption to provide for inheritance, and requiring proof of an express or implied contract to adopt, was also rejected.

Finally, the court briefly considered and then rejected an argument that they should apply a definition of "functional parenthood"—"anyone who maintains a functional parental relationship with a child when a legally recognized parent created that relationship with the intent that the relationship be parental in nature"—to determine when to place someone into the legal category of "parent." The court rejected this as a "novel theory," the application of which would then leave the courts facing "years of unraveling the complex practical, social, and constitutional ramifications of this expansion of the definition of parent" (Polikoff 1990).

The 1991 New York Court of Appeals decision in *Alison D. v. Virginia M.* also denied visitation to a lesbian co-mother, on the basis that she had no standing to seek visitation because she was not biologically related to the child. Although the statute did not define the term *parent*, the court read the term to refer only to biological parents, rejecting alternative legal theories that would have provided a basis for recognizing the co-mother's right to seek visitation.

The first reported case of a custody dispute between two lesbian parents in which a court even expressed the possibility of giving any "parental" recognition to the role of the nonbiological mother is a 1992 New Mexico case, *A. C. v. C. B.* The women had lived together for fourteen years, and had a six-year-old child who had been conceived through insemination. The women had joint responsibility for child care and child support, and there was strong evidence of joint parenting. The nonbiological mother had been designated guardian and trustee for the child, and the women had a joint trust fund, savings account, and life insurance for the child's benefit.

In reversing summary judgment for the biological mother, the Court of Appeals said that the co-mother had made a prima facie showing that authorized consideration of her right to continue her relationship with the child. The court stopped short of issuing an opinion on the question of whether the nonbiological mother had standing to contest custody and visitation, but did say that she had alleged facts sufficient to state a colorable claim. Remanding the case, the court expressly noted that someone in the shoes of the co-mother may be able to establish deprivation of a legally recognized right to maintain some type of continuing relationship with the child. The court did not say that a visitation agreement would not be enforceable, although it noted that it would be subject to some modification if it were in the best interests of the child, and stated that sexual orientation was not a ground for denial of custody or visitation in New Mexico.

Unfortunately, the approach adopted in New Mexico diverges from the dominant trend of decisions in parenting disputes between lesbians who have co-mothered a child. As the cases in Wisconsin, New York, and California suggest, there is still little judicial recognition of alternative forms of family structures and a rigid unwillingness to extend the legal category of parent to include women who have acted as functional mothers but who lack a biological connection with the child.

The dominance of this approach to analyzing the rights of the co-mother carries important implications for the approach courts might be expected to take in determining the rights of limited fathers. In Wisconsin, California, and New York, the degree of functional parenting and involvement with the child was not a relevant factor in determining the co-mother's rights, since the decisions denying her access were based on her lack of standing as a nonparent. In the three cases denying visitation to the co-mother, her parenting history and behavior simply had no legal relevance. Taking equal responsibility for child care and financial support did not have an impact on her legal status. Equally, her involvement in the decision to have the child, the decision as to who would become pregnant, how pregnancy would be achieved, or the decision about the role of the donor was also irrelevant. In a situation where the key feature distinguishing the roles of the two women in relation to the child was the genetic tie, the majority of the courts opted for honoring biology and ignoring other aspects of connection with the child.

If the fact that a nonbiological mother helped to design and assisted in the actual conception, and then behaved in all respects as if she were the child's parent, can be completely discounted by adherence to legal categories, then in a perverse mirror image of this approach, we might also expect the fact that a donor had only limited contact and involvement with the child to be equally irrelevant, since it does not change the fact that he does have a genetic connection to the child, and hence falls within the legal category of "parent." If the courts follow the approach established in most of the lesbian co-mother cases, then neither agreements limiting the donor's role nor the fact that his responsibility for or contact with the child may have been minimal should be relevant to an analysis of his parental rights.

Indeed the judicial treatment of lesbian mothers suggests that little, if any, reliance will be placed on agreements altering the legal parenting rights of the parties. In *In Re the Interest of Z. J. H.* the court held that rights as to custody and visitation could not be contracted away, and that the statutes establishing the paramountcy of parental rights over the rights of nonparents could not be displaced by agreement. It appears that agreements that aim to vary the legal status of the parenting parties will carry little or no weight in assessing custody or visitation petitions. With respect to the position of limited fathers, contracts defining the man's parental rights or limiting the role of the donor have uncertain validity at best, and cannot be relied on as providing protection for the mother(s) against his claims for increased access.

Just as the majority of courts have declined to base co-mother visitation decisions on any implied parenting agreements, they have also declined to adopt a "best interests" approach to reach a determination. Such an analysis would have invoked consideration of the specific relationship between the child and the nonbiological mother. In the three cases denying visitation, there is no discussion of the children's understanding of their relationship with the co-mother, nor do the courts appear to consider that it is possible that the children may never have distinguished between the two women in terms of their day-to-day connections to them. In *Alison D.*, for example, the child called both women "mommy," and visitation continued for three years after the separation. In *Nancy S.*, after the separation one of the children lived with the nonbiological mother for three years. In denying visitation, the courts failed to acknowledge that from the perspective of the child they were cutting off access to the child's mother—an outcome that was never examined in terms of the best interests of the child.

In terms of the position of the limited father, determining the issue of standing prior to any consideration of the issue of the best interests of the child reinforces the perspective that it is the biological relationship of the party to the child that is critical; this perspective places the genetic connection as the threshold issue for having the court hear the claim. When biology is given such a central place in the legal test of parent, it will hardly be surprising that after that hurdle is crossed, consideration of the best interests of the child might tend to focus on the child's interest in having two parents and, more particularly, role models of both a mother and a father. Indeed the mother's or mothers' decision to have a known donor, acting as a limited father, might in itself be interpreted as an endorsement of the view that a father is a necessary presence for the child.

Ultimately, the courts must be criticized for not trying to apply the law in a way that recognizes the unusual positions of the parties in a case involving lesbian mothers; rather, co-mother disputes have been analyzed under a rigid and doctrinally formalistic legal approach, simply applying laws clearly devised for heterosexual parents to situations falling outside those parameters. The consequence is that one of the child's parents is excluded from the legal process of determining what is in the child's best interests.

In the majority of lesbian co-mother cases, the courts have seemed unable to escape the concept of the two-sexed family. As a result, they "read down" the role of the nonbiological mother, to a point where she is not even the functional equivalent of one member of the heterosexual couple. Rather than standing in a privileged position within a parenting couple, she stands as an outsider, in a supposedly long line of people the courts see as in similar positions—child care workers, babysitters, and housekeepers, all of them "outsiders" who the courts fear might seek visitation if the legal category of "parent" were relaxed.

An inflexible application of the traditional legal custody and visitation framework will lead to an inevitable privileging of a limited father's position, purely by virtue of the biological relationship. As the child's biological father, under a rigid application of the law he will fall within the definition of a legal parent; he would then have all the rights that position entails, including standing to seek custody or visitation. Applying the dominant approach in the lesbian co-mother cases to the situation of a limited father means that the limited father is advantaged, centralized, and accorded full legal rights to the same extent that the nonbiological lesbian mother is disadvantaged and rendered invisible by her exclusion from the category of parent.

Hence the exclusionary themes that dominate the cases regarding the parenting rights of lesbian co-mothers become inclusionary for donor fathers. The same legal doctrines and approaches used to remove a co-mother from an ongoing relationship with the child she once parented could be used to restore the man in that relationship.

Litigating the Position of the Donor/Father

The position of the donor/father was litigated in 1993 in the extremely controversial New York case *Thomas S. v. Robin Y.*[6] This was the first reported judicial consideration of the position of a limited father of an older child, raised by a lesbian couple, where the donor had some history of involvement with the child and was known to the child as her biological parent. The trial level decision of Family Court Judge Kaufmann, although hotly debated in the lesbian and gay community and now reversed on appeal, does attempt to look past formal legal categories and grapple with the underlying issue of what it means to be "a parent" in the context of a relationship with a child.

In *Thomas S.* the role of the donor had changed over the course of the child's life. Although there was no written agreement, the initial understanding between the two lesbian mothers and the donor, a gay man, was that he would have no parental rights or obligations but would make himself known to the child, Ry, if she asked questions about his identity. The women had the same agreement with a different donor who had provided sperm resulting in the birth of an older child, Cade. From the time of Ry's birth in 1981 until 1985, Ry's donor had virtually no contact with the child or the mothers.

In 1985, following questions from the older child about her biological origins, the mothers asked both donors to meet the children and traveled from their residence in New York to California, where both of the men lived. After this meeting, a relationship developed between the family and Thomas S., after which he visited the women and children several times a year, with contacts always remaining at the discretion of the mothers. In essence, during this period Thomas S. was acting as a "limited father," maintaining contact with the child within the limits established by the mothers, not asserting any parental rights, not contributing financially, and not taking parental responsibility for the child.

By 1991 Thomas S. wanted visitation with Ry apart from the mothers, and sought to change the pattern of interaction. He asked that both the children come to California to spend time with him and meet his biological family, without the mothers being present. His request could be seen as an attempt to step out of the role of "limited father," demanding greater recognition as a "parent." Concerned about possible future custody claims by Thomas S. or his family, the mothers refused the request for visitation without their being present. Thomas S. then commenced paternity and visitation proceedings. After he began proceedings, the mothers stopped all contact between him and the family.

In a surprising decision, although Thomas S. established that he was Ry's biological father, the Family Court ruled that he was equitably estopped from establishing paternity or seeking visitation.[7] The court differentiated biological and functional parenthood, holding that even though Ry did have some relationship with Thomas S., and knew him to be her biological parent, that given the initial period of absence from the child's life and the nature of the relationship that he later established with Ry and her family, he was equitably estopped from claiming parental rights. In applying the doctrine the court took into account the fact that Thomas S. initially said he had no interest in asserting parental rights. The fact that he did not contribute financially was also relevant, confirming his initial intent not to act as a parent. The court saw Thomas S. as "attempting to change the ground rules" that had been established.

Significantly, however, rather than simply relying on the donor's history, the court's approach turned on a best interests analysis, which considered the child's place within her existing family. Indeed, the decision was notable for the degree of respect shown for the specific, individualized concept of "family" that had been created by the mothers, and that was shared by the children:

> Ry has been brought up to view Robin Y. and Sandra R. as equal mothers raising two children and to view Thomas S. as an important man in her family's life. In her family there has been no father. Robin Y. and Sandra R. are deeply committed to this concept of their family, and Ry, who has been raised by them, must also be committed to the concept at this point in her life. (380)

Specifically, the court said that although Ry knew that Thomas S. was her biological parent, and sensed his affection for her, that did not mean that she ever "viewed him as a parental figure."

> The reality of her life is having two mothers . . . working together to raise her and her sister. Ry does not now and has never viewed Thomas S. as a functional third parent. To Ry, a parent is a person who a child depends on to care for her needs. To Ry, Thomas S. has never been a parent, since he never took care of her on a daily basis. (380)

This deference to a child's perception of whether someone is a part of their family or their "functional parent" (a term the court fails to define) is an unusual basis on which to resolve a paternity or visitation claim. Visitation decisions do not generally, as the lesbian co-mother cases indicate, recognize a category of "functional parent," and do not normally turn on a child's subjective view of whether someone is a functional parent.

Indeed the Family Court's use of a "functional parent" standard based on the child's perception has critical implications. Most significant, by relying on Ry's understanding of who was a parent, the court drew a line around the adults who were directly involved in her day-to-day care; this analysis would exclude anyone in a noncustodial parental position, including someone who was acting as a "limited father."

In fact the decision sets a high performance threshold for someone trying to establish they are a functional parent, almost assuming that only daily carers, living with the child, will qualify. In this case, the parties lived on opposite coasts, and Thomas S. saw the child several times a year, and had other contact, such as letters or calls. Certainly Thomas S. had more contact with Ry than many noncustodial fathers have with their children, without losing their visitation rights. Perhaps this case can be distinguished because his failure to qualify as a functional parent was combined with an initial absence from the child's life, which the court saw as a failure on his part.

The lesbian and gay community is divided over the outcome of this case. At one level the court's analysis has been welcomed as a reaffirmation of lesbian family autonomy, but at another level the approach underlying the decision raises concerns for gay and lesbian families. The first issue of concern is that the donor in this case appears to have been penalized for doing precisely what the lesbian mothers wanted him to do—stay out of the child's life until they invited him into it. His initial absence provided the factual predicate for the invocation of the estoppel doctrine. Even after taking on the role of limited father, his position was still weakened in the eyes of the court by the fact that he allowed his contacts with the child to be at the mother's discretion—all of which suggests that greater pushiness in the early years may have enabled him to avoid denial on the grounds of estoppel.

The second implication of concern to lesbian and gay families is the underlying sense that the court's analysis was motivated by the fact that the child already lived in a two-parent family, and that granting a third person parental rights would jeopardize the quasi-nuclear structure long judicially favored for child rearing. In this case, the court arguably overlooked the sex of the two parents out of respect for the higher value of a "coupled" approach to the family. Allowing a third party to assert parental rights would threaten the implicitly sanctioned two-parent family structure.

Both these aspects of the Family Court decision are troubling. Using the donor/father's compliance with the mothers' wishes as a basis for denying him parental rights creates an obvious incentive for others to assert claims more strongly and earlier, to protect their positions. Any suggestion that two-parent family structures should be protected denies both the reality and the transformative potential of the different kinds of parenting relationships that are being developed by lesbians and gay men. The gay and lesbian community is marked by an array of diverse types of family structures and parenting relationships. This diversity can be distinguished from the diversity of heterosexual family structures by precisely the issue raised by the *Thomas S.* case—the fact that in gay and lesbian families the genetic connection is not central to either the meaning of parenthood or the role of functional parent.

Within a lesbian/gay politics, the exclusion of Thomas S. as a parent can therefore be read positively, as a recognition that the position of parent should not be determined solely by genetics, or negatively, as an exclusion that denies the most radical aspect of many lesbian and gay families: that children do have ongoing relationships with multiple "parents," some biologically related and some not, who live both inside and beyond their household, with differing levels of responsibility for them and different types of relationships with them. Many lesbian families have been successfully constructed around men who have agreed to, and are acting as, limited fathers. The *Thomas S.* decision suggests that such limited roles will not be given legal recognition, just as lesbian co-mothers have not been recognized.

Reformers would argue that it is the reality of diverse family structures that should be respected within the law, rather than trying to squeeze back into a more acceptable nuclear model a variety of different significant relationships that a child may have with adults who have a close and committed bond with the child. Multiple adult/child relationships with differing levels of connection and involvement could be recognized by the adoption of a more flexible legal approach to families. It is the lack of flexibility in the law—and the fact that the category of legal parent is perceived as an "all or nothing" category with full parental rights to those within it and none to those outside—that enables the law to be applied in a restrictive and exclusionary way, both for co-mothers and for limited fathers.

In a majority decision reversing the Family Court's, the Appellate Division found for Thomas S., holding that his biological fatherhood mandated entering an order of filiation and remanding the case for a hearing on visitation. In the majority's view, his parental rights could be terminated only in accordance with statutory criteria, not through the application of an estoppel analysis. As to the parties' mutual understanding, the majority thought public policy barred the enforcement of any oral agreement regarding parental rights that did not comply with the statutory criteria for terminating parental rights. In contrast, the dissenting judges followed the trial court approach, asking whether Thomas S. had a "true parental relationship" with the child—and finding that his involvement was too limited for him to be recognized as a parent. Both approaches—one based in biological connection and one in functional behavior—miss the point. Both analyses, denying any parental rights or granting full parental rights, fail to grasp the mid-point reality of a limited father's position. For Thomas S., recognizing the reality of his position would mean acknowledging both the validity and the limitations of his claim. Until the law develops a capacity to deconstruct the concept of parental rights, the unique position of the limited father will continue to be misinterpreted in one direction or the other.

These issues will undoubtedly come before the courts over the next few years, in litigation over written agreements granting donors visitation but limiting parental rights in other respects. The reformist position may be to propose a more flexible approach to granting standing for visitation petitions. Under a more flexible approach, more than two people could be granted visitation rights with respect to the child, allowing relationships with a co-mother and with a limited father to be protected without impinging on each other. Equally, if the mother(s) were protected against a custody claim, it could be argued that in opening the door and allowing a known donor to form a bond with his child, lesbian mothers have helped to create a significant relationship in the child's life, one that then warrants legal protection. The equitable estoppel argument used in the *Thomas S.* case could in fact flow the other way: since Thomas S. relied on the mothers' encouragement of his relationship with Ry, changing his position as a result and becoming actively involved with the child, the mothers should not subsequently be able to deny him visitation with the child.

Another interesting question that arises from the *Thomas S.* decision is whether it is consistent with the line of lesbian co-mother cases. There appears to be a fundamental inconsistency—the lesbian co-mother cases suggest that biological parenting alone will be used to determine parental rights legally, and that a strong evidence of functional parenting has no relevance in a visitation claim by a nonparent, while in *Thomas S.* the biological parent was granted no rights, based on his lack of functional parenting. Nor can the cases be reconciled by resort to the intent of the parties, since intent was not the determinative factor in any of the cases.

One analysis, which resolves any apparent inconsistency, would be to accept that the relationship between biology and functional parenting in determining parental rights is not symmetrical: while the absence of a biological connection is in itself a sufficient basis on which to determine that someone has no parental rights, the presence of such a connection will not alone warrant the recognition of parental rights without the presence of a functional parent relationship. One might conclude that in lesbian and gay families parental rights will only be recognized where there is both a genetic connection to the child and the person has acted as a functional parent. Such an approach can be readily criticized both for the inconsistency of the significance it places on functional parenting and for its privileging of biology as the essential element, which would always exclude the nonbiological mother despite her actual parenting of the child. Moreover, while the recognition of functional parenting as a relevant element in such decisions may have the support of many commentators who promote the use of a functional parent definition for custody and visitation disputes, its use as the standard in lesbian and gay families involving a limited father, where it was never envisaged or intended that the donor would act as a functional parent but always intended that he would have more limited rights and responsibilities with respect to the child, would be peculiarly inappropriate.

An alternative analysis might seek consistency between *Thomas S.* and the dominant line of lesbian co-mother cases in the courts' ultimate deference in both instances to the wishes of the biological mother. Faced with an assortment of parties who claim rights with respect to the child but who fall outside the usual family structures or types of relationships, the courts, although neither theorizing nor articulating the outcome as such, may then find cause to defer to the wishes of the biological mother. Again, this explanation of the cases would find support from some commentators. Martha Fineman has presented a strong case for centralizing and respecting the mother-child unit in family law disputes, and for allowing the mother, as the person who is the ongoing carer in the child's daily life, control over visitation (Fineman 1994).

Adopting this approach, however, obscures important features distinguishing lesbian and gay from heterosexual family disputes—primarily the fact that the parties may have embarked upon the conception with a very different understanding of their respective, and possibly multiple, parenting roles than might have been anticipated by heterosexual parents. If two women and a donor have agreed that he will play the role of a limited father and the lesbian partner will play the role of an equal mother, should the law recognize a change of mind by the biological mother, without other supporting reasons, as a sufficient ground for denying the other parties any rights to maintain their relationships with the child? It is this issue that is key—what rights persist through the parties changing their minds, such as when the lesbian couple are no longer together, or the couple falls out with a donor acting as a limited father? What weight, if any, should be given to past intentions? What responsibility should be placed on the parties to allow continuation of any established relationships with the child, after the relationship between the adults breaks down? What type of adult/child relationships do we want the law to recognize?

Parenting by Contract?

The legal category of parent in its current form cannot be sensibly applied to the variety of different sorts of "parents" who exist in nontraditional family situations. The courts have had to come to terms with family situations including stepparents or open adoptions, but the resistance toward recognizing lesbian and gay family relationships seems particularly entrenched.

A biologically predetermined approach to parental rights fits neatly into a framework where parental rights are exclusive and indivisible—not to be broken down, rearranged, or shared out with "strangers" to the biological connection (Bartlett 1984). The status of the parent is also inherently connected with the court's perception of the status of the child. The children of lesbian couples are not perceived to be children of the couple, but the children of the biological mother raised with the assistance of her partner.

There are specific reforms that could be made in family law that would ensure that the law reflected the experience and intentions of the parties in lesbian and gay families. First, the legal concept and statutory

definition of the term *parent* needs to be broadened to cover the variety
of parental situations that now exist. The courts generally appear to be
resistant to such moves, opting for a narrow definition of parent even
where statutes leave discretion. Polikoff's critique of the use of the legal
doctrines that have been relied on in attempts to have the courts broaden
their understanding of the term—such as the doctrines of de facto parenthood or in loco parentis, and her proposal for a definition based on
"functional parenting"—would resolve the problem in a fundamental
way, by removing the definitional obstacle that now faces the nonbiological parent under the law (Polikoff 1990). However the limits of this
approach must also be recognized, in that it envisages a model recognizing primary, custodial parenting but not the different quasi-parental role
played by someone such as a limited father. Polikoff's analysis fails to recognize that someone in the position of Thomas S. arguably has visitation
rights, even if not equal parental rights to the mother(s).

A second valuable reform would be for adoption law to allow the
adoption of a same-sex partner's biological child. This could be
achieved through statutory reform, clarifying that if the biological
mother consents to an adoption she does not have to terminate her own
parental rights. Alternatively, state courts could follow the approach of
the New York court in *Evan* and construe the provisions of existing
statutes that require termination of parental rights on adoption as inap-
plicable to these situations. Such an approach presents a direct challenge to notions of the exclusivity of parental rights, however, and is
unlikely to be followed in more conservative states.

In any event, if the donor is known, the option of second-parent
adoption will generally only be available where he has agreed to the
adoption, or waived his parental rights. Second-parent adoptions are of
considerable value to lesbian mothers since they do resolve the legal
position of the nonbiological mother; if the donor is known, however,
they are only a viable option where all the parties are in agreement. The
adoption process is unlikely to become the judicial avenue for resolving
disputes between lesbian mothers and sperm donors.

A third reform option is to encourage the parenting parties to draw up
contracts setting out their intentions and to allow the parties to enforce
those contracts against each other. It has been argued that if parties wish
to order their reproduction and parenting by enforceable contractual
agreements, including the creation of a position of "limited" parent, then
they should be able to do so (Shultz 1990). For lesbian mothers, enforceable contracts would mean that if insemination was contingent on the

donor signing a contract renouncing any parental rights with respect to the child, and agreeing in advance to consent to legal proceedings terminating his parental rights, then the contract could be enforced against the donor, who would be legally precluded from asserting any parental rights beyond those which had been agreed on in the contract. Suggestions of enforceable contracts in the context of ordering parental rights, however, must set off a series of ethical alarm bells.

Strong feminist criticisms have been leveled at proposals for greater reliance on contractual ordering of reproduction and parenting to determine rights in situations of assisted reproduction, and the issue of contract enforceability in the area of reproductive rights has been extensively analyzed in relation to surrogate mother contracts, with the majority of feminist writers arguing that surrogate contracts should not be enforceable against the biological mother (Field 1988; Pateman 1988; Shanley 1993). Do the ethical arguments against allowing surrogacy contracts to be enforced also persuade us that contracts limiting a donor's parental rights would be equally unethical and should not be enforced to deny a donor the full panoply of his paternal rights?

The arguments presented by surrogacy opponents include concerns that pregnancy contracts are intrinsically gendered transactions that exploit women's economically subordinated status; that they diminish the humanity of pregnancy and birth by an inherent commodification of bodily processes; that they embody an objectification of the female body and its reduction to reproductive organs; and that (not unlike slavery contracts) they offend the freedom essential to human dignity and selfhood (<u>Shanley 1993</u>). Further arguments against surrogacy stress the distinction between reproductive labor and other labor, and focus on the self-alienation resulting from the forced disjuncture of the emotions and the body in a surrogate pregnancy (Pateman 1988).

Underlying the problem surrounding surrogacy contracts, of course, is the fact that the woman who seeks to break a surrogacy contract does so because she changes her mind in the course of the deeply personal and intrinsically individual experience of pregnancy and birth. If the woman, despite her intentions to the contrary, finds that she feels an unanticipated and uninvited sense of connection to the fetus/child, then it is argued that this is a sense of connection that deserves recognition, respect, and even primacy. It is this sense of the intense personal significance of the experience of pregnancy, and the primacy of an embodied mother-child bond developed over the course of pregnancy and birth, which lies at the heart of the strongest feminist objections to contract pregnancy (Shanley 1993). The centrality of the experience of pregnancy explains why most feminists do not distinguish between surrogacy contracts where the surrogate is the genetic mother and those where the role of the surrogate is purely gestational, carrying a laboratory-fertilized embryo to which she has no genetic relationship. It is the experience of pregnancy, and not the fact that the child is the genetic product of the mother, which is presented as the determining factor in the resolution of a surrogacy conflict.

The centrality of the experience of pregnancy and the significance that it is accorded suggest that the arguments against enforcing surrogacy contracts where a woman trades away her parental rights cannot be similarly called upon as arguments against the enforceability of a contract against a man who agreed to limit his parental rights but who is later seeking to assert such rights beyond those agreed to. Perhaps, however, pregnancy is not the essential distinguishing factor. A donor who agrees to a limited father contract because he genuinely believes that a limited involvement with the child is all he wants, only to find after the pregnancy or birth that his feelings have changed and that he has misjudged his desire to establish or foster his own relationship with the child, is in a situation that is superficially similar to that of the surrogate mother. As feminists then, just as we reject the notion of enforceable surrogacy contracts, should we also reject the option of enforcing limited parenting agreements against sperm donors who change their minds after the birth of the child, and want to re-claim the parental rights they contracted away?

It could also be argued, however, that at a more fundamental level the donor who agrees to a limited role but then changes his mind is not the equivalent of the surrogate who wants to go back on her agreement to give up a child. Two fundamental differences distinguish the situations. First, the transactions of surrogacy and sperm donation are differently gendered. In surrogacy, a man initiates the transaction, selects the surrogate, makes payment to the woman, and imposes the requirement that the woman give up all rights to or interest in the child after birth. In donor insemination, it is the woman who is in the position of power and control. She initiates the transaction, selects the donor, acquires the sperm, and determines the level of involvement or recognition, if any, which she is willing to allow. She decides what rights or what level of control she is willing to give away. While not ignoring the more subtle ways in which women may be unwilling to assert power in relation to men, in contrast to surrogacy agreements the insemination agreement structurally places the woman in the controlling position.

The second critical difference is that the insemination contract, unlike the surrogacy contract, reflects and acknowledges the unequal value of the reproductive contributions of the two parties. The surrogacy contract discounts pregnancy and follows the genetic dictate that the man and the woman contribute equally to the creation of the child. The lesbian insemination contract is not based on such notions of biological equality; rather, in proscribing a variable (but always lesser) role for the donor/father, it reflects the significance of the fact that the woman has a more profound connection with the child because she has undertaken the pregnancy and given birth to the child. In insemination "limited father" contracts, motherhood is valued over fatherhood. Since the structure of lesbian insemination contracts integrates and recognizes pregnancy and begins with the premise that the woman's rights with respect to the child are superior to those of the man, such contracts avoid many of the feminist criticisms of surrogacy contracts.

Further distinctions between surrogate and insemination contracts are also significant. Insemination transactions with known donors do not involve payment, and hence are not subject to criticisms based on the financial exploitation of the woman, the commodification of her reproductive capacity, or the equating of pregnancy to wage labor.

Perhaps the most fundamental distinction between surrogacy contracts and lesbian insemination contracts with known donors is that in surrogacy the intention is that one of the biological parents will have no parenting rights in relation to the child while the other will have full parental rights. The surrogacy contract adopts an all-or-nothing approach—the man takes the child and all the rights, while under the agreement the woman has no continuing contact with child and no rights. For lesbian mothers with known donors and limited fathers, first, there is no similar standard intention as to the proposed roles of the parties, and questions of the rights and responsibilities of the donor have to be individually negotiated and addressed. Second, and more important, the insemination contract does not leave the limited father with nothing. Although it endeavors to remove the traditional legal rights of the donor, the insemination contract replaces them with a set of rights that have been contracted for; it also allows a continuing connection with the child. This distinction is critical, shifting the nature of the contract from "ownership" in surrogacy to "access" in insemination. It does not deny parenthood, it merely seeks to confine or limit the extent of the parenting role and create a "designer parent" to agreed specifications. The distinction between repudiating and limiting the position of a parent is arguably critical in overcoming the arguments against surrogacy that are based on the need to respect the child's position in relation to its biological parents.

However feminists have also criticized reproductive contracts in a broader sense, with some writers going beyond the case of surrogacy and arguing at a more fundamental level that the existence of any contractual relationships in the reproductive process raises serious ethical problems, imposing an alienation of the body and emotions and rejecting a relational view of the individual (Ryan 1990). In this analysis, the concept of limited fatherhood could raise particular concerns in that it attempts to dictate and constrain the nature of a parent-child relationship in advance, without honoring the potential the relationship between the donor and the child has to find its own shape as the child grows and the relationship develops (Ryan 1990). Imposing such constraints can be seen as an attempt to treat the most intimate of human relations as the equivalent of trade dealings, reducing the delicacy and dignity of an evolving relationship between an adult and a child to a set of agreed "rights."

Parenting contracts thus embody an even more problematic issue: they embrace a concept of the child as the object of negotiated rights, suggesting that parents have an inherent "ownership" right with respect to their children, which can properly and ethically be varied between the parties or contracted away. Even more than reproductive contracts, parenting contracts suggest a model for the structuring of relationships that centers on a concept of the child fulfilling the needs and desires of the parents rather than on the parents fulfilling the needs and desires of the child. Despite the absence of monetary exchange in most lesbian/sperm donor conceptions, the conceptual commodification of the child produced under the agreement may be as effectively accomplished by the imposition of a contract that is entered into even before conception has occurred and that sets limitations and restrictions on the potential relationship between the donor and the child.

These broader ethical concerns about parenting contracts, however, must be measured against the present reality of a legal system that rejects parenting contracts in favor of a rigid and inflexible approach to parenting, an approach that in practice and application has failed to recognize the primacy of those who are parenting children, and has at times chosen to grant parental rights to those who are not. The inadequacy of the law's current approach in dealing with lesbian and gay family disputes is well established, and the question of whether limited parenting contracts are unethical must be assessed against that background.

Another possible analogy to the limited parent contract is to be found in some private adoption agreements, where the adopting parent(s) agree to allow the biological mother continued visitation with the child—even involving her in their family circle in a role akin to that of a nonparental relative (Nathan 1984). In the adoption situation, however, the legal status of the parties is clearer, since the biological mother has agreed to the termination of her parental rights and the adopting parent(s) have exclusive parental status. The open adoption situation also differs from the limited parent contract, since the biological mother, the party whose rights with respect to the child are restricted, has surrendered those rights after the birth of the child rather than negotiated them away in advance in order to procure the conception.

In both the lesbian mother cases and future limited father cases the courts need to be more willing to look at the nature of the decision-making processes that led up to the conception of the child. With lesbian mother(s) and limited fathers, agreements establishing a "limited father" role are negotiated and discussed as part of the process of selecting the appropriate person as the donor. The fact that the decisions about parental roles are an essential element of the decision to parent strengthens the argument that courts should honor the intentions of the parties in such cases. Enforcement of this form of "limited parent" agreement could always be made subject to any clear detriment to the child that would result if the agreement was enforced. Beyond these concerns, the law needs to recognize that lesbians and gay men want to form families, become parents, and assume parenting roles in a variety of ways; it needs to provide them with a legal framework within which they can do so. Until then, lesbian mothers need to recognize the high legal risks involved in selecting known sperm donors over unknown. Frozen, anonymous sperm remains legally the safest option for lesbian mothers. For mothers and donors alike, however, the practice of giving donors limited fathering rights raises new ethical dilemmas, which should challenge us toward further analysis of what being a "parent" really means, both conceptually and legally.

NOTES

1. Since the HIV virus has been identified in semen, using fresh sperm for insemination poses a major risk of HIV transmission.

2. The *Jhordan* decision noted that this was illegal in Connecticut, Georgia, Oklahoma, and Oregon.

3. The prohibition was upheld as constitutional in *Opinion of the Justices* 530 A.2d 21 (N.H. 1987). The New Hampshire Supreme Court also recently upheld the right of the State Division for Children and Youth Services to require all foster parents to complete forms indicating whether they or any member of their household is homosexual (*Stuart v. State* 134 N.H. 702; 597 A.2d 1076 [1991]).

4. The adoption of a lesbian partner's biological child has also been allowed in other states, including Alaska, California, Massachusetts, New Jersey, Oregon, and Washington. See, for example, *In Matter of a Petition of L. S. and V. L. for the Adoption of Minors (T) and (M)* (D.C. Super. Ct. Fam. Div. 17 F. L. R. (BNA) 1523, [1991]); *In re Adoption of Tammy*, 619 N.E.2d 315 (Mass. 1993); *In the Matter of an Adoption of a Child by J. M. G.*, 632 A.2d 550 (N.J. 1993). However, other courts in New York have not all followed the approach taken in the Evan case. See *Matter of Dana*, Putnam Co. Fam. Ct. N.Y.L.J., January 26, 1994.

5. *In Re the Interest of Z. J. H.*, 471 N.W.2d 202 (Wis. 1991); *Nancy S. v. Michele D.*, 228 Cal.App.3d 831 (1991); *Alison D. v. Virginia M.*, 572 N.E. 2d 27 (1991); *A. C. v. C. B.*, 829 P.2d 660 (N.M.App. 1992). See also *Curiale v. Reagan*, 272 Cal.Rptr. 520 (1990).

6. 599 N.Y.S.2d 377 (Fam. 1993). The decision has been reversed on appeal: N.Y.A.D. 1 Dept., Nov. 17, 1994, no. 51466.

7. The doctrine of equitable estoppel can be applied in situations where one party, by either taking or failing to take action, induces a second party to rely on the first party's action or inaction to the second party's detriment, such as where a delay in asserting a right has created circumstances where it would be inequitable to allow it to be exercised.

PART THREE

Regulating Mother

9 | Images of Mothers in Poverty Discourse

MARTHA A. FINEMAN

This essay focuses on the construction of the concept of Mother in poverty discourses. It addresses the role of patriarchal ideology in the process whereby a characteristic typical of a group of welfare recipients has been selected and identified as constituting the cause as well as the effect of poverty. I am particularly interested, in this regard, in those political and professional discourses in which the existence of single mother status is defined as one of the primary predictors of poverty. Such association of characteristic with cause has fostered suggestions that an appropriate and fundamental goal of any proposed poverty program should be eradication of the status and practice of single motherhood. This goal is to be accomplished through appropriate coupling of the single mother with the child's father, who would then assume his rightful place in the family and fulfill his financial obligations. By his so doing, the paramount welfare reform objective—letting the state off the economic hook—will have been achieved.

While it is true that many commentators prefer sanctified relationships, the coupling of single mother and financially endowed male anticipated by such reforms need not be accomplished through the formation of a formal marital bond. The objective of such proposals is the creation of a legal tie between the presumed to be economically viable male and the dependent single mother and child. It is through this legal tie that child support obligations can be established and enforced. Neither the mother's nor the father's wishes in regard to the establishment of such a tie are considered relevant.

The legal process through which this tie is accomplished is the paternity proceeding. Increased reliance on this process as the essential step in assuring family responsibility for children has been a mainstay of recent welfare reforms. For the most part, these reforms seek to ensure that children are firmly anchored (financially, morally, and legally) within the nuclear family. The socially and economically based deprivations poor children and their mothers suffer are thus transformed into deprivations attributable to and based upon the deviant family form they occupy. It follows that economic salvation is to come through the refashioning of these families to conform as closely as possible to the "natural" family so as to perpetuate traditional roles. The reforms are driven by the perceived compelling need for the reestablishment of patriarchy, redefined for the contemporary context where divorce is common and increasing numbers of never-married women choose to become mothers (Wegman 1989:944–45).

In earlier work, I explored the transformation of the concept of Mother that father-centered reforms have wrought in the divorce context (Fineman 1991a). Upon reading poverty discourses, I was struck by how similar both the articulation of the "problem" (absent father) and the creation of an ideal "solution" (bring him [back] into the family in some form) were in both areas. The ideological spaces occupied by the discourses of poverty and divorce, with their two unique categories of single mothers, was different enough that the existence of a common articulation of problems and solutions suggested to me the need for further thought.

Perhaps the similarity in creation and definition of problems and solutions should not have been surprising since many single mother families are created by divorce and many of these mothers initially or eventually need state assistance. In poverty discourses, however, the single mother family under consideration is not typically presented as the once-married, formally middle-class housewife and mom and her children who now find themselves upon hard times as the result of divorce. The single mother crafted and located within poverty discourses is not constructed with the same characteristics as the single mother fashioned by divorce discourses—she is differentiated by race and by class from her divorced sister. In spite of such differences, the core and common problem facing mothers within each group is identified as the missing male. It follows, therefore, that the solution to the problem for both categories of single mothers lies in the legally coerced [re]establishment of a paternal presence, physically outside of, but metaphysically completing, the family structure.

As a result of these observations, I became interested in what I now call the phenomenon of "crossover discourses." I define this phenomenon as the propensity for rhetorical images associated with being female in our culture, generated and perpetuated in one context, to spill over and define our understanding of women in other contexts. In other words, Mother as a socially defined and symbolic institution has transsubstantive implications. The concept of Mother conceived of as "true" in forging images in poverty discourse inevitably will be a definitive presence in our understanding and grand construction of the institution of "Mother." Any process in which the Mother is explicitly the focus of attention generates images that ultimately are significant in shaping societal attitudes toward regulation of motherhood through the creation of rules governing such things as reproduction, custody at divorce, and a variety of other areas of law in which the institution of Mother is implicated.

I have concluded that the tendency of discourses in this area to cross over is directly related to the continued vitality of patriarchal ideology. Even though our social circumstances have altered substantially during the past several decades, patriarchal concepts have remained at the center of how we define and understand all families in our culture. As I discuss in the last section of this essay, the ideology of patriarchy is the most instrumental force in the creation and acceptance of discourses about mothers in our society.

In focusing on the institution of Mother, I do not mean to suggest that it represents the only appropriate, or even a necessary, role for individual women. I realize that not all women are mothers (although we all have or have had mothers, but that raises a different set of issues). However, motherhood as an institution with significant and powerful symbolic content in our culture has an impact on all women. This impact is independent of individual choices about whether or not to become a mother. It comes from the durability and tenacity of the assumptions made about any individual woman, assumptions that are forged in the context of the cultural and social forces that define an "essential" or idealized women. For this reason, all women must care about the social and cultural presentation of concepts of motherhood that are part of the process whereby a unitary, essentialist, social understanding of women is constructed and perpetuated. Mother is so interwoven with the notion of what it means to be a woman in our culture that it will continue to have a defining impact on individual women's lives, even where that impact is manifested primarily in the extent of resistance to the dominant cultural ideology.

The New Poverty Discourses

Poverty Reform Discourse

Recent proposals for welfare reform further the themes of the Family Support Act of 1988, which is the first major legislation addressing poverty to pass Congress in several decades. It reflected the belief that welfare dependency is a significant problem requiring dramatic reorientation of welfare policy. The primary objective seemed to be the attachment of welfare recipients to the workforce. This was accomplished for the single mother either through mandating her to work (or train for work) and/or by substituting for the state the employed father as the child's primary source of support. The legislation's focus on reinforcing the work ethic and dominant individualistic norms of self-sufficiency through the imposition of "workfare" provisions for mothers of young children was the major emphasis of most commentators. The Jobs Opportunities and Basic Skills Program (JOBS) component of the reform legislation represented one instance in the long history of welfare to promote work and discourage welfare dependency among the poor. Most often the term *workfare* has been reserved for the requirement that recipients work off their benefits, usually by accepting some form of public or community work assignment. The JOBS program was called the "new workfare" in that, while requiring work, it also offered opportunities for education, job training, skill development, job counseling, and placement in the private sector, along with other supportive services such as extended child care and health insurance. The JOBS program, then, was workfare with supportive services. The JOBS program replaced the Work Incentive Program (WIN), which was initiated in 1967.

Jencks and Edin have indicated that the increases in employment workfare programs produced were hardly a solution to the poverty problems of poor, female-headed families if the earnings needed to enable these families to be able to get out of poverty are taken into account. They suggest that mothers of these particular families would on average need jobs that pay in the vicinity of two to three times the minimum wage before they could be reasonably expected to leave welfare and on their own cover their expenses, including child and health care:

The essence of the so-called "welfare trap" is not that welfare warps women's personalities or makes them pathologically dependent, though that may occasionally happen. The essence of the "trap" is that while welfare pays badly, low-wage jobs pay even worse. Most welfare mothers are quite willing to work if they end up with significantly more disposable income as a result. But they are not willing to work if working will leave them as poor as they were when they stayed home. . . . All these calculations lead to one inexorable conclusion. An unskilled single mother cannot expect to support herself and her children in today's labor market either by working or by collecting welfare. If she wants to make ends meet, she must either get help from someone else (usually an absent father, parent, or boyfriend) or she must combine work and welfare. At present, the only way she can combine work and welfare is to collect AFDC [Aid to Families with Dependent Children] and then work without telling the welfare department.   (Jencks and Edin 1990:31)

The work requirement sections of the legislation seemed to provide greater supportive services than previous schemes, and liberals could conclude that it was offered and would operate to do more than merely discourage welfare (Garfinkel 1987; Walsh 1988:32; Abramovitz 1988:24).

The work provisions were only part of the legislative scheme, however. Other provisions of the Family Support Act mandated stricter enforcement of child support orders, including wage-withholding (Family Support Act of 1988, Title I). States were required to meet federal standards for establishing paternity for children born out of wedlock as a means of obtaining child support from absent fathers (Family Support Act of 1988, Title I, Subtitle B). For impoverished two-parent families, the Family Support Act mandated that all states were to adopt the Aid to Families with Dependent Children-Unemployed Parent Program (AFDC-UP), which provided welfare benefits to two-parent families in which the principal wage earner was unemployed (Family Support Act of 1988, Part A).

The significance of these provisions in reinforcing traditional norms of the male-headed family and its responsibility for children was evident in the political rhetoric surrounding the reforms. In addressing the Family Support Act in the Senate, for example, Senator Daniel Patrick Moynihan of New York began his address by commending President Bush for his remarks at the United Nations World Summit for Children. Senator Moynihan stated:

One sentence [of President Bush's remarks] is especially notable. "We want to see the day when every American child is part of a strong and stable family." The importance of this statement is elemental. Unlike the problems of children in much of the world, age-old problems of disease, new problems of ecological disaster, the problems of children in the United States are overwhelmingly associated with the strength and stability of their families. Our problems do not reside in nature, nor yet are they fundamentally economic. Our problems derive from behavior. (136, Cong. Rec. S14416, S14417 [daily ed., October 3, 1990:14416–05])

Having established his basic premise, Moynihan continued:

There is a mountain of scientific evidence showing that when families disintegrate, children often end up with intellectual, physical, and emotional scars that persist for life. . . . We talk about the drug crisis, the education crisis, and the problems of teen pregnancy and juvenile crime. But all these ills trace back predominantly to one source: broken families.   (Ibid.)

Moynihan's rhetoric, which attributes the problems of the poor to their own behavior, tracks the simplistic tendency in current as well as poverty discourses to categorize mothers negatively according to their relationship or connection with men. Single mothers, for the most part, are deemed to present potential social problems for which they alone are responsible. There is an exception to such condemnation for women who became single mothers through the death of their spouse and therefore may be excused their status and considered worthy of sympathy as widows (McLanahan and Garfinkel 1989:94). This view is clearly expressed by Butler and Kondratas:

The typical AFDC parent today is not the "worthy widow" envisaged in the original legislation but a divorced, deserted, or never-married woman. Regardless of extenuating circumstances behind any particular out-of-wedlock birth or the justification for any particular divorce, the fact remains that illegitimacy and divorce have an element of personal choice and responsibility that widowhood does not. . . . Regardless of how difficult it is for individuals to pay for making irresponsible or unfortunate choices, that does not absolve those individuals of dealing with the consequences as best they can, before society is asked to step in to support them and their children. . . . Social assistance has always been based on social norms and expectations. One of the assumptions underlying AFDC was the idea that a mother has an important role to play in the upbringing and socialization of her children. It was the humane intention of the program in 1935 [designed for widows] to enable a mother to take care of her children—in other words, to encourage what was left of a family to stay together. It was, in today's parlance, a "profamily" measure. But now the program finances a subculture whose citizens argue . . . that they want children but not marriage, because "you don't want the commitments" and male figures are not substantially important in the family.   (Butler and Kondratas 1987:138–39)

Increasingly, at least in some discourses over the past several decades, poor women who become single mothers because of divorce are also included within the category of deserving mothers (Weitzman 1985). This classification is permitted by the recent changes in the way we consider marital dissolution, epitomized by the advent of no-fault divorce built upon the popular perception that the failure of a marriage is a joint responsibility. Children, of course, continue to be portrayed as innocent victims—usually of their parents' selfishness and hostility at divorce—but there has been a decline in the insistence that there be a designated villain and victim between the spouses.

The imagery of welfare discourse, however, remains laden with moral and normative judgments centered on stereotypical assumptions about single mothers in the poverty context. The decision to become and/or to remain a single mother, particularly when undertaken by a woman who has never been married, is decisive in the issue of whether one is to be considered a "good" mother. Poor mothers, if they are not single mothers as a result of death or, perhaps, divorce, are "bad" mothers. Their conduct is considered to have "earned" them this designation, and stereotypes about their motivations and behavior abound. Michael Katz reports the comment of an "otherwise sympathetic radio talk show host" who told him: "I don't mind paying to help people in need, but I don't want my tax dollars to pay for the sexual pleasure of adolescents who won't use birth control." Katz concluded the host's "outrage summed up popular stereotypes about the relation among adolescent pregnancy, welfare, and the underclass" (Katz 1989:215).

The characterization of some single mothers as "bad" corresponds to the popular and political classification of the poor as either "deserving" or "undeserving." This classification is often based on the public's perception as to whether the impoverished individual is poor because of personal choices and actions or as a result of forces beyond her control (Katz 1989:185–86). Furthermore, this distinction between deserving and undeserving has concrete material implications attached to its ideological categories in that the way one becomes a single mother quite often dictates the source of public assistance to which one may turn. Widows are typically entitled to more generous social security benefits to aid their single mother families, while single mothers who arrive at their status through divorce or by choosing never to formalize their relationship with their child's father are left to the variability of the child support system or AFDC.

Ironically, Senator Moynihan in arguing for the Family Security Act noted the inequity of financial support for children that has resulted from the difference in services. He pointed out that while survivors insurance benefits had increased by 53 percent, AFDC benefits were down an average of 138 percent—the end result being children who were receiving social security benefits getting over twice the benefits of those relying on AFDC. The Senator questioned this: "[T]hese are identically situated children. They are children living in a single-parent, female-headed household." He continued, "There is no way you can distinguish these children excepting one brutal reality: The majority of the children receiving Survivors Insurance are white, and the majority of the children receiving AFDC are nonwhite." He asked why this situation has come about and answered, "[V]ery simply it came about because the welfare program has become stigmatized as a program for people who did not work in a world where others did." While he recognized this as a stigma, he concluded, "it also reflects a certain reality," and also concluded that, in order to change "the public's unwillingness to fund these programs fully, we must remedy this stigma through work programs" (Moynihan 1988:7631–02). Such distinctions, therefore, go beyond stigma (which in and of itself is significant) to have real material impact on the future and fortunes of a large number of single mothers and their children.

Yet stigma is the conceptual basis for the disparate economic outcomes certain groups of single mothers may experience. The parsimonious treatment of poor women who have chosen to become mothers and not marry, or those whose choices have been limited because of circumstances that themselves grow out of poverty, are justified because they can be considered undeserving poor. Recently, such women in poverty discourses emanating from a wide spectrum of groups have been lumped together with drug addicts, criminals, and other socially defined "degenerates" in the newly coined category of "underclass." The undeserving nature (underclass status) of single mother families in this context is partly established by their lack of relationship to the workforce (either through their own jobs or through attachment to a male breadwinner) and partly by their asserted role as mothers in the perpetuation of poverty. Consider this set of assumptions and conclusions, for example:

> The link between female-headship and welfare dependency in the urban underclass is also well established, leading to legitimate concerns about the intergenerational transfer of poverty. At the root of this concern is

the paucity of employment among welfare mothers and how this affects attitudes of their children toward work.

After citing statistics as to how little welfare mothers work and how long they stay on welfare, the author continues:

One does not require a deep sociological imagination to sense the attitudinal and behavioral consequences of growing up in an impoverished household where there is no activity associated with the world of work and in a household that in turn is spatially embedded in a commercially abandoned locality where pimps, drug pushers, and unemployed street people have replaced working fathers as the predominant socializing agents.					(Kasarda 1989:44)

What seems to unify the category of the underclass is not only that its designated members are perceived to be the chronically poor but that their poverty results from their own failings. Single motherhood is taken as a sign of degeneration on the same level with crime and other social pathology. Single mothers are implicated by their asserted role in the intergenerational transmission of poverty through complicity within a "culture of poverty."[1]

Many commentators assume not only that individual behavior causes poverty but that choosing to make personal changes can solve the problems of this category of the poor. Consider, for example, the analysis of the problems of the underclass and recommendations emanating from the American Enterprise Institute:

Today, for example, significant numbers of American adults are not demonstrating the behaviors expected of free and responsible citizens. Linked to poverty among an important fraction of the poor is a high incidence of dropping out from school, of failure to prepare themselves for future employment, of begetting children out of wedlock, of crime, of drug use, and of other visible disorders. Such persons—whose numbers appear to be growing—are the behaviorally dependent, since their need for help from others springs in significant measure from their own behaviors.

The report continues:

It is not entirely a mystery how many climb from poverty. Some specific behavior empowers them. The probabilities of remaining involuntarily in poverty are remarkably low for those who

- complete high school
- once an adult, get married and stay married (even if not on the first try)

- stay employed, even if at a wage and under conditions below their ultimate aims.

(American Enterprise Institute for Public Policy Research 1987:4–5)

Note that marital status is central to the self-help schemes proposed
for the poor. Further, as the following quotation from William Julius
Wilson indicates, concern with the marital choices of the poor is shared
by liberal commentators. Marriage is viewed from a variety of political
positions as stabilizing and as an appropriate objective to be fostered by
public policy:

> [P]erhaps the most important factor in the rise of black female-headed
> families [is] the extraordinary rise in black male joblessness. . . . [T]he
> decline in the incidence of intact marriages among blacks is associated
> with the declining economic status of black men. . . . Black women
> nationally, especially young black women, are facing a shrinking pool of
> "marriageable" (i.e., employed) black men. This finding supports the
> hypothesis that the sharp rise of black female-headed families is directly
> related to increasing black male joblessness. . . . We conclude, therefore,
> that the problem of joblessness should be a top-priority item in any pub-
> lic policy discussion focusing on enhancing the status of families.
>
> (Wilson 1987:104–5)

Singular Pathology

In poverty discourses such as those set out above, Mother is modified
by her legal relationship, or lack thereof, to a male. Mothers are classified by whether or not they are single, a fact that is positioned as both
central and significant in the discourses. The absence of the formal legal
tie to a male has ideological implications and is far more than just a
descriptive term or classifying category. In addition to providing a basis
for determining who is undeserving in our culture, single motherhood
is often seen as "dangerous" and even "deadly" not only to those who
are single mothers and their children but to society as a whole.

Illustrative of the typical ways in which the threat of single motherhood is discussed are the comments of the then Chancellor of the University of Wisconsin at Madison (now Secretary of Health and Human
Services): Donna Shalala is reported to have stated that unwed teen
pregnancy is "an issue that threatens the future of Milwaukee and is as
dangerous and crippling to young lives as polio" (*Milwaukee Sentinel*
1990:1). Describing the enormity of the problem as "frightening," Shalala warns that "the stakes are very high. The stakes are our future, not
only in Milwaukee, but our future as a state."

Joanne Jacobs, a columnist for the San Jose, California, *Mercury News*, asserted in a column entitled "Illegitimacy Biggest Killer of Our Babies" that the leading killer of young children in America is not drugs, cancer, or accidents but illegitimacy (*Wisconsin State Journal* 1990:11A). This article is offensive beyond the author's use of the antiquated term *illegitimate*, a term that suggests the marital status of the child's mother has implications for the quality of the child. Jacobs was reporting the results of a study by Nicholas Eberstadt of Harvard University's Center of Population Studies and the American Enterprise Institute. In so doing, she popularized and publicized the rather amazing assertion that the high death rate for "illegitimate" children was not related to the mother's age, nor to her race or education or income, but was due to "the lack of care that leads to illegitimacy [which] also leads to poor care for children."

Jacobs dutifully lists, although she ultimately disagrees with, Eberstadt's conclusions that this lack of care warrants such drastic action as the denial of welfare benefits to mothers who "deliberately give birth to and raise a fatherless child." She also rejects his suggestion to alter the law "to grant divorce only for cause [such as] adultery, abuse, or desertion—and to deny women custody of their children," thereby removing the "incentives" to divorce provided by easy no-fault divorce combined with maternal custody and mandatory child support payments. Jacobs, however, concludes the column with her own normative observation that "we've become way too accepting of an 'alternative lifestyle' in which fathers are dispensable. It's bad for kids" (*Wisconsin State Journal* 1990:11A).

These popular characterizations of single motherhood are crude echoes of single-mother images prevalent in political, legal, and professional discourses that speculate about the impact of single motherhood on the institution of the family in the first instance and the fate of society in the long run. Such labels indicate the nature and degree of harm and threat as we speak of the "broken family," the "disintegration" of the family, the "crisis" in the family, the "unstable" family, the "decline" of the family, and—perhaps inevitably from some perspectives—the "death" of the family. Underlying such labels is the specter of single motherhood—statistically on the upswing—pathological and diseaselike, contaminating society, contributing to its destruction and degeneration (Moynihan 1990:14416–05). It is little wonder that with this perspective so pervasive many reformers urge that efforts must be made to curb the practice of single motherhood. Even liberal commentators,

such as Irwin Garfinkel of the Institute for Poverty Research, are mind-
ful of the role of deterrents and incentives in supporting welfare
reforms. Garfinkel states: "The problem with providing more aid to
single-parent families is that doing so creates incentives for the formation and preservation of single-parent families." Garfinkel, unlike some
conservative commentators, recognizes that single-parent families may
not be all bad:

> Of course, it is possible that society is better off—or at least no worse
> off—as a result of whatever additional single-parent families are created
> by more favorable treatment of those groups. Not all marriages are made
> in heaven. Some men beat their wives and children. . . . In some of these
> cases, all the parties may be better off separate rather than together.

Nonetheless, he concludes: "Despite the fact that increases in single
parenthood may not be socially pernicious, prudence would suggest
that in the face of ignorance we should seek to minimize incentives for
single parenthood" (Garfinkel 1982:12).

Single motherhood has been designated as the source and origin of
other social phenomena such as crime and poverty. Indeed, in the public's mind, in spite of the overwhelming evidence to the contrary (Katz
1989:216–17),[2] the face of poverty has increasingly become that of a
single mother, particularly an African-American single mother. Single
motherhood both represents the cause and is characterized as the result
of the disintegration of the family and society; it is a demographic category embedded with political and moral significance and as such is
viewed as having both explanatory and predictive powers. This is so not
only in popular discourse (Passell 1989) but also in more "reflective"
areas of discourse such as the social sciences, policy, and law.

Why has this casting of single motherhood, as pathological, as a social
disease, as one of the core explanations of poverty, been so readily
accepted and perpetuated in a variety of contexts and by people who
occupy a range of political viewpoints? Certainly it must seem evident to
liberals that this stereotyping may be viewed as both misogynistic and
racist. In attempting to answer this question, I have reached certain conclusions about the role of ideology in constructing and perpetuating the
single mother images contained in poverty discourses. The pathological
representation of single motherhood is inextricably linked to the
medium of patriarchal ideology—a constellation of symbols and beliefs
about the "natural" or "normal" family, which is widely shared in our
culture and through which all motherhood discourses are processed.

Ideology and Motherhood

If, as I do, one defines ideology as the rationalizing set of principles and concepts that link discourses to power, a close examination of discourse will reveal implicit aspects of an underlying ideology. Discourses are stylized appeals to ideology, and therefore ideology is what defines and confines the contours of the discourses. Poverty discourse discloses that patriarchy is the dominant family ideology that fixes the core concepts and images about motherhood and also facilitates, and even mandates, the crossover effect of such discourses. In this regard, the discourses concerning poverty and single motherhood are consistent with other stereotypes and myths fashioned under the influence of patriarchal ideology in which the dominant family form is that of a male-headed reproductive unit with defined gender role divisions. While it is true that this traditional image has undergone some revisions in light of the modern concern with gender equity and equality, the focus is still on the sexual affiliation between man and woman as the paradigmatic intimate associational bond. Patriarchal ideology might have had to adapt to twentieth-century shifts in expressions of sexuality and redefinitions of gender roles, but the fundamental composition and nature of the core images remain constant.

Motherhood has always been, and continues to be, a colonized concept—an event physically practiced and experienced by women but occupied, defined, and given content and value by the core concepts of patriarchal ideology. The existence of single motherhood, particularly when it represents a deliberate choice in light of the availability of birth control and abortion, can be viewed as a practice of resistance to patriarchal ideology. As such, single motherhood as an expanding practice threatens the hold of the dominant ideology.

Patriarchy as Ideology

In discussing patriarchy as ideology, I want to make it very clear that I view the term as constituted by a set of concepts and symbols that are much more complex and convoluted than the simplistic notion (a parody of patriarchy) that men are the formal holders of power within the family and society. Gerda Lerner has defined patriarchy as the "manifestation and institutionalization of male dominance over women and children in the family and the extension of male dominance over women in society in general" (Lerner 1986:239). The trouble I have with that definition is in its emphasis on and attention to notions of "manifestation" and "institutionalization" of dominance. Such a focus presupposes and mandates that societal structures such as the family become the focal point for critical assessment. This result would be unfortunate because there is a danger that in so directing inquiry, the beliefs that structural changes are sufficient and structural solutions are all that are necessary will be fostered. It seems to me to be essential to go beyond mere critique of structure, to a consideration of the power of dominant ideology, a much more elusive and intransigent social and cultural product than any mere structure. It is power of ideology that explains why individuals can resist or reject structure (by refusing to participate in a nuclear family, for example) but still find themselves defined and ultimately controlled by the ideology underlying the institution.

My preoccupation with ideology leads me to a much more pessimistic assessment of the possibility for social transformation than those generated by social critics who focus on structures. Dominant ideologies are subtly and conclusively expressed in the very creation of social norms and conventions. They define the contours of culture and of society and its institutions. A dominant ideology is transmitted through everyday language symbols and images as well as through the operations of formal institutions and structures of power.

Patriarchy is such a dominant ideology. It has as one of its organizing premises the belief that the primary affiliation or connection in society is the sexual bond. In our culture, consistent with the demands of the ideology, it is this affiliation that is privileged as the paradigmatic manifestation of connection. In popular culture, sexual expression, particularly heterosexual expression, is portrayed as the quintessential indication of maturity, of completeness, and of success and power. Traditionally, this is realized through marriage. Deviance from this paradigm has brought with it social and occasionally legal sanctions, as well as the potential for condemnation in the discourses of psychology, social work, and medicine. In recent years the legalistic and heterosexual aspects of the paradigm have been challenged with demands to include other forms of sexual intimacy as equally privileged with formal marriage. Alternative family legislation has been proposed that would recognize sexual affiliations other than heterosexual formal marriage. I consider these reforms to be complicit with the patriarchal core because in seeking to duplicate the privileging based on heterosexual affiliation, same-sex relationships merely affirm the centrality of sexuality to the fundamental ordering of society and nature of intimacy. The nexus or affiliating circumstances of these "alternatives" is still the sexual connection.

The institution of single motherhood is therefore considered deviant and threatening simply because it is a rejection of the primacy of the sexual connection as the core organizing familial concept and the privacy basis for social organization. The very label "single mother" separates some practices of motherhood from the institution of Mother by reference to the mother's marital status. Mother as constructed and defined in this discourse is modified by her relationship (formal and legal) to father. By contrast, the institution when practiced in its "normal" form is not so modified. No one speaks of a "married mother"—the primary connection of husband and wife is assumed in the unadorned designation of mother. It is only the deviant form of motherhood that needs qualification. It is important to note that in this process of distinguishing the deviant variation from the norm of motherhood a complementary cluster of stereotypical designated family roles are involved that together form the contemporary images of the "ideal" family.

The Role and Function of Ideology

As a specific matter thus far, I have been asserting a relationship between ideology and discourses about motherhood. As a methodological point I am assuming that the study of rhetoric about motherhood reveals something about the existence and content of dominant ideology that in turn reveals something about the location of power within society. In defining these relationships, I am pursuing the suggestion made by Terry Eagleton in his book *Literary Theory* that "most rhetoric shapes our reality in ways that ensure the continuation of the existing systems of power" (Eagleton 1983:210). Eagleton goes so far as to assert that ideology can be taken to indicate no more than the connective link or nexus between discourse and power (Eagleton 1983:73).

My interpretation and application of Eagleton's conception of ideology begin with an understanding of ideology as a system constituted by a more-or-less complementary collection of symbols, beliefs, and assumptions that, in combination, rationalize and give meaning to discourses in the context of power. Ideology in this regard can be considered a selection and sorting mechanism in that it provides coherence, structure, and form to social and political discourses. This functional definition of ideology as having systemic implications has theoretical as well as practical implications. First, on a practical level, it means that ideology will be much more likely to function as a conservative force. It will serve to "tame" or "domesticate" discourses by exerting a confining pressure on their initial development, ultimately channeling even the most radical ideas into set categories approved by the existing conceptual system. Within this perception of ideology, meaningful conflict and competition are confined to the level of discourse. To be labeled "dominant"—providing the recognized rhetorical links between power and discourse—an ideology may not be too explicitly contested. A dominant ideology, therefore, is relatively stable although it may alter over time, making some adaptation in response to the tensions generated by too violent or prolonged demands from discourses upon power.

In addition, if ideology is posited as a system of symbols and beliefs, it must be experienced as both complex and dynamic; this means that it will seldom be totally revealed in the context of any specific political debate or contest of discourses. It will also not be easily expressed abstractly, outside the context of a specific set of assumptions. As a dynamic system, ideology represents a process that is not facilely reduced to a finite set of clearly stated principles operational outside of any specific application. A cluster of social and cultural symbols and beliefs, ideology is referenced in seemingly disassociated discourses—it can be imagined as a series of synapses that together form possible permeations for various appeals (discourses) to institutions of formal power in our society. The definitive shape and content of an ideology are only partially revealed in its symbols: fragmented and shadowed traces discernible within discourses, from their initial formulation to their ultimate translation and transformation within institutions of power.

The assertions I have made have implications in regard to the methodology I have adopted in examining discourses about motherhood. The task is to uncover and understand the appeal to ideological components—the link to power. Ideology, as I understand it, is a shared cultural construct. Its core images define and confine the discourses produced by both the proponent of the status quo and its critic. For example, I find in examining discourses about motherhood that the underlying symbols and values are more uniformly shared than the differences in discourses would superficially indicate. Conflicts developed and located in these discourses concern the political implications or meanings of symbols and beliefs that comprise the ideology but do not dispute its existence or power. Oppositional discourses reference the shared aspects of the ideology in what are attempts to compel and convince.

An examination of motherhood in terms of its changing manifestations reveals that patriarchy as an ideology is elastic. It has adapted to ostensibly challenging discourses, absorbing seemingly significant challenges while ensuring the relatively undisturbed continuation of power distributions within the family structure. Such adaptation or modification of patriarchy has been necessitated by the "crisis" of the rising divorce rate in the twentieth century. Traditional intact family formation has been disrupted, but joint custody and the ideal of shared parenting have ensured continued male control over children and, through them, over their mothers even as divorce has become available virtually on demand (Fineman 1991a).

In response to the increasing number of women choosing to become single mothers (also designated as a "crisis") mandatory paternity laws were fashioned. This occurred first in the context of AFDC single mothers, but represents an expanding practice. In Wisconsin, for example, under a rhetorical bludgeon that dictates that every child has a "right" to a father (at least to a father's name on a birth certificate), legislation has been passed that requires all single mothers to participate in paternity proceedings. These proceedings are mandated even if the state is not likely to ever be asked to become a source of economic support for the child. The core tenets of the ideology of patriarchy—that "natural" families have two parents and that the patriarchical position is one of financial primacy and family control—are thus ensured. The major architect of this legislation has stated:

> We have now in Wisconsin a law that I authored that will become the model for the nation regarding paternity. It has as its foundation that every child born in Wisconsin has a legal right to a father. Children without legal fathers have started down a slippery slope that leads to poverty. Our new paternity law is a radical departure in that the interests of the child will become equal if not paramount to the interests of the natural parents. The law seeks to ensure that at the time of birth the state and the mother will pursue, for non-marital births, the establishment of paternity and the subsequent collection of support.
>
> But the philosophy of the law is not punitive. Rather, it assumes that families are natural and that it is not appropriate to have laws that have as their result that in one out of every two births outside of marriage the child will have no legal father—paternity will never be established.
>
> Under our new law the birth certificate will be the vehicle to establish paternity early on. A presumption of paternity will be created with the filing of a statement. It will go with the birth certificate in most cases when the baby leaves the hospital. It will provide the basis for courts to order child support. But most important, it will give that child a legal father.
>
> Both our child support law and our new paternity law are designed to ensure parental responsibility and to help families form and most importantly give new rights to children.   (Loftus 1988:427–28)

The legislator does not mention that the mother's cooperation, which will necessitate her revealing details of her sexual and personal life, will be compelled under the potential sanction of incarceration by use of the contempt power. Nor does he note that the "legal" father's paternal involvement with the child will not be mandated by the court beyond (perhaps) payment of child support. Also absent is any mention of the fact that a legal father can exercise legal rights, becoming an unwanted, perhaps abusive, presence in the mother and child's life merely because it was he who fathered the child.

Changes in behavior precipitated by alterations in divorce rules and expanding economic security for women that allow them to choose to become single mothers have required the remodeling of patriarchy. The remodeling has not substantially altered, let alone led to the rejection of, the core images of the ideology, however. The foundation remains stable. We may now be forced grudgingly to accept single mother households as an unfortunate by-product of the social and economic dislocations that characterize the latter part of this century, but they are seldom treated as an "acceptable," let alone a "desirable" family form. In expressions of popular culture as well as in public policy, single motherhood, at best, may be perceived as requiring, out of necessity, an uneasy accommodation with the dominant ideology. The societal aspiration, however, remains to complete the "family" by the addition of a man.

In the context of the treatment of single mothers in poverty discourses, the focus on family form obscures the economic deprivations that make it difficult for single women to raise their children. Rather than addressing their needs as single mothers, reforms take the form of pushing them into a model of family life increasingly discredited, even in the middle class from which it arose. The dominance of family imagery contained in the ideology of patriarchy has required rejection of economic subsidies that would truly support single mother families. Their deviation must be punished and deterred, their practice of resistance curtailed.

NOTES

This chapter is a summary of arguments appearing in chapter 5 of Martha Albertson Fineman, *The Neutered Mother: The Sexual Family and Other Twentieth-Century Tragedies* (1995).

1. Maxine Baca Zinn asserts that there are two models that describe the urban underclass: cultural and structural. The cultural model first gained recognition with the "culture of poverty" theory popularized by Daniel Patrick Moynihan in the late 1960s. Zinn concludes that the cultural model blames welfare for the disintegration of the family, for providing disincentives to work, and for encouraging a lifestyle where women have children out of wedlock and depend on the system to support the children, thus allowing men to avoid financial responsibility for children (Zinn 1989:856).

2. The statistics are summarized by Katz:

Most poor people in America do not live in families headed by adolescent mothers or even by women. In 1980, 37 percent of poor people lived in female-headed families. Poverty is not synonymous with single parents. Nor does adolescent pregnancy consume a large share of the social welfare budget or gross national product. In 1980, the money spent on AFDC represented only about 4 percent of all the costs of major public assistance and social insurance programs for the elderly, totally disabled, and all others, and only a fraction of AFDC payments go to adolescent mothers. In 1984, all means-tested cash transfer payments by federal, state, and local governments used 0.8 percent of GNP or 2 percent of the share of GNP spent by governments.

Consider, next, the question of birth rates. Among blacks, adolescent birth rates have fallen; among whites they have increased. Between 1970 and 1980, the birth rate of unmarried black women dropped 13 percent, in contrast to a 27 percent increase among unmarried white women. Nonetheless, black marital fertility fell even faster (38 percent), which means that the fraction of births occurring to unmarried women increased. Among just 15- to 19-year-old black women, the nonmarital fertility rate (births per 1,000 women) rose from 76.5 in 1960 to a peak of 90.8 in 1970 and has declined since then; by 1980 it had dropped to 83.0. Among whites, the rate, always lower than blacks', has risen steadily from 6.6 in 1960 to 10.9 in 1970 and 16.0 in 1980. In other words, between 1970 and 1980, the fertility of unmarried black 15- to 19-year-old women dropped almost 10 percent, while the rate for unmarried white women of the same age increased by 48 percent. Although the black rate remained more than five times as great as the white, adolescent pregnancy is not an issue just for blacks.

See also Edelman 1987:68–74.

10 | Racism and Patriarchy in the Meaning of Motherhood

DOROTHY E. ROBERTS

This essay starts with the presumption that women experience gender in different ways. For example, Black women experience various forms of oppression simultaneously, as a complex interaction of their race, gender, and class that is more than the sum of its parts. This is a critical observation that is transforming feminist thought. Mainstream feminist legal thought has typically focused on gender as the primary locus of oppression. This focus has forced women of color to fragment their experience in a way that does not reflect the reality of their lives. The racial critique of gender essentialism in feminist theory has inspired the ongoing reconstruction of a feminist jurisprudence that includes the historical, economic, and social diversity of women's experiences (Crenshaw 1989:152–60; Harris 1990; Kline 1989; Spelman 1988). The recognition of women's differences, however, does not negate the fundamental premise of feminism that women are oppressed "as women." It is still, therefore, useful to make patriarchy a focus of feminist inquiry and opposition. What I wish to examine in this essay is the relationship between racism and patriarchy.

Racism and patriarchy are not two separate institutions that intersect only in the lives of Black women. They are two interrelated, mutually supporting systems of domination, and their relationship is essential to understanding the subordination of all women. Racism makes the experience of sexism different for Black women and white women. But it is not enough to note that Black women suffer from both racism and sexism, although this is true. Racism is patriarchal. Patriarchy is racist.

We will not destroy one institution without destroying the other. I believe it is the recognition of that connection—along with the recognition of difference among women—that is truly revolutionary.

This essay explores how racism and patriarchy interact in the social construction of motherhood. Feminist thinking has established that motherhood is a role through which women often experience gender subordination. My aim is to show how any feminist account of motherhood as gender oppression must also include an account of race oppression.

Adrienne Rich distinguishes between the "experience of motherhood"—the relationship between a woman and her children—and "motherhood as enforced identity and political institution" (Rich 1979:196). This is a particularly useful distinction, as it begins with a conception of "motherhood" as contested and not essentialized. An unwed Black teenager, for example, may experience motherhood as a rare source of self-affirmation, while society deems her motherhood to be illegitimate and deviant. She may experience caring for her child as a determined struggle against harsh circumstances, while society sees in her mothering the pathological perpetuation of poverty. Some women may experience mothering as debilitating and intrusive, even though patriarchal ideology defines it as woman's instinctive vocation. Some women may experience fulfillment and happiness in mothering, even though some feminist theory calls it oppressive.

There are joys and sorrows that most mothers share: the pleasure of nursing her baby; the exhaustion from chasing after her toddler; the gratification of watching her child achieve whatever goal; the terror of unwanted pregnancy; the despair of surrendering yet another dream in order to care for her child. There are also experiences mothers do not share, in part because of race. Most white mothers do not know the pain of raising Black children in a racist society. It is impossible to explain the depth of sorrow felt at the moment a mother realizes she has birthed her precious brown baby into a society that regards her child as just another unwanted Black charge. Black mothers must perform the incredible task of guarding their children's identity against innumerable messages that brand them as less than human.[1]

There are features of motherhood as a political institution that subordinate women because we are women: our status as childbearer determines our identity; we are assigned the enormous responsibility of childrearing; our work is unpaid and degraded; and, to the extent our role as mother is valued, it is only when it "is attached to a legal father" (Rich 1979:196–97). Adrienne Rich argues that motherhood in its present form denies women their potential as full human beings. She writes:

> Institutionalized motherhood demands of women maternal "instinct" rather than intelligence, selflessness rather than self-realization, relation to others rather than the creation of self. Motherhood is "sacred" so long as its offspring are "legitimate"—that is, as long as the child bears the name of a father who legally controls the mother.   (Rich 1976:42)

Society's construction of mother, its image of what constitutes a good mother and a bad mother, facilitates male control of all women. Women who fail to meet the ideal of motherhood (unwed mothers, unfit mothers, and women who do not become mothers) are stigmatized for violating the dominant norm and are considered deviant or criminals. Martha Fineman calls motherhood "a colonized [concept]— an event physically practiced and experienced by women but occupied, defined, and given content and value by the core concepts of patriarchal ideology" (Fineman, this volume:217).

This is patriarchy's meaning of motherhood, one designed to serve the interests of men. The meaning of motherhood in America, however, is shaped on the basis of race as well as gender. Patriarchy does not treat Black and white motherhood identically. In America, the image of the Black mother has always diverged from, and often contradicted, the image of the white mother.

There are several areas to be examined in the study of racism and patriarchy in the meaning of motherhood. This essay is directed to a diverse community of feminist thinkers. It concerns the construction of motherhood by those in power. The essay also raises issues for discussion within the Black community, issues that Black feminist scholars are continuing to address, including: the meaning of motherhood within communities of color (Austin 1989:553); sexism by Black men (Crenshaw 1989:160–66; hooks 1981:87–117); and the need for Black women to confront our own differences and to develop solidarity among ourselves. Audre Lorde writes about Black women's need for one another: "There are two very different struggles involved here. One is the war against racism in white people, and the other is the need for Black women to confront and wade through the racist constructs underlying our deprivation of each other. And these battles are not at all the same" (Lorde 1984:164). Black mothers' self-definition is a critical aspect of the meaning of motherhood, as well, an aspect that influences both the dominant society's construction and the feminist reconstruction of mother (Collins 1990:91–113).

In this essay I explore the social meaning of motherhood during various periods of American history, from slavery to contemporary poverty discourse. While a complete historical analysis is beyond its scope, my review indicates that the social definition of mother changes along with other social developments. The systems of patriarchy and racism interact in different ways throughout history to produce diverse constructions of motherhood. The dynamic quality of subordination and resistance suggests that my inquiry will not produce a grand theory of the relationship between patriarchy and racism. Rather, my inquiry seeks a better understanding of how racism and patriarchy shape the meaning of motherhood in particular contexts, the ways in which women resist those meanings, and the implications for future action.

Slavery: The Foundation of Racist Patriarchy in America

The intimate intertwining of race and gender in the very structure of slavery makes it practically impossible to speak of one without the other. The social order established by white slaveowners was founded on two inseparable ingredients: the dehumanization of Africans on the basis of race, and the control of women's sexuality and reproduction. The American legal order is rooted in this horrible combination of race and gender oppression. America's first laws concerned the status of children born to slave mothers and fathered by white men: a 1662 Virginia statute made these children slaves (Marcus 1988–89:217–18; Higginbotham 1978:252).

The experiences of Black women during slavery provide the most brutal examples of the denial of autonomy over reproduction. Female slaves were commercially valuable to their masters not only for their labor but also for their capacity to produce more slaves. White masters, therefore, could increase their wealth by controlling their slaves' reproductive capacity—by rewarding pregnancy; punishing slave women who did not bear children; forcing them to breed; and raping them (Jones 1985:34–35; Sterling 1984:24–26). Racism created for white slaveowners the possibility of unrestrained reproductive control. As Henry Louis Gates, Jr., writes about the autobiography of a slave named Harriet A. Jacobs, she "charts in vivid detail precisely how the shape of her life and the choices she makes are defined by her reduction to a sexual object, an object to be raped, bred, or abused" (Gates

1987:12). The radical feminist model of motherhood, which is characterized by the patriarchal male's use of woman's body for reproduction,
is epitomized in slavery (Allen 1984:317). Slavery allowed the perfec-
tion of patriarchal motherhood. Patriarchy devised the most dehuman-
izing form of slavery.

Compulsory childbirth was a critical element of the oppression of
both Black and white women of the time. A *racist* patriarchy required
that both Black and white women bear children, although these women
served different and complementary functions. Black women produced
children who were legally Black to replenish the master's supply of
slaves (A. Davis 1983:7). White women produced white children to
continue the master's legacy. The racial purity of white women's children was guaranteed by a violently enforced taboo against sexual relations between white women and Black men and by antimiscegenation
laws that punished interracial marriages (Collins 1990:50). There was
a critical difference in the white patriarch's relationship to these two
classes of women. White men accorded some degree of respect and protection to white women, who were their wives, mothers, daughters, and
sisters. White patriarchs, however, owed nothing to their female slaves,
who were denied even the status of "woman" (Fox-Genovese 1988:293;
Omolade 1987:242–43). Black mothers reproduced for white patriarchy, but gained nothing from it.

Paradoxically, the role of Black slave women—who were forced to
serve white patriarchy—often contradicted the fundamental structure of patriarchy. First, the sexual relationship between female slaves
and their white masters impugned the value that white women held
under patriarchy as wives and mothers. For example, some Southern
white women cited in their divorce actions their husbands' "affection" for slave women as the cause for the dissolution of the marriage
(Clinton 1985:29–30). Some denounced slavery because of their
anger and humiliation at their husbands' sexual exploitation of Black
women (hooks 1981:28). Second, giving children born of the union
between white masters and Black women the status of slaves violated
a central tenet of patriarchy: that the status of the child follow the
male line. The slave's *mother* determined her child's identity as slave.
Thus, Frederick Douglass saw no hope for freedom in a biological tie
to his master:

> The whisper that my master was my father, may or may not be true; and,
> true or false, it is of little consequence to my purpose whilst the fact
> remains in all its glaring odiousness, that slaveholders have ordained,

and by law established, that the children of slave women shall in all cases
follow the condition of their mothers.   (Douglass 1982:49)

Maintaining racial hierarchy required that the patriarchal bloodline be
broken, that white men deny their own sons entitlement to patriarchal
power.

The Value of Motherhood

Society exerts structural and ideological pressures upon women to
become mothers. In this way, motherhood under patriarchy is virtually
compulsory. As Fineman has argued, however, only certain kinds of
motherhood are valued (Fineman, this volume). Nevertheless, the performance of an idealized conception of motherhood is women's major
social role. All women are socially defined as mothers or potential mothers. No woman achieves her full position in society until she gives birth
to a child. Pronatalism is so deeply imbedded in our consciences that
even feminist reproductive freedom discourse usually centers on the tim-
ing of births and the social arrangements surrounding motherhood; it
does not question the assumption that all women will eventually be
mothers (Gimenez 1984:290). Historically, the sanctity of motherhood
not only encouraged women to become mothers, it also relieved some of
the pain women experienced from their exploitation under patriarchy
(Gimenez 1984:304). Women's labor in the home has been compensated by the ideological rewards of motherhood, rather than economic
remuneration or the opportunity for self-determination. Thus the voluntary motherhood advocates in the nineteenth century opposed birth
control partly because they realized that motherhood was the only
source of dignity for women of their time (Gordon 1992:140).

Compulsory motherhood under patriarchy is complicated, however,
by racism. Contemporary society views childbearing by white women as
desirable.[2] Procreation by Black mothers, on the other hand, is devalued
and discouraged (Austin 1989:549–58; D. Roberts 1991:1436–50).
The devaluation of Black motherhood is a way of undermining Black
humanity. The value society places on individuals determines whether it
sees them as entitled to perpetuate themselves in their children. Denying a woman the right to bear children deprives her of a basic part of her
humanity. Patriarchy values white women primarily for their procreative
capacity, but it denies to Black women even this modicum of value.
Black women are deemed not even worthy of the dignity of childbearing. Discouraging Black procreation is also a means of subordinating the

entire race; under patriarchy, it is accomplished through the regulation of Black women's fertility.

A popular mythology about Black women, rooted in slavery, portrays them as less deserving of motherhood (D. Roberts 1991:1436–50). One of the most prevalent images of slave women was as the character of Jezebel, a woman governed by her sexual desires (D. White 1985:28–29). The ideological construct of the licentious Jezebel legitimated white men's sexual abuse of Black women and defined Black women as the opposite of the ideal mother. Jezebel contradicted the prevailing image of the True Woman, who was virtuous, pure, and white. The myth of the sexually loose, impure Black woman was deliberately and systematically perpetuated after slavery ended and persists in American culture today (Omolade 1989:16).

If the "bad" Black Jezebel represented the opposite of ideal motherhood, the asexual and maternal Black Mammy was the embodiment of the patriarchal ideal (Austin 1989:570; hooks 1981:84–85). Mammy was both the perfect mother and the perfect slave: whites saw her as a "passive nurturer, a mother figure who gave all without expectation of return, who not only acknowledged her inferiority to whites but who loved them" (hooks 1981:85). It is important to recognize, however, that Mammy did not reflect any virtue in Black motherhood. The ideology of Mammy placed no value in Black women as the mothers of their own children. Rather, patriarchy "claimed for the white family the ultimate devotion of black women, who reared the children of others as if they were their own" (Fox-Genovese 1988:292). Because of racism, Black mothers could not be moral authorities as white mothers were in relation to their children. Mammy, while she cared for the master's children, remained under the moral supervision of her white mistress (Ferguson 1984:171).

This ideological devaluation of Black motherhood has been manifested in many ways throughout American history. During slavery, Black women were systematically denied the rights of motherhood, including any legal claim to their children (A. Allen 1990:140, n. 9). Slave masters owned both Black women and their children. Slaveowners alienated slave women from their children through the sale of either mother or child to other slaveowners and through the control of childrearing. In *Beloved*, Tony Morrison recounts a slave mother's experience of separation from her loved ones:

> Anybody Baby Suggs knew, let alone loved, who hadn't run off or been hanged, got rented out, loaned out, bought up, brought back, stored up, mortgaged, won, stolen or seized. . . . What she called the nastiness of

life was the shock she received upon learning that nobody stopped playing checkers just because the pieces included her children. Halle she was
able to keep the longest. Twenty years. A lifetime. Given to her, no
doubt, to make up for *hearing* that her two girls, neither of whom had
their adult teeth, were sold and gone and she had not been able to wave
goodbye.   (Morrison 1987:23)

Patriarchy denied to Black mothers the authority, the joy, and the gratification of mothering that it allowed white mothers. Once again, patriarchy was perfected in the treatment of slave women.

A contemporary example of the way in which society devalues Black
motherhood is the welfare system's disproportionate denial of Black
mothers' parental rights (Gray and Nybell 1990:513). Malcolm X
called foster care a system of legalized slavery (Little 1965:21–22). He
described the state's disruption of his own family in terms that mirror
white slavemasters' control of slave families:

> Soon the state people were making plans to take over all of my mother's
> children. . . . A Judge . . . in Lansing had authority over me and all of my
> brothers and sisters. We were "state children," court wards; he had the
> full say-so over us. A white man in charge of a black man's children!
> Nothing but legal, modern slavery—however kindly intentioned. . . . I
> truly believe that if ever a state social agency destroyed a family, it
> destroyed ours.   (Little 1965:21–22)

The state intervenes more often in Black homes in part because Black
mothers are more likely to be supervised by social workers, because child
welfare workers apply culturally biased standards to Black families, and
because the state is more willing to intrude upon the autonomy of Black
mothers (Stack 1983–84:541). Government bureaucrats often mistake
Black childrearing patterns as neglect when they diverge from the norm
of the nuclear family (R. Hill 1977; Stack 1974:62–107).

One of the most extreme forms of devaluation of Black motherhood
is the coerced sterilization of Black women (Davis 1983:215–21). The
disproportionate sterilization of Black women enforces society's determination that we do not deserve to be mothers. Black women have
experienced sterilization abuse in the form of blatant coercion, trickery,
and subtle influences on their decision to be sterilized (Petchesky
1979:32). The procedure is performed by individual doctors who
encourage Black women to be sterilized because they view Black
women's family sizes as excessive and believe we are incapable of using
contraceptives (D. Roberts 1991:1443). It is also accomplished through

government policies that penalize women on welfare for having babies, but make sterilization the only publicly funded birth control method readily available to them (D. Roberts 1991:1443–44).

Currently, the image of the undeserving Black mother legitimizes the prosecution of poor Black women who use drugs during pregnancy. Although prenatal substance abuse cuts across racial and socioeconomic lines, the vast majority of women charged with such crimes are poor and Black (D. Roberts 1991:1432–36). These women are more likely to be detected and reported to government agencies, in part because of the racist attitudes of health care professionals (D. Roberts 1991:1432–34). On a deeper level, it is their failure to meet society's image of the ideal mother that makes their prosecution acceptable. The state does not punish poor crack addicts simply because they may harm their unborn children. Rather, the state punishes them for having babies because it deems them unworthy of procreating (D. Roberts 1991:1472).

Angela Harris uses the example of beauty to demonstrate the qualitative difference between white and Black women's failure to meet patriarchal standards (Harris 1990:596–98). She observes that Black women's frustration at being unable to look like the "All-American" woman is not simply a more intense form of white women's frustration. This is because beauty is constructed according to race, as well as gender (hooks 1991:4). Thus, the despair felt by Pecola Breedlove, the character in Toni Morrison's *The Bluest Eye* who spends her childhood praying for blue eyes, is something other than the disappointment felt by a little white girl who despises her features (Morrison 1970). Pecola Breedlove despairs "not because she's even further away from the ideal of beauty than white women are, but because Beauty [sic] *itself* is white, and she is not and can never be, despite the pair of blue eyes she eventually believes she has" (Harris 1990:597).

Similarly, Black women can never attain the ideal image of motherhood, no matter how much we conform to middle-class convention, because ideal motherhood is white. The maternal standards created to confine women are not sex-based norms that Black women happen to fail. They are created out of raced, as well as gendered, components.

Motherhood and Domesticity

During the nineteenth century, the ideology of separate spheres for men and women reinforced women's devotion to motherhood within the orbit of patriarchy. Under this construct, the husband sustained the family economically and represented the family in the public sphere; the wife cared for the private realm of the home (Olsen 1983:1498–1501). The separate spheres ideology gave women a place, role, and importance in the home, while preserving male dominance over women. "The cult of domesticity" legitimized the confinement of women to the private sphere by defining women as naturally suited for motherhood and naturally unfit for public life. Justice Bradley expressed this view of women in his notorious concurring opinion in *Bradwell v. Illinois*, 83 U.S. 130 (1872), which upheld the exclusion of women from legal practice:

> The natural and proper timidity and delicacy which belongs to the female sex evidently unfits it for many of the occupations of civil life. The constitution of the family organization, which is founded in the divine ordinance, as well as in the nature of things, indicates the domestic sphere as that which properly belongs to the domain and functions of womanhood. . . . The paramount destiny and mission of woman [sic] is to fulfil [sic] the noble and benign offices of wife and mother. This is the law of the Creator.   (141–42)

The gendered division of labor continues to be an aspect of women's subordination. The American wage labor system is structured as if workers have no child care responsibilities (Frug 1979:56–61). This assumption systematically disadvantages women, because they are assigned the task of childrearing. Men have the privilege of performing as ideal workers (i.e., workers with no child care responsibilities) and consequently earn more money (Mossman, this volume:303; J. Williams 1989:823). Although most mothers now engage in wage labor, typically they must limit their work commitments to accommodate their child care duties. According to Joan Williams, this gendered system results in the economic marginalization of women workers who are mothers because, by virtue of their mothering, they fail to perform as ideal workers. Often this "failure" is what makes it possible for their husbands to perform that role, while mothers ensure that their children receive high-quality care (J. Williams 1989:823–24).

Black women have historically defied the norm that defines motherhood in opposition to wage labor. The separate spheres ideology dissolved within slavery. While Victorian roles required white women to be nurturing mothers, housekeepers, and companions to their husbands, the slave women's role required strenuous labor (White 1985:27–29). Slave women's lives of hard physical labor shattered the myth that women were weaker than men and unfit for the public sphere. Thus, in 1851 Sojourner Truth could present to a women's rights convention in Akron, Ohio, a unique denunciation of male justifications for the disenfranchisement of women. Unlike most of the white women's rights advocates, she could point to her personal experience of field labor as proof that women could perform the same work as men:

> Dat man ober dar say dat women needs to be helped into carriages, and lifted ober ditches, and to have de best place every whar. Nobody eber help me into carriages, or ober mud puddles, or gives me any best place . . . and ar'n't I a woman? Look at me! Look at my arm! . . . I have plowed, and planted, and gathered into barns, and no man could head me—and ar'n't I a woman? I could work as much and eat as much as a man (when I could get it), and bear de lash as well—and ar'n't I a woman? I have borne thirteen chilern and seen em mos' all sold off into slavery, and when I cried out with a mother's grief, none but Jesus heard—and ar'n't I a woman?   (Gilbert 1878:134)

Sojourner Truth not only attacked patriarchal images of women, she also challenged white feminists to relinquish their racial privilege (Crenshaw 1989:154). As bell hooks notes, "White women saw black women as a direct threat to their social standing—for how could they be idealized as virtuous, goddesslike creatures if they associated with black women who were seen by the white public as licentious and immoral?" (hooks 1981:31). In this way, the construction of an ideal mother that excluded Black women actually encouraged white women's allegiance to an oppressive concept of their own womanhood. In order to embrace Ms. Truth's message, the white women present had to reject the racist assumption that because Black women were unworthy of the title "woman" their experiences had no bearing on true womanhood. In fact, at an antislavery rally in Indiana, Sojourner Truth bared her breasts to prove that she was indeed a woman (hooks 1981:159). The women present had to accept Ms. Truth as truly woman and to sacrifice their personal stake in the white ideal of womanhood.

After slavery, Black women continued to work in patterns that diverged drastically from those of white women. Black women joined the wage-earning labor force in proportions three or four times higher than white women (Ferguson 1984:179, n. 12). After the Civil War, Black women were encouraged by white politicians and entrepreneurs, as well as by the depressed wages of Black men, to earn a living outside the home (Omolade 1987:252). In 1880, 50 percent of Black women were in the labor force, compared to only 15 percent of white women

(Omolade 1987:252). The racial disparity among married women was even greater: in 1870 in the rural South, more than four out of ten Black married women had jobs, mostly as field laborers, while 98.4 percent of white wives were housekeepers (Jones 1985:63). In Southern cities, Black married women worked outside the home five times more often than white married women (Jones 1985:113).

The demands of labor within white homes undermined Black women's own roles as mothers and homemakers (Jones 1985:127). Black domestics, of course, were unable to attend to their children during the day. They returned home late in the evening (if not on weekends) and had to entrust their children to the care of a neighbor, relative, or older sibling, or leave them to wander in the neighborhood (Jones 1985:129). The preoccupation with the virtue of white women justified not only the persecution of Black men but also the condemnation of "insolent" Black female servants (Jones 1985:149). Black women holding menial jobs were portrayed as unfeminine in order to justify subjecting them to working conditions that conflicted with the image of delicate womanhood: "The image of Mammy, 'Aunt Jemima,' Beulah, and even the emasculating matriarch is that of an overweight, rotund female, devoid of the curves that are indicative of the more seductive examples of her sex. Outfitted in an unflattering dress, apron, and scarf (a 'headrag'), she is always ready for work and never ready for bed" (Austin 1989:583).

Women of color continue to do most of the domestic service in America, filling jobs such as maids, child-care workers, nurse's aides, sewing machine operators, and food preparation workers (National Committee for Pay Equity [NCPE] 1987:20–26). In the early twentieth century, nearly two-thirds of all employed Black women in the North were domestic servants and laundresses (Jones 1985:164). It was not until 1970 that Black women were no longer employed primarily as domestic workers or farm laborers (Omolade 1987:258–59). Nevertheless, these jobs remain segregated on the basis of both race and gender, and they pay the lowest wages (NCPE 1987:20–26; hooks 1981:132–36).

The experience of Black working mothers complicates the feminist response to domesticity in two ways. First, white feminists' view of work, as resistance to motherhood and a liberating force for women, does not account for Black women's experiences. This ideology often focuses on a romanticized, middle-class quest for entrance into an elite workforce rather than on the women who have always been exploited as a source of cheap surplus labor (hooks 1981:146). Black women historically experienced work outside the home as an aspect of racial subordination and the family as a site of solace and resistance against white oppression (Y. Davis 1983:16–17; Spelman 1988:132). Black women's attention to domestic duties within their homes has defied the expectation of total service to whites. Elizabeth Spelman has observed that the oppressive nature of the "housewife" role must be understood in relation to women's other roles, which are raced as well as gendered: "The work of mate/mother/nurturer has a different meaning depending on whether it is contrasted to work that has high social value and ensures economic independence or to labor that is forced, degrading, and unpaid" (Spelman 1988:123).

Second, Black mothers' work experience raises one way in which racial privilege has helped to maintain the gendered division of domestic work. The employment of Black women as domestic servants in white homes reproduced the mistress-houseslave relationship (Y. Davis 1983:90–91). White mothers who could afford it reduced the burdens of childrearing by shifting their duties to Black maids (Palmer 1989:65–87). Judith Rollins found in her study of domestics and the women who employ them that the increased participation of middle-class women in the workplace did not change their attitudes toward their role in the home. According to Judith Rollins:

> The middle-class women I interviewed were not demanding that their husbands play a greater role in housekeeping; they accepted the fact that responsibility for domestic maintenance was theirs, and they solved the problem of their dual responsibilities by hiring other women to assist.
>
> (Rollins 1985:104)

Thus, white middle-class women gained entry to the male public sphere by assigning female domestic tasks to Black women, rather than by demanding a fundamental change in the sexual division of labor (Crenshaw 1989:154 and n.5).

Single Motherhood and Poverty

The sharp increase in the number of single mothers is changing the practice of motherhood in America. As more and more women raise children without husbands (Wegman 1989:944–45), the state has responded by increasing its interference in their families and by instituting programs and policies designed to restore the traditional nuclear family through reinstatement of the missing male (Fineman, this volume).

Contemporary welfare reform measures exemplify this effort. Martha Fineman demonstrates how the new poverty rhetoric blames single mothers for perpetuating poverty and how it proposes as the solution the coupling of poor single mothers with financially secure males (Fineman 1994, this volume:205–6). She links the representation of single motherhood as pathological to patriarchal ideology that defines mother and child by their relationship to fathers (Fineman, this volume). Single mothers are considered deviant because they reject the primacy of sexual affiliation as the basic organizing concept of the family. Fineman concludes that the condemnation of single mothers in current poverty reform discourse is primarily a reflection of patriarchy. Indeed, she declares: "The ideology of patriarchy is the most instrumental force in the creation and acceptance of discourses about mothers in our society" (Fineman, this volume:207).[3]

Race is very much implicated both in the correlation between poverty and single motherhood and in the discourses that explain it. While the proportion of poor families maintained by women has risen in all racial and ethnic groups, the proportion of poor Black families headed by women is far larger (Rowe 1991:74). Black single motherhood also has a unique history. During slavery, masters forcibly separated many Black mothers from their husbands (Omolade 1987:242). Some slave men escaped to freedom or purchased themselves from their masters, leaving their women and children behind (Omolade 1987:248). For example, Mississippi marriage registration records from 1864 show that nearly one in five Black women aged thirty and older were separated from their husbands by force (Gutman 1976:146). One study of slave women in Georgia revealed that over half of the women known to have been mothers appeared to have been living apart from their husbands (Wood 1987:609).

Suzanne Lebsock's research on free Black women in early-nineteenth-century Petersburg, Virginia, revealed that the most common household structure among free Blacks was the female-headed family containing one woman and her children (Lebsock 1982:285–86). Lebsock notes that free Black women had a unique incentive to remain single, arising from their ability to retain legal control over their property.

> For the woman who hoped to buy an enslaved relative, legal wedlock meant that her plan could be sabotaged at any time by her husband or by her husband's impatient creditors. The common-law disabilities of

married women added an ironic twist to chattel slavery's strange fusion of persons and property: [m]atrimony could pose a threat to the integrity of the free black woman's family.   (Lebsock 1982:285)

This pattern of Black single motherhood continued after Emancipation. Between 1880 and 1915, 25 to 30 percent of all urban Black families were headed by women (Jones 1985:113).

Ideologically, in America single motherhood is Black. The current condemnation of unwed mothers is rooted in the myth of the Black matriarch, the domineering female head of the Black family. White sociologists have held Black "matriarchs" responsible for the disintegration of the Black family and the consequent failure of Black people to achieve success in America (Giddings 1984:325–35).[4] Senator Daniel Patrick Moynihan of New York popularized this theory in his 1965 report, *The Negro Family: The Case for National Action* (Moynihan 1965). According to Moynihan:

> At the heart of the deterioration of the fabric of Negro society is the deterioration of the Negro family. It is the fundamental cause of the weakness of the Negro community. . . . In essence, the Negro community has been forced into a matriarchal structure which, because it is too out of line with the rest of the American society, seriously retards the progress of the group as a whole.   (Moynihan 1965:5, 29)

Thus, Moynihan attributes the cause of Black people's inability to overcome the effects of racism largely to the independence and dominance of Black mothers.

Underlying the current campaign against poor single mothers is the image of the lazy welfare mother who breeds children at the expense of taxpayers in order to increase the amount of her welfare check (Collins 1991:77; Fineman 1995:117–18). In society's mind, that mother is Black. Writers in the 1980s, most notably Charles Murray, author of *Losing Ground*, claimed that welfare induces poor Black women to refrain from marriage and to have babies (Murray 1984:154–66). Society penalizes Black single mothers not only because they depart from the norm of marriage as a prerequisite to pregnancy but also because they represent rebellious Black culture (Austin 1989:557; Solinger 1992a:25). To some extent, society punishes white single mothers because they are acting too much like Black women (Collins 1991:74).

An analysis of Black single motherhood focused entirely on race would be incomplete. The role of gender also needs to be explored. Black feminists have criticized William Julius Wilson's assessment of female-headed households in *The Truly Disadvantaged* (Wilson 1987), for example, for being essentially an endorsement of patriarchy (Austin 1989:567–68; Zinn 1989:870–72). While Wilson rejects the theory that poverty is culturally transmitted, he accepts the premise that family structure causes poverty and that rebuilding the traditional family is therefore the key to solving Black poverty (Wilson 1987:57–62, 71–92). It is true that families headed by single Black females are poorer than families with an adult male present (Simms 1986:143, 144, table 1). Wilson, however, fails to investigate the economic and social forces that marginalize Black single mothers. He also fails to explore the extent to which Black women have deliberately created single mother families by dissolving unwanted relationships in response to sexism in their homes or other disadvantages of marriage (Omolade 1987:273). Wilson's suggestions for reform, aimed at returning Black men to the family, do not include ways directly to empower Black women to improve their economic well-being (Crenshaw 1989:165).

In fact, it is questionable that marriage alone will transform Black women's lives. For pregnant teenagers, marriage is actually correlated with "dropping out of school, having more babies, and ultimately being divorced or separated" (Austin 1989:565–66). Although fundamental social change is required, expanding women's access to day care, low-income housing, nontraditional job markets, and health care are more viable short-term remedies for Black female poverty (Rowe 1991:77). Using both race and gender in understanding Black single motherhood clarifies that Black women's welfare will not be improved simply by restoring the patriarchal family structure.

In some ways, white mothers' lives are becoming structurally more similar to the lives of Black mothers.[5] Patriarchy in the modern capitalist welfare state is marked by an increased devaluation of motherhood that cuts across racial lines. Indications of this change include: the rise in "illegitimate" single motherhood for both Black and white women; the abandonment of the moral mother ideology and women's diminished control over childrearing; the replacement of the father by the patriarchal welfare state; the decrease in the amount of mothers doing domestic work and the increase in the numbers of women in the labor force; and the growing isolation of mothers (Ferguson 1984:172–75; Fineman 1992:658–66). In late-twentieth-century America, more and more white mothers will occupy social positions that have been historically defined for Black mothers only.[6] Just as Black women must identify and oppose patriarchy in the social control of families, white women must identify and oppose the operation of racism in the social control of families.

It may be in the lives of those most outcast by patriarchy that we will catch a glimpse of a liberated motherhood (Rich 1979:271–73; West 1988:47–48). Those mothers considered the most deviant may help us to imagine what motherhood might be like in a society where women are "free to develop a sense of self that is our own, and not a mere construct of patriarchy" (Cain 1990:212). In other words, we could move from deconstructing society's view of these women to actually claiming their oppositional insights as part of our reconstruction of motherhood. Regina Austin challenges us to consider whether Black single motherhood is an example of resistance against patriarchy.

> A black feminist jurisprudential analysis . . . must seriously consider the possibility that young, single, sexually active, fertile, and nurturing black women are being viewed ominously because they have the temerity to attempt to break out of the rigid economic, social, and political categories that a racist, sexist, and class-stratified society would impose upon them.   (Austin 1989:555)

Of course, this is risky territory. It is difficult to identify the emancipatory moments that spark within the vast realm of subordination. How can we claim what is liberating in the lives of the oppressed without denying all that remains oppressive? How can we discern the transformative potential in what is basically a response to subjugation? We must do the hard work of distinguishing between self-destructive and self-affirming behavior, between resistance and accommodation, between what merely reproduces illegitimate hierarchy and what destroys it.

Disloyalty to Feminism

What does this connection between racism and patriarchy mean for the feminist project? How does it test our commitment to a feminist vision of motherhood and of society in general? What does it tell us about the requirements for unity among women who are different? In this section, I explore the ways in which the interaction between racism and patriarchy tempts both white and Black women to be "disloyal" to feminism.[7]

White Women and White Privilege

One of the most painful parts of recognizing the relationship between racism and patriarchy is confronting white women's participation in the racial subordination of Black women. During slavery, for example, most white women either silently cooperated with the practice of own-ing Africans as chattel or actively abused the slaves in their households (Clinton 1985:28–32; hooks 1984:49). Elizabeth Fox-Genovese explains that, although Southern white women grumbled in private about cer-tain aspects of slavery, they were not willing to attack the entire system that benefited them in many ways: "Slavery, with all its abuses, consti-tuted the fabric of their beloved country—the warp and woof of their social position, their personal relations, their very identities" (Fox-Gen-ovese 1988:334). Some white women used their power over the slaves their husbands owned as compensation for their own subjugated posi-tion in marriage (hooks 1981:153). bell hooks suggests that the cruelty that white men inflicted on female slaves in the presence of white women served as a warning to their wives, sisters, and daughters to remain obedient.

> Surely, it must have occurred to white women that . . . [if] . . . enslaved black women were not available to bear the brunt of such intense anti-woman male aggression, they themselves might have been the victims. . . . Their alliance with white men on the common ground of racism enabled them to ignore the anti-woman impulse that also motivated attacks on black women.   (hooks 1981:38–39)

Thus, the subjugation of Black women encouraged white women's alle-giance to the patriarchy. This is a critical lesson about the relationship between racism and patriarchy: racism did not perfect patriarchy only by allowing slavemasters the possibility of unrestrained control of Black women. It also secured the compliance of white women by promising them the privileges denied to slaves and threatening them with the pun-ishments meted out to slaves.

Black feminists at the turn of the century criticized white women for allowing their affiliation with white men and their interest in the system to limit their opposition to white supremacy. Ida B. Wells, for example, saw the patriarchal idealization of white womanhood as license for white women's willing or unwilling silence (Harris 1990:599–660). Anna Julia Cooper charged the contemporary women's movement with opposing only women's domestic confinement rather than the entire system of racial patriarchy (Harris 1990:600, n. 88). My intention here is not to assess the level of white women's guilt but to show how white women's stake in patriarchy largely determined their complicity in institutions of white supremacy. This complicity, in turn, enabled their acquiescence in their own inferior status.

Racism within feminist advocacy concerning motherhood in particular has neglected and even harmed Black women.[8] The feminist birth control movement in the early twentieth century collaborated with the racist eugenics movement of the time (Davis 1983:213–15; Gordon 1976:274–90 and 329–40). Leading advocates of birth control, such as Margaret Sanger, made accommodations with eugenicists and used racist rhetoric urging the reduction of the birthrates of "undesirables" (Gordon 1976:274–90). For example, in "Why Not Birth Control in America?," published in *Birth Control Review* in 1919, Sanger stated as the feminist movement's objective, "More children from the fit, less from the unfit—that is the chief issue of birth control" (Gordon 1976:281). In *The Pivot of Civilization*, published in 1922, Sanger advocated society's use of stockbreeding techniques, warning that uncontrolled procreation by the illiterate and "degenerate" might destroy "our way of life" (Gordon 1976:281).

Feminists during this period advocated birth control, not as a means of self-determination for all women but as a tool of social control by the white elite (Gordon 1976:276–86). Their private birth control clinics evaluated clients based on their eugenic worth and advised them on the desirability of their procreative decisions (Gordon 1976:286–87). The first publicly funded birth control clinics were established in the South in the 1930s as a way of lowering the Black birthrate (Gordon 1976:314–29), and during the Depression, birth control was promoted as a means of lowering welfare costs (Gordon 1976:329–40). In 1939 the Birth Control Federation of America proposed a "Negro Project" designed to reduce reproduction by Blacks who "still breed carelessly and disastrously, with the result that the increase among Negroes, even more than among whites, is from that portion of the population least intelligent and fit, and least able to rear children properly" (Gordon 1976:332).[9]

The focus of contemporary reproductive rights discourse on abortion also neglects the broader range of reproductive health issues that affect Black women. White middle-class women concern themselves mainly with laws restricting choices otherwise available to them, such as statutes making it more difficult to obtain an abortion. Poor women of color, however, remain primarily concerned with the material conditions of poverty and oppression restricting their choices.[10] For example, the denial of access to safe abortions through lack of government funding, as well as the lack of resources necessary for a healthy pregnancy and parenting relationship, limits the reproductive freedom of poor women of color. Because of racism, it is more likely that the government will interfere with their reproductive decisions; because of their poverty, they are more likely to need the government's assistance to facilitate those decisions.

The mainstream opposition to sterilization reform in the 1970s exemplifies how the focus on "choice" has contradicted the interests of Black women. The Committee to End Sterilization Abuse introduced, in New York City, guidelines designed to prevent sterilization abuse by requiring informed consent and a thirty-day waiting period (D. Roberts 1991:1461, n. 213). Planned Parenthood and the National Abortion Rights Action League openly opposed the guidelines on the grounds that they restricted women's access to sterilization.

Women's false hope in white privilege continues to thwart any radical assault on gender hierarchy. I have discussed earlier in this essay how many white women gained entry into the white male working world by shifting female domestic work to Black women rather than by demanding a fundamental change in the sexual division of labor. Dolores Janiewski describes how racism prevented unity among Southern working women in the 1930s:

> White women prized the tangible benefits of their privileged position as workers and sometimes employers of black women. The intangible benefits of white supremacy's pseudo-homage to white womanhood remained deeply entrenched in these women's notions of self-respect and respectability. Taught to view themselves as "lady-like" when they refrained from heavy labor but to call black women "lazy" when they made the same claims, these women resisted any imputation of "social equality" which would place them on the same level with those they regarded as unclean, immoral and unlike themselves. Black women's demands for equal treatment threatened white women's deeply held beliefs in a natural, God-given order that established their moral as well as economic superiority over their black co-workers. Organized, whenever such organization was successful, by unions that failed to confront white domination, these women never met their black counterparts on equal terms in the workplace, the community, or the union.
>
> (Janiewski 1983:33–34)

Privileged racial identity has always provided whites with a powerful incentive to leave the existing social order intact (Bell 1990:402–3). W. E. B. DuBois explained white resistance to labor reform during Reconstruction, for example, by the fact that "the white group of laborers, while they received a low wage, were compensated in part by a sort of public and psychological wage" (Du Bois 1976:700–701). Similarly, the white laboring class never demanded free public education during slavery because they relied on the possibility of becoming slaveholders themselves as their means of social advancement (Du Bois 1976:64). Freed slaves, not working whites, led the first mass movement for publicly funded education in the South. Women's common oppression has not been any more successful than workers' common oppression at overcoming the stifling effect of racial privilege on movements for radical social change.

Sojourner Truth's challenge to the women's movement of her time was to relinquish any perceived advantage in the cult of white womanhood. Her challenge—the racial challenge to feminism—is the giant step necessary for radical change. To point out white women's racial privilege is not to deny that white women are oppressed (Hurtado 1989:834). Indeed, it is to point out a principal means by which white women remain oppressed. Adrienne Rich sees the need to confront racism as a white woman because she understands that only by giving up white privilege will white women be fully capable of dismantling patriarchy. Otherwise, Rich argues, white feminists "might still possess the capacity to delude themselves into some compromise of inclusion into patriarchy, into the white male order" (Rich 1979:309).

Black Women and Black Nationalism

Catharine MacKinnon has recently suggested that some Black women may be disloyal to feminism because of our common struggle with Black men for racial justice.

> I sense here that people feel more dignity in being part of any group that includes men than in being part of a group that includes that ultimate reduction of the notion of oppression, that instigator of lynch mobs, that ludicrous whiner, that equality coat-tails rider, that white woman. It seems that if your oppression is also done to a man, you are more likely to be recognized as oppressed, as opposed to inferior. Once a group is seen as putatively human, a process helped by including men in it, an oppressed man falls from a human standard.   (MacKinnon 1987:21–22)

I would imagine that most Black women would find it farfetched to seek a greater claim to humanity (in the eyes of the dominant culture) by identifying with Black men, who are also viewed as less than human. Our unity with men in the struggle for Black liberation is grounded in the reality that being Black in America is part of *our* identity, critical to what it means for us to be women. We are bound to Black men through the day-to-day struggles of living in a racist society. We know that our liberation as women is linked to the liberation of Black people as a group.

Black women may be guilty of another kind of disloyalty, however. Some of us remain silent about sexism in our own communities or decline to align with white feminists because of the response of Black men. We fear we will be charged with betraying our common interests as a people. Nationalist and Afrocentric accounts of the African past and of ideal gender relations often propose a conservative utopian model of Black family life that discounts conflict between Black men and women (E. White 1990:73–77). This model expects Black women to accept an unequal, "complementary" role that will arguably help to further the nationalist struggle. Audre Lorde has explained that "[t]he necessity for and history of shared battle have made us, Black women, particularly vulnerable to the false accusation that anti-sexist is anti-Black" (Lorde 1984:120).[11]

The relationship between racism and patriarchy, then, also holds a challenge for Black women. It calls upon Black feminists to inform our communities that patriarchy contributes to Black men's oppression and that feminism is essential to the struggle for the liberation of all Black people.[12] E. Francis White describes, for example, "the emergence of a black feminist discourse that attempts to combine nationalist and feminist insights in a way that counters racism but tries to avoid sexist pitfalls" (E. White 1990:74).

Perhaps women who occupy different social positions possess differing abilities to identify particular aspects of oppression in each instance of domination. Perhaps some feminists see more clearly the patriarchy in discourses about single mothers, for example, while others see more clearly their racism. We can help each other to understand how the discourses really contain both. We can remind each other that, whatever attraction racist patriarchy holds for us, it is not *our* order. Comparing oppressions ("I experience sexism the same way you experience racism," or "I experience sexism more painfully than you experience racism," or vice versa) can only be destructive. These comparisons lead us to think, "What you are experiencing is only [or less than] what I have experienced, and therefore I do not need to listen to your story" (Grillo and Wildman 1991:409, n. 36). Recognizing the connection between different forms of subordination leads to a more productive response: "What you are experiencing is linked to what I have experienced, and therefore I need to listen to your story to better understand my own (and our) oppression."

Feminism and Antiracism

> In the past, I don't care how poor this white woman was in the South she still felt like she was more than us. In the North, I don't care how poor or how rich this white woman has been, she still felt like she was more than us. But coming to the realization of the thing, her freedom is shackled in chains to mine, and she realizes for the first that she is not free until I am free.
>
> — Fannie Lou Hamer,
> "The Special Plight and Role of Black Women"
> (Lerner 1973:611)

Understanding the connection between racism and patriarchy expands the feminist project. Its goal cannot be to liberate women without taking issues of race into consideration. Racism subordinates women (Spelman 1988:14–15). "If feminism is to be a genuine struggle to improve the lives of *all* women, then all feminists must assume the responsibility for eliminating racism" (Kline 1989:117). The struggle against racism is also a necessary part of uniting women in political solidarity. Racism divides women (hooks 1981:156). Some feminists may find their motivation to oppose racism within the dreams of feminism: "It can spring from a heartfelt desire for sisterhood and the personal, intellectual realization that racism among women undermines the potential radicalism of feminism" (hooks 1981:157–58). I do not mean that feminists should see opposition to racism as an important extracurricular project. Racism is part of the structure of patriarchy in America, and opposition to racism is critical to dismantling it.[13]

Difference is such a pleasant word. It applies to everyone. It does not call anyone to action. We need only acknowledge that it exists and then move on with our preconceived plans. *Racism* is quite different. It destroys. It condemns. It speaks of power. It demands a response. Adrienne Rich calls on feminists to use the word *racism*:

> If black and white feminists are going to speak of female accountability, I believe the word *racism* must be seized, grasped in our bare hands, ripped up out of the sterile or defensive consciousness in which it so often grows, and transplanted so that it can yield new insights for our lives and our movement.   (Rich 1979:301–4)

Acknowledging each other's differences is not enough. Relationships of power produce some of our differences. We must face the awful history and reality of racism that helps to create those differences. We do not need to focus less on gender; we need to understand how gender relates to race. If we see feminism as a "liberation project" that seeks the emancipation of all women we must address the complexity of forces that bind us (Romany 1991:23). bell hooks describes the feminist project that embraces this holistic understanding of oppression:

> To me feminism is not simply a struggle to end male chauvinism or a movement to ensure that women will have equal rights with men; it is a commitment to eradicating the ideology of domination that permeates Western culture on various levels—sex, race, and class, to name a few—and a commitment to reorganizing U.S. society so that the self-development of people can take precedence over imperialism, economic expansion, and material desires.   (hooks 1981:194–95)

When we not only acknowledge our differences but also take up the struggle they demand, we stand a chance of creating that world.

NOTES

I presented my preliminary thoughts on the subject of this essay at Martha Fineman's February 1992 seminar on Reproductive Issues at Columbia University School of Law. I am grateful to the students for their discussion and to Professor Fineman for her generous encouragement. I presented drafts of this essay at the September 1992 symposium "Discovering Our Connections: Race and Gender in Theory and Practice of the Law," sponsored by the American University Journal of Gender & the Law, *and at the Feminism and Legal Theory Project's Workshop on Motherhood at Columbia University School of Law. I benefited from the comments of participants, particularly Nancy Erickson, Linda McClain, Barbara Omolade, and Ann Shalleck. Kim Taylor provided valuable research assistance.*

1. Patricia Williams mused about a lawsuit brought by a white woman against a clinic that negligently sold her a Black man's sperm:

> I ponder this case about the nightmare of giving birth to a black child who is tormented so that her mother gets to claim damages for emotional distress. I think about whether my mother shouldn't bring such a suit, both of us having endured at least the pain of my maturation in the

racism of the Boston public school system. Do black mothers get to sue for such an outcome, or is it just white mothers?

(Williams 1991:186–87)

2. Ruth Colker tells the story of her law school classmate who decided to be sterilized. The university physician refused to allow her to undergo the procedure unless she agreed to attend several sessions with a psychiatrist, presumably to dissuade her from her decision. Colker recognized that the "physician's actions reflect the dominant social message—that a healthy (white) woman should want to bear a child" (Colker 1989:1067, n. 196).

3. I credit this declaration as the inspiration for my article. I was initially taken aback by Martha Fineman's statement attributing the condemnation of single mothers in new poverty discourses primarily to patriarchy. When I read these discourses, I thought, "the ideology of *racism* is the most instrumental force" in their creation and acceptance. In fact, that reaction was the thesis of an article I wrote about the prosecution of women who use drugs during pregnancy (D. Roberts 1991). The strange thing about my response to Fineman's arguments was that I mostly agreed with them. I understood more clearly that both racist and patriarchal ideology work together to construct the meaning of motherhood in our society.

4. hooks explains how white male scholars assume that Black men vacate their parenting roles because of domineering Black women. As hooks points out, the term *matriarch* does not accurately describe the Black woman's role in our society. As the most socially and economically marginalized group in America, Black women do not hold the power the term *matriarch* implies (hooks 1981:70–83).

5. Statistics demonstrate that since 1980 there has been a 40 percent increase in the number of births to unmarried white women, thereby narrowing the gap between the percentage of Black unmarried mothers and white unmarried mothers (Fineman 1995:124–25).

6. This does not mean that white and Black mothers will be treated in the same way. It means that racism helps to determine the social constructs that regulate white as well as Black mothers. For example, Fineman argues that "[t]he 'public' single mother family is distinguished from her counterpart in the 'private' family' and is subjected to greater state intervention" (Fineman 1991c:961). It should be further noted, however, that the construction of "public" and "private" families is based on racist, as well as patriarchal, norms. The state has always considered Black mothers, whether married or single, to need public supervision and not to be entitled to privacy. Thus, the "public" single mother has never had a *Black* counterpart in the "private" family. When white single mothers and their children are considered "public" families, they are placed in a category that has historically been occupied by Black mothers. I suspect that many poor single white mothers will be harmed by welfare reforms really meant for Black women.

7. This phrase is a play on the title of Adrienne Rich's essay, "Disloyal to Civilization: Feminism, Racism, Gynephobia," in which Rich refers to women's disloyalty to patriarchy (Rich 1979:295).

8. For general accounts of racism in American women's movements during the nineteenth and twentieth centuries, see Davis 1983:46–86; hooks 1981:119–49.

9. It is arguable that a contemporary version of the "Negro Project" (not connected to feminist reproductive rights advocacy) can be seen in recent attempts to implement incentives for welfare mothers to use the long-term contraceptive Norplant. For more information on this see "Poverty and Norplant: Can Contraception Reduce the Underclass?" The *Philadelphia Inquirer*, December 12, 1990:A18 (suggesting that Black women on welfare be given incentives to use the contraceptive Norplant), and Tamar Lewin, "Implanted Birth Control Device Renews Debate over Forced Contraception," *New York Times*, January 10, 1991:A20 (reviewing the debate on forced use of Norplant).

10. Thus, the prochoice movement remained relatively complacent about the effective denial of access to abortions for poor women with the Supreme Court's decisions in *Maher v. Roe*, 432 U.S. 464 (1977) and *Harris v. McRae*, 448 U.S. 297 (1980), which upheld the denial of public funding for abortion. See Stearns 1989:7. The belated mobilization of the prochoice movement triggered by the Supreme Court's decision in *Webster v. Reproductive Health Services*, 492 U.S. 490 (1989) (upholding the state's ability to restrict access to abortion services), and the resulting spate of state restrictions on abortion seemed motivated by their threat to the reproductive rights of affluent women (7–9).

11. Barbara Omolade suggested to me that Black women's reluctance to challenge sexism is manifested more outside the Black community than in our communications with Black men.

12. Audre Lorde wrote of wanting to teach her son this lesson:

> I wish to raise a Black man who will not be destroyed by, nor settle for, those corruptions called *power* by the white fathers who mean his destruction as surely as they mean mine. I wish to raise a Black man who will recognize that the legitimate objects of his hostility are not women, but the particulars of a structure that programs him to fear and despise women as well as his own Black self.   (Lorde 1984:74)

13. This view of racism and patriarchy rejects the claim that one institution is more fundamental than the other, that one derives from the other, or that it is more critical to destroy one before the other.

11 | A "Tangle of Pathology": Racial Myth and the New Jersey Family Development Act

NINA PERALES

On January 21, 1992, New Jersey Governor James Florio signed into law the Family Development Act (the Act), a set of state welfare reform laws focused on changing the size and composition of the Aid to Families with Dependent Children (AFDC) family unit.[1] Although the Family Development Act includes some changes generally regarded as positive by welfare advocates (including the call for integrated support services for public assistance recipients), two aspects of the Act caused strong community and advocate opposition.

One of the controversial provisions, bill 4703, commonly referred to as the "child exclusion" provision, eliminates the increase in cash benefits normally granted to a woman who has a child while on AFDC. The other controversial provision, embodied in bill 4702, and referred to as the "bridefare" provision, allows children to keep their AFDC and Medicaid benefits, while the family earns income up to 150 percent of the poverty line, if the AFDC mother marries a man who is not the natural father of the children. Significantly, a related bill and another of the "bridefare" provisions, bill 4704, gives higher AFDC benefits to two-parent families in which the parents are married, compared with those where the parents are simply cohabiting.

On June 26, 1992, the Puerto Rican Legal Defense and Education Fund (PRLDEF), as part of its Latinas' Rights Initiative, filed a federal administrative complaint against the state of New Jersey with the Office for Civil Rights of the U.S. Department of Health and Human Services (HHS OCR).[2]

The complaint argues that New Jersey's "child exclusion" provision intentionally discriminates against Latinos and African Americans on the basis of race and national origin, in violation of Title VI of the Civil Rights Act of 1964. The complaint was filed on behalf of a pregnant Latina, who was receiving AFDC and using the pseudonym "Maria Garcia," and a number of advocacy organizations whose membership included African American women and Latinas on welfare: Union y Progreso, Together Against Poverty, Standing Up for Justice, and the Monmouth County Coalition for the Homeless. The complaint is still under investigation by HHS OCR.[3]

New Jersey's Family Development Act is part of a growing trend among states to enact welfare laws that punish or reward women for particular marriage and childbearing decisions. Other states considering similar measures include California, Colorado, Illinois, Maine, Maryland, Mississippi, and Pennsylvania. Welfare reform laws intended to "improve" the behavior of recipients include provisions in Ohio and Wisconsin that condition a family's AFDC grant on the children's school attendance (Center for Law and Social Policy 1992:7).

The rhetoric and the coercive measures in the New Jersey Family Development Act are aimed directly at African American and Latina mothers, who make up the majority of AFDC recipients in the state.[4] The Act's explicit goal, couched in the language of self-help and increased personal responsibility, is to restrict childbearing and force the creation of more "traditional" nuclear family units among mothers on welfare.

In this essay, I will examine elements of the Family Development Act (the "bridefare" and the "child exclusion" provisions) with an eye to three things: first, how racial stereotypes, or myths, are the driving force behind punitive welfare laws; second, how the welfare reform debate in New Jersey and generally uses racially laden concepts to de-legitimize African American and Latina motherhood and justify punitive welfare laws; and third, how welfare reform laws send disempowering messages to the African American and Latina mothers in New Jersey.

A basic premise of this essay is that racist and sexist discriminatory intent are tightly knit together in the Family Development Act and that this same combination of racism and sexism enables the production of derogatory images of African American and Latina mothers. I suggest, further, that compound discrimination is responsible for the urge felt by many people to restrict and dominate the practice of motherhood by these women. A combination of sexism, classism, and racism forms the real "tangle of pathology" within the Family Development Act (Moynihan 1965:4). The goal of this essay, therefore, is not to separate out racism from sexism in the Family Development Act but rather to try to expose how racism operates within the Act. Race discrimination is an integral part of the African American and Latino experience. It would thus be inappropriate to ignore the operations of racial stereotypes and racism when analyzing a policy designed for African Americans and Latinos on welfare.[5]

By highlighting the racism in the Family Development Act, one can see that the Family Development Act is part of a broader attack on the integrity of African Americans and Latinos. In this way it is possible to connect the Family Development Act to other discriminatory governmental practices that may not appear to target women specifically or even welfare specifically.

Finally, it is my aim in this examination of the Family Development Act to help civil rights attorneys, including those at PRLDEF, to understand better how racism is disguised by policymakers who create burdensome and discriminatory laws. I want to encourage civil rights attorneys to be creative in challenging this type of discrimination.

The New Jersey Family Development Act

According to the state of New Jersey, the goal of the Family Development Act is "to attack head-on the nation's urgent problems of long-term and inter-generational welfare dependency" (Draft Summary:1). The Family Development Act is made up of six laws referred to as bills 4700 through 4705. Bills 4701 and 4705 do not affect benefits; they establish a 24-hour hotline for social service referrals and a Council on Community Restoration to advise the governor on community restoration projects.

Bill 4700 establishes the Family Development Program (FDP). The FDP implements New Jersey's federally mandated Job Opportunities and Basic Skills (JOBS) program and calls for increased coordination of support services for families in the JOBS program.[6]

The remaining three provisions, bills 4702–4704, are the provisions I have outlined in the first part of this essay. I want now to turn to those bills and discuss them in detail.

Bill 4702, one of the "bridefare" provisions, creates a financial incentive for marriage by establishing that:

> An eligible parent who is married to a person who is not the parent of one
> or more of the eligible parent's children shall not be eligible for benefits
> if the household income exceeds the State eligibility standard for benefits;
> however, the eligible parent's natural children shall be eligible for benefits
> according to a sliding income scale established by the Commissioner
> which does not take into account the income of the eligible parent's
> spouse, if the total annual household income does not exceed 150 per-
> cent of the official poverty level[.]   (N.J. Stat. Ann. §44:10-3.4 [1993])

The effect of this stepfather bridefare provision is as follows: a woman
with two children who marries a man can keep her children's welfare
benefits and the family may keep up to $21,000 of earned income per
year. This bridefare provision denies a similar working mother who
does not have a husband the "income disregards."[7]

Perhaps the most bizarre aspect of the Family Development Act is
that the best bridefare package only applies to families with stepfathers.
If a woman marries the *natural* father of her children, the family is only
eligible for the regular combination of cash grant and income disregards.

Bill 4704 creates another marriage incentive by providing for payment of the full AFDC cash grant to families with two married parents.
Previously, New Jersey only gave 60 percent of the full grant to two-parent families on AFDC. Under bill 4704, unmarried two-parent families will continue to receive only 60 percent of the grant. Bill 4704
states:

> The welfare system in this State should be designed to promote family
> stability among AFDC recipients by eliminating the incentive to break
> up families created by AFDC program regulations, which undermines
> the ability of AFDC-enrolled mothers to achieve economic self-suffi-
> ciency and thereby perpetuates their dependence, and that of their chil-
> dren, on welfare.   (N.J. Stat. Title 44:10-3.7)

The regulations promulgated by the newly named Division of Family Development are justified in the following way:

> The rules and the legislation upon which the amendments are based are
> intended to encourage parental responsibility, promote the value of
> work, and encourage the development of nuclear families through mar-
> riage. The rules are not intended, nor should they be viewed, as dis-
> criminatory, but rather as a positive step forward in the evolution of
> public assistance programs which lead to self-reliance and self-determi-
> nation.   (Division of Family Development:1992a)

The result of these provisions is that unmarried women living with the fathers of their children are placed at the bottom of the benefit scale: they will receive only 60 percent of the normal welfare grant.

Bill 4703, the "child exclusion" provision, imposes financial sanctions upon women who have a baby while on welfare by denying the increase in cash benefits usually granted upon the baby's birth. It states that the Commissioner of welfare must eliminate "the increment in benefits under the program for which that family would otherwise be eligible as a result of the birth of a child during the period in which the family is eligible for AFDC benefits" (N.J. Stat. Ann. §44:10-3.5 [1993]). In New Jersey, this amount is $64 per month for a child born to a woman who already has two or more children.

Racial Stereotypes of African Americans and Latinos

Racial stereotypes that characterize African Americans and Latinos as inherently degenerate—shiftless, lazy, childlike, dependent, and also animal-like and impulsive—have evolved into the "culture of poverty" rhetoric so widespread today.[8] The older and newer expressions of racism share the same basic theme: it is the defective character of people of color themselves that causes their oppressed condition.

In the mid-1800s the theory of the inherent degeneracy of African Americans held that without slavery to structure their lives, African Americans declined "into vice and pauperism accompanied by the bodily and mental afflictions incident thereto—deafness, blindness, insanity, and idiocy" (Calhoun 1884).

Today, we are subjected to more subtle theories about racial inferiority; they feature the same ideas about defective character but are usually wrapped in anthropological or sociological jargon. In 1965, Daniel Patrick Moynihan wrote his infamous report, "The Negro Family: The Case for National Action," in which he asserted that African Americans live in a "tangle of pathology" that is "capable of perpetuating itself without assistance from the white world" (Moynihan 1965:47). The pathological behavior of African Americans included a "matriarchal" family structure, high rates of criminal activity, unemployment, divorce, and childbearing out of wedlock. He theorized that African Americans could only succeed if they changed their self-destructive and abnormal behavior and acquired mainstream American values.

In the 1980s, there was a revival of the rhetoric that linked people of color to degeneracy through the idea of pathological culture. A 1986 television special called "The Vanishing Family: Crisis in Black America" visited a housing project in Newark, New Jersey, and depicted young mothers on welfare and the fathers of their children as sexually irresponsible, unmotivated, and devoid of morality (Moyers 1986). The television show had the result of "reinforcing, with 'liberal' authority, the most archetypal of racist myths, fears, and stereotypes—a picture of 'jungle' immorality and degeneracy, inarticulateness and sloth . . . [and] to make the situation seem so hopeless that 'realistically' there is nothing to be done about it anyway" (Gresham 1989:118).

Although the stereotype of inherent degeneracy is most commonly analyzed in its application to African Americans, stereotypes about the degenerate character of Latinos are just as negative and just as pervasive. These stereotypes vary between subgroups and create particular images (the lazy Mexicans, the dirty Puerto Ricans who bring cockroaches to apartment buildings) but they have more similarities than differences.

Like African Americans, Latinos are commonly portrayed as having abnormal or deficient character and morals. Latinos are stereotyped as slick womanizing machos (the Latin Lovers) who are impulsive and violent with their women. On television, Latinos are most often ruthless and cold-hearted young gangsters and drug traffickers. Latinos are also stereotyped as simple-minded and lazy peasants/Indios, superstitious, uncivilized, and vulgar, who sleep through the day and lack ambition. Latinos are also "illegal aliens," criminals who sneak into the United States to get jobs, conceal themselves in dirty overcrowded houses, speak no English, and are passive in the face of neglect or exploitation.

Stereotypes of African American Women and Latinas

Within the paradigm of racial inferiority, specific images of African American women and Latinas include all those I have already discussed and a few more that are created from a combination of racism and sexism.

The African American woman is most commonly stereotyped as lazy and sexually permissive. In popular culture, "the predominant image is that of the 'fallen' woman, the whore, the slut, the prostitute" (hooks 1981:52). This stereotype is often referred to as the "Jezebel." The Jezebel is not only promiscuous, she is sexually insatiable and indiscriminate in her choice of lovers.

Another stereotype, which becomes an important part of the image of African American women on welfare, is that of "Sapphire." bell hooks discusses the image of Sapphire as "iron-willed, effectual, [and] treacherous toward and contemptible of black men, the latter being portrayed as simpering, ineffectual whipping boys" (hooks 1981:85).

The Black Matriarch is a stereotype made more pervasive by scholarship like the Moynihan report. The Matriarch is a too-strong woman who dominates the men and boys in her family and prevents them from developing a normal self-image. She is responsible for the oppressed status of all African Americans. "Female dominance, Moynihan concluded, had created a 'tangle of pathology' . . . responsible for the chaos, promiscuity, drug abuse, and crime that allegedly afflicted the Negro family" (Aptheker 1982:132).

There is a strong connection between the negative stereotypes of African American women and Latinas.[9] The themes of laziness and promiscuity are often applied to both African American women and Latinas. The Latina may be seen as having a more violent temperament than her African American sister (hot Latin blood), but she is similarly described as oversexed, impulsive, manipulative, and lazy. As a mother, she has too many children, is slovenly, and does not encourage them to succeed.

Racial Myths in the Welfare Debate

Racial myths like the ones described above have justified systematic discrimination against African Americans and Latinos in the United States. In the area of welfare, we see that the "inherent degeneracy" of African Americans and Latinos has been used to deny benefits to women of color; it also informs the core theory of contemporary policies that reduce and restrict benefits in order to control mothering by African American women and Latinas.

Social welfare has always been influenced by negative stereotypes about poor people. Historically, common belief held that idle and shiftless paupers were drawn to welfare programs and that welfare encouraged people with "normal" working values to become demoralized and slothful. In 1935 Franklin D. Roosevelt himself gave this description of welfare: "Continued dependence upon relief induces a spiritual and moral disintegration fundamentally destructive to the national fiber. To dole out relief in this way is to administer a narcotic, a subtle destroyer of the human spirit" (Roosevelt 1935).

As the welfare rolls have become increasingly composed of African Americans and Latinos, welfare has more often been described as an "enabler" for poverty and social disintegration. Under this theory, welfare allows people of bad character to avoid working for a living and to deviate from the social norms of traditional marriage and legitimate births.

According to the conservative writer and editor Mickey Kaus:

Welfare may not have been the main cause of the underclass, but it *enabled* the underclass to form. Without welfare, those left behind in the ghetto would have had to move to where the jobs were. Without welfare, it would have been hard for single mothers to survive without forming working families. . . . Welfare is how the underclass (unhappily, unintentionally) survives. Change welfare, and the underclass will have to change as well. (Kaus 1992:38)

In this view, then, welfare and people of color make a potent mix. According to the logic of Kaus and the racial stereotypes prevalent today, welfare is something people get dependent on and people of color are *naturally* dependent. Welfare enables people to live jobless lives without moral restraint and people of color are *naturally* lazy and immoral. In the public consciousness, welfare and people of color interact as naturally as the drug and the addict. This explains the effectiveness of descriptions of African Americans and Latinos as "hooked on welfare."[10]

The Family Development Act and its sponsor, New Jersey State Assemblyman Wayne Bryant, promote the idea that welfare is an opiate and that people on welfare lack a work ethic and personal responsibility. Mr. Bryant argues that "a system that is built on being nonproductive and nonresponsible is a detriment to those who receive" (Bryant October 22, 1991:41). He elaborates:

I don't understand why we believe that we should set up some sheltered kind of existence that makes them live in an unreal world. . . . Why would we want to insulate, and to bring a group of people into a false existence like that, for some reason, if you're in this pot, you have no obligations? Everything is going to be done free, and good for you. . . . They can't think for themselves [and] we have to worry about everything that happens in their life. (Bryant July 9, 1991:34–35)

Making use of the negative images of women of color, welfare rhetoric generates the picture of the full-blown "welfare queen." The welfare queen is a woman of color who manipulates and exploits the welfare system, scorns lasting or legalized relationships with men, and has a series of children out of wedlock in order to continue her welfare eligibility. The Milwaukee County Welfare Rights Organization quoted the following example of welfare rhetoric to demonstrate the hostility against women on welfare:

> You give those lazy, shiftless good-for-nothings an inch and they'll take a mile. . . . I'm tired of those niggers coming to our state to get on welfare. I'm tired of paying their bills just so they can sit around home having babies, watching their color televisions, and driving Cadillacs.
>
> (Quoted in D. Roberts 1991:1444)

In the Northeast, where Puerto Ricans and other Latinos are concentrated in urban centers with African Americans, the welfare queen has become Puerto Rican:

> [T]here is a grave family problem in Puerto Rican ghettos where there are thousands of single mothers, very young, who try to escape poverty through welfare or by means of new companions who then leave them and leave them with other children to aggravate the problem. With these conditions it is impossible to raise and educate correctly one's children so that they can then triumph in life. In sum, what is missing, what fails among Puerto Ricans in the ghettos of the United States are the families, and that is the problem.   (Montaner 1990)

The welfare queen is a mother, of course, but an unfit and careless one. She is the welfare Brood Sow, who reproduces to increase her welfare check.

The images of welfare as an opiate and the immoral welfare queen fit closely with stereotypes of racial degeneracy; together they function to justify policies that seek to marginalize, limit, and control the activities of people of color.

Welfare has become a way for whites to articulate their race anxiety without seeming to be outright bigots, and in this way, welfare is used as a symbol of the racial decline of the nation.

For example, a recent article in the *New York Times* by Nobel Prize–winning economist Gary Becker suggested that the United States should auction immigration permits to people seeking entry into the United States in order to avoid an influx of "welfare dependent" immigrants. He argues that:

> Because of the expanded welfare state, open immigration is no longer a practical policy. These days, open immigration would merely induce people in poorer countries to emigrate to the U.S. and other developed countries to collect generous transfer payments.   (G. Becker 1992:114)

Mr. Becker, apparently without checking to see if most immigrants are eligible for welfare, uses the image of the immigrant on welfare to symbolize a racial threat to the country.

Similarly, a poem written by California Assemblyman William Knight ties welfare to the specter of being overwhelmed by Latino immigrants. Written in broken English, it states in part:

> They come in rags and Chebby trucks,
> I buy big house with welfare bucks . . .
> We have a hobby; it's called breeding.
> Welfare pays for baby feeding.
>   (Knight 1993:1)

Racial Code Words

The Family Development Act and its supporters use phrases such as "personal responsibility" and "dependency" to construct an image of a dysfunctional welfare culture. These words connect in a subtle way to the stereotypes I have discussed in this essay and create an image of African American and Latino parasitism within the welfare program.

In the welfare debate, words such as *underclass*, *pathology*, and *matriarch* imply racial degeneracy without actually mentioning race. Sometimes, the racial nature of these code words is revealed to us forcefully. In February 1992 Frederick Goodwin, former administrator of the U.S. Alcohol, Drug Abuse, and Mental Health Administration, stated in a meeting:

> If you look . . . at male monkeys in the wild, roughly half of them survive to adulthood. The other half die by violence. That is the natural way of it for males, to knock each other off and, in fact, there are some interesting evolutionary implications. . . . The same hyperaggressive monkeys who kill each other are also hypersexual, so they copulate more and therefore they reproduce more to offset the fact that half of them are dying.

Mr. Goodwin then made an analogy with inner-city crime and the "loss of some of the civilizing evolutionary things we have built up. . . . Maybe it isn't just the careless use of the word when people call certain areas of certain cities, jungles" (Goodwin 1992).

Racial code words surround and describe African American and Latina mothers in particular and serve as useful vocabulary to the promoters of the Family Development Act. Perhaps the most popular

phrase for poor African Americans and Latinos today is the "underclass."
Maxine Baca Zinn describes the underclass as a "category, by definition
poor, [that] is overwhelmingly Black and disproportionately composed
of female-headed households. . . . The underclass is permanent, being
locked in by its own unique but maladaptive culture" (Zinn 1989:857).

Assemblyman Wayne Bryant accepts the concept of the "underclass"
and believes that the solution for the underclass is to become "main-
streamed." He made this clear when he stated that the Family Development Act will make "our system of welfare more in line with where
we say we want to get them [welfare recipients]. We want them to
matriculate into the mainstream, and therefore adopt the policies we
have as their policies" (Bryant October 22, 1991:4).

The welfare queen, herself not explicitly racially identified, plays a
central role in the world of racial code words. In her article about the use
of racial myths in the 1991 Clarence Thomas/Anita Hill hearings, Wahneema Lubiano argues that references to women on welfare bring with
them a whole package of words and concepts that imply racial degeneracy. She argues that the welfare queen is "omnipresent" in debates about
urban blight and the decline of the nation (Lubiano 1992:332).

One of the most blatant yet unacknowledged rhetorical feats in the
Family Development Act is the equation of marriage with the economic
advancement of poor women of color. Wayne Bryant and the text of the
Act itself state that the primary purpose of the child exclusion and
bridefare provisions is to encourage welfare recipients to be less dependent and to take responsibility for their families' support. However,
rather than encouraging the self-sufficiency of women, the two bridefare provisions provide a financial incentive to marry. It is assumed that
the presence of a husband will result in the financial support of the
woman and her children. The logical dissonance between the stated
purpose of the Family Development Act and its incentive structure
reveal that the "problem" of welfare dependency is located in the
unmarried status of the welfare mother, and not in her inability to earn
a living wage for her children.

Wayne Bryant explained that his proposed reforms were necessary
because:

> [W]e cannot continue to operate a system that sets up a set of norms
> which are almost completely contrary to the norms of the rest of our
> society . . . because you have now taught them a pattern of life which is
> different than how to become successful, responsible, and self-sufficient
> in our society.   (Bryant October 22, 1991:42)

In light of the Act's obvious bias toward marriage as the escape route from poverty, Wayne Bryant's statement begs the question, "How exactly is a woman on welfare supposed to 'take responsibility' and become 'self-sufficient'?"

When they enacted the Family Development Act, New Jersey legislators relied on the stereotype of the dependent brood sow without checking into the real facts of welfare in New Jersey. For example, the women on welfare in New Jersey have the same average number of children as all women in the state. The average AFDC case lasts twenty-six months. Most importantly, state welfare records reveal that the vast majority of births to women on AFDC are within ten months of the case opening, proving that most babies were not conceived while their mothers received welfare. When reality contrasts so sharply with the proposed "remedy" of the Family Development Act, one can only conclude that the Act was created to respond to a mythical image of people on welfare, and not the reality. Unfortunately, when racial rhetoric is expressed in code words about culture and personal responsibility, it becomes harder to attack using traditional civil rights definitions of intentional discrimination. African American and Latina mothers are, as Patricia Williams has stated, "subsumed in a social circumstance—an idea, a stereotype—that pins [them] to the underside of this society and keeps [them] there, out of sight/out of mind, out of the knowledge of mind which is law" (P. Williams 1991:121).

Support for the Family Development Act Among African Americans and Latinos

It must be noted that the Family Development Act receives approval from some African Americans and Latinos as well as some whites. Much of this support can be said to spring from sexism within our communities and the belief that the proper place for a woman is to be subservient to a husband. bell hooks writes that in the wake of the Moynihan Report, "Black men were able to use the matriarchy myth as a psychological weapon to justify their demands that black women assume a more passive subservient role in the home" (hooks 1981:79).

However, the support for these provisions is more than a wish of African American and Latino men to subjugate and control the women in their community. There is also internalized racism and class alienation at work when people of color approve of punitive welfare laws aimed at people of color.

Assemblyman Wayne Bryant, sponsor of the Family Development Act, is an African American man. He did not grow up poor but believes that what poor African Americans need is harsh welfare laws to get them back on their feet. "I am saying, as an African American, I will not tolerate anyone having my people disproportionately in a system that is going to keep them permanently in poverty, without them having some responsibility" (Bryant October 22, 1991:41).

Bryant believes in the "culture of poverty" although he himself grew up outside of poverty. Accepting uncritically the stereotype of African American women and Latinas on welfare, he twists punitive welfare provisions into an opportunity for success for "his" people. Bryant has described the current welfare system as a "system of slavery" and the new provisions as a chance to "empower" people on welfare (Bryant July 30, 1991:5, 10). He promotes the child exclusion provision this way:

> So therefore, when folks say it's a denial of benefits—no, I just came up with another way that folks could be responsible like the rest of us. I often wonder why no one focuses on that point, that we have given folks an opportunity to . . . do like other folks do—work for their kids.
>
> (Bryant July 9, 1991:45)

Worst of all, Bryant has been used happily by white legislators as the "front" for the Family Development Act. One white New Jersey senator stated that "[i]t would be very difficult for a white to raise [the subject of welfare dependency]. . . . A white raising the same concerns would be called a racist. . . . [Wayne Bryant] is doing us all a favor by focusing the debate" (Payne 1992:30).

Even some poor African Americans and Latinos on welfare share the widespread belief that women on welfare have more children to continue eligibility and don't want to work. In one meeting between PRLDEF representatives and the organizational plaintiff Union y Progreso, a Latina who was a poor single mother and had been on welfare in the past expressed support for the punitive provisions of the Family Development Act. After some discussion, she agreed that she herself had never conformed to the stereotype of the welfare queen and she decided that it was wrong to apply the stereotype to all women on welfare. Not surprisingly, the Latinas in Union y Progreso considered the stepfather bridefare provision the most outrageous. Under this provision, wage-earning mothers on welfare can keep a large portion of their wages and their welfare benefits only if they are married to a man who is not the father of their children. The women were furious that their own earnings are counted against their cash grants to a larger extent than the same earnings of married women receiving welfare.

The Impact of the Family Development Act on African American and Latina Mothers

By denying the increase in cash benefits to African American women and Latinas who give birth to an additional child, the Family Development Act makes life that much more difficult for this struggling population. Although most women do not have children in order to receive more welfare, they do have children for a variety of other reasons, and a woman's decision to bear a child (whether the baby was planned or not) will now result in a severe financial penalty for the family.

A woman with a job who has an additional child under the new law might appear to be in a better economic position than the woman with an additional child who received the $64 under the old law. The reduction in cash benefits plus the "income disregards" given to a working woman with a new child mean that she will not receive the $64 but she can keep her earnings until they equal one-quarter of her monthly grant. However, it is unrealistic to think that women will benefit from this provision unless they begin work in the month the baby is born and they have no child care costs.

The bridefare provisions are equally egregious. If women on welfare in New Jersey respond to these options as purely economic actors, will single welfare mothers with earned income try to maximize their cash grants by bribing the men they know to marry them? Will women married to the fathers of their children swap husbands with their friends in order to get the better package? The Family Development Act is unclear about the treatment of certain families; when a welfare mom marries a welfare dad and each person becomes the stepparent of the other's children, do they get to keep their earnings or do they cancel each other out? These images would be humorous if not for the depressing reality of mothers trying every day to do the best that they can for their children. While people on welfare struggle with inadequate grants and an incompetent bureaucracy, the bridefare provisions and the child exclusion provision attempt to solve a fantasy problem and ignore the real problems of welfare.

Based on myths of the irresponsible brood sow and the castrating matriarch who scorns valid offers of marriage, the bridefare and child exclusion provisions send a very clear message to the African American women and Latinas on welfare: "You have caused your own poverty through pathological behavior. You are not fit to have any more babies and you should climb out of poverty by marrying a man who will provide for you and your children."

By establishing a standard for having a baby that includes having an independent source of money (apart from welfare), the Act places "acceptable" childbearing beyond the reach of women on welfare.[11] By suggesting that all births are intended, the Act can legitimately punish any woman for bearing a child while she is on welfare.[12]

The image of "unfit" motherhood exists in contrast to the "fit" motherhood engaged in by women who can afford the costs of child-rearing without welfare. Unable to meet the standard of appropriate motherhood, the woman on welfare who has another baby is acting outside societal norms and should be punished. In this way the Family Development Act criminalizes African American and Latina mothers for having babies and blames them for the poverty of their children and themselves.

The Family Development Act *also* blames them for welfare "dependency" and social "blight" in general. Women on welfare are told that when they reproduce, they do more than have a baby. Their "reproduction" is the perpetuation of social decay. Like the Moynihan Report, enactment of the Family Development Act told African American and Latina mothers that they "enforced the structure of poverty and delinquency" (Aptheker 1982:133).

The Family Development Act promotes the idea that women's traditional role in the family is the key to economic success:

> We want to do . . . away with what I call the "invisible man," [where welfare allows] men and women [to] conjugate [sic] together and yet not encourage the family like we do in middle-class families. . . . We want to encourage them to form families in order that this family value can be reborn again in the most vulnerable of our society.
>
> (Bryant July 9, 1991:4–5)

Wayne Bryant's image of the "invisible man" evokes its partner image: the domineering and rejecting woman who made him "invisible."

The Family Development Act, with its revival of "tangle of pathology" theory, has held out the African American and Latina mother for indictment:

> She is the agent of destruction, the creator of the pathological, black, urban, poor family from which all ills flow; a monster creating crack dealers, addicts, muggers, and rapists—men who become those things because of being immersed in *her* culture of poverty.   (Lubiano 1992:339)

Reproductive Rights

The Family Development Act's absolute restriction on childbearing, no matter how few children a woman has borne, is a straightforward attempt to limit the number of babies born to African American women and Latinas. With the history of the African American and Latino communities in mind, this provision can be viewed as the latest assault in a series of coercive reproductive policies imposed upon African American women and Latinas.

The devaluation of African Americans and Latinos generally has resulted in a very high level of governmental interference with the bodies of African Americans and Latinos, especially those of women. People of color in the United States have often been the targets of eugenics campaigns, and even today African American women and Latinas are sterilized at much higher rates than white women (D. Roberts 1991:1442 n. 125; Garcia 1982). Additionally, African Americans and Latinos have been used for medical experiments that might never have been conducted upon white people.[13] This history of control and limitation informs the way in which women of color experience the Family Development Act.

Ultimately, the Family Development Act can be seen as a withdrawal from, as opposed to an engagement in, the problems facing the African American and Latino communities. Although it is phrased in terms of empowerment, the Family Development Act blames the victims of poverty for poverty itself and seems only to want to reorganize and *contain* people on welfare. Jerome Miller makes a similar point in his discussion of high rates of incarceration of young African American men and the popularity of the call for more prisons and longer prison sentences:

> The "nothing works" school of criminology having run its course, we are ready for a new slogan—"They're not worth the effort." We will have moved from disciplining an incorrigible population to controlling a disposable one. This new adventure avoids the murkiness of "root causes" and offers a decidedly more comforting analysis to the majority.
>   (Miller 1992:40)

The enactment of the Family Development Act, and the popular support for punitive welfare reform nationwide, is an intentional targeting of a small number of women of color as the cause of the nation's woes. As middle-class people feel the pinch of the economic crisis, politicians turn to race baiting as a convenient escape from the demands for an improved economy. Syndicated cartoonist Jim Bergman drew a cartoon in which an African American welfare mother is described in successive frames as a parasite on the economy, the cause of the Savings and Loan crisis, the head of the Defense Department that wasted billions of tax dollars, and the leader of a decade of junk bonds and leveraged buyouts. At the end of the cartoon he writes, "Doesn't it feel better now knowing who to blame?"(Bergman 1992:A9).

By blaming the victim for the problem and presenting "family values" as the only solution, the Family Development Act allows all people not on welfare to stop seeking justice and simply walk away. This attitude can be heard in the chilling statement made by former Vice President Quayle in his "Murphy Brown" speech:

> I believe the lawless social anarchy which we saw [in the L.A. riots] is directly related to the breakdown of family structure, personal responsibility and social order in too many areas of our society. For the poor the situation is compounded by a welfare ethos that impedes individual efforts to move ahead in society. . . . The intergenerational poverty that troubles us so much today is predominantly a poverty of values.
>
> (Quayle 1992:2–4)

By attempting to restrict births to women and impose a married-parents structure on all welfare families, the Act is intended to promote men's control of women and to promote white control of African Americans and Latinos. New Jersey targeted African American and Latina mothers for racial and sexual control because they are a disempowered population and because the damaging combination of stereotypes renders them even more vulnerable to attack.

Theories that blame African American women and Latinas for poverty make it easy for laws like the Family Development Act to penalize welfare recipients. In fact, as long as people of color "cause" the devastation in their communities, the best public policy will be to abandon them. As George Frederickson explains:

> If the blacks were a degenerating race with no future, the problem ceased to be one of how to prepare them for citizenship or even how to make them more productive and useful members of the community. The new

prognosis pointed rather to the need to segregate or quarantine a race liable to be a source of contamination and social danger to the white community, as it sank ever deeper into the slough of disease, vice, and criminality.   (Frederickson 1971:117)

The Family Development Act carries implications that go beyond the imposition of a standard of motherhood that cannot be met by many African American and Latina mothers on welfare. When viewed in the context of the deplorable social and economic conditions forced upon communities of color, with people homeless and hungry, in prison, and dying of AIDS, victim-blaming rhetoric such as the "culture of poverty" is part of a larger message about who is fit to be free, who is fit to be able to eat, and who is fit to have a home. In short, this rhetoric sends a message to communities of color that they are not fit to survive.

NOTES

I would like to thank Dorothy Roberts for inspiring me through her writing to think critically about the legal construction of women of color. I also want to thank Martha Fineman for inviting me to present the first version of this essay at the December 1992 Feminism and Legal Theory Workshop at Columbia University. Finally, I am deeply grateful to Javier Maldonado for his insightful comments and steadfast support during the writing of this essay.

1. Regulations implementing the Family Development Act became effective October 1, 1992, after New Jersey obtained the necessary federal waivers from the U.S. Department of Health and Human Services.

2. The NAACP Legal Defense and Educational Fund and the NOW Legal Defense and Education Fund are co-counsel in the complaint.

3. In meetings with counsel for the complainants, HHS officials have expressed concern over the potential racially disparate impact of the New Jersey child exclusion policy but stressed that President Clinton wants to give states "flexibility" in seeking solutions to poverty (September 9, 1993, meeting between counsel for complainants, Michael Wald, Deputy Counsel General for HHS, and Dennis Hayashi, Director, HHS Office for Civil Rights).

4. Most other states and the United States as a whole have a majority of whites on the welfare rolls. New Jersey is exceptional because the majority of its recipients are African American and Latino.

5. It is critical to look beyond a view of the Family Development Act as an attack on women's rights of privacy and reproductive freedom, as they have

been traditionally defined by the mainstream feminist movement. An examination of the racism in the Family Development Act helps reveal most fully why and how the Act burdens the rights of African American women and Latinas.

6. Because of deep cuts in the New Jersey budget, the state was unable to implement the full range of support services described in bill 4700.

7. Under the current system, a woman's earnings are subtracted from her cash grant, dollar for dollar, after a certain amount is "disregarded." Every month, the first $120 she earns is disregarded, and one-third of what she earns is disregarded after that. After some months, only a $90 disregard is applied, and every dollar earned above that amount is subtracted from the grant. So, even if a woman earns very low wages in a marginal job, she may find her grant reduced to practically nothing, or her cash and Medicaid benefits may be terminated because she earns more than the amount of her cash grant.

8. I use the term *race* to describe Latinos as well as African Americans; I use the term *race discrimination* similarly to describe discrimination against both Latinos and African Americans. Although Latinos come in many different colors, I have chosen for the purposes of this paper to refer to them as a discrete race of people. For a more in-depth discussion of racial identification and resistance to Black/white racial categorization among Puerto Ricans in particular, see Rodriguez 1989:chap. 3.

9. In many scholarly works by women of color, the contemporary devaluation of African American women is described as a direct result of their historical treatment under slavery in the United States (see hooks 1981:52). Latinas are subjected to similar devaluation, but it springs from a different history, a history of invasion, conquest, enslavement of indigenous and African peoples, serfdom, and modern colonialism.

10. Puerto Ricans are seen by many as already "hooked" on the United States and therefore ripe for welfare dependency. Clara Rodriguez describes the common belief that

> [b]ecause of Puerto Rico's long periods of political dependency, first with Spain and then with the United States, Puerto Ricans are afflicted by political passivity; indeed, they have formed a colonial or welfare mentality with regard to the government.   (Rodriguez 1989:15)

This theory was also used by Daniel Patrick Moynihan to explain low voter turnout by Puerto Ricans in New York: "attitudes developed toward the paternalistic government of Puerto Rico were easily transferred to the government of New York" (Glazer and Moynihan 1970).

11. The regulations for the Family Development Act state that the Act's goal is to "foster parental responsibility by permitting public assistance recipients to deal with the same constraints faced by employed families where there is no automatic increase in salary when another child is born into the house-

hold" (24 N.J.R. 3346). This argument reveals the myopia of the creators of the Family Development Act and their fixation with the idea of welfare "dependency." In fact, working people get a $1,500 state tax exemption when they have a child (which is more than a woman on welfare would normally get per year for her baby). See also Roberts (1991:1474–75) discussing the imposition of a racially discriminatory procreation standard for drug-addicted women.

12. Regulations promulgated by the New Jersey Department of Human Services exclude from the child exclusion sanction any baby born within ten months of the woman's case opening. This may have been a defensive move by the department when it realized that it could not justify punishing births to women who did not conceive while on welfare.

13. Two examples of this kind of human experimentation are the forty-year-long Tuskeegee Syphilis Study conducted upon African American men and the testing of early high-dosage versions of the birth control pill upon Puerto Rican women living in housing projects in Puerto Rico during the 1950s.

12 | "Making Sense": Notes for Studying Black Teen Mothers

BARBARA OMOLADE

Just as the slave woman's sexuality, maternity, and labor were demonized and stigmatized in order to mask the oppressions of the American slave systems, contemporary Black teen and single mothers have become symbols of "the breakdown of the Black family"; this obscures the depths of their poverty and oppressions. While experiencing the most dire consequences of poor schooling, unemployment, racial inequities, and physical and ideological sexist attacks, Black teen mothers have become the centerpiece of debates between liberal and conservative approaches to public policies and government programs that deal with race, the family, poverty, and governmental funding of social programs. Both sides of this debate view Black teen and single mothers as social pariahs exhibiting pathological behaviors that call for greater efforts to limit their access to public assistance and other government programs and entitlements while admonishing them to change their sexual, marital, and maternal practices.

Increasingly, however, irrespective of whether government intervention or changed behavior is advocated, Black women's actual experiences and views are bypassed in public policy discussions. Since so much of public discourse and public policy is based upon the writings and findings of social scientists, especially sociologists, the ignored experiences of Black teen and Black single mothers have their origins in the failure of the social sciences to study Black women accurately. In fact, the very existence of Black single and teen mothers, irrespective of their experiences and backgrounds, has been constructed and construed by social scientists and public policymakers into a "social problem."

In order to make sense of the Black teen mother's experience from a social science perspective, we need to critically deconstruct its current theories and methodologies, which bypass *both* the personal and the political, *and* the individual structural aspects of their lives. There is an absence of a self-conscious critique of existing studies about Black teen mothers. There is even a lack of an appropriate social scientific language for describing this phenomena. By "language" I do not simply mean the vocabulary and words used, but rather the entire range of methods, theories, and tools used by the investigator, as well as the investigators's context and assumptions. Most significant in this context is the question of voice—who is speaking for whom and why?

The value of novels and stories by and about Black women suggests that their experiences are best represented in oral histories and life story narratives unimpeded by the methodological, linguistic, and ideological requirements of disciplines that often denigrate and ignore them. Black women are able to bear witness to themselves through testifying, recollection, and oral analysis.

Kesho Scott notes that the personal stories of the African American women in her ethnography *The Habit of Surviving* "are self-conscious testimonies—what they want to tell—about themselves as victims and survivors who exist on the margins of American culture. In the process of storytelling, each woman has exposed how black female identity is socially constructed" (Scott 1991:7).

Life Stories and Leticia's Family

Joelle Sanders's *Before Our Time* offers us a text revealing the "self-conscious" testimony of four generations of teenage mothers; Leticia, a twenty-year-old African American mother of two; Leticia's thirty-nine-year-old mother, Denise Benjamin; her sixty-three-year-old grandmother, Rena Wilson; and her eighty-three-year-old great-grandmother, Louise Eaton. Though separated by circumstance and historical context, each of these women has a narrative to tell about becoming a teenage mother.

The stories of these four women reveal what Patricia Hill Collins aptly calls "the multilayered texture of Black women's lives" (Collins 1990). These narratives reveal a great deal more than traditional sociological accounts of the "social problem" of Black teen mothers. They reveal how Black women who are daughters, wives, lovers, and workers, as well as mothers, have complex and multilayered life experiences. Their stories demonstrate relationships of care and concern among themselves and amplify the impact of fathers, stepfathers, lovers, and brothers—Black men—on the families they share. Their experiences provide insights into public policies, bureaucracies, and institutions because navigating family court systems, prisons, drug rehabilitation services, schools, and—of course—public assistance are integral parts of their lives. The narratives also reveal changing cultural norms, social contexts, and labor patterns as well as generational differences about sexuality and marriage among these Black women.

Louise Eaton was born in Maryland and had twelve brothers and sisters. When she was in her early teens, she moved to Washington, D.C., with one of her sisters. She became a domestic and met and married Williams Chambers in 1921 when she was fifteen years old. She subsequently moved to New York City and gave birth to two daughters. When her husband couldn't find work, Louise worked as a domestic. Her husband eventually abandoned the family when their eldest daughter, Rena, was thirteen years old. Rena became pregnant by her first lover when she was fifteen years old. He was her closest friend and had comforted her after her father left the family. They wanted to marry, but his mother prevented it. Rena graduated from high school when two months pregnant and stayed at a home for unwed mothers until she married Lewis Cadden, a marriage that lasted for one year. Years later Rena's daughter, Denise, ignorant about contraception, became pregnant by Charles Johnson when she was a senior in high school. She graduated when she was four months pregnant.

When her daughter, Leticia, was five years old, Denise married Reginald Benjamin and remained with him for nineteen years despite his sexual molestation of Leticia. After a suicide attempt when she was in the tenth grade Leticia began living with her boyfriend, Terrence, and his family. When she was sixteen years old, Leticia became pregnant by Terrence, dropped out of school, and became part of a "YWCA program in New York City that offered a long-standing comprehensive program for teenage mothers" (Sanders 1991:2). Sanders met Leticia at that program and was "taken and moved by her extraordinary memory . . . which summoned up details from her earliest years. She was unafraid to remember and was tremendously driven to talk about the particulars of her life" (3).

Sanders's ethnography focuses on Leticia and her relationships with money, men, motherhood, and drugs. Soon after the birth of her first child, Leticia's two-and-a-half-year relationship with Terrence deteriorated into violence and mutual adultery, which Leticia attributed to the negative influences of his family. She moved into an apartment that her grandmother "was renting out to someone else" (1991:48). Leticia eventually took in a roommate whose boyfriend sold drugs. The money he paid for using her apartment and the easy availability of drugs soon hooked Leticia into both violence and prostitution. She "wanted the money to buy a lot of nice things" and "do better for [her] kids" (102).

The short lived "high" that ensued—nine months from May 1985 to February 1986—left Leticia in a drug rehabilitation program and pregnant with her second child. After her rehabilitation she then moved to Queens to live with her great-grandmother. At this time she considered getting an apartment, passing her high school equivalency tests, and gaining permanent custody of her son, whom she had relinquished during the time she was addicted.

Leticia was clearly conflicted about whether to establish a long-term relationship or marriage with her child's father or continue having casual sexual relationships. Rejecting the traditional role of wife, she described her vision of marriage: "I know I can't live with Terrence. We both know that. But if he asked me to marry him, I would. But only on one condition. He'd stay where he's at and I'd stay where I'm at. We just don't belong in the same house. We argue too much and I like to do my thing" (105). Leticia said she met new men easily, or "wherever she goes." She got involved quickly and soon tired of them. She wanted personal, not merely sexual, satisfaction. She desired the power to mold men to meet her needs, "to raise them to be the men she would want to marry" (128).

Leticia viewed herself as a working mother. She "is not on welfare to depend on welfare," and stated, "I feel it's just something temporary until I'm able to go and get me a job . . . then, too, I feel that I have worked. I have had taxes taken out of my paycheck. So I'm only getting my taxes back" (102). At one point, Leticia worked at the same time as she received public assistance while her grandmother cared for her youngest child and babysat other children in the apartment they shared. She brought home $175 a week—$190 before taxes—yet public assistance cut her out of the budget at the same time that her child's father owed $9,000 in back child support.

During this same period, Leticia was unable to pass the high school equivalency exam because of the demands of her job and family. After failing she felt overwhelmed and depressed. She told her grandmother, "Everything is so overwhelming, I can't make any money on my job. I have to take Hazela and Terry for appointments, and I can't miss my work. It's too much. I can't take this kind of responsibility" (133). Leticia's grandmother felt she returned to drugs more out of defeat than desire. While addicted to drugs, Leticia lost custody of her children. Her son was sent to his father. Her daughter was cared for by her grandmother, who also attempted to find Leticia a drug rehabilitation program.

Eventually, Leticia's younger married brother took her south with him, telling her, "If you come with us, you've got to get it all together" (155). She stops using drugs, goes to work, and eventually returns to New York married to "a man her father's age" and pregnant with her third child (164). Although it is not certain that she won't return to drugs, Leticia tells Sanders that she no longer wants to experience the risks and losses associated with addiction. Leticia's life shows us the difficult levels of survival, struggle, loss, and hope associated with the maturing of a young adolescent girl into Black womanhood.

In her afterword, Sanders says that the experiences of Leticia and her maternal line indicate "the economic, psychological, and social struggles they faced as children and how these factors influenced their becoming adolescent mothers" (177). Sanders points to the policy and program initiatives implied by the persistent poverty with "little to call their own," paternal losses through either abandonment or mental illness, poor schooling, and lack of information on contraception of her subjects.

Sanders's account respectfully allows the women to speak about their lives in their own words, but her afterword ignores the content of criticisms and issues raised by Rena Wilson and the other women. It is hard to understand why Sanders feels it is unrealistic "to imagine that interventions in lives like these can make a difference in how teenagers think about themselves," when the women themselves describe their needs quite articulately and suggest some possible interventions.

Leticia's mother, Denise Benjamin, suggests that unrealistic notions about marriage influence sexual and reproductive choices. "You always think you're gonna be different from your parents. Do it differently. It's really a hopeful thing at the beginning. But we were too idealistic. I just thought if only I had a husband everything would be fine" (43). These remarks suggest that the choices of poor Black women who were teen mothers have also been influenced by the dominant culture's idealization of marriage. Yet, in her commentary, Sanders maintains a social-problems approach that focuses on deficiencies and lack.

Sanders does not analyze how the racism these women encounter creates even more difficulty in their lives. Rena Wilson points to the impact of racism in the family court's decision to separate Leticia's children:

> It's such a shame. The whole breakup of this family. In the end, the courts are a circus. They give you what they want. You get what they dole out. Our family is separated. And this white judge . . . could care less about what happens to a black family. . . . One would want people to take the view that family life is so very important. That the lack of a close knit family, the lack of something to hold on to, disorients people.   (62)

Further, while Sander's account emphasizes paternal loss, Rena Wilson focuses on the impact of maternal loss and her daughter's tolerance of incest, which she believed caused Leticia to feel emotionally abandoned and alienated. She suggests that the incest and loss of her mother's love were factors in understanding Leticia's self-destructive behaviors. "I attach a lot of importance to a mother's love. So sometimes when I think about Leticia I get very upset. I think about her childhood. . . . My own daughter, her mother—I can't understand how she could continue to live with a man who molested her daughter" (141).

Most telling is the fact that although Sanders laments that these girls should have "postponed the need to re-create mother-child bonds until they made something more of their lives as individuals," their stories, to the contrary, demonstrate that they did make a great deal out of their lives. Louise Eaton owns a house in Queens and has never been on public assistance. Rena Wilson was a civil service secretary until she retired and now cares for children to supplement her pension "and assure herself an independent life, one that now includes 'cruises to nowhere' and vacations, the theater, and dinners out" (174). She also seems to have access to apartments and always seems able to help her granddaughter Leticia and her children find places to live. Although on welfare when her children were young, Denise Benjamin now works as a medical technician. She remained married for nineteen years and her younger son is a gifted student. Her other son is married and living in the south. Although they were poor and badly schooled, the women in this family were able to make a great deal out of their lives and to support each other in the process. They made difficult and pragmatic decisions that helped them sustain their lives and the lives of their children.

The nuanced layers and personal insights revealed in these women's narratives simply do not fit popular views about the pathology and deviance of Black teen mothers. An analysis that suggests an unreflective cycle of self-destructive behaviors is not justified given a careful reading of these narratives.

Scott's discussion of survival habits helps us understand how Black women, like those in Sander's study, "make external and internal adaptations to economic exploitation and racial and gender related oppression." These habits of survival, "first and foremost, are responses to pain and suffering that help lessen anger, give a sense of self-control, and offer hope. They can also be responses to unexpected happiness—ways of keeping 'good times' going." They work, so oppressed people use them over and over again to defeat pain or prolong pleasure (Scott 1991:10).

Constructing a Social Problem: Are Black Teen Mothers Like Alcoholics?

Social events, such as teen pregnancy, are constructed as "problems"—human behaviors and phenomena that are bracketed, designated (labeled), categorized, and usually quantified as "pathological" and "problematic" within the overall society. Class, gender, and race are critical factors shaping this construction as well as selecting those constructors empowered to designate social phenomena as problematic.

The lives of Black people have always been considered and constructed as problems within American society because of fundamental views of Black inferiority based on ideas about genetic make-up and African origins. These views, which rationalized the position and condition of Black people during slavery and segregation, continue to operate to stigmatize their gender roles and personal choices.

Although sexuality, marriage, and family continue to be considered "private" issues for most Americans, slavery and segregation established patterns that unscrupulously exposed and subjected these arenas to public scrutiny for Black people. Furthermore, the resistance of Blacks to both white supremacy and their debased positions has been perceived to be a threat to the social order. In a classic "blame the victim" process, nearly everything African Americans have done, whether positive or negative, has been at one time or another considered a "social problem." This is then used as a rationale for the continued debasement and destitution of Black people.

The "social problems" associated with the Black family are fostered by a blindness to the disjuncture between white expectation of Black performance and behavior and pervasive social practices that deny African Americans equal access to resources and opportunities. Negative or positive Black coping mechanisms, individual mistakes and unorthodox practices, are viewed as evidence of group pathology, while structural displacement and historic legacies, whether positive or negative, are masked or omitted from the analysis. Hence, Black "social problems" are viewed like alcoholism—as sickness and character weakness—rather than evidence of long-standing societal problems with the racial, gender, and class inequality perpetuated by white supremacy and experienced by African Americans.

Teen pregnancy and childbearing in the 1970s "turned away from a focus on the consequences to mother and child" to the "negative consequences to 'society' caused by welfare dependency among teenage mothers" (Huling 1987:11). "The consistent focus of the popular media on teenage parenthood among black welfare recipients in the 1980s and the particular focus on welfare expenditures to teenage mothers in large cities . . . has shaped the public's current image of the typical welfare recipient as a black teenage mother" (12). This shift in perspectives must be seen within the larger context of the report issued by Senator Patrick Moynihan in March 1965, which equated the persistence of racism with the "atypical" nature of many Black families, especially the enhanced role of women. The report framed the argument for racial social reform solely in terms of strengthening the Black male patriarchy or male control over Black women. After decades of debating about the Black family and questioning the attacks of Moynihan and others, the current dominant paradigm is still in alignment with Moynihan's basic premise, which characterizes single mother families and marriages where Black women do not have traditional roles as a "tangle of pathology" (Moynihan 1965:29).

By regarding family forms as instrumental in creating pathology, Moynihan and others have simply fostered notions of Black female deviance based on Black women's personal reproductive and marital choices. Hence studies of Black teen motherhood are characterized by their "sharp lines between the normal and the deviant." Rather than teen motherhood's being viewed as the outcome of the normal behavior of heterosexual intercourse in a society where young people are influenced by a culture perpetuating romance and sex, Black teenagers are considered deviants because they have sex before either marrying or becoming adults.

Like the alcoholic, the teen mother (or father) is perceived as a particular kind of person with a major "social problem," a perception that places the researcher in the position of the "society" concerned with the welfare of "troubled persons" (Gusfield 1992:124). This positioning draws attention away from the "nonpathological aspects" of teen motherhood and the commonality of adolescent sexuality evident across racial and national boundaries.

Unwed teen mothers, like drinkers, are assumed to be malevolent and manipulative. Gusfield uses the phrase "malevolent assumption" to describe the ways those who are involved in drunk driving and drunkenness are assumed to cause "accidents" every time "alcohol is in use when an accident occurs" (Gusfield 1992:125). By confusing "statistical generalizations based on aggregate relationships" with causality, researchers continue to make most drinking a social problem. Likewise, irrespective of the circumstances, *all* Black teen mothers are assumed to be on welfare and to have strange and psychopathic reasons for having children. They are preemptively considered neglectful mothers with no prospect of succeeding in school or work.

It has "been repeatedly documented that, compared to youths who postpone childbearing, teenage mothers have lower educational attainment, less income, higher unemployment, are more dependent on welfare, are more likely to experience psychological problems associated with pregnancy, have higher levels of completed fertility, are more likely to abuse or neglect their children, experience higher rates of marital dissolution and are more likely to have daughters who also become unwed teenage mothers" (Taylor 1991:219). Yet these findings are challenged by other studies that indicate that over long periods of time the differentials in income between Black teen mothers and non-teen Black women are small. Mayfield's study of Black teen mothers indicates that they are more likely to complete their education and have positive supports and role models than white teen mothers (Mayfield 1991:227).

By critiquing studies that emphasize the negative impact of Black teen motherhood, I am not, of course, advocating teen mothering or understating the social and personal consequences of motherhood for young Black women. However, these studies fail to differentiate Black teen mothers on the basis of class, education, supportive family, positive relationships with the father of the child, and their own personalities. This failure divides Black, white, and Latin teen mothers from each other and ignores the lives of Black teen girls before they became mothers, or those who do not become mothers. In addition, it obscures the difficulties faced by all adolescent females. Teen parenthood should be viewed as a mainstream social phenomena rather than exclusively as a social problem of the Black poor.

Perhaps teen motherhood in the United States is nothing more than a socially unacceptable and difficult rite of passage from adolescence to womanhood for young women who are shaped by the persistence of traditional values that posit motherhood as evidence of womanhood. Society sends mixed messages to adolescents about womanhood; puritanical values regarding sexuality compete with images that emphasize sexuality as a male-dominated terrain in which women are perceived as sexual objects. There is confusion in society's promise of gender equality in which education and work supposedly release women from the traditional roles of marriage and motherhood. Many women desire sexuality and motherhood precisely because they offer an identity and domain outside the public and marketplace spheres.

Contemporary American society does not offer the average adolescent girl the tools and/or education to prevent pregnancy; the jobs and/or education to prevent pregnancy; the means to improve her life after becoming a mother; or even the housing or employment legitimacy necessary to establish a viable adolescent marriage. Black teenage girls and other adolescents have had to embark on their own perilous courses toward fulfillment and adulthood without adult guidance or support.

The construction of Black teen motherhood as a catastrophic social problem plays into widely held but false racial and gender notions that are also the context for empirical and sociological studies. Negative representations of Black women, held by society at large, interlock with and reinforce many social scientific studies that reify race and gender stereotypes. Black teen mothers are Black and, hence, seem to embody negative and pejorative beliefs about the inferiority and debased sexuality of people of African descent. They are female, so are subject to universal beliefs about women's inferiority. Because they are both Black and female, these teenagers are seen as continuations of the negative legacies of both their gender and their race, while also embodying the distorted images of Black women as sexually loose "mules of the earth." In this society sexually active adolescent girls of any racial or ethnic background are considered wayward and delinquent. All women who mother outside of marriage are stigmatized and viewed as "incubators of the underclass" and sexually promiscuous. Black adolescent poverty and unemployment are equated with personal failure; the fact that they are caused by structural processes outside of individual control is ignored. The "personal failure" viewpoint lends itself to equating the difficulties Black adolescents face with criminality.

Many white and Black sociologists and public policymakers negate and vilify the experiences of Black adolescents and teen mothers. Like Gusfield's description of those who construct alcoholism and social drinking as a social problem, these sociologists as "authors of research have appeared in the guise of spokespersons of the society. The subject has been identified by constructing its deviance. The impact of research in these areas has been to convince audiences that the author, the researcher, the scholar represents the 'society,' that the issue or phenomenon is the action of the abnormal, the deviant, the unusual" (Gusfield 1992:132). An understanding of how studies about Black teen mothers are constructed should enable us to learn "how public phenomena are given body and how authority is created and seized in the arena of public problems" (Gusfield 1992:132).

Black Families in Public Policy Discourse

One of the more recent public discussions of the Black family can be found in Andrew Hacker's *Two Nations, Black and White: Separate, Hostile, Unequal.* He summarizes the "dismaying" statistics: "Nearly two-thirds of black babies are now born outside of wedlock, and over half of black families are headed by women. The majority of black youngsters live only with their mother; and in over half of these households, she has never been married. At last count, over half of all single black women have already had children, and among women in their mid- to late thirties, less than half have intact marriages. These figures are from three to five times greater than for white households, and markedly higher than those recorded for black Americans a generation ago" (Hacker 1992:67). According to Hacker, "single-parent households—which in most cases means homes headed by the mother—have become increasingly common in America and the rest of the world. That this arrangement now accounts for over half of black families has aroused great concern. For one thing, the loss of male breadwinners has done much to perpetuate poverty. . . . In addition, some observers perceive an erosion of potential controls especially over teenagers—which were once maintained by fathers in the home" (68–69).

Although he cautions against generalizations about Black families, the very language he uses is one of generality. The data upon which his assertions are made, statistics produced by the government, are necessarily generalized. While he does concede that "this is not the place to debate whether optimal family life requires the full time presence of two parents bound by a legal marriage" (72–73), his chapter does not *discuss* either the successes of Black single mother families or the reasons for Black marital failure and the situations when marriage does not provide the optimal circumstance for childrearing.

Black women speak a different language from public policymakers and social scientists who study and view their experiences as "social problems." Again, *language*, here implies more than merely vocabulary. It implies context, culture, the perspective of the speaker (interpreter) as well as that of the listener. Everyone has a language and everyone speaks a "mother's tongue" in their interior, routinized daily lives. A person's language is a reflective and self-conscious way of describing and understanding oneself and one's world. More than a collection of the private musings of an individual, language also constructs and frames historical context, cultural syntax, and the grammar of experiences that creates the speakers, their audiences, and a public dialogue and debate.

To imagine a conversation between Hacker and Leticia, unmediated by Sanders, would reveal the disparity between the social scientist and his language and the subject and her language. Hacker—the social scientist—and Leticia—the subject—represent different races, classes, and genders. Hacker's voice has more authority than Leticia's, not simply because he is white, male, and professional but because his status and training reinforce his authority to generalize and surmise about human behavior. He is an intellectual whose "job" is to study, read, and write about society. Leticia's voice has authenticity, by contrast, because she has lived the experience and mastered the routines necessary for her life. His voice is that of society looking at her as an example of a generalization—the social problem of Black teenage mother. Hers is the "voice of the self" (Etter-Lewis 1991:52).

Leticia has authenticity, but she lacks authority. Sanders, another kind of social scientist, has also not lived as a Black teen mother but has been trained to enhance Leticia's voice by (re)presenting it in written and oral forms. As an oral historian or life history recorder, Sanders gives Leticia's authentic voice authority. Locating Leticia culturally and historically would further enhance her voice's authority without losing its authenticity. Hacker, by contrast, has authority, but lacks the authenticity derived from having lived the experience of his subjects—

in this case, having been a young Black mother. The stories and analysis of Black teen mothers have rarely been informed by a Black historical and cultural perspective focusing on Black women's experiences. This perspective could ultimately lead to discourses about unequal gender and racial power relations, stratification, white supremacy, and the cultural and coping strategies developed by African and slave women.

Although Leticia is portrayed as having a great deal of personal and individual power, which she uses to negotiate complex bureaucracies, garner resources and goods, and express and explore her own needs, the limitations of that power are obvious. The state and public institutions ultimately, control, contain, and limit her abilities. There are few efforts or recommendations for improving the lives of women like Leticia by increasing the numbers and salaries of their wage-earning work, or providing decent housing and child care. The jobs available to such women do not enable them to adequately support their families. Leticia's work ethic prevented her from merely accepting welfare and created problems with balancing her education, family, and work responsibilities. Her attempts to be sexually independent failed when confronted with male power especially in family court: her child's father gained custody of their child but was not forced to make child support payments. Leticia discovered she could not achieve both liberty and commitment in her relationships with men. There were virtually no safety nets and social supports available to a substance-abusing mother desiring to "kick her habit."

Because the structures of power are so subtle and pervasive, even social scientists are unaware of how these structures shape the lives of both themselves and their subjects. Sociologist Dorothy Smith describes social scientists as those whose positions of reflection and analysis of the world enhance the viewpoints and strategies of those who rule. She uses the term *relations of ruling* to go beyond the traditional concepts of "power, organization, direction, and regulation" to include "patriarchal forms of our contemporary experience." She continues by saying that we are "ruled by forms of organization vested in and mediated by texts and documents, and constituted externally to particular individuals and their personal and familial relationships" (D. Smith 1987:3). In their attempts to objectify human experiences, the sociologist and others in the academy are implicated in creating the texts and representations used by those who rule. Irrespective of their goals, uncritical social scientists speak in the language of the state and the dominant discourse, in part because they ignore the authenticity and perspectives of those who live on the other side of the "fault line"—those whom they study.

While aware and outspoken about a racial and class "fault line," for nearly a century most African American sociologists paid little attention to the social construction of gender, especially its interconnections with race in Black women's lives. These sociologists often uncritically support Black patriarchal solutions to Black female employment and racial marginality. For example, some support the promotion of male-headed households and families. This is often done without examining women's perspectives and experiences regarding relationships and marriages with Black men.

The most well-known, profound, and intelligent insights into the Black female psyche in the public culture tend to have been written by Black women novelists and poets. Disciplines such as sociology or political science have not been transformed or infused with in-depth analysis or critical studies by and about Black women. Sociological works on gender and race that challenge the existing sociological canon, especially writings by Black women sociologists such as Patricia Hill Collins, Rose Brewer, and Cheryl Townsend Gilkes, have not been given the recognition nor have they had the impact of the writings of Black women writers such as Toni Morrison, Maya Angelou, Terry McMillian, and Alice Walker. Black female literature has become a genre in which myth, autobiography, and fiction combine to present the most accurate written accounts of Black women's lives. The most popular works about Black teen mothers are, for example, the novel *The Color Purple* by Alice Walker and the autobiographical *I Know Why the Caged Bird Sings* by Maya Angelou. The lack of powerful and challenging studies of Black teen and single mothers has meant that Moynihan's analysis and Wilson's underclass theories influence virtually all social scientific research and government policy on the Black family (Wilson 1987).

Statistics are a significant instrument for studying general aspects and providing demographic information about groups. In making macro or micro conclusions about social phenomena, sociologists and others have relied heavily on the data produced by statistics to study social facts.

Most sociological studies about Black teen mothers are not life stories. They are statistical studies analyzing discrete phenomena, such as comparisons of the onset and frequency of sexual intercourse for Black and white teen mothers. These studies use the same methodology of measuring the statistical significance of variables and then attempt to discuss the relationship of their findings to general theories and conclusions about their subjects. This quantitative approach reveals a great deal about what aggregate numbers of teen mothers *do* in terms of what variables the observers select as important to their research agenda. Researchers attempt to measure particular behaviors and reveal patterns, but they indicate little about who these girls *are*. Careful formulations can examine specific behaviors and attitudes, but they cannot reveal complex motives and emotions. The twists and turns of the lives of individual women or the multilayered levels of the Black female experience are ignored.

What is obliterated by the reliance on statistical data is that the lives and experiences of individuals are also social facts. However, Black teen mothers or anyone else do not live their lives to provide social facts to be used by social scientists. They do not make decisions to confirm or deny public policy trends. Teens do not consider the rates of teen pregnancy when they have sex. They, like the rest of us, are living their lives based upon their feelings and thoughts. Each oral history and life story reveals that each individual is a statistical outlyer—an anomaly whose life is an intricate and complex construction of their individual self. These selves are social facts, and in order to understand them it is necessary to first respect their subjective and real-life existence. Generalizations about human behavior are a necessary shorthand for sociologists, investigators, and others to understand what is going on; they must not, however, be allowed to become a substitute for a discussion of the discrete, specific lives of the individual, even and especially that individual who is young, Black, and female.

Black women have unique experiences that result from racial and gender interconnections as well as from being oppressed by racism and sexism. Scott notes that "the women in my own family and community seemed to be poised on a 'tightrope,' suspended between overlapping worlds—the worlds of being black and being woman. Their experiences were colored by their own cultural invention—their creation of themselves and their personal stories" (Scott 1991:7). "A critical component of the black female self is her tie to the African-American community. In many instances she is simultaneously a stabilizing force from within the community and an agent of change" (Etter-Lewis 1991:53). Black women are not always capable of performing these stabilizing roles or of acting as agents of change, but many do. Leticia, for example, in spite of her difficulties, was a leader of her support group and spoke publicly on many occasions about being a Black teen mother. Her mother is active in the church. It is essential to ask, then, what kinds of formal and informal groups exist in the Black community that have an impact on the lives of Black teen mothers and their families. Why are the patterns and processes of those groups ignored in discussions of Black teen mothers?

Life stories must be the center of all social scientific inquiry about Black women, irrespective of other methodologies used. The Black community, with its history and culture, is integral to this inquiry, because it locates Black women's lives within a social context that nestles their individual and family life. Their stories should shape the quantitative social scientists' choice of variables and their analysis of data. They should inform discussions of power, stratification, and ideology, as examples of how these systems are reproduced, manipulated, and resisted. The routine and everyday experiences of Black women should undergird public discourse and social science scholarship. All levels—the personal life story, the historical and cultural dimensions of Black life, and the structures and processes of the larger society—should be included or referenced in each study about the Black teen and single mother.

The Black teen mother "crisis" is not due simply to the difficulties faced by young Black women and children; it is also due to the inability of public policy to meet their needs successfully. This inability is reinforced by the very social science that is supposed to explain and analyze human behavior and therefore inform public policy.

Social scientists, as part of the dominant discourse, are reluctant or unable to distance themselves from their role of supporting the state, the patriarchy, or the institution of white supremacy long enough to authenticate Black women's experiences. These social scientists hence lack a methodology and a language for making sense of the lives of Black women. Although they speak with different levels of authority and authenticity, social scientists choose variables, construct questions, and interpret data in the same way that Black teen girls decide whether they should have sex—that is, subjectively. The human endeavor, no matter what it may be, is subjective and has its own specific language for explaining and understanding its activity. This subjectivity and specific language need therefore to be at the center of all our inquiries.

PART FOUR

Mother in Practice

13 | Challenging "Hidden" Assumptions: (Women) Lawyers and Family Life

MARY JANE MOSSMAN

This essay reexamines, from the current perspective of the 1990s, a question that was asked in 1889 by a woman lawyer in Boston named Lelia Robinson: "Is it practicable for a woman to successfully fulfill the duties of wife, mother, and lawyer at the same time? Especially a young married woman?" (Drachman 1989:222).

This question has been asked more often as the number of women seeking admission to the legal profession has dramatically increased during the past two decades in both Canada and the United States. Robinson's question requires us to confront directly the issue of whether women should agree to conform to the existing work patterns of the legal profession as a condition of entry, or whether there is a need for the profession itself to change to accommodate new kinds of entrants. Buried within this question, are hidden[1] assumptions about the roles of men and women in our society, assumptions that become evident if we reverse the gender in Robinson's question and ask whether it is practicable for a man to be a "husband, father, and lawyer" at the same time; clearly, this combination of familial and professional roles has always been regarded as entirely compatible for men.

The entry of women in large numbers (including women who are mothers) to the paid workforce has become a widespread feature of North American life in the second half of the twentieth century (Armstrong and Armstrong 1988:143; Government of Canada 1989; Vanier Institute 1992). However, the entry of women into the legal profession in ever increasing numbers has occurred only quite recently, against a background of previous legal and social exclusion. This pattern has two consequences for our current examination of Lelia Robinson's question. First, due to the numbers of women now entering the legal profession, the answer to the question is no longer simply one of individual choice, a choice that traditionally required women to be either lawyers or wives and mothers, but not both. Instead, the issue has now become one about equity within the profession as a whole. Second, the pattern of exclusion of women from the legal profession only reversed in significant numbers within the past two decades. This means that about 80 percent of all women who have ever been lawyers in North America were admitted after 1970 (Epstein 1990:309; Weisberg 1982; Harvey 1970–71:9; Mossman 1988b:252; Dranoff 1972:177). Thus, the demographic profile of women lawyers is not evenly spread across the adult life span. Indeed, the largest proportion of women who are lawyers is found in age groups that correspond to childbearing years, a factor that accounts for the recent, more vocal expressions of concern about alternative work arrangements among members of the legal profession.

The entry of women to the legal profession represents only one example of the pattern of women seeking employment in nontraditional workplaces. At the same time, the example of women lawyers is particularly interesting for a number of reasons. Law's traditional role in shaping public policy means that lawyers and law firms may provide a leadership role in the creation of an integrated workforce in our society. Such a view was espoused, for example, by Judge Judith Kaye in the United States, when she suggested that law firms should apply their enormous resources to create a "genuinely integrated profession," one that could be a model for achieving gender equality in society (Kaye 1988:126; see also Rhode 1988:1163). In Canada, the entrenchment of sex equality guarantees in the constitution arguably creates special obligations on the legal profession to ensure that it meets standards of sex equality *within* the profession. These men and women have professional responsibilities to deliver legal services that accord with these constitutional guarantees of sex equality (Smith 1992:211). The existence of such constitutional guarantees of sex equality in Canada, coupled with a significant number of official surveys of the differing roles of men and women lawyers by provincial law societies and the Canadian Bar Association, makes this issue one of particular interest for lawyers in Canada as well as in the United States.

All these factors suggest that women who are both lawyers and mothers may be especially well positioned, *as women*, to challenge the hidden assumptions that are at the root of the work and family dilemma that currently exists in North American society.

"Hidden" Issues About Work and Family

A reexamination of the work and family dilemma in the legal profession must start by questioning underlying (and hidden) assumptions about three matters: the nature of legal work, the different and "gendered lives" (Fineman 1990:25; 1992a:1) of men and women in North American society, and the complexity of the idea of "family." Assumptions about these matters influence not only the shape of proposed solutions but also the extent to which such solutions will either constrain or enhance the goal of gender equality in workplace arrangements for the future.

The Nature of Legal Work

Reexamining the nature and organization of legal work requires a critical appreciation of the extent to which existing arrangements reflect current needs on the part of clients and their lawyers and the extent to which our existing practices are the result of traditions that do not now serve society as well as in the past. Do current arrangements, for example, take advantage of the flexibility of new technologies, particularly innovations that allow effective long-distance communication? Is a legal culture of long hours at the workplace always necessary, or does it reflect a tradition that thrives on work for its own sake? From a critical perspective, how might we organize legal work in the 1990s so as to accomplish two objectives that are of equal importance: highly efficient and effective client services, as well as meaningful work and family lives for lawyers?

As Joan Williams has suggested, our current arrangements for legal work reveal a hidden assumption about the availability of full-time domestic labor to support the activities of lawyers in the workforce (Williams 1990:352–53). That assumption is evidenced by the fact that a typical lawyer expects to work twelve hours per day (perhaps not including travel time to work), often six days per week. Such a model of lawyering offers three alternatives for women: one is to have no children, a "choice" adopted by many more women lawyers than their male colleagues; another is to have children but, adopting the life pattern of the typical workaholic father-lawyer, spend little time with them and consign most of the care to someone else; or finally, to depart from the model of "ideal worker" by arranging work responsibilities so as to meet family obligations (Esau and Penner 1990).

Recent lawyer surveys in Canada confirm that women lawyers do not enter the *private* practice of law at the same rate as their male colleagues, a conclusion that seems to suggest that many women lawyers "choose" the third alternative. A recent Ontario survey, for example, compared men and women entering the legal profession since 1975, and found that 81 percent of male lawyers entered private practice while only 68 percent of women did so. There were similar disparities in the rates of men and women who remained in private practice; women were more likely to be employed by government (Law Society 1991:15; see also Curran 1986:19; R. Abel 1988:203). These conclusions are interesting because the work done by lawyers employed by government (litigating, drafting, negotiating, and creating large-scale agreements among multiple parties) is similar to that done by private-practice lawyers. Thus, the different patterns of employment among male and female lawyers cannot be explained by differences in the legal *work* that is being done in each setting. However, there are important differences in working *conditions*, which may indeed be affecting employment choices. It is crucial therefore to identify the hidden assumptions that underlie the working conditions of lawyers in private practice, "the legal culture of the large firms" (Menkel-Meadow 1989:314).

After identifying the hidden assumptions about current arrangements for legal work in differing work contexts, it is important to reexamine them critically because the pattern of women lawyers' work presently operates to systematically limit their equal access to prestigious positions in the legal profession. Thus, one of the consequences of a pattern of disproportionate "segregation" of men in private practice firms and women in government is the glass ceiling for women lawyers. As the Ontario survey suggested:

> Underrepresentation of women in the private practice of law has important implications for women's opportunities for advancement within the profession. High standing, as regards income and prestige, is achieved most often in the realm of private practice. . . . The underrepresentation of women in private practice translates into reduced opportunities for advancement to some of the most prestigious positions within the profession.
>   (Law Society 1991:4)

Such problems clearly have an adverse impact on equality objectives for men and women within the legal profession. At the same time, it is arguable that society is also not well served by the demands of the current legal culture; as Eleanor Fox has stated so bluntly:

> The hyper-technician, honed down and homogenized by the bureaucracy and driven by the constant reminder of private short-term profit-maximizing interests, will not have the human capacity to solve the legal problems of the twenty-first century.   (Fox 1989:963)

For all these reasons, our search for solutions to the work and family dilemma for members of the legal profession must begin by challenging the status quo of work arrangements for lawyers and unmasking those practices that, in reality, depend more on tradition than on client needs for efficient and effective legal services. We should be especially wary of many such arrangements that reflect a gendered model of lawyering, a model that imagines a worker, typically male, with full-time domestic labor, typically female, in the home. The critical point is that our search for a solution to the dilemma of work and family cannot rest on an assumption that current arrangements for legal work are neutral in their impact on men and women who are lawyers. Rather, they embody hidden assumptions about the nature of legal work, assumptions that privilege those without familial responsibilities and that are, for that reason, incompatible with the creation of an integrated legal workforce now and in the future.

Lawyers and "Gendered Lives"

We must also rethink the idea that women lawyers make different "choices" in relation to work and family life. As Deborah Rhode has suggested, women lawyers in the United States are routinely constrained in terms of their occupational "choices" by traditional understandings of sexual roles for men and women in our society (Rhode 1988:1182). The recent survey reports in Ontario confirm that women lawyers experience the relationship between their family roles and their work as lawyers in ways that are different and gendered by contrast with male lawyers. For example, women lawyers reported larger shares of responsibility for child care (an average of 49 percent of the total child care responsibility), by contrast with male lawyers (an average of 26 percent of the total) (Law Society 1991:46, table 35).[2] Similarly, surveys in British Columbia, while demonstrating a range of women lawyers' responses to responsibility for child care, confirmed that women lawyers experienced a disproportionate share of the responsibility by contrast with their male colleagues (Brockman 1991:31–34; 1992a:91; 1992b:747).[3] These results are consistent with those achieved in the 1987 survey of Stanford law graduates in which male lawyers committed significantly less time than female lawyers to child care (Taber et al. 1988:1209).

For women lawyers, these hidden assumptions about women's greater responsibilities for child care clearly conflict with a model of legal work that assumes the existence of full-time domestic labor in the home. Taken together, these two hidden assumptions constrain the "choices" available to women lawyers, by contrast with their male colleagues, and contribute to a gendered experience of lawyering. In other words, "[M]en and women are not similarly situated with respect to work, a fact veiled by the view (held widely by women as well as men) that women's different work patterns result from 'choice' " (J. Williams 1990:353). Even though some women lawyers are now "choosing," like their male colleagues, to make professional work their priority, such a choice frequently has different consequences for them. As the American Bar Association Report on Women in the Legal Profession noted, "Women who stick it out and make partner may wake up and find themselves, as one woman testified, 'forty-three, single, childless, and typical' " (Barnett 1990:217). At the same time, workplaces with more willingness to examine the structures of legal work have demonstrably benefited. They have received an influx of large numbers of energetic women lawyers who want to engage in serious professional work as well as enjoy their family lives, a result that suggests that workplaces make "choices" as well.

The question of "choice" is misleading, however. There are many women lawyers who cannot take advantage of the limited choices that are available. For these women there is no choice at all. For instance, women lawyers who are sole-support parents or sole providers within their families must work in legal positions that accommodate family responsibilities. Other women find themselves locked into certain kinds of job settings because of discriminatory reasons such as race or ethnicity.[4] Thus, solutions to the work and family dilemma need to be responsive to the needs of women lawyers in differing contexts and with different experiences of the nature of "choice." Women's gendered lives mean that there are societal expectations about their family roles that not only differ from those of their male colleagues but also reveal differences among women especially if they are not white, not middle-class, and not heterosexual.

The gendered experiences of women lawyers must also be under-stood in the context of a legal profession in transition from exclusivity to a more integrated workforce. The pattern of women's entry to the profession has been characterized in terms of three phases: first, the pio-neer phase when there were very few women lawyers in North America; a second phase of "superwoman" lawyers who were intent on meeting the requirements of the male model of lawyering even if it meant "revis-ing loan agreements in the labor room"; and, more recently, a phase in which women lawyers more often decide that the "hard-won prize" is not worth the sacrifice of their personal and family lives (Kaye 1988:121; Lyne 1992:F27). This kind of analysis is consistent with data in the Canadian surveys of women lawyers, data that reveal a higher rate of exit from the profession for women than for men, especially for those in age cohorts that correspond to childbearing years (Law Society 1991:64, esp. table 48).[5] Yet it is also important to understand that these three phases overlap: some women lawyers may be in the pioneer phase at the same time that others are in the "superwoman" phase, and still others are questioning the price and moving out of the profession altogether. For women lawyers who are not white, the category of pio-neer may be more frequently experienced than any of the others.[6] And for some women lawyers, it is possible to experience all three of these phases at different times in a career.

At the same time, however, this analysis shows that, because of our society's unstated assumptions about roles for men and women, women's experiences as lawyers are different from those of their male colleagues. Indeed, these gendered expectations are sometimes reflected in judg-ments about women lawyers even when those women lawyers do con-form to the model for legal work in private-practice firms. As Epstein commented, "Women in firms who want to leave early to be with their children have a hard time, but women who stay late are regarded as heartless by the same men who set the standards" (Epstein 1990:334). For this reason, effective solutions to the work and family dilemma require that we confront the gendered roles of men and women in North American society, and the ways in which these gendered roles have an impact on women lawyers in differing circumstances.

The Idea of "Family"

In addition to the nature of legal work and gendered experiences among women lawyers, we must also question hidden or unstated assumptions about the idea of "family." Most of the recent surveys of women lawyers in Canada have focused on the issue of child care as the primary aspect of the work and family dilemma. Such a focus reflects the extent of the current crisis for women lawyers, but it needs to be understood in broader terms as well. The issue of child care for members of the legal profession needs to be expanded beyond the context of the traditional nuclear family (and the legal definitions of family) to include common-law unions, second marriages with stepchildren, and same-sex relationships with and without children, to name just a few. In this way the discussion will reflect family life in contemporary North America more accurately.

The gendered roles for women and men in North American society must be taken into account with respect to family responsibilities in a wide variety of familial contexts. Some anecdotal evidence suggests that both male and female lawyers conceal the existence of same-sex relationships for fear of reprisal, particularly in private-practice firms. For these lawyers, the work and family dilemma thus presents the double burden of discharging significant family responsibilities and, moreover, doing so in secret. While little is known about how the dilemma is resolved, it is possible to speculate that the gendered roles of men and women in our society may impose greater burdens on women lawyers than on their male colleagues in the context of these family relationships, as in others.

The idea of family responsibilities should be expanded to include care for dependents other than small children. Even when physical care may be provided by others, there is evidence that women, more often than men, are responsible for the emotional care of both children and adults. According to Monica Boyd, "social norms dictate that women are the main care givers" and thus "the need to extend aid—either financial, emotional, or social—to their elderly relations will have the greater impact on women" (M. Boyd 1988:92). In light of these gendered responsibilities, even women lawyers who remain single may have familial responsibilities for others, which differ in kind and degree from those of their male colleagues.

Thus, it is not enough that our solutions take account of the pressing problems currently experienced by mothers who are lawyers (including those who are married and cohabiting and those who are sole-support parents). They must also recognize the broader range of familial demands and human needs that constitute important and lasting relationships. We need to identify hidden assumptions about the idea of family if we are to ensure that our solutions match the complexity of the familial relationships in which women and men lawyers are actually involved. Identifying the hidden assumptions underlying the idea of family is thus as critical to the process of designing solutions to the work and family dilemma as revealing the hidden gendered assumptions about the organization of legal work. Only by questioning these assumptions will meaningful and lasting solutions to the work and family dilemma be possible.

Work and Family: Solutions for the 1990s

[T]he legal profession has changed in recent years, making room for mothers, and, indirectly, fathers. But so far the changes are like a crack in a granite foundation, and the women who form the blade of the chisel may find themselves as pinched as the metaphor suggests.

(Freeman 1986:36)

Changes have been taking place in arrangements for accommodating work and family within the legal profession. Yet, all too often, these changes have been piecemeal, representing token efforts to accommodate the needs of some women lawyers without in any way challenging the underlying issues: the nature of legal work, the "gendered lives" of men and women who are lawyers, and the need to fully define "family" responsibilities. In such a context, women lawyers have been generally expected to conform to the traditional pattern of the lawyer's professional life, perhaps with some modest and short-term alterations to suit their childbearing roles. Yet the profession itself has not been required to change, and lawyers have not altered their fundamental expectations about the roles of men and women or about the "hidden" familial responsibilities most often borne by women, including women who are lawyers.

Any discussion of proposed solutions to the work and family dilemma needs to start by acknowledging that such proposals must address the need for fundamental, not merely Band-Aid, changes.

Designing Guidelines: A Problem for "Women" or for "Parents"?

One issue that must be addressed when solutions are being considered is whether it is more appropriate to make policies gender-neutral or gender-specific. Much of the pressure on the legal profession to change to accommodate work and family responsibilities has come from women, as increasingly large numbers of women enter the profession. For this reason, the work and family dilemma has often been perceived as "a woman's problem," requiring law firms and other employers to create special policies for women who are lawyers. Such a characterization obviously reflects the reality that women are more likely to be adversely affected by the work and family dilemma. Indeed, it seems that the failure of law firms to respond effectively to these needs has resulted in women's higher rate of departure from private practice in Canada (Law Society 1991:64–70; Brockman 1991:31). Such concerns led Chief Judge Patricia Wald to urge the profession to respond to the needs of "present-day women," and not to worry about the possibility that they might be thereby reinforcing women's traditional responsibilities for child care (Wald 1988:75).

By contrast, some firms have approached these issues as a more general problem of balancing work and family responsibilities, a problem that affects men who are lawyers as well as women. For these firms, a gender-neutral approach has seemed the preferable means of ensuring that women enjoy equal opportunities with men in professional work. A woman lawyer involved in drafting a "parenting policy" for her U.S. law firm stated emphatically: "It was important to me to indicate that the firm regards the issue as parenting, not solely as a woman's issue" (Freeman 1986:36; cf. Fineman 1992b:301).

The gender-neutral approach has also been suggested as a way of overcoming the problem of the segregation of mothers within the profession. Recent evidence has indicated, for example, that a woman who "chooses" the "mommy track" (Kingston 1988; Mezey 1992:206) is likely to face permanent and often insurmountable barriers in her legal career thereafter: the "glass ceiling" problem. According to Carrie Menkel-Meadow, women must therefore look carefully at these "hidden" consequences of their "choices" (Menkel-Meadow 1983:197). Yet, even a gender-neutral "parenting track" might lead to the same problems for both men and women who choose it. To avoid this result such an arrangement must be accompanied by a commitment to rethink the nature of legal work in light of lawyers' needs to balance their work and family lives. Thus, a gender-neutral approach is not, at least by itself, a panacea for solving the work and family dilemma.

Indeed, by focusing on the relative usefulness of special policies for women lawyers on one hand, or gender-neutral policies on the other, we risk obscuring what is fundamentally at issue in relation to such policies: the "hidden" issues about the structure of legal work, the gen-

dered lives of men and women who are lawyers, and a broader conception of what constitutes family. Instead of the debate about special
needs versus gender-neutral policies, the legal profession needs to
develop policies about work and family that both respond to the needs
of women lawyers who currently experience disproportionate pressures
and also to take account of the need for changes in parenting arrangements that are more suited to an integrated workforce in the legal profession and more widely throughout North America.[7] Thus, whether a
policy is framed in gender-neutral language is much less important than
its content and whether it can respond to both present needs and future
aspirations.

Designing Solutions: Alternative Work Arrangements

Law firms and other workplaces in Canada and the United States have
been developing a number of different kinds of alternative work
arrangements, especially but not only for women lawyers (American
Bar Association 1990; Boston Bar Association 1991). In general, alternative work arrangements fall into four categories: restructured full-ime
work; reduced work-time options; leaves; and technological innovations. Some or all of these alternatives may be useful in a variety of legal
workplaces, although it is always necessary to tailor solutions to the particular circumstances of workplaces and of lawyers. Moreover, in light
of the "hidden" issues I have already discussed, it is critical not to
assume that just because they are rare, alternative work arrangements
are therefore "unworkable"; as the ABA manual has stressed, there is a
need for both workplaces and lawyers to be flexible and accommodating in seeking solutions and in assessing their merits.

   Restructured full-time work is an option that includes flexible working hours (all employees work during core hours, but make up a weekly
total according to their individual schedules) and compressed work
weeks (employees work the total allotment of hours per week compressed into fewer days). These alternatives are less useful in private-
practice law firms because the total number of hours makes it difficult
to have time left over for flextime or to compress such hours into fewer
days. As Linda Marks has stated: "It is hard to compress a seventy-hour
workweek into fewer than five days and still do anything else" (Marks
1990:363); such an alternative fails to challenge the ethos of long hours
of work for lawyers. At the same time, it is important not to eliminate
this alternative too readily without considering its usefulness in partic-

ular circumstances; for example, it may be an excellent alternative for a divorced parent (male or female) whose custodial responsibilities are heavier on weekends than during weekdays.

Reduced work-time options include arrangements for working part-time, job sharing, and phasing out, all of which involve working fewer hours per week than the norm. This arrangement may also be less useful for lawyers, where the norm is often much longer than forty hours per week. It works in a number of different ways: working fewer than the normal number of days per week, working a total number of hours per year but with fewer regular hours, or billing a defined number of hours per year with flexible time. According to the ABA manual, the key to making part-time work depends on specifying the exact requirements of a part-time lawyer. It is also necessary for both the lawyer and the firm to accept the need for some flexibility in the arrangements.[8] According to Linda Marks, "part-time in law firms seems to work best when figured in terms of billable hours or billable plus nonbillable hours worked per year, rather than a certain number of hours per week" (Marks 1990:364).

Part-time work may also be combined with job sharing to reduce overhead costs involving space and support staff. While job sharing can mean that two lawyers share cases and clients, it can also mean that two lawyers "share an office or secretary, and provide backup to one another on cases" (Marks 1990:365). Flexibility on the part of the firm and the lawyer is also needed to make job sharing effective. By contrast with part-time and job sharing, which are relatively new developments, phasing out is well-established as an option; it has been used traditionally for senior members of firms who want to retire gradually. Indeed, widespread acceptance of the practice of phasing out among private-practice firms weakens the argument that other kinds of reduced work-time options are unworkable.

Leaves from practice, with or without pay, are other options for alternative work arrangements. The provisions of federal legislation in Canada concerning maternity, paternity, and adoptive parental leaves with partial pay offer a useful starting point for the creation of such leave programs for lawyers.[9] As the ABA has suggested, it is important to design specific leave policies for childbirth and adoption, and to distinguish them clearly from other kinds of policies for purposes of child care.[10]

By contrast with leaves for childbirth and adoption, leaves for child care, other "dependent-care," or "family illness" are relatively rare in the legal profession. The Canadian surveys of lawyers suggested that the absence of such arrangements was a major reason for the disproportionately low number of positions held by women in large private-practice firms. According to the Law Society survey, for example, women lawyers accommodated their family demands (especially child care responsibilities) by exiting from law-firm workplaces, and reentering (if at all) a few years later in different workplaces (Law Society 1991:58). In the United States, serious concerns have been expressed about the costs to law firms of these patterns of "erosion" of valuable personnel (Marks 1990:366). There is reason to reconsider the usefulness of leave arrangements in avoiding the exit and loss of valuable personnel, particularly in light of the relatively more usual pattern of leaves for educational or political purposes, or for purposes of a "sabbatical." While the purposes of these latter arrangements are clearly different from leaves required to meet familial responsibilities, it is less clear why the former should be available and the latter not. A firm policy that takes no account of lawyers' needs to respond to family responsibilities sends a message (to men as well as to women) about the firm's values in terms of family life, values that are unrealistic and inappropriate in the context of an integrated workforce of men and women lawyers.

Telecommuting or "flexiplace" refers to new arrangements for working away from the workplace, generally accomplished by means of new technology. For most professionals, the idea of working at home full-time is not attractive, both because of the isolation experienced and because of human needs to create a sense of home that is separate from the workplace. Yet arrangements involving technology can probably offer the extra flexibility needed to make part-time and other alternative arrangements work effectively (Brooks 1992). Thus, these options should be considered along with other possible alternative arrangements.

Alternative Arrangements and the Need for Fundamental Change

The goal of creating a fully integrated workforce cannot be achieved without policies that enable men and women to balance work and family responsibilities. However, in order for such policies to be effective, we need to confront the "hidden" issues in the work and family dilemma. It is only then that we can negate the adverse connection that now exists between accommodating work and family by alternative work strategies and the "glass ceiling" (Mossman 1988a:567; Hagan, Huxter, and Parker 1988:9). The fundamental problem is that the conception of lawyering currently accepted as inevitable is an outdated conception based on the idea of a lawyer as a male worker without significant familial responsibilities. Effective solutions to the work and family dilemma require "a direct challenge to the gendered structure of wage labor" (J. Williams 1990:356).

In considering this problem, Joan Williams identified and then rejected two possible changes. One would require men to give up their right to the domestic labor of women, a solution Williams regarded as unrealistic for most men who are lawyers. A second alternative was that women lawyers be relieved of child care responsibilities. This alternative, Williams recognized, does not really change existing practices, since it still permits fathers to shift family responsibilities to women; the only difference would then be that female caregivers would no longer be these male lawyers' wives but would be "less privileged women" who would provide child care and household help for wages. Such a solution seems undesirable in societal terms, since it means that an integrated workforce of men and women lawyers would be achieved at the expense of those women who provide caregiving. It is not insignificant that these women are often the most marginalized workers and the most disadvantaged women in North America in terms of race and class (Macklin 1992:682). In spite of the fact that many women lawyers have "chosen" this solution on an individual basis, therefore, it is unlikely to be accepted as a general societal solution.

Thus, fundamental change requires that we confront the model of lawyering that now creates "inconsistency between the roles of ideal worker and responsible parent" (Williams 1990:356). We need a new model of lawyering and a new definition of an "ideal lawyer" as someone *with* family responsibilities (Williams 1990:356; Hochschild and Machung 1989; Czapanskiy 1991:1415). Williams has argued that the legal profession is an excellent place to begin to develop policies that truly challenge existing norms, particularly because of the legal profession's current search for more meaningful work:

> The legal context seems particularly promising as an educational tool because the time demands are often so excessive that even male lawyers see them as disfiguring the broader goals they have set for their lives. This may make it easier to see women's childrearing aspirations as part of a larger pattern of aspiration in which work demands are balanced with other goals. (356)

Negative views about the practice of law (on the part of some women lawyers) have appeared recently in the United States (R. Hirsch 1989:22) and were evident in the comments of women lawyers who participated in the surveys in Canada (Law Society 1991:78). Similar frustrations were expressed in the Canadian surveys by some men who wished that they had more time "to pursue nonprofessional activities and to spend with [their families]" (78). Thus, the result of the work and family dilemma, for both men and women lawyers but especially for women, is high rates of exit from the profession.

The "choice" to exit from the profession is an individualized solution, but not one that addresses the fundamental need for change within the profession. Indeed, the irony is that those who remain in the profession, especially in large law firms, are more likely to be those who conform most closely to the traditional concept of the ideal worker (a male lawyer without family responsibilities). Such a pattern also means that there will be more men than women, and that mothers will be present only rarely. The tragedy is that the legal profession's current search for renewal is occurring at the same time as many women (and some men) who are abandoning it are the very people most willing to think about the need for fundamental change. Such a situation can be reversed only if the legal profession affirmatively offers leadership in terms of alternative work arrangements that do not penalize "choices" on the part of men and women who want to balance their work and family responsibilities. The profession can offer leadership in the North American work context in terms of the effective creation of an integrated workforce of men and women:

> Attracting and retaining the best legal talent in the 1990s will require accommodating management policies to the new demographics of the legal profession: female and male lawyers in roughly equal numbers, many of them balancing the demands of dual careers and new families, others struggling with single parenthood or ailing parents, still others needing windows of flexibility to accomplish a variety of important life goals. These lawyers are committed to the profession, but have competing demands in their lives which must be balanced.
>
> (American Bar Association 1990:5)

Responding to Lelia Robinson's Question for the Twenty-First Century

There is abundant evidence of the search for solutions to the work and family dilemma in the current literature on the legal profession (American Bar Association 1990; CBA Task Force 1993; Nielsen 1990:369; Schafran 1990:181; Simms 1990:385). Some suggestions are specifically directed to (women) lawyers as individuals (Nielsen 1990:369), while others focus more on the responsibility of leaders in the legal profession to encourage and support needed changes. The ABA manual is explicit about the need to avoid policies that reinforce a glass ceiling and the importance of challenging traditional myths about alternative work arrangements that merely confirm the status quo (American Bar Association 1990:2:14, 2:22–26). On this basis, one might reasonably conclude that fundamental change is not only possible but perhaps inevitable within the legal profession, and that solutions to the work and family dilemma will be found before the twenty-first century.

In spite of the optimism this literature inspires, it is still necessary to challenge the inherent barriers to fundamental change in the legal profession, barriers that are often hidden and that operate subtly to discourage such change. For instance, there may be reluctance among the members of private-practice firms, especially women, to consider alternative work arrangements. Such reluctance is demonstrably reasonable in light of the many sanctions that have so often applied to these arrangements in the past (Martin 1992). In addition, women's needs for such arrangements change over time, and some women will be less interested in new developments, particularly if they have succeeded without them (Simms 1990:388). What is critical, however, is that the fact that there are differing points of view about both the problems and the appropriate solutions must not be a reason for the legal profession failing to confront the work and family dilemma.

Another barrier to change is the profession's traditional stance toward criticism and dissent. Any process of fundamental change that also relies on mutual education through discussion must necessarily relinquish a definition of "loyalty" (either to the profession as a whole or to any individual workplace) that requires the absence of criticism or challenge to the status quo. There is abundant anecdotal evidence in Canada that women lawyers must choose either to remain "loyal" through the absence of such criticism or to suffer the consequences of their challenges in reduced workplace opportunities. For all of us who want to engage seriously in discussions about fundamental change within the legal profession, it is important to deal with the ways in which the consequences of criticism and dissent operate to stifle the voices of those who need to be heard (Mossman 1993:147).

It is also important to understand this process of change in the pro-

fession as ongoing and incremental. It is a process that continues to
exact costs from women lawyers that are disproportionate to those of
their male colleagues and that also operates to exclude some women
more than others because of their race, class, sexual orientation, or marital status. While it may no longer be necessary for most women to
remain unmarried or childless in order to be lawyers, an unmarried
woman without children often seems more likely to "succeed" in a traditional legal career, even in 1994, by remaining so. Such considerations do not, of course, so systematically constrain men who are
lawyers.

The point, however, is that women experience the costs of their
"choices," whatever they are, disproportionately to men in the legal
profession. Indeed, all too little is known of the costs experienced by
women of earlier generations. What happened to those women lawyers
who made the first claims for part-time work arrangements, claims that
were routinely denied? Where are these "lost" women lawyers now?
How can their experiences and expertise help us in shaping the kinds of
policies that will make the legal profession as egalitarian as it needs to
be in the context of an integrated workforce of men and women? And
how can we use the ideas and energies of men and women who, often
from very different perspectives, share the goal of achieving equality in
the legal profession before the advent of the twenty-first century?[11]
Only by taking these questions seriously can we answer Lelia Robinson's one hundred year-old question with a resounding "Yes!"

NOTES

*Earlier versions of this paper were presented at the National CBA Confer-
ence on Gender Equality—A Challenge for the Legal Profession in Toronto
(1992); and at the Feminist Legal Theory Workshop at Columbia Law
School (1992). I would like to acknowledge here the helpful comments and
ideas, and especially the collegial support of Martha Fineman and Isabel
Karpin, as well as the excellent research assistance of Michael Gardner and
Elizabeth Nastasi at Osgoode Hall Law School.*

1. The idea of gender as a "hidden" issue in law has been addressed most
comprehensively in Graycar and Morgan 1990.

2. The survey also confirmed that women lawyers experienced a lower proportion of responsibility for child care being borne by a partner or person they
lived with than did their male counterparts; women lawyers reported that their

partners shouldered 21 percent of this responsibility, while men lawyers reported that their partners assumed 61 percent of it.

3. According to Brockman's 1991 report, the second most frequent category of discrimination against women lawyers (according to 68.4 percent of women lawyers and 33.8 percent of men lawyers) was "lack of accommodation for family commitments."

4. Epstein has suggested that middle- and upper-class white women in the United States have the greatest opportunities to attain the highest-ranking jobs, but they also have the greatest "choice" to decide that the time demands of these jobs are not compatible with their other interests, including family life. By contrast, economic motivation on the part of women lawyers who are not white and middle-class may reduce or eliminate the amount of choice they experience (Epstein 1990:333).

5. The largest percentage of males departing from the practice of law reported, as their reasons for leaving, "improved career opportunities elsewhere" (26 percent) and "general dissatisfaction with the practice of law" (25 percent). Among women lawyers, the top-ranked reasons for leaving practice were "general dissatisfaction with the practice of law" (30 percent) and "to look after my children" (15 percent).

In a similar study of men and women in public and private sector workplaces in Canada (6,000 public sector employees and 15,000 private sector workers), researchers reported significant differences by sex in responses to a question about the reasons such employees may have considered quitting their jobs. For mother employees, 40.9 percent gave as their reason "not enough time with my children"; by contrast, 27 percent of the same group gave as a reason "work too stressful." For father employees who had considered quitting, 27.7 percent gave as their reason "unhappy in my job" and the same percentage gave "work too stressful" as their reason. Only 9.2 percent of father employees gave "not enough time with my children" as their reason for considering quitting (Duxbury, Higgins, and Lee 1993:12)

6. In commenting on this paper, Jacinthe Herbert confirmed this assessment in relation to Black women in the legal profession in Ontario; it probably also applies to other women lawyers who are not white (including Asian women and First Nations women and Black women) throughout Canada. The context may be somewhat different in the United States.

7. For an interesting analysis of the consequences of taking work and family seriously at an institutional level at Levi Strauss & Co., see J. White 1993:8.

8. The American Bar Association manual, *Lawyers and Balanced Lives*, also emphasizes that part-time arrangements must be distinguished from the "reduced work schedule" made available to a woman lawyer returning to the firm after maternity leave (2:4); the reduced work schedule after giving birth should thus be treated quite separately from requests for part-time work.

9. See *Unemployment Insurance Act*, S.C. 1990, c. 40, §9 (repealing and

replacing §11); and for a recent court challenge that resulted in the current statutory language, see *Schacter v. Canada* (1992), 93 D.L.R. (4th) 1. In the United States, the *Family and Medical Leave Act* was enacted in 1993, requiring employers with fifty or more workers to provide up to twelve weeks of unpaid leave for family medical emergencies, childbirth, or adoption (see the *New York Times*, August 15, 1993, E-3).

10. *Lawyers and Balanced Lives* identified the goals of maternity, paternity, and adoptive leaves; it also suggested a three-stage process for maternity leave, followed by the possibility of a reduced work schedule on return to work because "a return to full billable hour workload from a zero billable hour workload would be jarring under any circumstances" (American Bar Association 1990:1:5).

11. For an interesting discussion of differing kinds of contributions by women to the process of fundamental change, see Fox 1989.

14 | Child Custody and Child Neglect: Parenthood in Legal Practice and Culture

ANN SHALLECK

The law, in its daily operation, helps to construct our concepts of parenthood. By examining the law, we can see the assumptions about parenting embedded within it, the ways the law works to reinforce those assumptions, and the spaces that the law creates to challenge those assumptions. Within family law, child custody and child neglect are two areas that are extremely powerful in shaping both our understandings and experience of parenthood. The legal regimes governing who gets custody of a child and when inadequate parental care permits state intervention into the care of a child implicate the most fundamental notions of what constitutes parenting. To understand the power of the law in the construction of parenthood, it is necessary to look beyond statutes, court rules, and the decisions of appellate courts to the multiple aspects of the legal world in which these formal statements of the law are given meaning (Alfieri 1991; Goldfarb 1992; López 1992; Sarat 1990; White 1990). In the interactions between lawyers and clients, in trial courtrooms and clerk's offices, in negotiations between opposing counsel, and in the structures and dynamics of the institutions charged with responsibility for children, we can see both the visions of parenting contained within child custody and child neglect law as well as the potential for, and limits to, attempts to challenge those visions.

In this essay, I will examine a child neglect and related child custody case that two of my students worked on in 1991 and 1992 and that I supervised in the Women and the Law Clinic, part of the clinical program at the American University, Washington, D.C., college of law. I will examine only one small part of a long and complicated case that in many respects is typical of cases within the Child Neglect Branch of the Family Division of the court. Sharon,[1] our client, a Black woman, wanted, after two years of litigation of her child neglect case, to transfer legal custody of her three children to her own mother, Louise, who had had physical and/or temporary legal custody of all of the children for varying periods. Although all of the participants in the case favored this result, the process of legally transferring custody from mother to grandmother took almost a year, consumed innumerable hours of the students' time, required the filing of many pleadings, dominated several court hearings, disrupted Sharon's life, and created potential danger for Sharon, Louise, and one of Sharon's children.

The difficulty of the students' efforts to accomplish for Sharon a seemingly uncontroversial result within the legal system revealed how gender and race shaped in different ways the assumptions about parenting embedded in the legal rules, legal processes, and distinct legal cultures of child custody and child neglect adjudication. A Black woman raising her children with her mother as they faced the challenges of their daily lives did not fit within the vision of parenting dominant within child custody law. This same woman, although a familiar figure within child neglect law, was seen against the background of the dominant visions in neglect law, a background that created a distorted understanding of her. Furthermore, both parts of the legal system devalued Sharon's experience as a parent and caregiver and also operated to marginalize further her efforts to create a stable and loving home for her children within the parameters of her own life. In isolating Sharon's experience from the vision of parenting dominant within custody law and practice, while submerging Sharon's experience in the dominant neglect vision, law and practice reinforced both visions.

To examine how the structure and operation of custody and neglect law affected Sharon's life, I will focus on one central incident arising from the legal requirement that the fathers of Sharon's children be notified of the transfer of custody from mother to grandmother. After describing this incident, I will examine three aspects of the custody transfer that reveal the assumptions embedded in the legal rules, legal processes, and legal culture encountered in this case: (1) the legal form of the consensual custody transfer from mother to grandmother; (2) the requirement that a child's father receive notice of the custody action; (3) and the attitude of the child advocate.

Sharon's Case

Background

Two students, Joan and Tom, were representing Sharon as part of their fieldwork in a two-semester, law-school clinical program. Joan and Tom were both white. Sharon was Black. At the time that Joan and Tom began their work in the clinic and assumed responsibility for the case, students in the clinic had been representing Sharon in her neglect case for over two years. Almost two years earlier, after extensive pre-trial litigation over drug use, Sharon had entered into a stipulation with the other parties in the case—the government and the *guardian ad litem* for the children[2]—that her three children, Denise, Malcolm, and Marie, ages six, five, and three respectively, were "neglected" due to her drug use.[3] She had also consented to their placement under court supervision with her own mother, Louise, who was also Black.[4] At the time that the petition initiating the case had been filed, the two older children were living with Louise and the youngest was with Sharon and Richard, a man with whom Sharon was living at that time. Richard, too, was Black. The stipulation set out Sharon's visitation rights with her children and also established conditions regarding her drug use that she needed to fulfill in order to get her children back.

Following the entry of the stipulated adjudication and disposition, there had been periodic court review hearings, each one involving a mandated investigation and report by a caseworker from the city child welfare agency.[5] Marla, the caseworker who had handled the case since the stipulation had been entered, was Black. During the period of court reviews, the children had remained with Louise. Louise moved once, causing a change in Denise and Malcolm's schools. Although there were instances of conflict between Louise and Marla over issues involving the older children's school placements and Louise's difficulties in bringing the children to scheduled appointments, the caseworker had made no attempts to remove the children from Louise's temporary custody under the neglect statute.[6] The caseworker's reports submitted to the court presented a basically favorable picture of the children's lives with their grandmother. At the same time that Joan and Tom took over representation of Sharon, the court, unbeknownst to the students, had appointed a new attorney, to replace one who was departing, as the *guardian ad litem*. Valerie, the new *guardian ad litem*, was white, as the prior one had been.

When Joan and Tom began their work on the case, Sharon had already indicated, both to her previous student lawyers and to the court, that she wanted to transfer legal custody of her children to her mother. Louise was agreeable. All the other participants in the neglect case favored this action. Everyone, including the judge, who was white, understood that once the transfer of legal custody was complete, the neglect case would be closed. Although the previous students had begun to do research and to draft the court documents, no legal action had as yet been started in the custody case when Joan and Tom took over.

The Incident

It was close to the end of Joan and Tom's time in the clinic. Finally it appeared that the custody transfer from Sharon to Louise was close to completion. Months earlier, Joan and Tom had filed the custody actions regarding Denise, Malcolm, and Marie, requesting the transfer of custody to Louise. In drafting the pleadings in the custody cases, the students had quickly discovered that under the governing statute the fathers of the children needed to be notified of the proposed action.[7] Although notice to the fathers of the children was also required in the neglect cases,[8] the government, as the petitioning party responsible for providing notice, had never given this notice and the *guardian ad litem* had never raised the issue. The court never inquired about or enforced the statutory notice provisions.

When Joan and Tom talked with Sharon about the statutory requirement that they give notice in the custody cases, they learned that Raymond, Denise's father, had been very abusive to Sharon. This information had never surfaced in the child neglect case. Both Sharon and Louise were very scared of him. Although he had occasionally sought to have some contact with his child, Denise, he had not provided any support for her at any time during her life. Denise had said she did not like being around him. Although Sharon and Louise had some information about Raymond through their extended network of family and friends, they had managed to keep their distance from him, even though he intruded upon their lives periodically. They believed that he now lived in a neighboring state, but maintained contacts in his former home. The students learned that Louise's move had been prompted by Raymond. Hoping to avoid contact with him, she had instructed family and friends not to reveal her whereabouts to him. Marla, the caseworker, had had some informal contact with Raymond while investigating the neglect case, and Louise believed that Raymond was aware of the neglect case. Both Sharon and Louise thought him capable of using Denise as a tool for tormenting Sharon, possibly by snatching and hiding her.

Because of this situation, Joan and Tom were deeply troubled by the notice requirement and began trying to find ways to deal with it. First they worked very hard on developing various legal theories to support a judicially created exception to the notice requirement in the custody statute. They did extensive research on the Uniform Child Custody Jurisdiction Act (UCCJA),[9] the statute governing proceedings in intrastate custody litigation, searching for any reported cases in any state in which a court had dispensed with notice. They studied the commentary of the Commissioners on Uniform State Laws regarding the UCCJA, as well as the legislative history in our jurisdiction. They analyzed the Constitutional limitations on dispensing with notice. Grappling with the complexities of the Constitutional parameters of notice to unwed fathers established by the Supreme Court in a series of cases, when a child is being adopted, they considered the extent to which these same parameters apply when only custody and not all parental rights are at stake (*Michael v. Gerald D.* 491 U.S. 110 [1989]; *Lehr v. Robertson* 463 U.S. 248 [1983]; *Caban v. Mohammed* 441 U.S. 380 [1979]; *Quillion v. Walcott* 434 U.S. 246 [1978]; *Stanley v. Illinois* 405 U.S. 645 [1972]). They tried to think of other situations in which the danger of violence permitted departure from standard procedures. As a result of their research, they identified several possible legal theories and some strategies for implementing those theories.

When they discussed these possibilities with Sharon, she initially favored attempting to dispense with notice, but later, after reflection, decided to proceed with giving notice. Among other reasons, if Joan and Tom were successful at persuading the judge to create an exception to the notice requirement, Sharon was concerned that the custody decree might be vulnerable to appellate or collateral attack. Sharon was quite anxious to be done with court proceedings. Providing notice as the statute required seemed to create a kind of security for her. In addition, because there was some possibility that, despite their best efforts, Joan and Tom might not be able to locate Raymond, Sharon hoped that the case might go forward without Raymond becoming involved. With Sharon's decision to attempt to give notice, Tom and Louise devised other mechanisms to create some protection for Sharon and Louise; for example, they omitted their addresses from the pleadings filed in the case.

The original pleadings included custody complaints for each of the children, together with motions to consolidate the custody cases with the neglect cases. Within the court's structure, custody cases are heard in a different branch of the Family Division than neglect cases. Without consolidation, the two kinds of cases would be handled by different clerk's offices, put on different calendars, and heard by different judges. Consolidation in Sharon's case was designed to serve two purposes. First, it would ensure that the judge who was already familiar with her neglect case and supported the transfer of custody to the grandmother would decide the custody case. Second, because of this familiarity, Sharon would probably not have to go through a separate hearing on the custody matter, so long as none of the fathers contested the custody transfer.[10]

Even before filing the pleadings, Tom and Joan undertook a long process of attempting to locate Raymond so they could give him notice of the custody case. Neither Sharon nor Louise knew where Raymond could be found, but they did know that he had been convicted of at least one crime in Virginia and had served time in jail. They also had other leads indicating that he was working in Virginia. In their investigation, Joan and Tom learned that Raymond was still on probation for one of his crimes, and they were able to locate the probation officer. Although the probation officer refused to divulge Raymond's address, he did agree to send the notice and complaint via restricted delivery, return receipt requested, as required by law, to the address he had for Raymond. In addition, Joan and Tom attempted to serve Raymond at the last known address and last known place of employment they had for him. When Raymond responded to none of these attempts at service, the students believed that Sharon's hopes of proceeding with giving custody to her mother, without the interference of Raymond, had been realized. Tom and Joan then filed a motion to waive publication and for leave to post service in lieu of publication, virtually always a formalistic step in the process of dispensing with notice to someone who cannot be found.

Astoundingly, Raymond responded to the motion for posting. He called the clinic requesting more information about the case. From the conversation with him, Joan and Tom could not tell what he planned to do. He did not say that he wanted custody, that he wanted to appear in court, or that he wanted to respond to the complaint. The students gave him information, but, in order to avoid encouraging him to frame an objective, did not press him about his plans. They reported the call to Sharon and Louise and with some apprehension decided to wait to see what if anything would follow. Perhaps Raymond would go no farther.

Joan and Tom then had to decide about informing the other participants in the neglect case about Raymond's call. After much work, the custody cases had been consolidated with the neglect cases. The participants in the two cases were, however, different. The District of Columbia, through its Corporation Counsel, is the moving party in all neglect cases,[11] but has no role in custody cases. Also, consistent with normal practice, in the neglect cases, the children had a *guardian ad litem* appointed to represent their interests, whereas in the custody cases, the children had no formal representative. Finally, the grandmother was one of the parties in the custody cases but had chosen in the neglect cases not to assert her right to be given party status.[12] Although, as a formal matter, neither the government nor the child advocate needed to be informed of Raymond's response to the notice of the child custody case, Joan and Tom decided that, in light of the consolidation and strategic concerns, it was best to let Marla, the Department of Human Services caseworker, and Valerie, the *guardian ad litem*, know of the contact that had been made.

Although Valerie was well aware of Raymond's history of violence, when she heard of Raymond's contact with the clinic, Valerie immediately stated to Joan her desire to set up a visit between Raymond and his daughter, Denise, as quickly as possible and requested his telephone number. She vigorously advocated the convening of an emergency hearing in the neglect case in order to get Raymond involved in Denise's life. Joan attempted to slow Valerie down by reminding her of the history of Raymond's violence and of Denise's stated dislike of being around him. She also told Valerie the information she had given to Raymond when he had called, explaining that she had advised him of the custody proceeding and of his right to participate in that proceeding. She resisted divulging Raymond's telephone number to Valerie.

Joan and Tom were very distressed, both by Valerie's response to Raymond's unanticipated appearance and by the possibility that she could, through aggressive action to get Raymond involved, seriously disrupt and endanger Sharon, Louise, and Denise's lives. They were not, however, surprised. This was not the first conflict they had had with Valerie.

The initial conflict began with the very first court action the students had taken on the case. When they got the case and reviewed the file, they noticed that the court order placing the children with their grand-

mother was due to expire approximately one month prior to the next
court hearing scheduled in the case. Court orders in neglect actions are
of limited duration and action must be taken to extend them for additional periods of time.[13] In order to insure that the legal status of the
children was maintained in a secure fashion until the next court hearing, Tom and Joan informed the judge by letter of the discrepancy
between the expiration date of the order and the date of the court hearing and enclosed a proposed order extending the placement with the
grandmother until the court hearing. They inadvertently forgot to
inform the *guardian ad litem* of their action. The judge signed the order
ex parte. When Valerie learned of the students' action, she was furious.
Her anger was, from any perspective, totally out of proportion to the
event. First, as a substantive matter, everyone agreed that the children
should remain with the grandmother. Second, statutory responsibility
for ensuring the stability of children's placements rests with the government, not with the parent. The students were, in effect, correcting the
government's mistake. Third, although Valerie had been appointed by
the court several months before Joan and Tom took over the case, neither she nor the court had ever informed the clinic of the change in the
guardian ad litem. Also, despite the appointment, she had taken no
action at all on the case so none of the other participants in the case
knew of her involvement. Therefore, had the students remembered to
inform the *guardian ad litem*, they would have informed the prior attorney who had withdrawn from the case without their knowledge.
Fourth, although the students were mortified and apologized profusely
for their mistake, Valerie refused to accept the apology and insisted on
criticizing them in open court.

Although embarrassing, this first conflict gave Joan and Tom much
information about Valerie that they could draw upon in evaluating her
behavior throughout the rest of the case. They had found that she often
failed to evaluate a situation from the point of view of the children, the
very people she was supposed to be representing. She did not think
about the effect that a particular action or situation would have on the
reality of their lives. Rather, she tended to approach situations from her
own point of view. Things that she liked or made sense to her were
assumed to be good for the children. Things that displeased her were
treated as harmful to the children. Related to this problem of perspective was her repeated failure to do the kind of investigation that would
yield information helpful in seeing things within the real parameters of
the children's experience. For instance, because she was annoyed at not

having notice of the brief extension of the court order, she equated that annoyance with harm to the children, without doing any investigation to discover if there was any actual or potential danger. The students hypothesized that her annoyance stemmed from her embarrassment that at the time of the students' letter to the judge she had been appointed to the case for six months but had taken no action whatsoever to find out about the children's welfare.

Subsequent incidents revealed a similar pattern. For example, for one of the hearings in the neglect case, Marla, the caseworker, submitted a court report that mistakenly included the grandmother's address. As part of their effort to protect Louise, Sharon, and Denise from Raymond, the students asked Marla to withdraw her report and submit a revised report in which the address was deleted. Although Marla agreed to this action, Valerie objected because she had no independent basis for knowing that they might be in danger. Without considering what, if any, effect the absence of an address would have on the children and without doing any investigation about potential danger, she took a position based solely on her own view that all relevant information should be in a report. In addition, throughout the litigation, Valerie had been quite hostile to Sharon, whom she was unable to see as a real person. Toward Louise, she was ambivalent, sometimes friendly and sometimes hostile. Even at her friendlier moments, she rarely expressed any understanding of or empathy for the obstacles that Louise faced in caring for the children. For example, at one point, Valerie decided that the children needed to attend counseling. Although Louise agreed to take the children to counseling, Valerie became angry when Louise had to cancel and reschedule appointments because of her work schedule. With strong opinions about almost everything connected to the case, Valerie was quick to reach her judgments.

As they evaluated what to do, the students were concerned that these aspects of Valerie's character made it more likely that she might actually take precipitous action to encourage Raymond's involvement. On the other hand, the students had encountered on many occasions the sporadic quality of her interventions. Although she reached her judgments quickly and spent great amounts of time expounding her views, she was not very effective at implementing her ideas. Therefore, since setting up a visit or convening an emergency hearing required action, Joan and Tom decided to wait and see if Valerie actively pursued her inclinations.

Joan and Tom informed both Sharon and Louise of Valerie's ideas.

Upon hearing of the *guardian ad litem's* reaction to Raymond's call, Louise commented, "Why do white people think that kids need to have two parents?"

Valerie never took action and Raymond never sought further involvement. Louise moved again, largely to ensure that Raymond would not find her. The custody transfer was completed and the neglect case was closed. Sharon was able to obtain the legal result that she wanted. The outcome, however, disguises the fear and the disruption that the custody proceeding caused in Sharon's life, her mother's life, and the lives of her children.

The Legal Rules, Legal Processes, and Legal Culture

This case is in no respect remarkable. Nothing particularly unusual happened. Nothing terrible resulted. I have chosen to write about it precisely because it reveals how the assumptions underlying the structure and operation of custody law affect the lives of women on a daily basis. There are three aspects of this custody transfer that are particularly noteworthy.

The Legal Form of the Consensual Custody Transfer

In drafting the custody actions, the students sought to convey the consensual nature of the change in legal status that was to occur. Tom and Joan perceived that the consensual quality of the transfer of custody was of great importance to both Sharon and Louise. They thought that during the two-year course of the neglect case, Sharon and Louise had worked very hard to construct a relationship characterized by warmth and trust, within which each of them could have significant responsibility for the children. For many reasons, this had not been an easy task for them.

At the outset of the neglect case, Sharon and Louise were adversaries. Louise was cooperating with the government in substantiating the allegations against Sharon. At one point it appeared that Louise would be the main witness against Sharon regarding her drug use. Although Sharon agreed to her children being placed temporarily with their grandmother, she was suspicious and wary of the situation, fearful that her children would be turned against her. She was also critical of her mother, finding fault with her own mother's qualifications as a mother.

As the neglect case proceeded, however, Joan and Tom learned of the

many ways that Sharon and Louise were able to come together in caring for the children. Louise was supportive of Sharon's attempts to stop
using drugs. She also recognized the difficulty of this task, knowing
both the severe inadequacies of the available treatment, as well as the
enormous pressures on Sharon to continue. Louise did not withdraw
her support when failures occurred. For her part, Sharon stayed away
from her mother and children when using drugs, but was involved with
and responsible toward the children when her behavior was not
affected. At times she would stay with Louise and participate in the
daily care of the children. At other times she would visit regularly.
When she was not able to be around, she called the children on the telephone. The children remained very attached ᵗᵒ Sharon. She also continued to seek out and try treatment. Whenever Sharon was working,
she gave a significant portion of her income to Louise for the children.
There were, of course, conflicts and tensions. Sharon and Louise found
ways, however, to resolve these within the dynamics of their relationship.

As Joan and Tom learned more about Sharon and Louise's relationship with each other, they developed greater insight into the effects of
other participants in the case on that relationship. In addition to the
difficulties within their own relationship, Sharon and Louise confronted obstacles created by those participants. The caseworkers and
the *guardians ad litems* involved in the neglect case throughout its history all began from a position of hostility toward Sharon. They almost
never looked at the strengths she brought to her relationship with her
children nor identified the loving and nurturing aspects of those relationships. All wanted to restrict Sharon's access to the children, letting
her be with them only under the supervision of her mother. They were
much more accepting of Louise, particularly when she expressed opposition to Sharon. They did not welcome signs of support between
Sharon and Louise, and the two quickly learned not to reveal the nature
and extent of their contacts with each other.

Despite this background, Sharon and Louise worked out ways to
share in the care of the children. Each often spoke of the other's
strengths to the students. They figured out how to make arrangements
and order their lives within the interstices of official scrutiny. They did
not bring their complaints about each other to those officials for resolution.

Although the students perceived that Sharon's decision to transfer
custody of her children to her mother was emotionally difficult for

Sharon, they thought that both Sharon and Louise placed a lot of value on the arrangement they had developed. Tom and Joan had worked closely and intensely over time with Sharon to make sure that she understood the legal consequences of the change in custody, knew of alternatives, and wanted this step taken. They explored with her multiple aspects of the custody transfer. They worked hard to counsel their client within the tradition and using the skills of client-centered counseling (Binder, Bergman, and Price 1991; Dinerstein 1990). The students thought that the voluntary transfer of custody to Louise enabled Sharon to express formally the arrangement that she and her mother had worked out within their relationship. In addition, the voluntary nature of the custody transfer was very important to Sharon in light of the compulsion of the government's intervention into her life in the neglect case. The custody case was not only a way to make the neglect case go away, it was also a form within which to assert her own agency in the situation.

As the students drafted the custody proceedings, they discovered that it was extremely difficult to make the legal form of the custody transfer reflect the meaning of the transfer in the client's life. First, how were they to caption the case? Although the rules of court prescribed no particular form, the practice was to caption the cases as one party versus another. The students reacted against a caption that seemed to place the mother and grandmother in an adversarial posture. Why file an action in the form of one party opposing another when competing claims or opposing interests did not create the underlying basis for the legal action? Second, who was the moving party? In researching the practice, they found that the person requesting custody was generally denominated the moving party, the one seeking something from another. It was, however, important to Sharon to be recognized as the one taking action, not the one against whom action was being taken. In order to make the form more truly represent their client's life, they decided to use a different type of caption, drawn from practice in other areas of family law. They captioned the cases *In re* the children with the mother making the allegations and requesting the relief. The substance of the allegations presented the consensual nature of the request, as did the affidavits of the mother and grandmother, which were attached. Although the result was not ideal, the students believed that it more effectively expressed what this legal action meant to their client.

Although there was nothing in the governing statutes or rules that prevented the students' action, they met with resistance. They were advised by court legal staff that the clerks would not accept the pleadings. When the clerk did accept the pleadings, the court jacket was labeled not as captioned but in accordance with common practice. It is worth wondering why the students encountered such resistance. Although there is enormous and increasing pressure in the litigation of custody cases to come to agreement on custody matters, why was there a problem? (Fineman 1988). Can the circumstances of this case help us understand better the different ways that different sorts of custody cases are handled?

Let me suggest two factors that might be operating here. First, the transfer of custody between mother and grandmother falls outside the dominant model of custody cases. The vision of fathers and mothers struggling over custody, either during or following divorce, shapes the dominant structures for legal action. The dissolution of the patriarchal, nuclear family creates the paradigm for legal action regarding custody. The transfer of custody between mother and grandmother falls outside this model. A custody transfer from a Black mother to a Black grandmother, whose familial relationships were denigrated under the legal and cultural practices of slavery, is in particular tension with the dominant model. Social structures, family relationships, and experiences surrounding custody issues between African Americans, who during slavery saw the law not only deny protection to their families but also countenance both random and systematic attacks on the integrity of those families, are removed from the implicit vision of custody law. The structures, relationships, and individual experiences behind these cases are treated as marginal. Instead, custody law squeezes divergent situations into the legal forms, rules, and procedures developed in the context of divorce. The social struggles behind the standard forms, rules, and procedures are different from those at work within these divergent situations.[14] The arrangements between these two African American women regarding the care of children are part of a different aspect of the social world (Stack 1974). In Sharon's case, the arrangement is part of a social structure within which a mother, raising her children with little or no involvement from the fathers, establishes other relationships within which her children receive care. Because this part of the social world is treated as marginal within the dominant system of custody decision–making, the efforts of individuals to use the legal system to create stability in these custodial arrangements are of little account. Attempts to shape that system to reflect the realities of the people living in this world are resisted.

Second, the effort at consensual decision making in Sharon's case was an individual one, carried out outside the realm of professional decision makers. Sharon and Louise were ordering their lives without the involvement of social service or legal professionals. In fact, much of that ordering went on in opposition to the involvement of both social service and legal professionals in the neglect case. To the legal system, the social world of Sharon and Louise, of mother and grandmother working out custody to accommodate the problems and crises of their lives, belonged in the neglect system where professionals could assert firm control over the events in their lives. Sharon and Louise's attempt to create a consensual resolution on their own outside the legal realm where they belonged could not be recognized.

Notice of the Custody Transfer

As with the legal form of the custody transfer between mother and grandmother, the rigid notice requirement of custody law needs to be viewed within the context of the patriarchal, nuclear family. If custody adjudication is understood as arising primarily from the dissolution of that family unit, then the biological father is a critical participant. Making sure that he knows about any possible legal action regarding that unit is essential to recognizing and affirming his central position within it. By firmly protecting his legal claims regarding the dismantling of that unit, the notice requirement of custody law reinforces his centrality within that unit.

The strength of the notice requirement in custody law becomes particularly apparent when seen in operation. It is striking to compare the notice requirements in Sharon's custody and neglect cases. In both written custody and neglect law, there are notice requirements. In Sharon's neglect case, as in countless others, however, the requirement was meaningless. The government, which has responsibility for providing notice, ignored its obligation. The court never inquired into or attempted to enforce the requirement. The child advocate never challenged the government's failure. No one worried that the fathers did not know what the court might do regarding the care of their children. No one was solicitous of their claims. The fathers were invisible.

Why should a father appear essential in the context of custody adjudication but irrelevant in the context of the neglect case? Within the neglect system, mothers are viewed as primarily responsible for harm that is done to the children. When something has gone wrong, the mother is viewed as the object of blame. The actions of the fathers that contribute to neglect or abuse are often not considered, except when they are clearly the central cause of harm. When fathers are uninvolved in the care of their children, their absence and lack of responsibility are virtually never considered in determining whether a child is "neglected" (District of Columbia Task Force on Gender Bias 1992). Therefore, in contrast to custody determinations, notice to absent fathers is rarely treated as important to neglect adjudication (Garrison 1983).

In Sharon's custody case, the students explored the possibilities for treating the notice requirement differently, for creating some small room within existing custody law to proceed without the involvement of fathers. Beginning from the particular social context and individual concerns that Sharon brought to the custody action, they attempted to craft legal arguments and case theories that reflected and validated Sharon's experience. Implicit in their arguments and theories was a vision of custody adjudication not rooted in nuclear family dissolution. Once custody adjudication is understood as arising from some other social context, the biological father can be viewed differently. Within these other contexts, his participation may not appear to be essential.

Joan and Tom wondered why, in the sort of custody transfer from Sharon to Louise, it was necessary for the fathers to be involved at all. Unlike adoption cases, a father's right to establish or retain a relationship with a biological child (*Lehr v. Robertson*, supra) was not being eliminated. Even with a transfer of custody from mother to grandmother, the father continued to be able to assert a right to custody or visitation. Joan and Tom explored alternative possibilities regarding the legal consequences to a father of a transfer of custody from mother to grandmother. For example, they discussed crafting a custody transfer between mother and grandmother to have no legal effect on the father's possible subsequent claim to custody or visitation. Under this scenario, the transfer could be made explicitly without effect on the father's rights. Whatever the legal standard would be governing his possible subsequent claim for custody or visitation, had no custody transfer been made, the standard would remain the same after the transfer. He need not be held to a more difficult standard in justifying his claim to custody or visitation just because a court had acted with respect to the mother and the grandmother. Alternatively, even if, in a subsequent claim for custody, he would have to demonstrate the need for modification of an existing court order, usually involving a higher standard than an initial claim for custody, he would retain a viable claim.

Either of these two possibilities identified by the students would permit the court to dispense with notice, act with respect to the needs of the child, and yet protect the father's ability to assert his claims in the future, should he decide that he wants to have custody or visitation. Believing that Raymond had no interest in having either custody or visitation, Sharon and Louise both saw the notice requirement as creating an opportunity for him to disrupt their own efforts to create a legally protected arrangement for caring for the children. In addition to worrying about the impact on Sharon, Louise, and Denise, the students also saw the notice requirements as protecting the father's right to have a say in that transfer, to voice his opinion. Although they thought that this interest was of some importance, they wondered why it, as distinct from the legally protected interest in having an opportunity to form a relationship with a child, was deemed worthy of such protection.

As the students explored these possibilities regarding notice, they saw that the possibilities they had identified raised questions about the finality of custody decrees that, under the existing framework of custody law, were likely to present problems. In looking at custody adjudication outside the context of nuclear family dissolution, the students confronted questions about finality that are implicated when custody is adjudicated. Is the involvement of the father important to achieving finality of custody adjudication? How strong is the interest in finality? If fathers are given notice and the court adjudicates their rights in the custody proceeding, then the decision may be more secure. However, custody decisions are, for a variety of reasons, notoriously insecure, subject to ongoing relitigation even in the context of divorce (Wexler 1985). Why is finality of greater importance here than in other situations? In addition, if the interest in finality is, at least partly, to create security for the child, is not that interest lessened when the very step meant to create finality instead creates insecurity for the child? If notifying a father may create disruption in the stability of the child's custodial arrangement, why the rigidity of the notice requirement? In Sharon's case, a statutory route for dispensing with the notice requirement would have given her the opportunity to proceed without involving Raymond. The actual and potential disruption in her life and her child's life would have been greatly lessened.

In developing their theories to support a departure from the notice requirement, Joan and Tom identified the importance of recognizing the history of prior violence as a significant factor in assessing when notice could be dispensed with. After examining challenges to other aspects of the treatment of violence against women within custody adjudication (Cahn 1991), they saw the need to address the implications of notice within situations of violence. The emerging understanding of how violence against women in intimate relationships is a frequent part of women's efforts to separate from those relationships (Mahoney 1991), as well as how violence is related, although certainly not confined, to the patriarchal, nuclear family, can help the students to challenge the dominant images of the family implicit in the notice requirements of custody law.

The Attitude of the Child Advocate

In Sharon's case, it was not only the legal procedures and legal rules that created problems; it was also the attitudes and behavior of the participants in the case. Valerie's reaction to Raymond's telephone call after receiving notice of the custody action illustrates the ways that the legal culture incorporates assumptions about the importance of fathers. Although Raymond had contributed virtually nothing to the raising of Denise and had also posed a grave danger to Sharon and Louise, Valerie jumped upon the opportunity to bring him into the family unit. Without any investigation or without any contact with Raymond, she was prepared to ignore or forgive any prior transgressions.

These responses are particularly striking in light of Valerie's formal role in the neglect proceedings. As a *guardian ad litem*, she was charged with representing the best interests of the child. She had reason to believe that the child, who was seven at the time, did not want to see her father. She sought Raymond's involvement without even speaking with Denise herself. She assumed that involvement would be beneficial despite the information she had about his prior care for, and commitment to, Denise. She did not even consider the effect of his involvement on the two individuals, Sharon and Louise, who had provided care and affection for Denise throughout her life. It is also noteworthy that, within the neglect case itself, she had made no efforts to secure his participation. So long as the focus was upon the neglect of the child, Raymond did not come to her mind. Once the focus was upon custodial arrangements, Raymond was welcome.

When Louise heard of Valerie's reaction, she immediately understood Valerie's attitude to be shaped by race. As the students spoke with Louise about Valerie, she communicated clearly to them that she saw race as an element in the dominant vision of the family. To Louise, it was a critical part of the model of the patriarchal, nuclear family as the essential unit for the raising of children. The model did not describe her own experience, the experience of her daughter, or the experience of many other Black people she knew. She saw the legal system as using the construct of the patriarchal, nuclear family against Black mothers to devalue their relationships with their children. She understood how that devaluation endangered the children and the family. She rebelled against this insult. She felt isolated from the values of the dominant culture as expressed through the reaction of the supposed advocate for the children.

Although Louise's comment ascribed these views to "white people," she made her comment to two white students, whom she had come to know quite well during the year. She had talked with them at other times about how race affected her experience in the child welfare system. To the students, she communicated an understanding of race as a factor in shaping a dominant vision of family relationships, a vision that discounted many of the relationships within the largely Black community within which she lived.

Another aspect of Louise's comment is also revealing. In asking why white people think children should have two parents, she is perhaps accepting a view that Sharon's children do not have two parents. Implicit in her comment is the understanding of a parent as a mother or a father, excluding herself from that category. Thus, perhaps her own understanding of her relationship to the children is also shaped by the heterosexual character of the patriarchal, nuclear family (Polikoff 1990).

NOTES

1. I use first names (although not actual names) throughout the article. The names used in addressing or discussing people engaged in the legal system are often of enormous symbolic significance. The many cultural meanings contained within terms of address, in particular the operation of power, race, and gender embedded in those meanings, take on particular significance within the dynamics of power in the legal system. Right at the beginning of their clinical experience when they are sending letters to the ongoing clinic clients, students confront for the first time decisions about how to address their client and how to identify themselves. In this case, the relationship between the students and the client came to be on a first-name basis. In the relationships with other participants in the case, first names were also used. In telling the story, I will adopt this practice.

2. D.C. Code §16–2304(b)(2): "The Division shall in every case involving a neglected child which results in a judicial proceeding . . . appoint a guardian ad litem who is an attorney to represent the child in such proceedings. The guardian ad litem shall in general be charged with the representation of the child's best interest."

3. D.C. Code §16–2301(9)(C): "The term 'neglected child' means a child: . . . whose parent, guardian, or other custodian is unable to discharge his or her responsibilities to and for the child because of incarceration, hospitalization, or other physical or mental incapacity."

4. D.C. Code §16–2320(a)(3)(C):

(a) If a child is found to be neglected, the Division may order any of the following dispositions which will be in the best interest of the child: . . .
(3) Transfer legal custody to any of the following—. . . (C) a relative of other individual who is found by the Division to be qualified to receive and care for the child except that no child shall be ordered placed outside his or her home unless the Division finds the child cannot be protected in the home and there is an available placement likely to be less damaging to the child than the child's own home.

5. D.C Code §16–2323(b): "At least 10 (ten) days prior to each review hearing the Division of the department, agency, or institution responsible for the supervision of the services to the child and his parent, guardian, or custodian shall submit a report to the Division."

6. D.C. Code §16–2322(2): "An order vesting legal custody of a child in an individual other than his parent shall remain in force for two years unless sooner terminated by order of the Division."

7. Louise had moved out of the District of Columbia to a nearby town. Notice was required under the District of Columbia's version of the Uniform Child Custody Jurisdiction Act, known as Uniform Child Custody Proceedings, D.C. Code §16–4504.

8. D.C. Code §16–2306(a).

9. 9 Unif. L. Ann. 111 (1979).

10. The process of consolidation proved to be amazingly complicated procedurally, despite the fact that there was a court rule governing neglect proceedings providing for the consolidation of neglect cases with related matters concerning the child or family. See D.C. Super.Ct.R. - Neglect 3(a). When the custody complaints were filed at the same time as the consolidation motions, the clerk required that the documents be filed in both the Intrafamily and Neglect Branch of the court, in which neglect cases are heard, and the Domestic Relations Branch, in which custody cases are heard. To prevent any confusion arising from the filing in two branches, the students included a praecipe with the pleadings filed in the Domestic Relations Branch, explaining the procedural posture of the case and indicating to the clerk that the judge who was

assigned to the neglect cases would be deciding the consolidation motions. At a subsequent hearing in the neglect cases, the judge granted the motions for consolidation (and also ordered the transfer of custody for Malcolm, whose father had consented to the transfer). Despite the students' efforts to avoid confusion, the Domestic Relations clerk sent the consolidation motions to the Domestic Relations Motions Judge, who, without knowing of the prior action of the judge in the neglect cases, denied the motions. The students then needed to file motions requesting the judge who had denied the consolidation motions to vacate her orders.

Although the difficulty of the consolidation can be attributed largely to bureaucratic ineptitude, it also reveals the consequences for individuals of having the legal system divide up the situations of their lives into different categories of cases. Even when there is a process for bringing together the different legal forms into which experience gets parceled out to create unified decision making regarding a particular human situation, the bureaucratic structure built up around those legal forms has a momentum and power of its own that requires considerable attention and energy to counteract.

11. D.C. Code §16–2305(c) & (f).

12. D.C. Code §16–2304(b)(2) permits a person who has had a child with them for more than twelve months to request to be designated a party, except as the proceedings pertain to the determination of neglect.

13. D.C. Code §16–2322.

14. One aspect of this phenomenon is the chaos within the law regarding the standard to be applied in "third party" custody cases, the category in which custody transfers from mothers to grandmothers are placed. For a discussion of the confusion in the legal rules regarding third party custody within the jurisdiction within which this case occurred, the District of Columbia, see Polikoff 1991.

15 | Older Mothers and Adult Children: Toward an Alternative Construction of Care

JOANNA K. WEINBERG

This essay looks at motherhood in the context of social constructions of care, caregiving and care-receiving. It explores the characterization of motherhood relationships during the course of a lifetime and looks at the relationship between adult children and older mothers. By choosing to focus on relationships of mothering over a lifetime I am attempting to shift the focus away from traditional conceptions of mothering and in so doing redefine motherhood as a social construction that is not necessarily connected to age, or even gender, but to roles that involve care and representation within a family structure. Because society perceives that mothers as well as mother-figures are always women, this analysis centers on the role of women. My purpose in examining the issue in this manner is (1) to explore the role of women as mothers defined by the process of care, particularly caregiving and representation; and (2) to relate this inquiry to the relationship of adult children and older mothers, especially as those relationships involve the implementation of existing social welfare policies. What follows is a preliminary exposition of some of the issues from perspectives drawn from policy, theory, and literature. This discussion of mother as caregiver/care-receiver incorporates the connected categories of care, representation, dependence, and autonomy.

The concept of mother-as-caregiver gives rise to several issues. First, this construction suggests that motherhood is a commodity—the commodity of caregiving. As such, its worth should depend both on the value placed on motherhood by society and on the value of the role of care in the marketplace. Care has always been valued highly in the language of everyday social life (which perhaps accounts in part for the continuing resonance of the "family values" theme, in one or another guise, as a political issue). However, it has traditionally received a very low value in the marketplace. This contradiction needs to be answered in any discussion of the value and construction of motherhood. Second, using the construction of care as a mechanism for talking about motherhood necessitates an examination of the existing body of theory and social evidence on this issue after its trappings of sentimentality have been pared away. Finally, constructing a theory of motherhood that stretches across the life course (of both mothers and children) is consistent with current demographic trends, since mothers are living longer and consequently are around for longer periods of their children's adulthood. That realization forces us to alter the manner in which the roles of motherhood are understood and evaluated.

In this essay I first examine ideas based in both literature and theory about motherhood and care across the life course. My aim will be to tease apart the strands of the mothering role. Next, I examine policy perspectives including: social science data on where and how care is provided, and on the distribution of caregiving roles across the life course; legislative and regulatory guidelines for the compensation of care, by mothers and mother-substitutes (role-mothers); and statements of policy and politics on the role of care within society (i.e., the "family values" discourse). For example, social welfare and health-related legislation often presume the provision of care by a relative but provide no or minimal compensation for the provision of care. Finally, these two explorations come together in an iteration of the changing role of motherhood in the twenty-first century.

Themes of Care: The Fallacy of Motherhood

Two visions of motherhood have haunted me as I worked on this essay. Both are fictional, or nearly so, and both provide an apt description of some of the conflicts inherent in the mothering role.

The Story of Hannah

The first account comes from the story of Hannah in the Bible. Hannah was the mother of Samuel, whose birth was preceded by many years of infertility for Hannah. According to the biblical story, Hannah was distraught by her inability to conceive (since in those days it was always the fault of the woman) and lamented to her husband that she had no sons. In response he attempted to comfort her with the words "Am I not better to thee than ten sons?" to which Hannah replied "no" (Hertz 1978:952). Hannah then went to the Temple to pray for a son and became so absorbed in prayer that the priest thought that she was drunk and scolded her. Finally, however, according to the biblical story, God answered her prayers and sent her a son.

My fascination with this tale is not Hannah's relationship with God and the conception of Samuel but rather Hannah's lamentation and her husband's response. Most interpretations of this story see Hannah's sadness as resulting from her lack of fulfillment—motherhood being the natural and expected goal for a woman. While this is undoubtedly one aspect of the Hannah story, there are also other possible reasons for her sadness and for her belief that however much she might love her husband, he could not be as good as ten sons. It is likely that the age/gender gap existed in biblical times as it does today, and that women lived longer than men. It is quite possible, then, that Hannah faced the likelihood that she would outlive her husband. Hannah also lived in a time when she was legally unable to own or inherit property or to make contracts. In other words, upon the death of her husband, her children would be her only source of support. In those days, sons could provide more support than daughters, as daughters generally had their husband's families to care for. So, not only would a husband not be better than ten sons but one son would be better for Hannah than ten husbands.

Dinner at the Homesick Restaurant

The second story I want to look at is a modern fable. The book *Dinner at the Homesick Restaurant*, by Anne Tyler, opens with a mother, Pearl Tull, on her deathbed telling her adult son, Ezra, that she wishes he had an "extra mother," so that there would be someone left to care for him (Tyler 1983:1). The notion of an "extra mother" is probably a reference to days when infant mortality was high and families had "extra" children to make sure there would be children to carry on even if one or more children died. The basis for the "extra child" notion was both emotional and economic, since children were necessary for the perpetuation of the economic family unit. The underlying point is clear. Even in their adulthood, Pearl wants to protect her children as if they were still young.

> Still, she thought, it had seemed like a good idea once upon a time: spare children, like spare tires, or those extra lisle stockings they used to package free with each pair. "You should have arranged for a second-string mother, Ezra," she said. Or she meant to say.   (Tyler 1983:2)

Today, we have neither extra mothers nor extra children. As the size and scope of the family has compressed, our understanding of the precise nature of the parent/child relationship is also changing. Motherhood, for many of us, looks like something between a nineteen-fifties sitcom with mom waiting at home with milk and cookies and the novel of the pioneer or dust bowl mother enduring her fate in stony, silent suffering. The reality is, of course, different. The complexity of this reality is explored in the 1992 movie *Baby Boom*, in which Diane Keaton plays the main character, a single mom who gives up her career for her child. The mother moves to the Vermont woods to confront her uncertainty about her venture into motherhood and to seek counsel. For counsel, she turns, not to her own mother, or her daughter (who is, in any event, too young), nor to her friends, but instead to the women who played those fifties sitcom moms. She turns to Jane Wyatt, who played the mother of Bud, "Princess," and "Kitten," and to Barbara Billingsley, who played Beaver's mom, "June, dear." And do they pat her on the head and tell her that she can be a great mom just like them? Not at all. They tell her: "[We were] just actresses playing parts . . . we reported to work and they tied aprons on us . . . we were working mothers putting in a twelve-hour day. . . . Except that we weren't called 'working mothers' back then" (Gerard 1992).

There is one more story that I would like to tell, but this one comes from "true" life.

Emma Mae Martin

When the Senate Judiciary Committee held hearings on Clarence Thomas's nomination to the Supreme Court in October 1991, there were many stories about how Clarence was the "successful" child—his sister, after all, had been on welfare. The real story is not quite as flattering to Clarence Thomas as it first appears. Clarence and his sister, Emma Mae, were raised, for a portion of their childhood, by an aunt. While Clarence was attending law school at Yale University, the aunt had a severe stroke and as a result needed constant care. Emma Mae was a divorced mother of three, holding down two minimum-wage jobs and receiving no assistance from her children's father. When the aunt had her stroke, Emma Mae quit her jobs in order to care for her. Clarence did not participate either socially or financially in the care of his aunt. It is likely that either he or the other members of his family considered his career of too great importance to make such a commitment (Stansell 1992:261).

The stories I have related have as their core a recharacterization of the mother-child relationship. Two aspects of this recharacterization are closely related to the theoretical underpinnings of motherhood; they form the basis of the central inquiry in this essay. The first is the characterization of the ethic of care as a central aspect of the motherhood role. As the stories of Hannah and Pearl Tull illustrate, care incorporates both what mothers do for young children and what adult children do for older mothers (or fathers). However, what is often missed in this characterization of caregiving as a transitory function is the fact that the care provided by mothers often extends into the adulthood of their children. This understanding leads to a second necessary recharacterization of the care-model of motherhood—the reciprocity inherent in the motherhood function. Hannah sees her role as both caring for the child to whom she gives birth and relying on that child for care in her old age. Pearl Tull sees her role, even at her death, as caring for her adult son, although she also recognizes the duality inherent in the fact that at the same time he is her caregiver.

These roles—the continuity and the reciprocity—are integral to the construction of motherhood. They are, however, aspects that are all but ignored in society's idealization of motherhood. That ideal incorporates a "traditional" family, in which the mother's role is almost entirely framed by a context of, and a connection to, young, nonadult children. Social policies also operate in accord with this image.

Policy Perspectives on the Ethic of Care

The Demographics of Care

The caregiving roles of women as mothers are well documented, at least with regard to mothers' roles in caring for young children (Skolnick 1991; Huber and Spitze 1983). Skolnick, for instance, refers to contemporary society as having undergone about "half a revolution" as, despite the rise of feminism and the increased numbers of women in the workforce in the 1970s, "most working women continue to do the bulk of family chores" (Skolnick 1991:122–23). The changing roles of mothers in the workplace are also well documented (Hochschild and Machung 1989; Huber and Spitze 1983). More recently, the impact of race and class on those roles has received attention, particularly as public policy has moved toward making participation in the workplace mandatory for women who request assistance from the government in raising their children (Rainwater and Yancey 1967; Weinberg 1992; Grillo and Wildman 1991). But there is a continuing need to assess issues relating to the continuity and reciprocity of caregiving roles, particularly as the stresses of poverty have effectuated profound alterations in the structure of family life.

While issues relating to the aging of the female baby boomers are receiving increased attention (Friedan 1993; Greer 1991), little attention has been given to the impact the caregiving role will have on this generation. The mass media and scholars are, however, beginning to address the dilemma of what has been called the "sandwich" generation: women of the baby-boom generation who, having had their own children in midlife, find themselves caring for their own (or their spouses') aging parents. This is a direct result of increased longevity (Stone et al. 1987; Stephens and Zarit 1989). Issues of race and class are also critical for an analysis of the impact of this phenomenon because the pressures of caregiving exact a greater price from women who have fewer economic resources with which to face the increased responsibilities. Women may have less resources for reasons of past discrimination or limited opportunity, because they have a marginal connection with the job market or no connections at all. In addition many of these women are seriously underpaid for the work that they do (Stacey 1990; Weinberg 1990; Katz 1989). The "graying baby boom"—the bulge in the demographic chart—means that people over sixty-five will constitute more than 20 percent of the population by the year 2030. It is likely that this trend will exacerbate the disparity between rich and poor, white and nonwhite into the next century.

Demographics suggest another issue to add to the complex mix of what relationships between young and old will look like in the twenty-first century. Most caregiving is provided by intimates—relatives, usually mothers, daughters, grandmothers, and daughters-in-law (Abel 1991:10–12; Stone et al. 1989:616). But "stranger caregiving"—paid or informal care performed by nonrelatives provided at home (home care) as well in hospitals, nursing homes, and other institutions—is an expanding field of care, in which the caregivers are predominantly women who are low-waged and working for agencies that are minimally regulated. The health care system is heavily dependent on such services, despite the low regard in which they are held (U.S. Senate Information Paper 1988). At the present time, many home care and low-skill hospital workers are nonwhite. This trend is likely to increase, since demographic forecasts suggest that the white non-Hispanic population will decline from 77 percent of the total U.S. population in 1990 to about 66 percent in 2010 and 62 percent in 2030 (Kingston 1991:21; U.S. Committee on Ways and Means 1987). But many of that white 77 percent who are now in midlife will be over 65 in 2030. This means not only that these old baby boomers will face the intergenerational class and race conflict that many scholars have discussed, but that they will do so in far more personalized ways than the statistics suggest because the people who will provide care for old baby boomers will most likely be of a different race or ethnicity (Estes, Swan, et al. 1993:156–57; Minkler 1986).

The demographic trends I cite here suggest two other conclusions. First, in the future, women will be even more likely than they are at present to be caregivers for older people than they will be for children. Second, women's caregiving responsibilities will not lessen as they themselves become older. They are also likely to remain the chief caregivers throughout their adult life course, whether through the provision of care to their own relatives or to others. Currently, 35 percent of all caregivers are women over 65. This proportion will probably increase with the overall aging of the population. Moreover, most family caregivers provide care for more than five years, and about 80 percent of these caregivers provide care seven days a week, without respite. As women now in the workforce take on these responsibilities, the burdens of balancing home life and family will become increasingly difficult (Collopy et al. 1990; Stone et al. 1987).

The Ethic of Care as a Gendered Responsibility

There are conflicting interpretations of the apparent gendered division of care. One interpretation posits women's caregiving role as coming from societally imposed conceptions about women's roles and, more important, being due to the noncompensable character of such roles. In other words, both the social structure of relationships as well as the legislative structure of the welfare state presume the unpaid labor of female relatives; relevant social policies are structured in such a way as to incorporate that labor (Aronson 1992:8). This is evidenced, for example, by Medicaid and Medicare provisions that provide for minimal compensation of home care services (U.S. Senate Special Committee on Aging 1988:4–6, 9–14).

Another interpretation sees the caregiving role as a consequence of the division of labor that confines women to the private sphere, constrains their access to market resources, and limits their capacity to be independent (Aronson 1992). Caregiving is inherently a private activity, not in the sense that caregivers are closed off from public view, but in the sense that the activity tends to be both isolating and invisible. The activity of family caregivers, for example, is simply not counted, for the most part, as an activity different from, for example, homemaking. Moreover, even paid caregivers tend to be invisible employees. Even when they are employed by home care agencies, they are often "contract" employees and as such are not entitled to health benefits and other insurance (U.S. Senate Special Committee on Aging 1988:16–17; Estes, Swan, et al. 1993:105–7).

While these interpretations describe similar consequences, they suggest different solutions. The first interpretation suggests that social policies may need to be restructured to provide for compensation for caregiving. The second interpretation suggests that the caregiving role itself might need to be restructured so that both men and women participate in the tasks (Aronson 1992). Both, however, make clear that "exploring women's own interpretations of their situations as caregivers in this contested and shifting context is crucial for understanding how the gender division of labor is sustained, and how we can think about possibilities for change" (Chafetz 1988:109).

Tronto suggests a third interpretation that classifies the ethic of care as essentially political in nature (Tronto 1993). Care is perceived as gendered primarily because of the gender identification of women with one level of care, the day-to-day provision of individual care. Other roles that involve the ethic of care focus more on legislative formulation or political development. In some sense, this characterization corresponds to the public/private characterization of gender roles, the history of which has been extensively documented (Tronto 1993).

I want to suggest another interpretation, one that incorporates the reciprocity inherent in the caregiving relationship that I have described at the beginning of this essay. This interpretation would agree with the three principles for reform that seem to be underlying the other interpretations: that social policies relating to the compensation of caregiving should be restructured; that alternatives to the woman-as-caregiver construction be explored as a means of altering the implicit underlying obligation; and that the essentially political nature of the public/private spheres of caregiving roles be recognized. It would also recognize the essentially subjective nature of the character of care. Studies of caregiver/care-receiver relationships suggest that even where a formal caregiver and care-receiver relationship is identified by public agencies, for example, or by researchers, in the case of an adult child caring for a parent, the person theoretically *receiving* the care often continues to perceive herself as a caregiver for the son or daughter (the role exemplified by Anne Tyler's fictional Pearl Tull). My interpretation of caregiving incorporates this understanding and articulates an ethic of reciprocity and continuity, thus altering the axis on which the ideology of caregiving is considered. This interpretation delimits the dichotomy between caregiver/care-provider and care-receiver and places the constructions inherent in the ethic of care on a vertical continuum of the life course rather than situating them as an isolated collection of disparate roles. It also legitimates and gives voice to the actual caregiving tasks that many women continue to play throughout their life course, even when they themselves are the recipients of care from others.

Caregiving: Hidden Limits on Autonomy

While the economic status of older people in American society has improved in recent years, primarily due to a combination of Social Security retirement benefits and the provision of medical care costs through Medicare and Medicaid, older women still lag behind (Quadagno and Meyer 1990; Estes, Swan, et al. 1993:158–60). There has also been a gradual but pervasive constriction of autonomy for older women. The constriction has come about in several interlinking areas of social policy—health care, income support, and workplace structure. I argue that this is closely linked with the role of women as caregivers throughout their life course and the failure of policymaking institutions to adequately value this role.

The construction of care and caregiving is an issue that has so far evaded close scrutiny. Because society continues to assess a person's value on the basis of one's ability to perform paid work, and because the worth of a person's work is determined by the free market, much of the traditional work of women—caregiving, homemaking, child care—has not been considered valuable or indeed "work." Government policies tend to limit the ability of working women to perform these "traditional" tasks and at the same time to participate meaningfully in the private work economy. President Bush's vetoes of the 1990 and 1992 Family and Medical Leave Acts were stark examples of this policy and contributed to the revival in awareness of the gendered construction of caregiving (28 Weekly Comp. Pres. Doc. 1722, September 22, 1992). Not only has social policy legislation failed to address this problem, it has played a major role in perpetuating a gender-biased policy for addressing the caregiving issue.

Health Care

In the area of health care, the focus has been on *health* not on *care*. The dilemmas of medical technology, health insurance, and treatment modalities all relate to health. The presumption that a significant portion of a woman's life cycle will be spent as a caregiver illustrates the blindness of policymakers to both the need to provide carer resources and the need to adequately compensate those doing the caring. The Commonwealth Fund projects that in the future problems of poverty among the elderly will be confined largely to women (Commonwealth Fund Study 1988). This is partly because women live longer, but it is also because women as caregivers are forced to "spend down" a greater proportion of their resources caring for an ill spouse or family member. In addition, women tend to accumulate fewer resources due to the more intermittent work history resulting from these care roles. Both private and public insurance programs view women as costless caregivers; the services provided by women as caregivers are rarely reimbursable or compensable.

The benefit/work connection also has an impact. President Clinton's and other health reform proposals considered in 1993 were tied to employer contributions to private insurance systems, with an expansion of a Medicaid-like program for the un- or underinsured (Skocpol 1993; Rice et al. 1993). This did not assure any improvement in the quality of care for those insured by public programs, although it did attempt to address the cost issues posed by the existing private insurance system. A Senate Special Committee on Aging reported in 1987 that most nursing-home patients are institutionalized only because they are so sick and frail that there is no alternative. Most such people typically receive months or even years of unpaid in-home care from relatives (usually female) before entering the nursing home. The Committee noted that in comparison with other industrialized nations, the United States relies far more heavily on informal unpaid caregivers. This population, largely middle-aged or elderly, is itself an underserved community whose problems have not been addressed by policymakers (Senate Special Committee on Aging 1988).

Home Care

Recently, of course, policymakers have been highly concerned with issues of cost containment. An interesting pattern has developed in the field of aging. It is less expensive for elderly people to live in the community, where that is physically and logistically possible, than to live in institutions (Halamandaris 1986; Collopy et al. 1990). This has given rise to an expansion in what is termed "home care," where elderly people continue living at home as they become more infirm but are provided with the necessary services. According to commentators, "home care promises to sustain personal independence, and social integration of the elderly" (Collopy et al. 1990:4). Home care is also seen as effecting a "paradigm of choice," enabling elderly individuals to live in a relatively independent manner. Nevertheless there are still some troubling questions.

As home care has evolved, it has become a "choice" based in large part on necessity. The "prospective payment" system of Medicare forces hospitals to release people earlier than was previously the case, and nursing home beds are scarce, expensive, and only minimally covered by public or private insurance systems (Koren 1986). At the same time, home care itself is undercompensated by insurance (Harrington and Swan 1985). Moreover, while home care may provide the elderly individual with more autonomy than he or she would have in an institutional setting, the major burden of providing this care (approximately 80 percent of all home care in the United States) is borne by families and primarily by the women in those families (Senate Special Committee on Aging 1987). The alternative to family caregivers is care through formal or informal home care agencies, but currently a complex set of funding streams exist, which provide only limited payment for such care (Collopy et al. 1990).

Clearly then, the issue of autonomy in the context of home care is double-edged. On the one hand, home care usually provides the care-receiver with increased autonomy, while on the other hand, the caregiver gives up substantial autonomy by providing the care. The alternative is a model of care that focuses on balancing the autonomy and interests of caregivers with those of the care-receivers as well as on providing an atmosphere of mutual accommodation and reciprocity. This is difficult to do, however, particularly given the constraints on funding for caregivers. It is also easy for caregivers to use the paternalistic medical model as the basis for care; many reimbursement structures rely on this model by providing reimbursement only for primarily medical services (Meltzer 1988; Rivlin and Weiner 1988; Oday 1985).

Older Women and the Workforce

The dilemma of caregiving suggests another flaw in the restructured welfare state: the "graying" of the welfare state. As women get older, their own social supports diminish. Aid to Families with Dependent Children (AFDC) recipients will no longer qualify for public assistance when their grown children leave home because AFDC requires a child under eighteen to be resident in the home. What will happen to their mothers who will still be young when their youngest child leaves home? (Weinberg 1991:450–52). If they do not have functional employment skills, they will again depend on welfare supports that the programs are not designed to provide. Moreover, women who are divorced are not automatically assured of a share in their former spouse's retirement or pension benefits (except for Social Security), and often do not consider this in the course of a divorce settlement (*Clearinghouse Review* 1991). The Family Support Act (FSA) of 1987 made some effort to address this issue by targeting women whose youngest child is near the age of eighteen for service priority. It is still too early to tell whether this strategy will work, or whether it will provide such women with sufficient education or wage-earning capacity to remain self-sufficient. The FSA statute mandated evaluation studies early in the administration of the Act, but funding for these studies was slow to get underway (P. L. 100–485, §406 102, stat. 2343, 2399 [1988]). A preliminary assessment by Judith Gueron and Edwin Pauley was somewhat pessimistic regarding the success of the employment strategy, finding that much depended on the idiosyncrasies of each labor market (Gueron and Pauley 1991). Further assesment of this is unlikely, as the "now politics" of 1995 has shifted emphasis toward "punitive" welfare reform.

Many of the social policies developed in the latter half of this century have also ignored the needs of midlife and older women, particularly those who have not worked or who do not have spouses who worked in the mainstream workforce (Hammond 1986). Training provisions in current welfare legislation are designed for young workers; they do not provide services necessary for older women, such as preparation for retirement or day care for husbands or parents who may be under their care. But the time for restructuring these social policies is short. In 1987, 12.2 percent of the population were over sixty-five (30 million people); forecasts are that people over sixty-five years old will comprise about 14 percent of the population in 2010 and that the population of people over eighty-five years old will grow from slightly over 1 percent of the population now to 5 percent of the population by the time the baby-boom generation reaches eighty-five (Kingson 1991).

Many older women have minimal employment, pension, and health insurance supports. Lives spent as caretakers often leave them with few resources to face old age, and with little training for the workplace. This has a great deal to do with the way in which aging is treated in federal and state legislation. Legislation providing benefits for older people has traditionally focused on the relationship of an individual's prior work life to the need for benefits. Social Security retirement income is entirely based upon a person's work history (or that of their spouse) (Weinberg 1991:440–42).

Theoretical Perspectives on the Ethic of Care

The Ethic of Family Status and Family Stories

As the demographics of aging changes, the social context for the motherhood relationship has also undergone reevaluation. Feminist theory suggests that context and methodology can provide a basis for developing an underlying theory (Fineman 1992a; Bartlett 1990). Interestingly, many of the studies that look at the relationship between mothers and adult children point to the passing along of family stories—some true and some myth—as an essential aspect of that relationship. But the stories, in great part, define the relationship.

> [R]elationships between proximate generations come to be mediated by cultural knowledge derived from two different sources: (1) an archival stock of family typifications . . . the family's historical and biographical way of defining roles and statuses, and (2) . . . cultural typifications about the elderly and aging . . . [for example,] the presumption of role reversal between elderly parents and adult children.
>
> (Eisenhandler 1992:243)

The intensity of the motherhood role gives these stories—the "family typifications"—a particular import in structuring a different kind of relationship for the elderly mother. The relationship changes from one that is based upon "first-hand" nurturing (as with infants and children) to one that encompasses changes in life-course and relationship cycles. The relationship between mothers and adult children contains elements of caregiving and receiving on both sides and changes during this phase. One dilemma for many mothers is in restructuring the relationship so that the stories have relevance to the adult child, and so that the mother's experiences of caregiving for young children can have continued relevance for the altered relationship between adult children and their older mothers. Literature also has some lessons here. In her two books, *The Joy Luck Club* and the *Kitchen God's Wife*, Amy Tan weaves the childhood memories of both mothers and daughters together with experiences of adulthood in a way that makes the connections between both the individuals and the life phases clear and continuous. In *The Joy Luck Club*, one mother describes her anguish when her adult daughter cannot "hear" her stories: "For all these years I kept my mouth closed so selfish desires would not fall out. And because I remained quiet for so long now my daughter does not hear me. . . . All these years I kept my true nature hidden, running along like a small shadow so nobody could catch me. And because I moved so secretly now my daughter does not see me" (Tan 1989:67). As if to make up for this lack of hearing and seeing, *The Kitchen God's Wife* is the story of a mother who *is* able to tell her stories to her daughter; in the process, mother and daughter achieve a relationship that incorporates reciprocity, both in understanding the past and in accommodating the present (Tan 1990).

If stories are necessary for the development of an ethic of caring that incorporates its reciprocal and continuous nature—and I am suggesting they are—then it is also important to examine what kinds of theoretical frameworks might give the stories a structure. The theoretical framework that I am exploring necessitates an analysis of what a feminist ethic of care might look like.

I argue that a feminist ethic of care requires "making visible questions and categories currently rendered invisible" (LeBacqz 1991:18–19). LeBacqz calls this "attending to the absences" (18–19). As Steingraber puts it:

> Only by listening to these voices that have not been heard previously will we have an adequate basis for doing ethics. For example, more women

die of breast cancer in the United States each year than men have died
in the first ten years of the AIDS epidemic. . . . Imagine what a quilt
embroidered with the names of the cancer dead would look like.

(Steingraber 1991:21)

It has been suggested that women are more likely to emphasize "vertical" or "intergenerational" relationships, while men are more likely to
emphasize "horizontal" or peer-connected relationships (Walker and
Allen 1991; Troll 1987). To the degree that this analysis is correct, any
alteration in family status becomes more significant for mothers,
because it represents an alteration in the most "connected" aspects of
their lives. Even those who disagree that the experience of being a
woman exerts a profound effect on a woman's moral structure recognize
the role of the experience of motherhood in shaping a view of morality:
"older women who have experienced both the negative prejudices and
the positive child-rearing experiences of the feminine role may bring to
moral dilemmas a more intense belief and hope in peaceful, enabling
strategies as the way to live cooperatively" (Callahan 1991:77). Callahan objects to the suggestion that women exhibit a different ideology
of morality or ethics from men. However, her argument, which is
intended to show that differences in views about ethics of morality
depend on life experience rather than gender, itself supports the feminist argument that individual stories are important in defining a morality or ethics.

Autonomy, Representation, and Relational Care

The conceptualization of care as relational, in all of its manifestations,
also plays a role in defining autonomy. Traditionally, autonomy has
been viewed as an ability to exist in a separate domain, to be independent, to exercise a certain degree of self-determination and self-control
(Collopy 1988; Beauchamp and Childress 1983). While most scholars
recognize that *autonomy* is a somewhat elastic term, there is, nevertheless a particular terminology that predominates in discussions of the
concept. Words and phrases such as *self-determination, freedom, independence, liberty of choice and action, control of decision making and other
activity* are prevalent in these discussions. *Autonomy* also refers to
human agency free of outside intervention and interference.

Much of the research on adult child/mother relationships focuses on
the preservation of autonomy for the older mother. However, as Collopy points out, the "autonomy" ideal encompasses two principles: the

concept of individual autonomy, as described above, and the concept of *respect* for autonomy, by others (Collopy 1990:12–17). Reciprocity is therefore inherent in the implementation of principles of autonomy. This is particularly true in relationships between older mothers and adult children, where the history of an autonomous past may appropriately affect the parties' current perspective on autonomy. As an individual's physical autonomy diminishes due to the frailties of age, the representational aspects of that relationship become more important.

A paradigm for autonomous relationships between older women/ mothers and their adult children could incorporate a "vertical" sense of relationships between mothers and their adult children, similar to that already described. Using this structure, relationships that appear to be "dependent and not autonomous" may well be perceived as autonomous within the perspective of a vertical mother/child relationship. This also comes very close to the way in which the mother/fetus dyad has been characterized in the context of decision making about abortion. Goldstein talks about the "dyadic relationship" that exists between mothers and their fetuses, a relationship that continues for the first few months of the life of the newborn (Goldstein 1988). The mother/fetus and even the mother/infant relationship can be characterized as a biological dyad, because the mother "provides the biological and psychological substrate for the later individuation and personhood of the infant" (Goldstein 1988:48). But application of a "relational" structure might allow for the application of another kind of dyadic relationship between mothers (parents) and their children, one that draws upon the earlier dyadic relationship (recast as one of mutual psychological and emotional support) but that recognizes the continuing need for autonomy of both participants.

Another aspect of motherhood is its cultural representation: the way that the older mother (parent) is represented to and in the outside world. An essential feature of a mother's relationship with her child is the mother's ability to "represent" the needs and perspectives of the child to the adult world. The same might be true of the relationship between older mothers or parents and adult children, with the positions reversed. Adult children acting as family caregivers might appropriately represent their elderly family members, within the context of an institutional setting or legal proceeding such as a competency hearing, because "there is an awareness and understanding of the elder's personal goals that family members implicitly apply" (Horowitz, Silverstone, and Reinhardt 1991:30). Others see the potential for conflicts over representation as a major pitfall of the older mother (or father)/adult child relationship: "Unlike relations with formal providers . . . familial relationships in later life imply a history of reciprocal exchanges and affective bonds. . . . [The] special characteristics of the familial relationship, in turn, serve to both motivate behavior and provide the context in which that behavior is evaluated by the participants" (Horowitz 1991:24). It is, therefore, appropriate to conceptualize the entire structure of autonomy as one of relationship rather than independence.

This essay brings together several themes concerning the construction of care for adult children and their mothers. First, the care role is posed as a critical factor in the way that the role of motherhood is contextualized, in part because that is the construction most commonly placed upon that role by society. Second, examples of social and legislative policies illustrate the fact that, despite the universal veneration of the role of care, it receives only minimal recognition and compensation in the overall structure of benefits in the American welfare state. It is also clear that this structure is only minimally effective for caregivers with young children, and exists in its present state at great cost to the caregivers' autonomy; however, it has a negative impact on caregivers who provide care for the elderly or for infirm adults. Third, I have placed this discussion in the context of the relationship between adult children and mothers, as a way of further examining the motherhood role. When that context is added to the examination, it becomes clear that motherhood is an elastic concept, and that for older mothers, roles may shift rapidly from caregiver to care-receiver, and from caring for adult children (or spouses) to being cared for by those children within a short span of time.

Finally, I have tried to build a theoretical structure based upon feminism that would provide a way to reconceptualize the role of motherhood. Central to that theory is a change in the characterization of the role of care: to a reciprocal relation rather than a one-directional one.

This conceptualization is important for more than theoretical reasons. It is necessary to be able to conceptualize the structure of motherhood in the context of adult relationships in order to devise social policies that will assist adult mothers and adult caregivers: "The assumption by women of the major portion of the responsibility for the care of ill and chronically impaired elders means that women are extending, and will continue to extend, their family caretaking responsibilities into the latter stages of their lives . . . [and] that the strains of conflict between the roles of worker and mother . . . will not decrease with age, but will simply be replaced by another conflict between responsibility to older parents and work responsibilities" (Montgomery and Datwyler 1990:38). Given the likelihood that demographic and economic changes will only increase the potential for conflict about roles, and given the rapid expansion of a medicalized view of older people as infirm (including elders who are still mother/caregivers), it is important that we now work to develop both policies and a politics that incorporate what Pearl Tull meant when she wished for an "extra mother" for her children.

16 | Reproductive Technologies, Surrogacy Arrangements, and the Politics of Motherhood

LAURA R. WOLIVER

New reproductive technologies and surrogacy arrangements are subtly altering women's lives by making conception, gestation, and birth something that predominately male authorities increasingly monitor, examine, and control. Motherhood is powerfully shaped by culture (Firestone 1970; Bernard 1974; Rich 1976; Chodorow 1978; Ruddick 1980; O'Brien 1981; Dworkin 1983:173–88; Sevenhuijsen and Vries 1984; Belenky, Clinchy, Goldberger, and Tarule 1986; Martin 1987; Tong 1989:chap. 3; Duden 1993). Even though motherhood has never had much power and prestige in many societies (despite the sweet talk about "motherhood and apple pie"), one power women did have was their ability to gestate and give birth to babies. Many feminists are very wary of these new reproductive arrangements, given the disappointing track record of the medical profession's treatment of women (Rich 1976; Daly 1978; Ehrenreich and English 1978; S. Rothman 1978:142–53; Graham and Oakley 1981; B. K. Rothman 1982; Edwards and Waldorf 1984; Oakley 1984; Pollock 1984; Corea 1985a, 1985b; Farrant 1985:103; Fisher 1986; Martin 1987; Dutton, Preston, and Pfund 1988, especially the case study on DES; Rowland 1992). Feminist scholars are also justly skeptical about modern science given its history and ethic of dominance, control, and insensitivity to women's lives (Griffin 1978; Merchant 1980; Gould 1981; Rothschild 1983; Bleier 1984; Arnold and Faulkner 1985; Keller 1985; Harding 1986; Rosser 1986, 1989).

Defining human sexuality and reproduction issues within a medical and scientific model also has the subtle power of displacing an alternative focus on the social, economic, and environmental issues of reproduction (Elkington 1985; Diamond 1990). A biological paradigm frames the issue medically and individually while distracting from the political and economic context of reproductive decisions. Medical technology, rather than social change, therefore is offered as the solution to reproductive problems and concerns. The medical profession's gate-keeping role and its monopoly over birth control information and services already display these tendencies to control and medicalization (Petchesky 1984; Jaquette and Staudt 1985; Hartmann 1987).

Additionally, many legal systems have already displayed a marked tendency to devalue and belittle the experience and desires of women (Finley 1986; Estrich 1987; MacKinnon 1987; Bumiller 1988; Eisenstein 1988; Fineman 1988; Pateman 1988; Woliver 1988; Rhode 1993–94). Changes in American divorce and child custody policies have actually harmed many women, for example, in part because reformers did not consider women's economic and emotional circumstances, but instead adopted a neutrality stance that was favorable to men (Fineman 1983, 1988). Medical technologies have engendered much debate and concern about their economic, legal, and ethical impact (see, for example, Hanmer 1984; Hubbard 1984; Raymond 1984; Saxton 1984; Wikler 1986; Kishwar 1987; Spallone and Steinberg 1987; Stanworth 1987; Diamond 1988; Elshtain 1989; Glover 1989; St. Peter 1989; Taub and Cohen 1989; Teich 1990; to name just a few). In addition, surrogacy arrangements and reproductive technologies, which are presented as seemingly "neutral" procedures that result in "fair" policies, in fact gloss over women's relative poverty and powerlessness in society, thus skewing these arrangements toward abuse of women. These technologies, then, might actually decrease women's power over their bodies.

"As with most technologies," Rosser points out, "intrinsically the new reproductive technologies are neither good nor bad; it is the way they are used that determines their potential for benefit or harm" (1986:40). Introduced into sexist and class-based cultures, though, the new reproductive technologies raise serious issues of eugenics, the specter of abortions for sex selection, and the diminution of women's relationship to reproduction (Hanmer 1981:176–77; Powledge 1981:196–97; Hoskins and Holmes 1984; Roggenkamp 1984:266–77; Corea 1985b:188–212; Warren 1985; Holmes and Hoskins 1987; Steinbacher and Holmes 1987; Weisman 1988:1, 6; Rowland 1992).

Surrogacy

Surrogacy illustrates the marginalization of the woman involved, while highlighting fetuses as distinct legal entities, children as commodities, and the primacy of father-rights. In fact, the term *surrogate* itself is a misleading and insensitive term for these arrangements, since the so-called surrogate is the biological mother, and the contracting or adopting wife of the genetic father is the actual surrogate. The highly publicized 1987 "Baby M" custody trial in the United States displayed many of the issues in surrogacy arrangements and, possibly, future innovative reproductive arrangements. The Baby M case illustrated that women's experience of maternity tends to be belittled even in the least technologically dependent situation of surrogacy (Harrison 1987; Ketchum 1987; Pollitt 1987; Rothman 1989; Woliver 1989:27–33).

In *Baby M*, a woman was artificially inseminated with the contracting man's sperm. The contract specified, among many things, that the birthmother would relinquish the baby to the contracting man and his wife at birth. Instead, she tried to keep her baby. In *Baby M*, the genetic father was the contracting man, and the genetic mother was the surrogate mother. When she tried to keep her baby, she at least was recognized as having a genetic tie to the child.

In the future, there will be many arrangements where the contracting man and woman are the genetic parents while the birthmother, who is not genetically related to the baby, has gestated and birthed the child. Here matters become very complicated and the powerlessness and vulnerability of these so-called full surrogates is acute. Already at least one case has highlighted many of these issues.

Anna M. Johnson contracted to gestate and birth a child conceived from the ovum and sperm of the contracting couple. When Johnson sued in a California court to have her contract invalidated, the court upheld the contract. Johnson appealed to the California Supreme Court, which upheld the contact and awarded custody of the child to the genetic (contracting) parents (*Johnson v. Calvert*, 1993 WL 167739, May 20, 1993 [Cal.]). In part, Johnson had no claim to the child, the court said, because she had no genetic link. At the time the contract was signed, Johnson was a single mother and the contracting couple were middle class.

Many feminist scholars, after studying the Baby M trial and other testimonials of surrogate mothers, oppose these arrangements. Pateman writes, "The surrogacy contract also indicates that a further transformation of modern patriarchy may be underway. Father-right is reappearing in a new, contractual form" (1988:209). A legal system based on the male standard as the norm rationalizes surrogate contracts as "fair" and impartial arrangements. This logic means that sexual difference becomes irrelevant to physical reproduction: "The former status of 'mother' and 'father' is thus rendered inoperative by contract and must be replaced by the (ostensibly sex-neutral) 'parent'" (Pateman 1988:216). But, as Pateman explains, this is dangerous to women:

> In classic patriarchalism, the father is *the* parent. When the property of the 'surrogate' mother, her empty vessel, is filled with the seed of the man who has contracted with her, he, too, becomes the parent, the creative force that brings new life (property) into the world. Men have denied significance to women's unique bodily capacity, have appropriated it and transmuted it into masculine political genesis. The story of the social contract is the greatest story of men giving political birth, but, with the surrogacy contract, modern patriarchy has taken a new turn. Thanks to the power of the creative political medium of contract, men can appropriate physical genesis too. The creative force of the male seed turns the empty property contracted out by an "individual" into new human life. Patriarchy in its literal meaning has returned in a new guise.
>
> (1988:216–17; emphasis in original)

Similarly, Mary Shanley analogizes surrogacy contracts to aspects of slavery: "In both contract pregnancy and consensual slavery, fulfilling the agreement, even if it appears to be freely undertaken, violates the ongoing freedom of the individual in a way that does not simply restrict future options (such as whether I may leave my employer) but does violence to the self (my understanding of who I am)" (1993:629; see also P. Williams 1988 and 1991:224–26).

Some scholars are concerned about the seemingly patronizing ideology behind prohibitions on surrogacy contracts. They believe it is based on the idea that women, unlike men, cannot make rational decisions about emotional issues like genetic parenthood, signing a contract, and then living up to the terms of the contract. One voice for this point of view is that of Lori Andrews:

> My personal opinion is that it would be a step backward for women to embrace any policy argument based on a presumed incapacity of women to make decisions. That, after all, was the rationale for so many legal principles oppressing women for so long, such as the rationale behind the laws not allowing women to hold property.
>
> (1989b:369–70; see also Andrews 1988 and 1989a)

On the other hand, some scholars argue that surrogacy, if seen as a contract for reproductive services rather than as baby-selling, can potentially empower women: "The idea of personal agency in contracting to become a parent seeks to empower women to reclaim the power of their wombs," Shalev writes, "and to wield it responsibly with due respect for the biological vulnerability of men who must be able to trust and depend on women if they are to become fathers" (1989:17). The ability of women to contract the sale of their reproductive services, Shalev believes, would diminish the prevalent view of women as passive in reproductive matters. These contracts would enable women to exercise "birth power" (Shalev 1989) and fulfill the procreative desires of contracting couples (Robertson 1988).

Taken as a given by pro-surrogacy scholars is the right to sell human beings, the government's lack of jurisdiction to regulate such personal freedoms and choices, and the belittling of those who doubt the wisdom of such arrangements as merely expressing "personal opinions." Governments have a legitimate role to play in determining the permissibility of these arrangements in part because of the effect on all people. Surrogacy challenges society to assert fundamental principles regarding human dignity. "What is probably most remarkable about the debate over surrogate motherhood is that it has necessitated defending a claim that was previously taken as self-evident: namely, that society has an interest in people being regarded as intrinsically valuable, not as monetized units in a marketplace" (Capron and Radin 1988:63; see also Holder 1988).

Surrogacy debates must be informed by what motherhood means to women and by the socioeconomic conditions that pressure women into "choosing" these arrangements. Careful reading of surrogate contract stories reveals the heartaches these women endure and the sexist and classist nature of these arrangements (see, for example: Ketchum 1987:5–6; Pollitt 1987; Annas 1988; Coles 1988; Field 1989; Rothman 1989; Rowland 1992:177–80). "We are asked not to look behind the resulting children to see their lower-middle-class and lower-class mothers. But the core reality of surrogate motherhood is that it is both classist and sexist: a method to obtain children genetically related to white males by exploiting poor women" (Annas 1988:43). Arguments by feminists who defend surrogacy "attribute freedom to the person only as an isolated individual and fail to recognize that individuals are also ineluctably social creatures" (Shanley 1993:636). Radin, for example, argues for some exchanges to be "market-inalienable," because they are "grounded in noncommodification of things important to person-hood" (1987:1903). Radin continues,

> In an ideal world markets would not necessarily be abolished, but mar-ket-inalienability would protect all things important to personhood. But we do not live in an ideal world. In the nonideal world we do live in, market-inalienability must be judged against a background of unequal power. In that world it may sometimes be better to commodify incom-pletely than not to commodify at all. Market-inalienability may be ide-ally justified in light of an appropriate conception of human flourishing, and yet sometimes be unjustifiable because of our nonideal circum-stances.   (1987:1903)

In our culture, "the rhetoric of commodification has led us into an unreflective use of market characterizations and comparisons for almost everything people may value," Radin points out, "and hence into an inferior conception of personhood" (1987:1936). With regard to paid surrogacy arrangements, therefore, "the role of paid breeder is incom-patible with a society in which individuals are valued for themselves and are aided in achieving a full sense of human well-being and potential-ity" (Capron and Radin 1988:62).

Discussions of surrogacy sometimes emphasize the sanctity of con-tracts ("She was a competent adult when she freely chose to sign this contract") and analogies to wet nurses and baby-sitters. Structuring dis-cussions in those terms ignores gestation and birth, exclusively female experiences. Women's services are not merely rented by surrogacy; a part of the woman is taken away. The gestalt of maternity—women's psychological as well as physical experiences—is compartmentalized and devalued by defining childbirth in discontinuous terms (a "rented womb") rather than as the woman's complete experience of maternity (O'Brien 1981; Rothman 1986, 1989).

Equating the male experience of genetic parenthood to the woman's, comparing men's abilities to separate their sperm from their bodies, sell it (as in artificial insemination), or pass it on to a "surro-gate" mother to women's "equal opportunity" to do the same through surrogacy, imposes male experience as the universal. As Pateman notes, "women's equal standing must be accepted as an expression of the freedom of women *as women*, and not treated as an indication that women can be just like men" (1988:231, emphasis in original; see also Woliver 1988). Similarly, Eisenstein argues, "because law is engen-dered, that is, *structured through the multiple oppositional layerings embedded in the dualism of man/woman*, it is not able to move beyond the male referent as the standard for sex equality" (1988:42, emphasis in original).

Feminist concern about surrogacy arrangements is grounded in what Binion calls "progressive feminism," which argues for the inclusion of women's values and experiences in our legal system (Binion 1991). Mary Shanley, for instance, points out that the woman's experiences of her pregnancy "trump" prior agreements in a contractual pregnancy because "enforcement of a pregnancy contract against the gestational mother's wishes would constitute a legal refusal to recognize the reality of the woman and fetus as beings-in-relationship, which the law should protect as it does many other personal relationships" (1993:632). Similarly, other progressive feminist scholars explain the need to incorporate the experiences and aspirations of teenage girls into public policy-making regarding teenage pregnancy issues (Gordon 1976:chap. 15; Rhode 1993–94).

In addition, surrogacy could shift the cultural meaning of "to mother," making it more biological, discontinuous, and distant. Presently, "to mother" means, among other things, to nurture, a long-term emotional commitment. "To father," in contrast, means the biological provision of sperm. Surrogacy and justifications voiced in its favor cloud the present meanings of these terms and might limit "mothering" to mere genetic connection, comparable to "fathering."

New Reproductive Technologies

Feminist scholars are concerned about the impact reproductive technologies will have on women as a group, possibly restricting the group's choices rather than modestly increasing individual choices (Corea 1985b; Rowland 1987; Merrick and Blank 1993). Women's physical and emotional experiences of childbirth are being drastically altered at the same time as we are told that these technologies are for our own good and are responding to our demands.

Behind seemingly benign, neutral, and objective scientific practices and research often lie subtle systems of power. Murray Edelman (1977: chap. 4), for example, displays the way phrases used by mental health professionals that apparently imply progress, therapy, and empathy toward patients in fact disguise and justify systems of control and dominance. Modern feminists also view medical and legal power over issues of reproduction skeptically.

Expanding indicators for these new technologies mean that they are becoming part of more and more women's experience of motherhood. Where once they were used for emergencies and special cases, now many of them (ultrasound and fetal monitors, for example) are used routinely on healthy women. In these and many other ways, the naturalness of pregnancy and childbirth has been transformed into an illness, an unnatural condition, with an assumption of risk to fetal and maternal health that only the medical profession can rectify. Eventually, it is feared, the definition of a "good mother" will include women whose pregnancies and births are "managed" by the medical establishment using these technologies. At the same time, an "abusive" mother might include one who refuses to utilize the available technologies. In 1979 the president of the American College of Obstetricians and Gynecologists, for example, referred to home births as "the earliest form of child abuse" (quoted in Oakley 1984:219). Indeed, there have already been cases where mothers have been reprimanded for staying away from doctors' prenatal care and having home births (Oakley 1984:219, 246; Sherman 1988a, 1988b; Maier 1989; Rowland 1992:129).

The modern women's movement includes a women's health component, disenchanted with many medical practices and seeking to empower women to be better informed and more assertive consumers of health care (see, for example, Gardner 1981; Boston Women's Health Book Collective 1971, 1984; Edwards and Waldorf 1984). The potential force of the women's health movement to critique and change the medicalization of pregnancy and birth, though, has been partially co-opted by the doctors and clinics themselves. What started out, for example, as exercise, nutrition, natural childbirth, and similar classes organized and staffed by community women have slowly been absorbed by the birthing centers of hospitals and the outpatient services of large ob-gyn clinics. The original classes were alternatives to, if not in opposition to, the traditional doctor's treatment of pregnancy and childbirth; their goals included encouraging mothers to keep healthy, strong, and fit, in body and mind, for the upcoming birth. Mothers were educated about their bodies, what to expect from doctors and hospital staff, what their rights as patients were, and how best to resist and avoid the unnecessary and demeaning aspects of the usual medicalized childbirth. In contrast, hospital- and clinic-based classes, while trying to educate women a little and encourage them to keep healthy, are not training them to challenge doctors or hospital routines but rather to be prepared and compliant future patients (see also Oakley 1984:238, 248–49). In addition, some health insurance policies might pay for doctor- and clinic-based prenatal classes, but not for those based in community organizations that, for instance, might tend to track women into the doctor-organized classes.

Oakley, for example, found from her study of the history of the medical treatment of pregnant women in Britain that "if one single message emerged, it was that pregnant women were themselves deficient: they lacked the necessary intelligence, foresight, education or responsibility to see that the only proper pathway to successful motherhood was the one repeatedly surveyed by medical expertise" (1984:72). Within this context, new reproductive technologies, such as ultrasound, seem "revolutionary" to Oakley because, "for the first time, they enable obstetricians to dispense with mothers as intermediaries, as necessary informants on fetal status and lifestyle" (1984:155). Ultrasound is like "a window on the womb," a long-desired goal for the professional providers of maternity care (Oakley 1984:156).

Researchers have noted that many women going through ultrasound are excited to see their fetus, relieved to learn it appears normal, and lovingly affectionate toward their future baby. "Ultrasound must, therefore," Oakley writes, "take its place in a long line of other well-used strategies for educating women to be good mothers. . . . Antenatal care has finally discovered mother love. Along with postnatal bonding, prenatal bonding will now in future be added to the repertoire of reproductive activities named and controlled by obstetricians" (1984:185; see also Rothman 1986:78–85, 114; Martin 1987:145–48).

The Changing Nature of Abortion Politics

New reproductive technologies add at least three new issues to political debates about abortion in the United States. First, new reproductive technologies are predicated on the availability of legal abortion, which is constantly under threat in this country. Amniocentesis, ultrasound, genetic screening, embryo transfer, test-tube babies, to name but a few, are procedures in which the option of abortion or destruction of excess embryos are inherent. Any changes in abortion laws will directly affect the use of these technologies. These technologies bring into abortion debates a new group of potential abortion users, who desire the abortion option for slightly different reasons than the original position on reproductive choice taken by the early women's movements. In addition, new medical knowledge is beginning to blur the boundaries between contraception and abortion. The controversy over introducing the French "abortion pill," RU-486, into the United States is one current example (Richard 1989:947–48).

Second, reproductive technologies such as ultrasound and fetal medicine are playing a significant, if subtle, role in the efforts to restrict abortion rights by furthering the construction of the image of the fetus as an entity distinct from the woman who carries and delivers it. These images are powerful symbols in United States prolife, antiabortion politics. "The idea that knowledge of fetal life, and especially confrontation with the visual image of the fetus, will 'convert' a woman to the pro-life position has been a central theme in both local and national right-to-life activism," Ginsburg found. "A popular quip summarizes this position: 'If there were a window on a pregnant woman's stomach, there would be no more abortions' " (1989:104). Images of the fetus used by antiabortion activists in the United States, it should be emphasized, usually exclude visualization of the woman the fetus is within (Petchesky 1984:353; Ginsburg 1989:107–9; Condit 1990:79–95; Duden 1993). These carefully constructed fetal images are powerful aspects of the antiabortion discourse,

> When pro-Life rhetors talk about why they believe as they do, the role of the photographs and films becomes quite clear. Without these pictures, pro-Life advocates would have only an abstract argument about the importance of chromosomes in determining human life or a religious argument about the "soul" . . . neither of those options could sustain the righteous fire of the public movement.   (Condit 1990:80)

Fetal images, combined with artful political commentary and voiceovers by antiabortion spokespeople, help the antichoice movement in its attempt to define the fetus as a human person (Petchesky 1987; Condit 1990:86–89). In ultrasound images, or microscopic views of zygotes, the viewer's eye must be trained to "see" the "life," since it is not clear to the uninitiated (Duden 1993:73–78; see also Rowland 1992); this training, as well as the viewing of women's innards, is an integral part of the politics and the cultural shift of re-visioning (Duden 1993). Technologies, therefore, that allow viewing, studying, and possibly treating fetuses medically "are likely to elevate the moral status of the fetus" (Blank 1988:148).

Fetal medicine and the technologies that allow the visualization of the fetus push women out of the center of medical attention in gestation and birth, except for efforts to control female behavior for the well-being of the fetus. Discussions and lawsuits about what pregnant women eat and drink (alcohol, tobacco, drugs) or how they live (working in unsafe occupations, engaging in unsafe sex, or practicing risky sports) have troubling implications in the United States for controlling women's behavior. Much of the emphasis in these discussions is on what the women do, not what the men in their lives are doing, or on the socioeconomic conditions that might influence women's habits, employment patterns, and prenatal care. Particularly chilling is the fact that some earlier medically recommended treatments and advice for pregnant women have subsequently proved very harmful (the use of X-rays in prenatal care is just one example). How do we know that the prevailing medical wisdoms of today will not be proven unsafe in the future? The inadequate, short-term testing of ultrasound is a troubling case in point (Oakley 1984:155–86; 1987:44–48).

Envisioning the fetus as a separate patient, combined with more detailed and heightened monitoring of the behavior of pregnant women, might have an impact on abortion choice. After all, if society oversees the nutrition and lifestyle of pregnant women in order to ensure the health of the fetal "patient," how would the women be allowed to abort this "patient"? The elevation of the fetus as a patient in medicine and politics, though, marginalizes the women involved. As Gallagher reminds us, "given the very geography of pregnancy, questions as to the status of the fetus must follow, not precede, an examination of the rights of the woman within whose body and life the fetus exists" (1989:187–98; see also Wingerter 1987).

Third, neonatal technologies are altering perceptions of fetal viability, and thus undermining one of the premises of *Roe v. Wade* (the 1973 U.S. precedent for legal abortion, based partly on the viability of fetuses). As U.S. Supreme Court Justice Sandra Day O'Connor noted, *Roe* is on "a collision course with itself" because of these changes (O'Connor, quoted from *City of Akron v. Akron Center for Reproductive Health, Inc.*:458). Neonatal technologies are pushing back the gestational age when fetuses might be viable outside the womb (Blank 1984b:584–602; Blank 1988:64–65). The result might be to pit the woman's rights against those of her fetus. Indeed, recent U.S. cases indicate that "when maternal actions are judged detrimental to the health or life of the potential child, the court has shown little hesitancy to constrain the liberty of the mother" (Blank 1984a:150). In reality only a very small number of women and babies have access to these neonatal technologies, but the experience of a privileged few is being generalized into the abortion debate as a whole. In addition to the attack by conservatives and antiabortion activists on abortion choice (see, for example, Steiner 1983; Luker 1984; Cohan 1986; Glendon 1987; Ginsburg 1989; Condit 1990; Himmelstein 1990:89–90; to name but a few), feminists now must respond to the pressure the new technologies exert on abortion politics.

Increased Marginalization of Women

The values inherent in these technologies are making women, as Rothman states it, "transparent" (1986). A cultural shift has occurred where women have been "skinned" and authorities are permitted to examine and monitor their innards (Duden 1993:7). The role of the woman is becoming secondary to that of the medical profession and those who can broker surrogacy and adoption contracts.

When they are used for contraception, sex-selective abortions, and sterilization, reproductive technologies have already seriously violated the rights, dignity, and indigenous cultures of poor women the world over while failing to address the underlying poverty and inequalities in these women's societies (Shapiro 1985; Hartmann 1987; Tobin 1990). The coercive "choices" presented to impoverished third-world women to "select" sterilization or dangerous contraceptives such as Depo-Provera in exchange for food, clothing, or other benefits show how professional medical technologies can be used to harm women, yet be justified with the language of individual choice (see, for example, Bunkle 1984; Clarke 1984; Akhta 1987; Hartmann 1987; Kamal 1987). "We will have to lift our eyes from the choices of the individual woman," writes Rothman, "and focus on the control of the social system that structures her choices, which rewards some choices and punishes others, which distributes the rewards and punishments for reproductive choices along class and race lines" (1984:33; see also Dworkin 1983:182; Corea 1985:2–3, 27; Rowland 1987:84; Gordon 1976, especially chap. 15; Rhode 1993–94).

In population control politics, the desires of women are largely ignored, their reproductive choices are narrowed, their knowledge of their own bodies is belittled, and traditional female and community-based healers are driven out of business. Contraceptive technologies emphasized by international aid agencies for less-developed countries, for example, sacrifice "women's health and safety in the indiscriminate promotion of hormonal contraception, the IUD, and sterilization, at the same time as they have neglected barrier methods and natural family planning" (Hartmann 1987:xv). The problem with barrier methods, from the point of view of many population planners, is that they are not effective enough, since they are under women's control and discretion. Hartmann found: "The thrust of contraceptive research in fact has been to remove control of contraception from women, in the same way that women are being increasingly alienated from the birth process itself" (1987:32).

Similarly, studies of the United States show that minority and poor women receive less quality health care, are subject to more intrusive medical procedures, and have limited "choice" to use expensive reproductive technologies (Martin 1987; Nsiah-Jefferson 1989; Davis 1990:53–65). Medical advice to poor and minority women is often uninformed regarding the language skills, cultural background, and desires of these patients. In these settings, therefore, "the graph she is asked to look at during her visit to the clinic only serves to mystify her experience. In ways that she cannot fathom, expert professionals claim to know something about her future child, much more, in fact, than she could ever find out by herself. Long before she actually becomes a mother she is habituated to the idea that others know better and that she is dependent on being told" (Duden 1993:29).

The marginalization of women in these new reproductive arrangements is shockingly clear in the language that is used to describe the women involved. Women are discussed in the new reproductive literature by bodily parts: "maternal environment" replaces a woman's womb, a pregnant woman becomes "an embryo carrier" (see, for example, Klein 1987:66). Surrogate mothers are likened to reproductive machines and are described as inanimate objects: "rented wombs," "incubators," "receptacles," "a kind of hatchery," "gestators," "a uterine hostess," or a "surrogate uterus" (see, for example, Ince 1984:99–116; Corea 1985:222; Hollinger 1985:901, 903). Fetal well-being appears more important than "invasions" of mother's bodies (Laborie 1987; Burfoot 1988:108, 110).

In vitro fertilization is sometimes described without once intimating that a human woman is involved. No woman, for example, is mentioned in the following overview of the 1978 birth of Louise Brown, the first "test-tube" baby:

> After many years of frustrating research, Drs. Edwards and Steptoe had succeeded in removing an egg from an ovarian follicle, fertilizing it in a dish, and transferring the developing zygote to a uterus where it implanted and was brought to term.   (Robertson 1986:943)

The women involved in these procedures are truly marginal. It is important to recall that "test-tube" babies are born from mothers who carried them during pregnancy. In addition, these women were sometimes experimented on without their full consent, or they participated based on misleading information concerning the probability of actually having a baby (Corea 1985:112–17, 166–85; Corea and Ince 1987; Lasker and Borg 1987:53–55).

The future role of mothers in a medical system oriented toward technological intervention and control in conception, gestation, and birth, where life itself is just another commodity and women's bodies producers of quality products, is very troubling. "To use the law for these complicated moral decisions," writes Rothman, "is to lose the nuances, the idiosyncrasies, and the individuality that protect us from fundamentally untrustworthy political institutions" (1989:87). In addition to the marginalization of women in these reproductive arrangements, these technologies deflect pressures for social reforms by promising technological fixes for reproductive difficulties. Some women delay motherhood and possibly increase reproductive risks, for example, to conform to male career timetables (such as the tenure system in universities or the partner process in law firms, to name but two). The new reproductive technologies allow this to continue by implying to women that they will suffer few consequences by delaying motherhood. Women's delay of motherhood is also used to justify the "demands" for the technologies by women. Potential pressures to change corporations, universities, and other employers, then, are blunted by this technological turn (Woliver 1989a:39; see also Woliver 1989b and 1990). New reproductive technologies and surrogacy arrangements are increasingly making women marginal in the new politics of motherhood.

An earlier version of this paper was presented at the 1990 Feminism and Legal Theory Conference on Motherhood, University of Wisconsin–Madison Law School.

BIBLIOGRAPHY

Abel, Elizabeth. 1990. "Race, Class, and Psychoanalysis?: Opening Questions." In Marianne Hirsch and Evelyn Fox Keller, eds., *Conflicts in Feminism*, pp. 186–243. New York: Routledge.

Abel, Emily. 1987. *Love Is Not Enough: Family Care of the Frail Elderly*. Washington, D.C.: American Public Health Association.

Abel, Richard. 1988. "United States: The Contradictions of Professionalism." In Richard Abel and Philip Lewis, eds., *Lawyers in Society: The Common Law World*, 1:186–243. Berkeley: University of California Press.

Abramovitz, Mimi. 1988. "Why Welfare Reform Is a Sham." *The Nation* (September 26): 24.

Abrams, Kathryn. 1989. "Gender Discrimination and the Transformation of Workplace Norms." *Vanderbilt Law Review* 42:1183.

——. 1990. "Ideology and Women's Choices." *Georgia Law Review* 24:761.

Akhtar, Farida. 1987. "Wheat for Statistics: A Case Study of Relief Wheat for Attaining Sterilization Target in Bangladesh." In Patricia Spallone and Deborah Lynn Steinberg, eds., *Made to Order: The Myth of Reproductive and Genetic Progress*, pp. 154–60. New York: Pergamon.

Alcoff, Linda. 1988. "Cultural Feminism Versus Post Structuralism: The Identity Crisis in Feminist Theory." *Signs* 13:405–36.

Alfieri, Anthony V. 1991. "Reconstructive Poverty Law Practice: Learning Lessons of Client Narrative." *Yale Law Journal* 100:2107.

Allen, Anita. 1990. "Surrogacy, Slavery, and the Ownership of Life." *Harvard Journal of Law and Public Policy* 13:139.

Allen, Jeffner. 1984. "Motherhood: The Annihilation of Women." In Joyce Treblicot, ed. *Mothering: Essays in Feminist Theory*. Totowa, N.J.: Rowman and Allanheld. Also published in Allen Jeffner, ed., *Lesbian Philosophy: Explorations* (Palo Alto, Calif.: Institute for Lesbian Studies, 1988).

American Bar Association. 1990. "Lawyers and Balanced Lives: A Guide to Drafting and Implementing Workplace Policies for Lawyers." Chicago: American Bar Association.

American Enterprise Institute for Public Policy Research. 1987. "The New Consensus on Family and Welfare: A Community of Self-Reliance." Working Seminar on Family and American Welfare Policy. Washington, D.C.: American Enterprise Institute for Public Policy Research.

Andrews, Lori B. 1988. "Surrogate Motherhood: The Challenge for Feminists." *Law, Medicine, & Health Care* 16, nos. 1–2: 72–80. Also published in Larry Gostin, ed., *Surrogate Motherhood: Politics and Privacy* (Bloomington: Indiana University Press, 1988), pp. 167–82.

——. 1989a. *Between Strangers: Surrogate Mothers, Expectant Fathers, and Brave New Babies.* New York: Harper and Row.

——. 1989b. "Alternative Modes of Reproduction." In Nadine Taub and Sherrill Cohen, eds., *Reproductive Laws for the 1990s*, pp. 361–403. Clifton, N.J.: Humana.

Annas, George J. 1988. "Fairy Tales Surrogate Mothers Tell." In Larry Gostin, ed., *Surrogate Motherhood: Politics and Privacy*, pp. 43–55. Bloomington: Indiana University Press.

Aptheker, B. 1982. "The Matriarchal Mirage: The Moynihan Connection in Historical Perspective." In B. Aptheker, *Women's Legacy: Essays on Race, Sex, and Class in American History.* Amherst: University of Massachusetts Press.

Arditti, Rita, Renate Duelli Klein, and Shelley Minden, eds. *Test-Tube Women: What Future for Motherhood?.* London: Pandora.

Armitage, A. 1993. "Family and Child Welfare in First Nations Communities." In B. Wharf, ed., *Rethinking Child Welfare in Canada*, pp. 131–71. Toronto: McClelland and Stewart.

Armstrong, P. and H. Armstrong. 1988. "Women, Family, and Economy." In Nancy Mandell and Ann Duffy, eds., *Reconstructing the Canadian Family: Feminist Perspectives*, pp. 143–74. Toronto: Butterworths.

Arnold, Erick and Wendy Faulkner. 1985. "Smothered by Invention: The Masculinity of Technology." In Erik Arnold and Wendy Faulkner, eds., *Smothered by Invention: Technology in Women's Lives*, pp. 18–50. London: Pluto.

Arnup, K. 1989. " 'Mothers Just Like Others': Lesbians, Divorce, and Child Custody in Canada." *Canadian Journal of Women and the Law* 3:18–32.

Aronson, J. 1992. "Women's Sense of Responsibility for the Care of Old People: 'But Who Else Is Going to Do It?' " *Gender and Society* 6, no. 1: 8.

Arthur, Stacey L. 1992. "The Norplant Prescription: Birth Control, Woman Control, or Crime Control?" *UCLA Law Review* 40, no. 1: 1–101.

Asch, A. and M. Fine. 1988. "Introduction: Beyond Pedestals." In A. Asch and M. Fine, eds., *Women with Disabilities: Psychology, Culture, and Politics*, pp. 1–32. Philadelphia: Temple University Press.

Ashe, Marie. 1987. "Mind's Opportunity: Birthing a Post Structuralist Feminist Jurisprudence." *Syracuse Law Review* 38:1129.

——. 1990. "Inventing Choreographies: Feminism and Deconstruction." *Columbia Law Review* 90:1123.

——. 1992. "The 'Bad Mother' in Law and Literature: A Problem of Representation." *Hastings Law Journal* 43:1017.

Ashe, Marie and Naomi Cahn. 1993. "Child Abuse: A Problem for Feminist Theory." *Texas Journal of Women and the Law* 2:75.

Austin, Regina. 1989. "Sapphire Bound." *Wisconsin Law Review*, p. 539.

Backhouse, C. 1981. "Shifting Patterns in Nineteenth-Century Canadian Custody Law." In David H. Flaherty, ed., *Essays in the History of Canadian Law*, pp. 212–48. Toronto: The Osgoode Society.

Bair, Deirdre. 1990. *Simone de Beauvoir: A Biography.* New York: Simon and Schuster.

Barnett, Martha W. 1990. "Women Practicing Law: Changes in Attitudes, Changes in Platitudes." *Florida Law Review* 42:209.

Barrie, J. M. 1985. *Peter Pan.* 1920. Reprint, New York: Bantam.

Barringer, Felicity. 1993. "Family Leave Bill: Peace-of-Mind Issue." *New York Times* (February 4): C1.

Bartlett, K. 1984. "Rethinking Parenthood as an Exclusive Status: The Need for Legal Alternatives When the Premise of the Nuclear Family Has Failed." *Virginia Law Review* 70:879.

——. 1990. "Feminist Legal Methods." *Harvard Law Review* 103:829.

Basch, Norma. 1982. *In the Eyes of the Law: Women, Marriage, and Property in Nineteenth-Century New York.* Ithaca: Cornell University Press.

Beauchamp, T. and J. Childress. 1983. *Principles of Biomedical Ethics.* New York: Oxford University Press.

Beauvoir, Simone de. 1985. *A Very Easy Death.* Trans. by Patrick O'Brien. 1965. Reprint, New York: Putnam.

Becker, Gary S. 1991. *A Treatise on the Family* (enlarged ed.). Cambridge: Harvard University Press.

——. 1992. "An Open Door for Immigrants—the Auction." *New York Times* (October 14): A14.

Becker, Mary E. 1986. "From *Muller v. Oregon* to Fetal Vulnerability Policies." *The University of Chicago Law Review* 53, no. 4: 1219–73.

——. 1989. "Obscuring the Struggle: Sex Discrimination, Social Security, and Stone, Seidman, Sunstein, and Tushnet's 'Constitutional Law.' " *Columbia Law Review* 89:264.

Belenky, Mary Field, Blythe McVicker Clinchy, Nancy Rule Goldberger, and Jill Mattuck Tarule. 1986. *Women's Ways of Knowing: The Development of Self, Voice, and Mind.* New York: Basic Books.

Bell, Derrick. 1990. "After We're Gone: Prudent Speculations on America in a Post-Racial Epoch." *Saint Louis University Law Journal* 34:393.

Bergman, Jim. 1992. Cartoon printed in the *Times* (January 30): A9.

Berke, Richard L. 1993. "Judge's Friends Try to Save Candidacy for High Court." *New York Times* (June 14): A11.

Bernard, Jessie. 1974. *The Future of Motherhood.* New York: Dial.

Bick-Rice, Judith. 1985. "The Need for Statutes Regulating Artificial Insemination by Donors." *Ohio State Law Journal* 46:1062.

Binder, David, Paul Bergman, and Susan C. Price. 1991. *Lawyers As Counselors: A Client-Centered Approach*. St. Paul, Minn.: West Publishing.

Binion, Gayle. 1991. "Toward a Feminist Regrounding of Constitutional Law." *Social Science Quarterly* 72, no. 2 (June): 207–20.

Blank, Robert H. 1984a. *Redefining Human Life: Reproductive Technologies and Social Policy*. Boulder: Westview.

——. 1984b. "Judicial Decision Making and Biological Fact: *Roe v. Wade* and the Unresolved Question of Fetal Viability." *Western Political Quarterly* 37:584–602.

——. 1988. *Rationing Medicine*. New York: Columbia University Press.

Bleier, Ruth. 1984. *Science and Gender: A Critique of Biology and Its Theories on Women*. New York: Pergamon.

Bloch, Ruth. 1978. "Untangling the Roots of Modern Sex Roles: A Survey of Four Centuries of Changes." *Signs* 4:237.

Bock, G. 1984. "Racism and Sexism in Nazi Germany: Motherhood, Compulsory Sterilization, and the State." In R. Bridenthal, A. Grossman, and M. Kaplan, eds., *When Biology Became Destiny: Women in Weimar and Nazi Germany*, pp. 271–96. New York: Monthly Review Press.

Boring, J. 1857. "Foeticide." *Atlanta Medical and Surgical Journal* 2:257–67.

Boston Bar Association. 1991. Task Force on Parenting and the Legal Profession. "Parenting and the Legal Profession: A Model for the Nineties." Boston: Boston Bar Association.

Boston Women's Health Book Collective. 1971. *Our Bodies, Our Selves*. Boston: New England Free Press. 1973–92. Reprint, New York: Simon and Schuster.

——. 1984. *The New Our Bodies, Our Selves*. New York: Simon and Schuster.

——. 1987. *Our Selves Growing Older*. New York: Simon and Schuster.

Bowlby, John. 1951. "Maternal Care and Mental Health." *Bulletin of the World Health Organization* 3:355–534.

Boyd, Monica. 1988. "Changing Canadian Family Forms: Issues for Women." In Nancy Mandell and Ann Duffy, eds., *Reconstructing the Canadian Family: Feminist Perspectives*, pp. 85–109. Toronto: Butterworths.

Boyd, S. 1989a. "Child Custody, Ideologies, and Employment." *Canadian Journal of Women and the Law* 3:111.

——. 1989b. "From Gender Specificity to Gender Neutrality? Ideologies in Canadian Child Custody Law." In C. Smart and S. Sevenhuijsen, eds., *Child Custody and the Politics of Gender*, pp. 126–57. London: Routledge.

——. 1991. "Some Postmodernist Challenges to Feminist Analyses of Law, Family, and State: Ideology and Discourse in Child Custody Law." *Canadian Journal of Family Law* 10:79.

——. 1993. "Investigating Gender Bias in Canadian Child Custody Law: Reflections on Questions and Methods." In J. Brockman and D. Chunn, eds., *Investigating Gender Bias: Law, Courts, and the Legal Profession*, pp. 169–90. Toronto: Thompson Educational Publishing.

Boydston, Jeanne. 1990. *Home and Work: Housework, Wages, and the Ideology of Labor in the Early Republic*. New York: Oxford University Press.

British Columbia. 1992. *Liberating Our Children/Liberating Our Nations: Report of the Aboriginal Committee, Community Panel, Family and Children's Services Legislation Review in British Columbia.* Victoria: Ministry of Social Services.

Brockman, Joan. 1991. "Identifying the Barriers: A Survey of Members of the Law Society of British Columbia." Vancouver Law Society of British Columbia Subcommittee on Women in the Legal Profession.

———. 1992a. "Gender Bias in the Legal Profession: A Survey of Members of the Law Society of British Columbia." *Queen's Law Journal* 17:91.

———. 1992b. "Bias in the Legal Profession: Perceptions and Experiences." *Alberta Law Review* 30:747.

Brooks, Andree. 1992. "Making Offices Compatible with Flexible Schedules." *New York Times* (October 4).

Brown, Wendy. 1993. "Jim Miller's Passions." *differences: A Journal of Feminist Cultural Studies* 5, no. 2: 140–49.

Bryant, Wayne. 1991. Testimony during public hearing before New Jersey Assembly Health and Human Services Committee.

Bumiller, Kristen. 1988. *The Civil Rights Society: The Social Construction of Victims.* Baltimore: Johns Hopkins University Press.

Bunkle, Phillida. 1984. "Calling the Shots? The International Politics of Depo-Provera." In Arditti, Klein, and Minden, eds., *Test-Tube Women: What Future for Motherhood?*, pp. 165–87. London: Pandora.

Burfoot, Annette. 1988. "A Review of the Third Annual Meeting of the European Society of Human Reproduction and Embryology." *Reproductive and Genetic Engineering: Journal of International Feminist Analysis* 1, no. 1: 107–11.

Butler, Judith. 1990. *Gender Trouble: Feminism and the Subversion of Identity.* New York: Routledge.

Butler, S. and A. Kondratas. 1987. *Out of the Poverty Trap: A Conservative Strategy for Welfare Reform.* New York: Free Press.

Cahn, Naomi. 1991. "Civil Images of Battered Women: The Impact of Domestic Violence on Child Custody Decisions." *Vanderbilt Law Review* 44:1041.

Cain, Patricia. 1990. "Feminist Jurisprudence: Grounding the Theories." *Berkeley Women's Law Journal* 4:191.

Calhoun, Arthur W. 1919. *A Social History of the American Family from Colonial Times to the Present.* Cleveland: Arthur H. Clark.

Calhoun, J. 1884. "Letter from Secretary of State to the British Ambassador." Quoted in J. H. Gresham, "The Politics of Family in America." *The Nation* (July 1989): 116.

Callahan, S. 1991. "Does Gender Make a Difference in Moral Decisionmaking?" *Second Opinion* 17, no. 2: 66, 77.

Canada Child and Family Services (CCFS) Task Force. 1987. *Indian Child and Family Services in Canada: Final Report.* Ottawa: Indian and Northern Affairs.

Canadian Bar Association Task Force on Gender Equality. 1993. Chaired by (former) Justice Bertha Wilson in Canada. *Touchstones for Change: Equality, Diversity, and Accountability.* Ottawa: Canadian Bar Association.

Canadian Royal Commission. 1993. Report on New Reproductive Technologies.

Capron, Alexander M. and Margaret J. Radin. 1988. "Choosing Family Law Over Contract Law as a Paradigm for Surrogate Motherhood." In Larry Gostin, ed., *Surrogate Motherhood: Politics and Privacy*, pp. 59–76. Bloomington: Indiana University Press.

Carasco, E. 1986. "Canadian Native Children: Have Child Welfare Laws Broken the Circle?" *Canadian Journal of Family Law* 5:111.

Carbone, June. 1990. "Economics, Feminism, and the Reinvention of Alimony: A Reply to Ira Ellman." *Vanderbilt Law Review* 43:1463.

Castro, Janice. 1991. "Watching a Generation Waste Away." *Time* (August 26): 10 (interview with economist Sylvia Ann Hewlett).

Center for Law and Social Policy. 1992. *Family Matters: A Quarterly Report on Welfare Initiatives* 4, no. 2 (April/May).

Chafetz, J. 1988. "The Gender Division of Labor and the Reproduction of Female Disadvantage." *Journal of Family Labor* 9:108–31.

Chesler, P. 1987. *Mothers on Trial: The Battle for Children and Custody*. New York: McGraw-Hill.

Chira, Susan. 1992. "New Realities Fight Old Images of Mothers." *New York Times* (October 4): L1 and L2.

Chodorow, Nancy. 1978. *The Reproduction of Mothering: Psychoanalysis and the Sociology of Gender*. Berkeley: University of California Press.

Chodorow, Nancy and Susan Contratto. 1982. "The Fantasy of the Perfect Mother." In Marilyn Yalom and Barnie Thorne, eds., *Rethinking the Family: Some Feminist Questions*. Also published in Nancy Chodorow, *Feminism and Psychoanalytic Theory* (New Haven: Yale University Press, 1988), pp. 79–96.

Clark, Homer Harrison. 1965. *Cases and Problems on Domestic Relations*. St. Paul, Minn.: West Publishing.

Clarke, Adele. 1984. "Subtle Forms of Sterilization Abuse: A Reproductive Rights Analysis." In Arditti, Klein, and Minden, eds., *Test-Tube Women: What Future for Motherhood?*, pp. 188–212.

Clearinghouse Review 25 (October 1991): 768.

Clinton, Catherine. 1985. "Caught in the Web of the Big House: Women and Slavery." In Walter J. Raser, ed., *The Web of Southern Social Relations*, pp. 19–34. Athens: University of Georgia Press.

Clymer, Adam. 1993. "Congress Passes Measure Providing Emergency Leaves." *New York Times* (February 5): A1.

Cochran. 1988a. "The Need for Cooperation on Welfare Reform." *Congressional Record* (Senate 134 Cong. Rec. §4712–01).

——. 1988b. "Welfare Reform—the Need to Attack Family Dependency." *Congressional Record* (Senate 134 Cong. Rec. §3069–01).

Coffey, M. A. 1986. "Of Father Born: A Lesbian Feminist Critique of the Ontario Law Reform Commission Recommendations on Artificial Insemination." *Canadian Journal of Women and the Law* 1:434.

Cohan, Alvin. 1986. "Abortion as a Marginal Issue: The Use of Peripheral Mechanisms in Britain and the United States." In Joni Lovenduski and Joyce Outshoorn, eds., *The New Politics of Abortion*, pp. 27–48. Newbury Park, Calif.: Sage.

Cohen, Jean L. 1992. "Redescribing Privacy: Identity, Difference, and the Abortion Controversy." *Columbia Journal of Gender and the Law* 3, no. 1: 43–117.

Coles, Robert. 1988. " 'So, You Fell in Love with Your Baby.' " *New York Times Book Review* (June 26): 1, 34–35.

Colker, Ruth. 1991. "An Equal Protection Analysis of United States Reproductive Health Policy: Gender, Race, Age, and Class." *Duke Law Journal* 2:324–64.

Collins, Patricia Hill. 1990. *Black Feminist Thought: Knowledge, Consciousness, and the Politics of Empowerment.* Boston: Unwin Hyman.

Collopy, B. 1988. "Autonomy in Long-Term Care: Some Crucial Distinctions." *The Gerontologist*, Supplement 28:10–17.

——. 1990. "The Place of Autonomy in Bioethics." *Hastings Center Report* 20 (January/February): 1.

Collopy, B., N. Dubler, and C. Zuckerman. 1990. "The Ethics of Home Care: Autonomy and Accomodation." *Hastings Center Report*, Special Supplement (March/April): 4.

Committee on Ways and Means. 1987. "Retirement Income for an Aging Society." Report prepared by Congressional Research Service, Library of Congress, U.S. Government Printing Office. Washington, D.C.

Commonwealth Fund Study: Commission on Elderly People Living Alone. 1988. "Aging Alone: Profiles and Projections." New York: The Commonwealth Fund.

Condit, Celeste M. 1990. *Decoding Abortion Rhetoric: The Communication of Social Change.* Urbana: University of Illinois Press.

Congressional Record. 1988. *Senate, Proceedings and Debates of the 100th Congress, Second Session, Family Security Act* (June 13, 1988, 134 Cong. Rec. §7631–02).

Cooper, D. and D. Herman. 1991. "Getting 'The Family Right': Legislating Heterosexuality in Britain, 1986–1991." *Canadian Journal of Family Law* 10:41.

Corea, Gena. 1985a, Updated Edition. *The Hidden Malpractice: How American Medicine Mistreats Women.* New York: Harper Colophon.

——. 1985b. *The Mother Machine: Reproductive Technologies from Artificial Insemination to Artificial Wombs.* New York: Harper and Row.

Corea, Gena and Susan Ince. 1987. "Report of a Survey of IVF Clinics in the USA." In Spallone and Steinberg, eds., *Made to Order: The Myth of Reproductive and Genetic Progress*, pp. 133–45.

Corea, Gena, J. Hanmer, B. Hoskins, J. Raymond, R. D. Klein, H. B. Holmes, M. Kishwar, R. Rowland, and R. Steinbacher, eds. 1987. *Man-Made Women: How the New Reproductive Technologies Affect Women.* Bloomington: Indiana University Press.

Cott, Nancy. 1979. *The Bonds of Womanhood: "Women's Sphere" in New England, 1780–1835.* New Haven: Yale University Press.

Crenshaw, K. 1989. "Demarginalizing the Intersection of Race and Sex: A Black Feminist Critique of Antidiscrimination Doctrine, Feminist Theory, and Antiracist Politics." *University of Chicago Legal Forum*, p. 139–67.

Cullum, C. S. 1993. "Co-Parent Adoptions: Lesbian and Gay Parenting." *Trial* 28.

Curran, Barbara. 1986. "American Lawyers in the 1980s: A Profession in Transition." *Law and Society Review* 20:19.

Currie, D. 1993. "Class, Race, and Gender: Re-Thinking the 'Motherhood Question' in Feminism." Paper presented at the Fifth International Interdisciplinary Congress on Women, San José, Costa Rica.

Curry, H., D. Clifford, and R. Leonard. 1993. *A Legal Guide For Lesbian And Gay Couples*. Berkeley, Calif.: Nolo.

Cushman, John Jr. 1993. "Illegal Workers: A Long Road to Legality." *New York Times* (February 4): C8.

Czapanskiy, Karen. 1991. "Volunteers and Draftees: The Struggle for Parental Equality." *University of California at Los Angeles Law Review* 38:1415.

Daly, B. O. and M. T. Reddy. 1991. *Narrating Mothers: Theorizing Maternal Subjectivities*. Knoxville: University of Tennesee Press.

Daly, Mary. 1978. *Gyn/Ecology: The Metaethics of Radical Feminism*. Boston: Beacon.

Davidoff, L., ed. 1992. "Motherhood, Race, and the State in the Twentieth Century." *Gender and History*, special issue 4:2.

Davidson, C. N. and E. M. Broner, eds. 1980. *The Lost Tradition: Mothers and Daughters in Literature*. New York: F. Ungar.

Davis, Angela Y. 1983. *Women, Race, and Class*. New York: Vintage.

———. 1990. *Women, Culture, and Politics*. New York: Vintage.

Davis, Peggy. 1989. "Law as Microaggression." *Yale Law Journal* 98:1559.

Dedger, Douglas. 1992. "Benefits in State and Local Governments Address Family Concerns." *Monthly Labor Review* 115:32.

Delaney, E. A. 1991. "Statutory Protection of the Other Mother: Legally Recognizing the Relationship Between the Nonbiological Lesbian Parent and Her Child." *Hastings Law Journal* 43:177.

de Man, Paul. 1979. "Autobiography as De-facement." *Modern Language Notes* 94:919–30.

Department of Indian and Northern Development. 1990. *Basic Departmental Data, 1990*. Ottawa: Ministry of Indian and Northern Development.

Dewar, John. 1989. "Fathers in Law? The Case of AID." In Robert Lee and Derek Morgan, eds., *Birthrights: Law and Ethics at the Beginnings of Life*. New York: Routledge.

Diamond, Irene. 1988. "Medical Science and the Transformation of Motherhood: The Promise of Reproductive Technologies." In Ellen Boneparth and Emily Stoper, eds., *Women, Power, and Policy: Toward the Year 2000*, pp. 155–67. New York: Pergamon.

———. 1990. "Babies, Heroic Experts, and a Poisoned Earth." In Irene Diamond and Gloria Feman Orenstein, eds., *Reweaving the World: The Emergence of Ecofeminism*, pp. 201–10. San Francisco: Sierra Club Books.

Diamond, Irene and Lee Quinby, eds. 1988. *Feminism and Foucault: Reflections on Resistance*. Boston: Northeastern University Press.

Dinerstein, Robert D. 1990. "Client-Centered Counseling: Reappraisal and Refinement." *Arizona Law Reviw* 32:501.

District of Columbia Task Force on Racial and Ethnic Bias and Task Force on Gender Bias in the Courts. 1992. *Final Report of the Task Force on Gender Bias in the Courts*. Washington, D.C.: District of Columbia Courts.

Division of Family Development (New Jersey). 1992a. "Response to Public Comments on Proposed Regulations." *New Jersey Register* 24:3345.

———. 1992b. "Assistance Standards Handbook." Amendments published in *New Jersey Register* 24:3352.

Doane, Janice and Devon Hodges. 1992. *From Klein to Kristeva: Psychoanalysis and the Search for the "Good Enough" Mother*. Ann Arbor: University of Michigan Press.

Dooley, David S. 1990. "Immoral Because They're Bad, Bad Because They're Wrong: Sexual Orientation and Presumptions of Parental Unfitness in Custody Disputes." *California Western Law Review* 26:395.

Douglas, Mary. 1966. *Purity and Danger*. Boston: Routledge and Kegan Paul.

Douglass, Frederick. 1982. *Narrative of the Life of Frederick Douglass: An American Slave*. Ed. Houston A. Baker, Jr. New York: Penguin.

Dowd, Nancy E. 1989. "Work and Family: The Gender Paradox and the Limitations of Discrimination Analysis in Restructuring the Workplace." *Harvard Civil Rights–Civil Liberties Law Review* 24:78.

Drachman, Virginia. 1989. "My 'Partner in Law and Life': Marriage in the Lives of Women Lawyers in Late 19th- and Early 20th-Century America." *Law and Social Inquiry* 14:221.

Draft *Summary of the Components of New Jersey's Welfare Reform Package*, at 1. On file with Nina Perales.

Dranoff, Linda Silver. 1972. "Women as Lawyers in Toronto." *Osgoode Hall Law Journal* 10:177.

Dreyfus, Hubert L. and Paul Rabinow. 1982. *Michel Foucault: Beyond Structuralism and Hermeneutics*. 2d ed. Chicago: University of Chicago Press.

Du Bois, W. E. B. 1976. *Black Reconstruction*. Milwood, N.Y.: Kraus-Thompson.

Duclos, N. 1993. "Disappearing Women: Racial Minority Women in Human Rights Cases." *Canadian Journal of Women and the Law* 2:25.

Duden, Barbara. 1993. *Disembodying Women: Perspectives on Pregnancy and the Unborn*. Cambridge: Harvard University Press.

Dutton, Diana B., Thomas A. Preston, and Nancy E. Pfund. 1988. *Worse Than the Disease: Pitfalls of Medical Progress*. New York: Cambridge University Press.

Duxbury, Linda, Christopher Higgins, and Catherine Lee. 1993. "Work-Family Conflict." *Vanier Institute of the Family: Transition* 23, no. 2: 11.

Dworkin, Andrea. 1983. *Right-Wing Women*. New York: Perigee.

Eagleton, T. 1983. *Literary Theory: An Introduction*. Minneapolis: University of Minnesota Press.

———. 1991. *Ideology: An Introduction*. London: Verso.

Edelman, M. W. 1987. *Families in Peril: An Agenda For Social Change*. Cambridge: Harvard University Press.

Edelman, Murray. 1977. *Political Language: Words That Succeed and Policies That Fail*. New York: Academic Press.

Edwards, Margot and Mary Waldorf. 1984. *Reclaiming Birth: History and Heroines of American Childbirth Reform.* Trumansburg, N.Y.: Crossing.

Ehrenreich, Barbara. 1990. *Fear of Falling: The Inner Life of the Middle Class.* New York: HarperCollins.

Ehrenreich, Barbara and Deirdre English. 1978. *For Her Own Good: 150 Years of the Experts' Advice to Women.* Garden City, N.Y.: Anchor.

Eisenhandler, S. 1992. "Lifelong Roles and Cameo Appearances: Elderly Parents and Relationships with Adult Children." *Journal of Aging Studies* 6:243, 246.

Eisenstein, Zillah R. 1988. *The Female Body and the Law.* Berkeley: University of California Press.

Elen. 1988. "Senator Moynihan Discusses Children in Poverty." (Introducing to the record an article written by Senator Moynihan.) (134 Cong. Rec. §16919–03).

Elkington, John. 1985. *The Poisoned Womb: Human Reproduction in a Polluted World.* New York: Penguin.

Ellman, Ira M. 1989. "The Theory of Alimony." *California Law Review* 77:1.

Elshtain, Jean Bethke. 1989. "Technology as Destiny: The New Eugenics Challenges Feminism." *The Progressive* 53, no. 6 (June): 19–23.

England, Paula and George Farkas. 1986. *Households, Employment, and Gender: A Social, Economic, and Demographic View.* New York: Aldine.

Epstein, Cynthia Fuchs. 1990. "Faulty Framework: Consequences of the Difference Model for Women in the Law." *New York Law School Law Review* 35:309.

Erdrich, Louise. 1987. *The Beet Queen.* New York: Bantam.

Erlich, Elizabeth. 1989a. "The Mommy Track." *Business Week* (March 20): 126.

——. 1989b. "Is The Mommy Track a Blessing—or a Betrayal?" *Business Week* (May 15): 98.

Ernaux, Annie. 1987a. *La Place.* London: Methuen.

——. 1987b. *Une Femme.* Paris: Gallimard.

——. 1991. *A Woman's Story.* Trans. by Tanya Leslie. New York: Four Walls Eight Windows.

Esau, A. and J. Penner, eds. 1990. *Lawyering and Legal Education Into the 21st Century.* Manitoba: Legal Research Institute of the University of Manitoba.

Esse Networks. 1990. *Together Today . . . For Our Children Tomorrow/ Our Most Valuable Resource: A Discussion of Indian Child Welfare.* Yukon Territories: Council for Yukon Indians.

Estes, C., James H. Swan et al. 1993. *The Long-Term Care Crisis.* Newbury Park, Calif.: Sage.

Estrich, Susan. 1987. *Real Rape.* Cambridge: Harvard University Press.

Etter-Lewis, Gwendolyn. 1991. "Black Women's Life Stories: Reclaiming Self in Narrative Texts." In Sherner Berger Gluck and Daphne Patai, eds., *Women's Words: The Feminist Practice of Oral History.* New York: Routledge.

Etzioni, Amitai. 1992. "Tough Medicine for a Sick America." *Los Angeles Times Magazine* (March 22): 32.

Eyer, D. E. 1993. *Mother-Infant Bonding: A Scientific Fiction.* New Haven: Yale University Press.

Falk, Marcia. 1994. "Reflections on Hannah's Prayer." In *Out of the Garden*, Christina Buchanan and Cecelia Spiegal, eds. New York: Fawcett Columbine.

Farrant, Wendy. 1985. "Who's for Amniocentesis? The Politics of Prenatal Screening." In H. Homans, ed., *The Sexual Politics of Reproduction*, pp. 96–122. Brookfield, Vt.: Gower.

Ferguson, Ann. 1984. "On Conceiving Motherhood and Sexuality: A Feminist Materialist Approach." In Joyce Treblicot, ed., *Mothering: Essays in Feminist Theory*, pp. 153–82.

Field, Martha A. 1988. *Surrogate Motherhood*. Cambridge: Harvard University Press.

Fineman, Martha A. 1983. "Implementing Equality: Ideology, Contradiction, and Social Change; A Study of Rhetoric and Results in the Regulation of the Consequences of Divorce." *Wisconsin Law Review*, pp. 789–886.

——. 1988. "Dominant Discourse, Professional Language, and Legal Change in Child Custody Decision Making." *Harvard Law Review* 101:727.

——. 1990. "Challenging Law, Establishing Differences: The Future of Feminist Legal Scholarship." *Florida Law Review* 42:25.

——. 1991a. *The Illusion of Equality: The Rhetoric and Reality of Divorce Reform*. Chicago and London: University of Chicago Press.

——. 1991b. "Images of Mothers in Poverty Discourses." *Duke Law Journal* 2:274–95.

——. 1991c. "Intimacy Outside of the Natural Family." *Connecticut Law Review* 23:955.

——. 1992a. "Feminist Theory in Law: The Difference It Makes." *Columbia Journal of Gender and Law* 2:1.

——. 1992b. "The Neutered Mother." *Miami Law Review* 46:301.

——. 1995. *The Neutered Mother, The Sexual Family, and Other Twentieth-Century Tragedies*. New York: Routledge.

Finley, Lucinda M. 1986. "Transcending Equality Theory: A Way Out of the Maternity and Workplace Debate." *Columbia Law Review* 86:1118–82.

Firestone, Shumalith. 1970. *The Dialectic of Sex: The Case for Feminist Revolution*. New York: Morrow.

Fisher, Sue. 1986. *In the Patient's Best Interest: Women and the Politics of Medical Decisions*. New Brunswick: Rutgers University Press.

Fiske, J. 1992. "Child of the State, Mother of the Nation: Aboriginal Women and the Ideology of Motherhood." Paper presented at the Joint Meetings of the Atlantic Canada Studies and British Columbia Studies Associations, 21–24 May, Charlottetown, P.E.I.

Fiss, Owen M. 1976. "Groups and the Equal Protection Clause." *Philosophy & Public Affairs* 5, no. 2: 107–77.

Fitzpatrick, P. 1987. "Racism and the Innocence of Law." *Journal of Law & Sociology* 14:119.

Floyd, Pink. 1975. "I Wish You Were Here." *Wish You Were Here*. CBS Records.

Foucault, Michel. 1979. *Discipline and Punish: The Birth of the Prison*. Trans. by Alan Sheridan. New York: Vintage.

——. 1980a. *The History of Sexuality*. Trans. by Robert Hurley. New York: Vintage.

——. 1980b. *Power/Knowledge: Selected Interviews and Other Writings, 1972–1977* Trans. by Colin Gordon et al. and ed. by Colin Gordon. New York: Pantheon.

Fox, Eleanor. 1989. "Being a Woman, Being a Lawyer, and Being a Human Being—Woman and Change." *Fordham Law Review* 57:955.

Fox-Genovese, Elizabeth. 1988. *Within the Plantation Household: Black and White Women of the Old South*. Chapel Hill: University of North Carolina Press.

Fraser, Nancy. 1989. *Unruly Practices: Power, Discourse, and Gender in Contemporary Social Theory*, pp. 144–60. Minneapolis: University of Minnesota Press.

Fraser, Sylvia. 1987. *My Father's House: A Memoir of Incest and Healing*. New York: Ticknor and Fields.

Frederickson, George. 1971. *The Black Image in the White Mind and the Debate on Afro-American Character and Destiny, 1817–1914*. Middletown: Wesleyan University Press. Quoted in J. H. Gresham, "The Politics of Family in America." *The Nation* (July 1989): 117.

Freedman, Monroe. 1975. *Lawyers' Ethics in an Adversary System*. Indianapolis: Bobbs-Merrill.

Freeman, Martha. 1986. "Writing Briefs and Changing Diapers." *California Lawyer* 6:36.

Friedan, B. 1993. *The Fountain of Age*. New York: Simon and Schuster.

Frug, Mary Joe. 1979. "Securing Job Equality for Women: Labor Market Hostility to Working Mothers." *Buffalo University Law Review* 59:55.

——. 1992. *Postmodern Legal Feminism*. New York: Routledge.

Furstenberg, Frank. 1990. "Divorce and the American Family." *Annual Review of Sociology* 16:379.

Fuss, Diana. 1991. "Inside/Out." In Diana Fuss, ed., *Inside/Out: Lesbian Theories, Gay Theories*. New York: Routledge.

Gallagher, Janet. 1985. "Fetal Personhood and Women's Policy." In Virginia Sapiro, ed., *Women, Biology, and Public Policy*, pp. 91–116. Newbury Park, Calif.: Sage.

——. 1989. "Fetus as Patient." In Nadine Taub and Sherrill Cohen, eds., *Reproductive Laws for the 1990s*, pp. 185–235. Clifton, N.J.: Humana.

García, Anna Maria. 1982. *La Operación*. Independent film.

Gardner, A. 1870. *Conjugal Sins Against the Law of Life and Health*. 1974. Photographic reprint, New York: J. S. Redfield.

Gardner, Katy. 1981. "Well Woman Clinics: A Positive Approach to Women's Health." In Helen Roberts, ed., *Women, Health, and Reproduction*, pp. 129–43. London: Routledge and Kegan Paul.

Garfinkel, I. 1982. "The Role of Child Support in Antipoverty Policy." Discussion paper #713, Institute for Research on Poverty, .

——. 1987. "Welfare: Reform or Replacement: Child Support Enforcement." Testimony Before the Subcommittee on Social Security and Family Policy, U.S. Senate Committee on Finance, Washington, D.C.

Garrison, Marsha. 1983. "Why Terminate Parental Rights?" *Stanford Law Review* 35:423.

Gates, Henry Louis Jr. 1987. "To Be Raped, Bred, or Abused." Review of *Incidents in the Life of a Slave Girl* by Harriet Jacobs, ed. by J. Yelin. *New York Times Book Review* (November 22): 12.

Gavigan, S. A. M. 1993. "Paradise Lost, Paradox Revisited: The Implications of Familial Ideology for Feminist, Lesbian, and Gay Engagement to Law" *Osgoode Hall Law Journal* 31:589–624.

Gavison, Ruth. 1992. "Feminism and the Public/Private Distinction." *Stanford Law Review* 45:1–45.

Gerard, J. 1992. "TV Generation Ages Into 'Baby Boom.' " *Detroit Free Press* (November 2): 1B.

Gerson, Kathleen. 1985. *Hard Choices: How Women Decide About Work, Career, and Motherhood.* Berkeley: University of California Press.

Getman, Karen. 1984. "Sexual Control in the Slaveholding South: The Implementation and Maintenance of a Racial Caste System." *Harvard Women's Law Journal* 7:115–52.

Giddings, Paula. 1984. *When and Where I Enter: The Impact of Black Women on Race and Sex in America.* New York: Marrow.

Giesbrecht B. (A.C.J.). 1992. *Report Respecting the Death of Lester Norman Desjarlais.* Winnipeg: Office of the Chief Medical Examiner, Queen's Printer.

Gilbert, Olive. 1878. *Narrative of Sojourner Truth: A Bondswoman of Olden Time.* Battle Creek, Mich.: privately printed.

Gimenez, Martha E. 1984. "Feminism, Pronatalism, and Motherhood." In Joyce Treblicot, ed., *Mothering: Essays in Feminist Theory*, pp. 290–304.

Ginsburg, Faye D. 1989. *Contested Lives: The Abortion Debate in an American Community.* Berkeley: University of California Press.

Ginsburg, Ruth Bader. 1985. "Some Thoughts on Autonomy and Equality in Relation to *Roe v. Wade.*" *North Carolina Law Review* 63, no. 2: 375–86.

——. 1992. "Speaking in a Judicial Voice." *New York University Law Review* 67, no. 6: 1185–209.

Glazer, Nathan and Patrick Daniel Moynihan. 1970. *Beyond the Melting Pot.* Quoted in Rodriguez 1989:15.

Glendon, Mary Ann. 1987. *Abortion and Divorce in Western Law.* Cambridge: Harvard University Press.

Glover, Jonathan et al. 1989. *Ethics of New Reproductive Technologies: The Glover Report to the European Commission.* De Kalb: Northern Illinois University Press.

Goldfarb, Phyllis. 1992. "Beyond Cut Flowers: Developing a Clinical Perspective on Critical Legal Theory." *Hastings Law Journal* 4:717.

Goldstein. 1988. *Mother Love and Abortion.* Berkeley: University of California Press.

Goodwin, Frederick. 1992. Quoted in speech delivered by Jerome Miller at the Civil Rights Training Conference, October 1992, in Airlie, Va.

Gordon, Linda. 1976. *Woman's Body, Woman's Right: A Social History of Birth Control in America.* New York: Grossman.

———. 1992. "Why Nineteenth-Century Feminists Did Not Support Birth Control and Twentieth-Century Feminists Do: Feminism, Reproduction, and the Family." In B. Thorne and M. Yalom, eds., *Rethinking the Family: Some Feminist Questions*, pp. 140–54. Boston: Northeastern University Press.

———. 1989. *Heroes of Their Own Lives: The Politics and History of Family Violence: Boston, 1880–1960.* New York: Penguin.

Gould, Stephen Jay. 1981. *The Mismeasure of Man.* New York: Norton.

Government of Canada. 1989. "Integration of Work and Family Responsibilities: Report on Strategies." Ottawa: Annual Conference of First Ministers.

Graham, Hillary and Ann Oakley. 1981. "Competing Ideologies of Reproduction: Medical and Maternal Perspectives on Pregnancy." In Helen Roberts, ed., *Women, Health, and Reproduction*, pp. 50–74. London: Routledge and Kegan Paul.

Gray, Silvia Sims and Lynn M. Nybell. 1990. "Issues in African-American Family Preservation." *Child Welfare* 69:513.

Graycar, R. and J. Morgan. 1990. *The Hidden Gender of Law.* Sydney: Federation.

Griffin, Susan. 1978. *Woman and Nature: The Roaring Inside Her.* New York: Harper Colophon.

Griffith, A. I. and D. E. Smith. 1987. "Constructing Cultural Knowledge: Mothering as Discourse." In J. S. Gaskell and A. T. McLaren, eds., *Women and Education: A Canadian Perspective*, pp. 87–104. Calgary: Detselig Enterprises.

Grillo, Trina and Stephanie M. Wildman. 1991. "Obscuring the Importance of Race: The Implications of Making Comparisons Between Racism and Sexism (or Other -isms)." *Duke Law Journal*, p. 397.

Grossman, Glenn M. 1992. "U.S. Workers Receive a Wide Range of Employee Benefits." *Monthly Labor Review* 115:36.

Gueron, J. and E. Pauley. 1991. *From Welfare to Work.* New York: Russell Sage.

Gusfield, Joseph R. 1992. "Listening for the Silences: The Rhetorics of the Research Field." In Richard Harvey Brown, ed., *Writing the Social Text: Poetics and Politics in Social Science Discourse*, pp. 117–34. New York: Aldine De Gruyter.

Gutman, Herbert G. 1976. *The Black Family in Slavery and Freedom.* New York: Pantheon.

Habermas, Jurgen. 1984. *The Theory of Communicative Action.* Vol 1. Trans. by Thomas McCarthy. Boston: Beacon.

———. 1985. *The Theory of Communicative Action.* Vol. 2. Trans. by Thomas McCarthy. Boston: Beacon.

Hacker, Andrew. 1992. *Two Nations Black and White, Separate, Hostile, Unequal.* New York: Ballantine.

Hagan, J., M. Huxter, and P. Parker. 1988. "Class Structure and Legal Practice: Inequality andd Mobility Among Toronto Lawyers." *Law and Society Review* 22:9.

Halamandaris, V. 1986. "The Future of Home Health Care in America." *Generations* 10:48–51.

Hale, Edwin M. 1867. *The Great Crime of the Nineteenth Century*. Chicago: C. S. Halsey.

Hammond, D. 1986. "Health Care for Older Women: Curing the Disease." In Marilyn Bell, ed., *Women as Elders: The Feminist Politics of Aging*, p. 59. New York: Harrington Park.

Hand, John. 1993. "Buying Fertility: The Constitutionality of Welfare Bonuses for Welfare Mothers Who Submit to Norplant Insertion." *Vanderbilt Law Review* 46:715–54.

Hanmer, Jalna. 1981. "Sex Predetermination, Artificial Insemination, and the Maintenance of Male-Dominated Culture." In Helen Roberts, ed., *Women, Health, and Reproduction*, pp. 163–90. London: Routledge and Kegan Paul.

——. 1984. "A Womb of One's Own." In Arditti, Klein, and Minden, eds., *Test-Tube Women: What Future for Motherhood?*, pp. 438–48.

Harding, Sandra. 1986. *The Science Question in Feminism*. Ithaca: Cornell University Press.

Harrington, C. and J. Swan. 1985. "Institutional Long Term Care Services." In C. Harrington et al., eds., *Long-Term Care of the Elderly: Public Policy Issues*. Newbury Park, Calif.: Sage.

Harris, Angela P. 1990. "Race and Essentialism in Feminist Legal Theory." *Stanford Law Review* 42:581.

Harrison, Michelle. 1987. "Social Construction of Mary Beth Whitehead." *Gender & Society* 1, no. 3: 300–11.

Hartmann, Betsy. 1987. *Reproductive Rights and Wrongs: The Global Politics of Population Control and Contraceptive Choice*. New York: Harper and Row.

Harvey, Cameron. 1970–71. "Women in Law in Canada." *Manitoba Law Journal* 4:9.

Hawthorn, H. B., ed. 1966. *A Survey of the Contemporary Indian of Canada: A Report on Economic, Political, Educational Needs, and Policies*. Ottawa: Indian Affairs Branch.

Hepworth, H. P. 1980. *Foster Care and Adoption in Canada*. Ottawa: Canadian Council on Social Development.

Herman, Judith L. 1981. *Father-Daughter Incest*. Cambridge: Harvard University Press.

——. 1992. *Trauma and Recovery*. New York: Basic Books.

Heron, Liz, ed. 1985. *Truth, Dare, or Promise: Girls Growing Up in the 50s*. 1992. Reprint, London: Virago.

Hertz, J. H., ed. 1978. *Pentateuch and Haftorahs*. Hebrew text, English translation and commentary. 2d ed. London: Soncino.

Higginbotham, Leon A. 1978. *In the Matter of Color*. New York: Oxford University Press.

Hill, John. 1990. "New Poll: Abortion Veto OK." Gannet News Service (September 7). Available in LEXIS, NEXIS Library, GNS File.

Hill, Kate. 1987. "Mothers by Insemination." In Sandra Pollack and Jeanne Vaughn, eds., *Politics of the Heart: A Lesbian Parenting Anthology*. Ithaca, N.Y.: Firebrand.

Hill, Robert B. 1977. *Informal Adoption Among Black Families.* Washington, D.C.: National Urban League.

Himmelstein, Jerome L. 1990. *To the Right: The Transformation of American Conservatism.* Berkeley: University of California Press.

Hirsch, Marianne. 1989. *The Mother/Daughter Plot: Narrative, Psychoanalysis, Feminism.* Bloomington: Indiana University Press.

Hirsch, Ronald L. 1989. "Will Women Leave the Law?" *Barrister* 16:22.

Hochschild, A. and A. Machung. 1989. *Second Shift: Working Parents and the Revolution at Home.* New York: Viking.

Hodge, Hugh. 1869. *Foeticide; or, Criminal Abortion.* Philadelphia: Lindsay and Blakiston.

Holder, Angela R. 1988. "Surrogate Motherhood and the Best Interest of Children." In Larry Gostin, ed., *Surrogate Motherhood: Politics and Privacy*, pp. 77–87. Bloomington: Indiana University Press.

Hollinger, J. H. 1985. "From Coitus to Commerce: Legal and Social Consequences of Noncoital Reproduction." *University of Michigan Journal of Law Reform* 18 (Summer): 865–932.

Holmes, Helen B. and Betty B. Hoskins. 1987. "Prenatal and Preconception Sex Choice Technologies: A Path to Femicide?" In Gena Corea et al., eds., *Man-Made Women: How the New Reproductive Technologies Affect Women*, pp. 15–29. Bloomington: Indiana University Press.

hooks, bell. 1981. *Ain't I a Woman: Black Women and Feminism.* Boston: South End.

——. 1984. *Feminist Theory: From Margin to Center.* Boston: South End.

——. 1991. "Theory as Liberatory Practice." *Yale Journal of Law and Feminism* 4:1–4.

Hooper, C. A. 1992. "Child Sexual Abuse and the Regulation of Women: Variation on a Theme." In Carol Smart, ed., *Regulating Womanhood: Historical Essays on Marriage, Motherhood, and Sexuality*, pp. 53–77. London: Routledge.

Horowitz, A., B. Silverstone, and J. Reinhardt. 1991. "A Conceptual and Empirical Exploration of Personal Autonomy Issues Within Family Caregiving Relationships." *The Gerontologist* 31, no. 1: 23, 30.

Horowitz, J. 1991. "Poof! The Mommies Vanish in Sitcomland." *New York Times* (May 26): H23.

Hoskins, Betty B. and Helen B. Holmes. 1984. "Technology and Prenatal Femicide." In Arditti, Klein, and Minden, eds., *Test-Tube Women: What Future for Motherhood?*, pp. 237–55. London: Pandora.

Hubbard, Ruth. 1984. "Personal Courage Is Not Enough: Some Hazards of Childbearing in the 1980s." In Arditti, Klein, and Minden, eds., *Test-Tube Women: What Future for Motherhood?*, pp. 331–55.

Huber, J. and G. Spitze. 1983. *Sex Stratification: Children, Housework, and Jobs.* New York: Academic Press.

Hudson, P. and B. McKenzie. 1983. "Child Welfare and Native People: The Extension of Colonialism." *Social Worker* 49:63.

Huling, Tracy. 1987. *Limited Options: An Analysis of Public Policy Trends in Teenage*

Pregnancy Prevention and Recommendations for New York State. Draft. New York: Center for Public Advocacy Research.

Humphreys, J. 1987. *Rich in Love*. New York: Viking Penguin.

Hunt, A. 1991. "Marxism, Law, Legal Theory, and Jurisprudence." In P. Fitzpatrick, ed., *Dangerous Supplements: Resistance and Renewal in Jurisprudence*, pp. 102–32. London: Pluto.

Hurtado, Aida. 1989. "Relating to Privilege: Seduction and Rejection in the Subordination of White Women and Women of Color." *Signs* 14:833.

Ince, Susan. 1984. "Inside the Surrogate Industry." In Arditti, Klein, and Minden, eds., *Test-Tube Women: What Future for Motherhood?*, pp. 99–116.

Indian Association of Alberta. 1987. *Child Welfare Needs: Assessment and Recommendations*. Calgary: Indian Association of Alberta.

Jack, Dana. 1991. *Silencing the Self: Women and Depression*. Cambridge: Harvard University Press.

Jacobus, Mary, Evelyn Fox Keller, and Sally Shuttleworth. 1990. *Body/Politics: Women and the Discourses of Science*. New York: Routledge.

James, P. D. 1980. *Innocent Blood*. New York: Fawcett.

Janiewski, Dolores. 1983. "Sisters Under Their Skins: Southern Working Women." In Joanne V. Hawks and Sheila L. Skemp, eds., *Sex, Race, and the Role of Women in the South*, pp. 13–35. Jackson: University of Mississippi Press.

Jaquette, Jane S. and Kathleen A. Staudt. 1985. "Women as 'at Risk' Reproducers: Biology, Science, and Population in U.S. Foreign Policy." In Virginia Sapiro, ed., *Women, Biology, and Public Policy*, pp. 235–68. Newbury Park, Calif.: Sage.

Jardine, Alice. 1985. *Gynesis: Configurations of Women and Modernity*. Ithaca: Cornell University Press.

——. 1986. "Death Sentences." In Susan Suleiman, ed., *The Female Body in Western Culture: Contemporary Perspectives*, pp. 84–98. Boston: Harvard University Press.

Jencks, Christopher and Kathryn Edin. 1990. "The Real Welfare Problem." *American Prospect* 1:31.

Johnson, Barbara. 1987. "My Monster, My Self." In Nancy K. Miller, ed., *A World of Difference*, pp. 144–54. Baltimore: Johns Hopkins University Press.

Johnston, P. 1983. *Native Children and the Child Welfare System*. Ottawa: Canadian Council on Social Development.

Jones, Jacqueline. 1985. *Labor of Love, Labor of Sorrow: Black Women, Work, and the Family from Slavery to the Present*. New York: Basic Books.

Kamal, Sultana. 1987. "Seizure of Reproductive Rights? A Discussion on Population Control in the Third World and the Emergence of the New Reproductive Technologies in the West." In Spallone and Steinberg, eds., *Made to Order: The Myth of Reproductive and Genetic Progress*, pp. 146–53.

Kantrowitz, Pat. 1993. "Being Smart About the Mommy Track." *Working Woman* (February): 48.

Kaplan, E. Ann. 1992. *Motherhood and Representation: The Mother in Popular Culture and Melodrama*. London: Routledge.

Karst, Kenneth L. 1977. "Foreward: Equal Citizenship Under the Fourteenth Amendment." *Harvard Law Review* 91:1–68.

——. 1983. "Why Equality Matters." *Georgia Law Review* 17:245–89.

Kasarda, J. D. 1989. "Urban Industrial Transition and the Underclass." *The Annals of the American Academy of Political and Social Science* 501:26.

Katz, M. 1990. *The Undeserving Poor: From the War on Poverty to the War on Welfare.* New York: Pantheon.

Kaus, M. 1992. "Yes, Something Will Work: Work," *Newsweek* (May 18): 38.

Kay, Herma Hill. 1987a. "An Appraisal of California's No-Fault Divorce Law." *California Law Review* 75:291.

——. 1987b. "Equality and Difference: A Perspective on No-Fault Divorce and Its Aftermath." *Cincinnati Law Review* 56:1.

Kaye, Judith S. 1988. "Women Lawyers in Big Firms: A Study in Progress Toward Gender Equality." *Fordham Law Review* 57:111.

Keller, Evelyn Fox. 1985. *Reflections on Gender and Science.* New Haven: Yale University Press.

Kelly, Michael. 1993. "Household Hiring Is Trickier with New Broom in Capital." *New York Times* (February 12): A1.

Kerber, Linda. 1988. "Separate Spheres, Female Worlds, Woman's Place: The Rhetoric of Women's History." *Journal of American History* 75:9.

Kern and Ridolfi. 1982. "The Fourteenth Amendment's Protection of a Woman's Rights to Be a Single Parent Through Artificial Insemination by Donor." *Women's Rights Law Report* 7:251.

Kerrison, Ray. 1990. "Backdrop to Bush's Court Selection; Pictures Show What Abortion Is About." *New York Post* (July 25): 2.

Ketchum, Sara Anne. 1987. "New Reproductive Technologies and the Definition of Parenthood: A Feminist Perspective." Paper presented at the June Feminism and Legal Theory Conference on Intimacy, University of Wisconsin Law School, Madison, Wisc.

Kiley, D. 1984. *The Wendy Dilemma: When Women Stop Mothering Their Men.* New York: Arbor House.

Kingston, E. 1991. "The Greying of the Baby Boom in the United States: Framing the Policy Debate." *International Social Security Review* 44 (January/February): 5–6.

Kingston. 1988. "Women in the Law Say Path Is Limited by 'Mommy Track.' " *New York Times* (August 8).

Kishwar, Madhu. 1987. "The Continuing Deficit of Women in India and the Impact of Amniocentesis." In Gena Corea et al., eds., *Man-Made Women: How New Reproductive Technologies Affect Women,* pp. 30–37. Bloomington: Indiana University Press.

Klein, Renate D. 1987. "What's 'New' About the 'New' Reproductive Technologies." In Gena Corea et al., eds., *Man-Made Women: How New Reproductive Technologies Affect Women,* pp. 64–73. Bloomington: Indiana University Press.

Kline, Marlee. 1989. "Race, Racism, and Feminist Legal Theory." *Harvard Women's Law Journal* 12:115.

——. 1992. "Child Welfare Law, 'Best Interests of the Child' Ideology, and First Nations." *Osgoode Hall Law Journal* 30:375.

——. 1994. "The Colour of Law: Ideological Representations of First Nations in Legal Discourse." *Social & Legal Studies* 3:451–76.

Knight, W. 1993. Poem left on members' seats at Republican caucus meeting of the California State Assembly, May 18, 1994. Reprinted in *Hispanic Link Weekly Report* 11, no. 22 (May 31): 1.

Koren, M. J. 1986. "Home Care—Who Cares?" *New England Journal of Medicine* 314, no. 14: 917–20.

Krauskopf, Joan M. 1985. "Maintenance: A Decade of Development." *Missouri Law Review* 50:259.

Kristeva, Julia. 1992. "Semiotics of Biblical Abomination." In *Powers of Horror: An Essay on Abjection*, pp. 90–112. Trans. by Leon Roudiez. New York: Columbia University Press.

Krosenbrink-Gelissen, L. E. 1991. *Sexual Equality as an Aboriginal Right: The Native Women's Association of Canada and the Constitutional Process on Aboriginal Matters, 1982–1987.* Saarbrucken, Germany: Verlag Breltenback.

Laborie, Françoise. 1987. "Looking for Mothers, You Only Find Fetuses." In Spallone and Steinberg, eds., *Made to Order: The Myth of Reproductive and Genetic Progress*, pp. 48–57.

Landes, Elisabeth M. 1978. "Economics of Alimony." *Journal of Legal Studies* 7:35.

Laqueur, Thomas. 1986. "Orgasm, Generation, and the Politics of Reproductive Biology." *Representations* 14:1–41.

——. 1990. *Making Sex: Body and Gender from the Greeks to Freud.* Cambridge: Harvard University Press.

Lasker, Judith and Susan Borg. 1987. *In Search of Parenthood: Coping with Infertility and High-Tech Conception.* Boston: Beacon.

Law, Sylvia A. 1983. "Women, Work, Welfare, and the Preservation of Patriarchy." *University of Pennsylvania Law Review* 131:1249.

——. 1984. "Rethinking Sex and the Constitution." *University of Pennsylvania Law Review* 132:955–1040.

Lawrence, Charles R., III. 1990. "If He Hollers Let Him Go: Regulating Racist Speech on Campus." *Duke Law Journal* 3:431.

Law Society of Upper Canada, Women in the Legal Profession Committee. 1991. *Transitions in the Legal Profession: A Survey of Lawyers Called to the Bar Between 1975 and 1990.* Toronto: Law Society of Upper Canada.

Leavitt, Judith Walzer. 1986. *Brought to Bed: Childbearing in America, 1750–1950.* New York: Oxford University Press.

Lebacqz, K. 1991. "Feminism and Bioethics: An Overview." *Second Opinion* 17, no. 2: 10, 18–19.

Lebsock, Suzanne. 1982. "Free Black Women and the Question of Matriarchy: Petersburg, Virginia, 1784–1820." *Feminist Studies* 8:271.

Lerner, Gerda. 1973. *Black Women in White America: A Documentary History.* New York: Vintage.

——. 1986. *The Creation of Patriarchy.* New York: Oxford University Press.

Lewin, Tamar. 1989. "View on Career Women Sets Off a Furor." *New York Times* (March 8): A18.

———. 1991a. "Implanted Birth Control Device Renews Debate Over Forced Contraception." *New York Times* (January 10): A20.

———. 1991b. "For Some Two-Paycheck Families, the Economics Don't Add Up." *New York Times* (April 21): sec. 4, 18.

———. 1993. "Laws Often Disregarded for Household Workers." *New York Times* (January 15): B16.

Lithwick, N. H., M. Schiff, and E. Vernon. 1986. *An Overview of Registered Indian Conditions in Canada.* Ottawa: Ministry of Indian and Northern Affairs.

Little, Malcolm. 1965. *The Autobiography of Malcolm X.* New York: Grove.

Little Bear, L. 1986. "Aboriginal Rights and the Canadian 'Grundnorm.' " In J. R. Ponting, ed., *Arduous Journey: Canadian Indians and Decolonization*, pp. 243–59. Toronto: McClelland and Stewart.

Loftus, T. 1988. Speech delivered to the National Child Support Enforcement Association in New Orleans, La.

López, Gerald P. 1992. *Rebellious Lawyering: One Chicano Vision of Progressive Law Practice.* Boulder: Westview.

Lorde, Audre. 1984. *Sister Outsider: Essays and Speeches.* New York: Crossing.

Lubiano, Wahneema. 1992. "Black Ladies, Welfare Queens, and State Minstrels: Ideological War by Narrative Means." In Toni Morrison, ed., *Race-ing Justice, En-gendering Power: Essays on Anita Hill, Clarence Thomas, and the Construction of Social Reality*, p. 323. New York: Pantheon.

Luker, Kristin. 1984. *Abortion and the Politics of Motherhood.* Berkeley: University of California Press.

Lyne, Barbara. 1992. "Women at the Top: Role Models or Relics?" *New York Times* (September 27): F27.

McDonald, S. P. 1980. "Jane Austen and the Tradition of the Absent Mother." In Cathy N. Davidson and E. M. Broner, eds., *The Lost Tradition: Mothers and Daughters in Literature.* New York: F. Ungar.

Macdonell, D. 1986. *Theories of Discourse: An Introduction.* London: Blackwell.

McLanahan and Garfinkel. 1989. "Single Mothers, the Underclass, and Social Policy." *Annals* 501:92.

MacKinnon, Catharine A. 1979. *Sexual Harassment of Working Women.* New Haven: Yale University Press.

———. 1983a. "The Male Ideology of Privacy: A Feminist Perspective on the Right to Abortion." *Radical America* 17, no. 4: 23–38.

———. 1983b. "Feminism, Marxism, Method, and the State: Toward Feminist Jurisprudence." *Signs* 8: 636–58.

———. 1987. *Feminism Unmodified: Discourses on Life and Law.* Cambridge: Harvard University Press.

———. 1989. *Toward a Feminist Theory of the State.* Cambridge: Harvard University Press.

———. 1991. "Reflections on Sex Equality Under Law." *Yale Law Journal* 100: 1281–328.

Macklin, Audrey. 1992. "Foreign Domestic Worker: Surrogate Housewife or Mail Order Servant?" *McGill Law Journal* 37:682.

Macnicol, John. 1980. *The Movement for Family Allowances, 1918–1945: A Study in Social Policy and Development.* London: Heinemann.

Macpherson, C. B. 1962. *The Political Theory of Possessive Individualism: Hobbes to Locke.* Oxford: Clarendon.

Mahoney, Martha R. 1991. "Legal Images of Battered Women: Redefining the Issue of Separation." *Michigan Law Review* 90:1.

Maier, Kelly E. 1989. "Pregnant Women: Fetal Containers or People with Rights?" *Affilia: Journal of Women and Social Work* 4, no. 2 (Summer): 8–20.

Mann, Judy. 1994. "Punishment Is Not a Contraceptive." *Washington Post* (March 2): E15.

Marcus, Isabel et al. 1988. "Looking Toward the Future: Feminism and Reproductive Technologies." *Buffalo Law Review* 37:203.

Marks, Linda. 1990. "Alternative Work Schedules in Law: It's About Time." *New York Law School Law Review* 35:361.

Marshall, G. 1993. "The Social Construction of Child Neglect." M.S.W. Thesis, University of British Columbia.

Martin, April. 1993. *Lesbian and Gay Parenting Handbook.* New York: Harper-Collins.

Martin, Emily. 1987. *The Woman in the Body: A Cultural Analysis of Reproduction.* Boston: Beacon.

Martin, Sheilah. 1992. "The Dynamics of Exclusion: Women in the Legal Profession." Paper presented at the National CBA Conference on Gender Equality: A Challenge for the Legal Profession, Toronto, Ontario.

Martinez, Al. 1991. "Babes in Machines and Babes in Arms." *San Francisco Chronicle Sunday Punch* (May 5): 2.

Mayfield, Lorraine. 1991. "Early Parenthood Among Low-Income Adolescent Girls." In Robert Staples, ed., *The Black Family: Essays and Studies.* Belmont: Wadsworth.

Means, Cyril C. Jr. 1968. "The Law of New York Concerning Abortion and the Status of the Foetus, 1664–1968: A Case of Cessation of Constitutionality." *New York Law Forum* 14, no. 3: 411–515.

Meltzer, J. 1988. "Financing Long-Term Care: A Major Obstacle to Reform." In S. Sullivan and M. Lewin, eds., *The Economics and Ethics of Long-Term Care and Disability,* pp. 56–72. Washington, D.C.: American Enterprise Institute.

Menkel-Meadow, Carrie. 1983. "Women in Law? A Review of Cynthia Fuchs Epstein's *Women in Law.*" *American Bar Foundation Research Journal,* p. 189.

——. 1989. "Exploring a Research Agenda of the Feminization of the Legal Profession: Theories of Gender and Social Change." *Law and Social Change* 14:289.

Merchant, Carolyn. 1980. *The Death of Nature: Women, Ecology, and the Scientific Revolution.* San Francisco: Harper and Row.

Merrick, Janna C. and Robert H. Blank, guest eds. 1993. "The Politics of Pregnancy: Policy Dilemmas in the Maternal-Fetal Relationship." *Women & Politics*, special issue 13, nos. 3/4.

Mezey, Susan Gluck. 1992. *In Pursuit of Equality.* New York: St. Martin's.

Middlebrook, Diane Wood. 1991. *Anne Sexton: A Biography.* Boston: Houghton, Mifflin.

Miller, Alice. 1984. *Thou Shalt Not Be Aware: Society's Betrayal of the Child.* Trans. by Hildegarde Hannum and Hunter Hannum. New York: Meridian.

——. 1990. *The Untouched Key: Tracing Childhood Trauma in Creativity and Destructiveness.* Trans. by Hildegarde Hannum and Hunter Hannum. New York: Doubleday Anchor.

——. 1991. *Breaking Down the Wall of Silence: The Liberating Experience of Facing the Painful Truth.* Trans. by Simon Worrall. New York: Dutton.

Miller, James. 1992. *The Passion of Michel Foucault.* New York: Simon and Schuster.

Miller, Jerome. 1992. "Search and Destroy: The Plight of African American Males in the Criminal Justice System." Paper delivered at the Civil Rights Training Conference in Airlie, Va., October.

Milwaukee County Welfare Rights Organization. 1972. *Welfare Mothers Speak Out: We Ain't Gonna Shuffle Anymore.* New York: Norton. Quoted in Dorothy Roberts, "Punishing Drug Addicts Who Have Babies: Women of Color, Equality, and the Rights of Privacy." *Harvard Law Review* 104:1419; 1444, n. 133.

Milwaukee Sentinel. 1990. "Teen Pregnancy Called Issue That Threatens State." (May 1): 1.

Minkler, M. 1986. " 'Generational Equity' and the New Victim Blaming: An Emerging Public Policy Issue." *International Journal of Health Services* 16:539.

Mohr, James C. 1978. *Abortion in America: The Origin and Evolution of National Policy, 1800–1900.* New York: Oxford University Press.

Mollison, Andrew. 1992. "Mom's Pay Kept Families Going in 80s, Study Says." *Atlanta Journal and Constitution* (January 17): H3.

Molloy, M. 1992. "Citizenship, Property, and Bodies: Discourses on Gender and the Inter-War Labor Government in New Zealand." *Gender and History* 4:293.

Monk, Ray. 1990. *Ludwig Wittgenstein: The Duty of Genius.* New York: Free Press.

Montaner, C. 1990. Statement made on the television program *Portada.* Univision Network (November 5).

Montgomery, R. and M. M. Datwyler. 1990. "Women and Men in the Caregiving Role." *Generations.* Special Supplement on Gender and Aging (Summer): 34, 38.

Monture, P. 1989. "A Vicious Circle: Child Welfare Law and the First Nations." *Canadian Journal of Women and the Law* 3:1.

Morrison, Toni. 1970. *The Bluest Eye.* New York: Holt, Rinehart, and Winston.

——. 1987. *Beloved.* New York: Knopf.

Mossman, M. J. 1988a. " 'Invisible' Constraints on Lawyering and Leadership: The Case of Women Lawyers." *Ottawa Law Review* 20:567.

——. 1988b. "Portia's Progress: Women as Lawyers: Reflections on Past and Future." *Windsor Yearbook of Access to Justice* 8:252.

——. 1993. "Gender Bias and the Legal Profession: Challenges and Choices." In J. Brockman and D. Chunn, eds., *Investigating Gender Bias: Law, Courts and the Legal Profession*, pp. 147–68. Toronto: Thompson.

Moyers, B. 1986. "The Vanishing Family: Crisis in Black America." Columbia Broadcasting System (CBS) Special Report (January).

Moynihan, Daniel Patrick. 1965. *The Negro Family: The Case for National Action*. Washington, D.C.: Department of Labor, Office of Policy Planning and Research.

——. 1967. "The Negro Family: The Case for National Action." In Lee Rainwater and William Yancey, eds., *The Moynihan Report and the Politics of Controversy*. Cambridge: MIT Press.

——. 1990. "The Family Support Act Is Underway." *Congressional Record*. 101st Congr., 2d Sess. vol. 136, pt. 14416:05.

Murray, Charles. 1984. *Losing Ground: American Social Policy, 1950–1980*. New York: Basic Books.

——. "The Coming White Underclass." *Wall Street Journal* (October 29): A14.

Nathan, J. E. 1984. "Visitation After Adoption: In the Best Interests of the Child." *New York University Law Review* 59:633.

National Committee for Pay Equity (NCPE). 1987. Pay Equity: An Issue of Race, Ethnicity, and Sex. Washington, D.C.: National Committee on Pay Equity.

National Council of Welfare. 1990. *Women and Poverty Revisited*. Ottawa: National Council of Welfare.

Nelson, Barbara J. 1990. "The Origins of the Two-Channel Welfare State: Workmen's Compensation and Mothers' Aid." In Linda Gordon, ed., *Women, the State, and Welfare*, pp. 123–51. Madison: University of Wisconsin Press.

Nielsen, Sheila. 1990. "The Balancing Act: Practical Suggestions for Part-Time Attorneys." *New York Law School Law Review* 35:369.

Nsiah-Jefferson, Laurie. 1989. "Reproductive Laws, Women of Color, and Low-Income Women." In Nadine Taub and Sherrill Cohen, eds., *Reproductive Laws for the 1990s*, pp. 23–67. Clifton, N.J.: Humana.

O'Brien, Mary. 1981. *The Politics of Reproduction*. Boston: Routledge and Kegan Paul.

O'Connell, Mary E. 1988. "Alimony After No-Fault: A Practice in Search of a Theory." *New England Law Review* 23:437.

O'Donnell, D. A. and W. L. Atlee. 1871. "Report on Criminal Abortion." *Transactions of the American Medical Association* 22:239.

Oakley, Ann. 1984a. *Taking It Like a Woman*. London: Cape.

——. 1984b. *The Captured Womb: A History of the Medical Care of Pregnant Women*. Oxford: Basil Blackwell.

——. 1987. "From Walking Wombs to Test-Tube Babies." In Michelle Stanworth, ed., *Reproductive Technologies: Gender, Motherhood, and Medicine*, pp. 36–56. Minneapolis: University of Minnesota Press.

Oday, L. 1985. "Medicare and Medicaid Update." In M. Knapp, H. Pies, Jr., and A. Doudera, eds., *Legal and Ethical Aspects of Health Care for the Elderly*. Ann Arbor, Mich.: Health Administration Press.

Okin, Susan Moller. 1991. *Justice, Gender, and the Family*. New York: Basic Books.

Olsen, Frances E. 1983. "The Family and the Market: A Study of Ideology and Legal Reform." *Harvard Law Review* 96:1497.

——. 1989. "Unraveling Compromise." *Harvard Law Review* 103:105–35.

Omolade, Barbara. 1987. "The Unbroken Circle: A Historical Study of Black Single Mothers and Their Families." *Wisconsin Women's Law Journal* 3:239.

——. 1989. "Black Women, Black Men, and Tawana Brawley: The Shared Condition." *Harvard Women's Law Journal* 12:12.

Pallen, Montrose A. 1869. "Foeticide, or Criminal Abortion." *Medical Archives* 3:193–206.

Palmer, Phyllis. 1989. *Domesticity and Dirt: Housewives and Domestic Servants in the United States, 1920–1945*. Philadelphia: Temple University Press.

Passell, Peter. 1989. "Economic Watch: Forces in Society and Reaganism Helped Dig Deeper Hole for the Poor." *New York Times* (July 16): 1.

Pateman, Carole. 1988. *The Sexual Contract*. Stanford: Stanford University Press.

Payne. 1992. "At $64 That Baby's a Steal." *Newsday* (January 26): 30.

Pearce, Diana. 1985. "Toil and Trouble: Women Workers and Unemployment Compensation." *Signs* 10:439.

——. 1990. "Welfare Is Not *for* Women." In Linda Gordon, ed., *Women, the State, and Welfare*, pp. 265–78. Madison: University of Wisconsin Press.

Pearlman, M., ed. 1989. *Mother Puzzles: Daughters and Mothers in Contemporary American Literature*. New York: Greenwood.

Pellatt, A. S. 1991. *An International Review of Child Welfare Policy and Practice in Relation to Aboriginal People*. Calgary: Canadian Research Institute for Law and the Family.

Petchesky, Rosalind P. 1979. "Reproduction, Ethics, and Public Policy: The Federal Sterilization Regulations." *Hastings Center Report* 9:29.

——. 1984. *Abortion and Woman's Choice: The State, Sexuality, and Reproductive Freedom*. New York: Longman and Boston: Northeastern University Press.

——. 1987. "Fetal Images: The Power of Visual Culture in the Politics of Reproduction." *Feminist Studies* 13:263–92. Also published in M. Stanworth, ed., *Reproductive Technologies: Gender, Motherhood, and Medicine*, pp. 57–80. Minneapolis: University of Minnesota Press.

Polikoff, Nancy. 1990. "This Child Does Have Two Mothers: Redefining Parenthood to Meet the Needs of Children in Lesbian-Mother and Other Nontraditional Families." *Georgetown Law Journal* 78:459.

——. 1991. "Custody Disputes Between Parents and Third Parties." In *Family Law: Child Custody Training Manual* 72. District of Columbia Bar.

Pollack, Sandra. 1987. "Two Moms, Two Kids." In Sandra Pollack and Jeanne Vaughn, eds., *Politics of the Heart: A Lesbian Parenting Anthology*. Ithaca, N.Y.: Firebrand.

Pollack, Sandra and Jeanne Vaughn, eds. 1987. *Politics of the Heart: A Lesbian Parenting Anthology*. Ithaca, N.Y.: Firebrand.

Pollitt, Katha. 1987. "Contracts and Apple Pie: The Strange Case of Baby M." *The Nation* 244 (May 23): 667, 682–688.

Pollock, Scarlet. 1984. "Refusing to Take Women Seriously: 'Side Effects' and the Politics of Contraception." In Arditti, Klein, and Minden, eds., *Test-Tube Women: What Future for Motherhood?*, pp. 138–152.

Pomeroy, H. S. 1888. *The Ethics of Marriage.* New York: Funk and Wagnalls.

Posner, R. 1987. "The Ethics and Economics of Enforcing Contracts of Surrogate Motherhood." *Journal of Contemporary Health Law and Policy* 5:21.

Powledge, Tabitha M. 1981. "Unnatural Selection: On Choosing Children's Sex." In Helen B. Holmes, Betty B. Hoskins, and Michael Gross, eds., *The Custom-Made Child? Women-Centered Perspectives*, pp. 193–99. Clifton, N.J.: Humana.

Quadagno, J. and M. H. Meyer. 1990. "Gender and Public Policy." *Generations* (Summer): 64.

Quayle, D. 1992. "Prepared Remarks by the Vice President, Commonwealth Club of California." Washington, D.C.: The Vice President's Office, Office of the Press Secretary.

Radin, Margaret Jane. 1987. "Market-Inalienability." *Harvard Law Review* 100: 1849–937.

Rainwater, L. and W. L. Yancey. 1967. *The Moynihan Report and the Politics of Controversy.* Cambridge: MIT Press.

Ratner, R. S. 1990. *Child Welfare Services for Urban Native Indians.* Vancouver: United Native Nations.

Raymond, Janice. 1984. "Feminist Ethics, Ecology, and Vision." In Arditti, Klein, and Minden, eds., *Test-Tube Women: What Future for Motherhood?*, pp. 427–37.

Regan, Donald H. 1979. "Rewriting *Roe v. Wade.*" *Michigan Law Review* 77: 1569–646.

Representations. 1986. Special issue. "Sexuality and the Social Body in the Nineteenth Century," Vol. 14 (Spring). Berkeley: University of California Press.

Rhode, Deborah L. 1988. "Perspectives on Professional Women." *Stanford Law Review,* 40:1163.

——. 1989. *Justice and Gender: Sex Discrimination and the Law.* Cambridge: Harvard University Press.

——. 1990. "Feminist Critical Theories." *Stanford Law Review* 42:617–38.

——. 1991. "The 'No-Problem' Problem: Feminist Challenges and Cultural Change." *Yale Law Journal* 100:1731.

——. 1993–94. "Adolescent Pregnancy and Public Policy." *Political Science Quarterly* 108, no. 4: 635–69.

Rice, T. et al. 1993. "Holes in the Jackson Hole Approach to Health Care Reform." *Journal of American Medical Association* 270, no. 11: 1357.

Rich, Adrienne. 1976. *Of Woman Born: Motherhood as Experience and Institution.* New York: Norton.

——. 1979. "Motherhood: The Contemporary Emergency and the Quantum Leap." In *On Lies, Secrets, and Silence.* New York: Norton.

——. 1991. "XIII. (Dedications) I Know You Are Reading This Poem." In *An Atlas of the Difficult World: Poems, 1988–1991.* New York: Norton.

Richard, Patricia Bayer. 1989. "Alternative Abortion Policies: What Are the Health Consequences?" *Social Science Quarterly* 70, no. 4: 941–55.

Richardson, Lynda. 1992. "No Cookie-Cutter Answers in 'Mommy Wars.'" *New York Times* (September 2): B1, B5.

Rivlin, A. and A. Weiner. 1988. *Caring for the Disabled Elderly.* Washington, D.C.: The Brookings Institution.

Roberts, Dorothy E. 1991. "Punishing Drug Addicts Who Have Babies: Women of Color, Equity, and the Right of Privacy." *Harvard Law Review* 104:1419.

Roberts, P. and R. Schulzinger. 1987. "Toward Reform of the Welfare System: Is Consensus Emerging?" *Clearinghouse Review* 21:3.

Robertson, John A. 1986. "Embryos, Families, and Procreative Liberty: The Legal Structure of the New Reproduction." *Southern California Law Review* 59: 939–1041.

——. 1988. "Procreative Liberty and the State's Burden of Proof in Regulating Noncoital Reproduction." In Larry Gostin, ed., *Surrogate Motherhood: Politics and Privacy,* pp. 24–42. Bloomington: Indiana University Press.

Robson, Ruthann. 1992. *Lesbian (Out)law: Survival Under the Rule of Law.* Ithaca, N.Y.: Firebrand.

Robson, Ruthann and S. E. Valentine. 1990. "Lov(h)ers: Lesbians as Intimate Partners and Lesbian Legal Theory." *Temple Law Review* 63:511.

Rodriguez, Clara. 1989. *Puerto Ricans Born in the U.S.A.* Boston: Unwin Hyman.

Roggenkamp, Viola. 1984. "Abortion of a Special Kind: Male Sex Selection in India." In Arditti, Klein, and Minden, eds., *Test-Tube Women: What Future for Motherhood?,* pp. 266–77.

Rollins, Judith. 1985. *Between Women: Domestics and Their Employers.* Philadelphia: Temple University Press.

Romany, Celina. 1991. "Ain't I a Feminist?" *Yale Journal of Law and Feminism* 4:23.

Roosevelt, Franklin. 1935. Testimony before Congress. Quoted in J. Anthony Lukas. 1992. "Declaring War on Welfare." *New York Times* (July 12): sec. 7, p. 1.

Rosaldo, Michelle Zimbalist and Louise Lamphere, eds. 1974. *Woman, Culture, and Society.* Stanford: Stanford University Press.

Rosser, Sue. 1986. *Teaching Science and Health from a Feminist Perspective.* New York: Pergamon.

——, ed. 1989. "Feminism and Science: In Memory of Ruth Bleier." *Women's Studies International Forum.* Special issue 12.

Rothman, Barbara Katz. 1982. *In Labor: Women and Power in the Birthplace.* New York: Norton.

——. 1986. *The Tentative Pregnancy: Prenatal Diagnosis and the Future of Motherhood.* New York: Viking.

——. 1989. *Recreating Motherhood: Ideology and Technology in a Patriarchal Society.* New York: Norton.

Rothman, Sheila M. 1978. *Woman's Proper Place: A History of Changing Ideals and Practices, 1870 to the Present.* New York: Basic Books.

Rothschild, Joan. 1983. "Introduction: Why Machina ex Dea?" In Joan Rothschild, ed., *Machina ex Dea: Feminist Perspectives on Technology,* pp. ix–xxix. New York: Pergamon.

Rowe, Audrey. 1991. "The Feminization of Poverty: An Issue for the 90s." *Yale Journal of Law and Feminism* 4:73.

Rowe and Associates. 1989. *The Vancouver Urban Indian Needs Assessment Study.* Vancouver: Ministry of Labour and Consumer Services.

Rowland, Robyn. 1987. "Technology and Motherhood: Reproductive Choice Reconsidered," *Signs* 12:512–28.

———. 1992. *Living Laboratories: Women and Reproductive Technologies.* Bloomington: Indiana University Press.

Rubenstein, Carin. 1993. "Consumer's World." *New York Times* (January 28): C1.

Ruddick, Sara. 1980. "Maternal Thinking," *Feminist Studies* 6:432–67.

Rush, Florence. 1980. *The Best-Kept Secret: Sexual Abuse of Children.* Engelwood Cliffs, N.J.: Prentice-Hall.

Ryan, M. A. 1990. "The Argument for Unlimited Procreative Liberty: A Feminist Critique." *Hastings Center Report* (July/August).

St. Peter, Christine. 1989. "Feminist Discourse, Infertility, and Reproductive Technologies." *NWSA Journal* 1, no. 3 (Spring): 353–67.

Sanders, Joelle. 1991. *Before Our Time.* New York: Harcourt Brace Jovanovich.

Sanger, Carol. 1992. "M is for the Many Things." *Southern California Review of Law and Women's Studies* 1:20.

———. 1996 (forthcoming). *Separating from Children.* Berkeley: University of California Press.

Sarat, Austin. 1990. ". . . The Law Is All Over: Power, Resistance, and the Legal Consciousness of the Welfare Poor." *Yale Journal of Law & Humanities* 2:343.

Sawicki, Jana. 1988. "Feminism and the Power of Foucauldian Discourse." In Jonathan Arac, ed., *After Foucault: Humanistic Knowledge, Postmodern Challenges.* New Brunswick: Rutgers University Press.

Saxton, Marsha. 1984. "Born and Unborn: The Implications of Reproductive Technologies for People with Disabilities." In Arditti, Klein, and Minden, eds., *Test-Tube Women: What Future for Motherhood?*, pp. 298–312.

Schafran, Lynn Hecht. 1990. "Gender and Justice: Florida and the Nation." *Florida Law Review* 42:181.

Schultz, Vicki. 1990. "Telling Stories about Women and Work: Judicial Interpretations of Sex Segregation in the Workplace in Title VII Cases Raising the Lack of Interest Argument." *Harvard Law Review* 103:1749.

Schwartz, Felice N. 1989. "Management of Women and the New Facts of Life." *Harvard Business Review* 67:65.

Scott, Kesho Yvonne. 1991. *The Habit of Surviving.* New York: Ballantine.

Sedgwick, Eve Kosofsky. 1990. *Epistemology of the Closet.* Berkeley and Los Angeles: University of California Press.

Sella, Carmel. 1991. "When a Mother Is a Legal Stranger to Her Child: The Law's Challenge to the Lesbian Nonbiological Mother." *University of California, Los Angeles, Women's Law Journal* 1:135.

Sennett, Richard and Jonathan Cobb. 1972. *The Hidden Injuries of Class.* New York: Random House.

Sevenhuijsen, Selma and Petra de Vries. 1984. "The Women's Movement and

Motherhood," In Anja Meulenbelt et al., eds., *A Creative Tension: Key Issues in Socialist-Feminism*, pp. 9–25. Boston: South End.

Sevilla, Graciela. 1994. "NAACP for Welfare Overhaul: Bid to Tighten Rules Gets Surprise Support." *Washington Post* (March 6): B1.

Sexton, Anne. 1981. "The Double Image." *The Complete Poems*. Boston: Houghton, Mifflin, p. 27.

Shalev, Carmel. 1989. *Birth Power: The Case for Surrogacy*. New Haven: Yale University Press.

Shanley, Mary Lyndon. 1993. " 'Surrogate Mothering' and Women's Freedom: A Critique of Contracts for Human Reproduction." *Signs* 18: 618–39.

Shapiro, Thomas. 1985. *Population Control Politics: Women, Sterilization, and Reproductive Choice*. Philadelphia: Temple University Press.

Sheehan, Susan. 1993a. "Reporter at Large: A Lost Childhood." *The New Yorker* (January 11): 54–85.

——. 1993b. "Reporter at Large: A Lost Motherhood." *The New Yorker* (January 18): 52–79.

Sheppard, Annamay T. 1985. "Lesbian Mothers II: Long Night's Journey Into Day." *Women's Rights Law Reporter* 8:218.

Sheridan, Alan. 1980. *Michel Foucault: The Will to Truth*. London: Tavistock.

Sherman, Rorie. 1988a. " 'Fetal Rights' Cases Draw Little Attention." *National Law Journal* 11, no. 4: 25.

——. 1988b. "Keeping Baby Safe from Mom," *National Law Journal* 11, no. 4: 1, 24, 26.

Shklar, Judith. 1984. *Ordinary Vices*. Cambridge: Belknap Press of Harvard University Press.

Shultz, M. M. 1990. "Reproductive Technology and Intent Based Parenthood: An Opportunity for Gender Neutrality." *Wisconsin Law Review*, p. 297.

Siegel, Reva B. 1985. "Employment Equality Under the Pregnancy Discrimination Act of 1978." *Yale Law Journal* 94:929–56.

——. 1992. "Reasoning from the Body: A Historical Perspective on Abortion Regulation and Questions of Equal Protection." *Stanford Law Review* 44:262–381.

——. 1994. "Home As Work: The First Woman's Rights Claims Concerning Wives' Household Labor, 1850–1880." *Yale Law Journal* 103:1073–217.

Silberman, L. 1991. "Transforming the Debate About Child Care and Maternal Employment." *American Psychologist* 46:1025.

Simms, Margaret C. 1986. "Black Women Who Head Families: An Economic Struggle." In Margaret C. Simms and Julianne M. Malveaux, eds., *Slipping Through the Cracks: The Status of Black Women*, pp. 143–44. New Brunswick, N.J.: Transaction Books.

Simms, Marsha. 1990. "Women in the Lawyering Workplace: A Practical Perspective." *New York Law School Law Review* 35:385.

Skocpol, Theda. 1993a. *Protecting Soldiers and Mothers*. Cambridge: Harvard University Press.

——. 1993b. "Is the Time Finally Ripe? Health Insurance Reforms in the 1990's." *Journal of Health Politics, Policy, and Law* 18, no. 13: 531.

Skolnick, A. 1991. *Embattled Paradise: The American Family in an Age of Uncertainty.* New York: Basic Books.

Smart, C. 1991. "The Legal and Moral Ordering of Child Custody." *Journal of Law and Society* 18:485.

——. 1992. "The Woman of Legal Discourse." *Social & Legal Studies* 1:29.

Smith, Dorothy E. 1987. *The Everyday World as Problematic: A Feminist Sociology.* Boston: Northeastern University Press.

Smith, Lynn. 1992. "Adding a Third Dimension: The Canadian Approach to Constitutional Equality Guarantees." *Law and Contemporary Problems* 55:211.

Smith-Rosenberg, Carroll. 1985. *Disorderly Conduct: Visions of Gender in Victorian America.* New York: Oxford University Press.

Solinger, Rickie. 1992a. *Wake Up Little Susie: Single Pregnancy and Race Before Roe v. Wade.* New York: Routledge.

——. 1992b. "Race and 'Value': Black and White Illegitimate Babies in the U.S.A., 1945–1965." *Gender and History* 4:343.

Spallone, Patricia and Deborah Lynn Steinberg. 1987. "Introduction." In Spallone and Steinberg, eds., *Made to Order: The Myth of Reproductive and Genetic Progress,* pp. 13–17. New York: Pergamon Press.

Spelman, Elizabeth V. 1988. *Inessential Woman: Problems of Exclusion in Feminist Thought.* Boston: Beacon.

Spence, J. and P. Holland, eds. 1991. *Family Snaps: The Meaning of Domestic Photography.* London: Virago.

Spivak, Gayatri Chakrovorty. 1988. "Can the Subaltern Speak?" In Cary Nelson and Lawrence Grossberg, eds., *Marxism and the Interpretation of Culture,* pp. 271–313. Houndmills: Macmillan.

Stacey, J. 1990. *Brave New Families: Stories of Domestic Upheaval in Late-Twentieth-Century America.* New York: Basic Books.

Stack, Carol B. 1974. *All Our Kin: Strategies for Survival in a Black Community.* New York: Harper and Row.

——. 1983–84. "Cultural Perspectives on Child Welfare." *New York University Review of Law and Social Change* 12:539.

Stansell, C. 1992. "White Feminists and Black Realities: The Politics of Authenticity." In Morrison, ed., *Race-ing Justice, En-gendering Power.*

Stanworth, Michelle. 1987. *Reproductive Technologies: Gender, Motherhood, and Medicine.* Minneapolis: University of Minnesota Press.

Stearns, Nancy. 1989. *"Roe v. Wade:* Our Struggle Continues." *Berkeley Women's Law Journal* 4:1.

Steedman, Carolyn. 1986. *Landscape for a Good Woman: A Story of Two Lives.* London: Virago. 1987. Reprint, New Brunswick: Rutgers University Press.

——. 1992. "Culture, Cultural Studies, and Historians." In Lawrence Grossberg, Cary Nelson, and Paula Treichler, eds., *Cultural Studies,* pp. 613–22. New York: Routledge.

Steinbacher, Roberta and Helen B. Holmes. 1987. "Sex Choice: Survival and Sisterhood." In Gena Corea et al., eds., *Man-Made Women: How the New Reproductive Technologies Affect Women,* pp. 52–63.

Steiner, Gilbert Y., ed. 1983. *The Abortion Dispute and the American System*. Washington, D.C.: The Brookings Institution.

Steingraber, S. 1991. "Lifestyles Don't Kill—Carcinogens in Food, Air, and Water Do." In Midge Stocker, ed., *Cancer as a Women's Issue*, pp. 91–102. Chicago: Third Side.

Stephens, M. P. and S. Zarit. 1987. "Symposium: Family Caregiving to Dependent Older Adults: Stress, Appraisal, and Coping." *Sociology and Aging* 4, no. 4: 387.

Sterling, Dorothy. 1984. *We Are Your Sisters: Black Women in the Nineteenth Century*. New York: Norton.

Still, L. 1993a. "Adopted Baby Caught in Legal Wranglings." *Vancouver Sun* (July 14): B2.

——. 1993b. "Adopters Push for New Evidence." *Vancouver Sun* (July 17): A3.

Stone, R., G. L. Cafferata, and J. Sangl. 1987. "Caregivers of the Frail Elderly: A National Profile." *The Gerontologist* 27, no. 5: 616.

Storer, Horatio R. 1866. *Why Not? A Book for Every Woman*. Boston: Lee and Shepard.

Storer, Horatio R. and Franklin Fiske Heard. 1868. *Criminal Abortion: Its Nature, Its Evidence, and Its Law*. Boston: Little, Brown.

Strauss, David A. 1989. "Discriminatory Intent and the Taming of *Brown*." *University of Chicago Law Review* 56, no. 3: 935–1015.

——. 1993. *The Partial Constitution*. Cambridge: Harvard University Press.

Strong-Boag, V. 1988. *The New Day Recalled: Lives of Girls and Women in English Canada, 1919–1939*. Toronto: Copp Clark Pitman.

Suleiman, Susan. 1985. "Writing and Motherhood." In Shirley Nelson Garner, Claire Kahane, and Madelon Sprengnether, eds., *The (M)other Tongue: Essays in Feminist Psychoanalytic Interpretation*, pp. 352–77. Ithaca: Cornell University Press.

——. 1994. *Risking Who One Is: Encounters with Contemporary Art and Literature*. Cambridge: Harvard University Press.

Sunstein, Cass R. 1992. "Neutrality in Constitutional Law (with Special Reference to Pornography, Abortion, and Surrogacy)." *Columbia Law Review* 92: 1–52.

——. 1993. *The Partial Constitution*. Cambridge: Harvard University Press.

Swift, K. 1991. "Contradictions in Child Welfare: Neglect and Responsibility." In C. Baines, P. Evans, and S. Neysmith, eds., *Women's Caring: Feminist Perspectives on Social Welfare*, pp. 234–71. Toronto: McClelland & Stewart.

Swigart, J. 1990. *The Myth of the Bad Mother: The Emotional Realities of Mothering*. New York: Doubleday.

Taber, Janet, Margaret Brant, Mary Huser, Risë Norman, James Sutton, Clarence Wong, Louise Parker, and Claire Picard. 1988. "Gender, Legal Education, and the Legal Profession: An Empirical Study of Stanford Law Students and Graduates." *Stanford Law Review* 40:1209.

Tan, A. 1989. *The Joy Luck Club*. New York: Putnam.

——. 1991. *The Kitchen God's Wife*. New York: Putnam.

Task Force on Gender Equality in the Legal Profession. 1993. *Touchstones for*

Change: Equality, Diversity, and Accountability. Ottawa: Canadian Bar Association.

Tate, Julia. 1992. *Artificial Insemination and Legal Reality*. ABA Section of Family Law.

Taub, Nadine and Sherrill Cohen, eds. 1989. *Reproductive Laws for the 1990s*. Clifton, N.J.: Humana.

Taylor, Ronald. 1991. "Black Youth in Crisis." In Robert Staples, ed., *The Black Family: Essays and Studies*, pp. 211–26. Belmont: Wadsworth.

Teich, Albert H., ed. 1990. *Technology and the Future*. 5th. ed. New York: St. Martin's.

Tobin, Richard J. 1989. "Environment, Population, and Development in the Third World," In Norman J. Vig and Michael E. Kraft, eds., *Environmental Policy in the 1990s*, pp. 279–300. Washington, D.C.: Congressional Quarterly Press.

Tong, Rosemarie. 1989. *Feminist Thought: A Comprehensive Introduction*. Boulder: Westview.

Treblicot, Joyce. 1991. "Ethics of Method: Greasing the Machine and Telling Stories." In Claudia Card, ed., *Feminist Ethics*, pp. 45–51. Lawrence: University of Kansas Press.

Tribe, Laurence H. 1988. *American Constitutional Law*. 2d ed. Minneola: Foundation Press.

———. 1990. *Abortion: The Clash of Absolutes*. New York: Norton.

Troll, L. 1987. "Mother-Daughter Relationships Through the Life Span." In S. Oskamp, ed., *Applied Social Psychology Annual*. Vol. 7, *Family Processes and Problems: Social Psychological Aspects*. Newbury Park, Calif.: Sage.

Tronto, J. 1993. Talk given at the Department of Social and Behavioral Sciences, School of Nursing, University of California, San Francisco.

Turpel, M. E. 1989–90. "Aboriginal Peoples and the Canadian Charter: Interpretive Monopolies, Cultural Differences." *Canadian Human Rights Yearbook* 6:3–90.

Tussman, Joseph and Jacobus tenBroek. 1949. "The Equal Protection of the Laws." *California Law Review* 37:341–81.

Tyler, A. 1983. *Dinner at the Homesick Restaurant*. New York: Berkeley, by arrangement with Knopf.

U.S. Congress, Office of Technology Assessment. 1988. *Artificial Insemination: Practice in the United States*. Washington, D.C.

U.S. Department of Labor. 1991. *Comparison of State Unemployment Insurance Law*. Washington, D.C.: U.S. Department of Labor.

———. 1992. *Comparison of State Unemployment Insurance Law*. Rev. ed. Washington, D.C.: U.S. Department of Labor.

U.S. Senate Special Committee on Aging. 1987. *Aging America: Trends and Projections, 1987–88*. Washington, D.C.: Department of Health and Human Services.

———. 1988. *Developments in Aging: 1987*. Vol. 3, *The Long-Term Care Challenge*. Report no. 100–291. Washington, D.C.: Department of Health and Human Services.

Vanier Institute of the Family. 1992. "The Pain of Choice, the Agony of None." *Transition* (June).

Wacquart and Wilson. 1989. "The Cost of Racial and Class Exclusion in the Inner City." *Annals* 501:8.

Wagner, W. J. 1990. "The Contractual Reallocation of Procreative Resources and Parental Rights: The Natural Endowment Critique." *Case West Law Review* 41:1.

Wald, Patricia M. 1988. "Women in the Law: Despite Progress, Much Still Needs to Be Done." *Trial* 24:75.

Walker, A. and K. Allen. 1991. "Relationships Between Caregiving Daughters and Their Elderly Mothers." *The Gerontologist* 31, no. 3: 389.

Walker, Alice. 1992. *Possessing the Secret of Joy.* New York: Harcourt Brace Jovanovich.

Wallerstein, Judith S. and Sandra Blakeslee. 1989. *Second Chances: Men, Women, and Children a Decade After Divorce.* New York: Ticknor and Fields.

Walsh, Joan. 1988. "Take This Job and Shove It." *Mother Jones* 13, no. 7.

Warner, Michael. 1991. "Introduction: Fear of a Queer Planet." *Social Text* 29:3–17.

Warren, Mary Anne. 1985. *Gendercide: The Implications of Sex Selection.* Totowa, N.J.: Rowman & Allanheld.

Washington Post. 1994. "Veering Off-Center on Welfare." (March 11): A24.

Wearing, B. 1984. *The Ideology of Motherhood: A Study of Sydney Suburban Mothers.* Sydney: Allen and Unwin.

Wegman, Myron E. 1989. "Annual Summary of Vital Statistics: 1988." *Pediatrics* 84:943.

Weinberg, J. K. 1991. "The Dilemma of Welfare Reform: 'Workfare' Programs and Poor Women." *New England Law Review* 26:415.

——. 1992. "Poverty, Autonomy, and Reproduction in the Welfare State." *Columbia Journal of Gender and Law* 3:377.

Weisberg, D. Kelly. 1982. "Barred from the Bar: Women and Legal Education in the U.S., 1870–1890." In D. Kelly Weisberg, ed., *Women and the Law,* vol. 2. Cambridge, Mass.: Schenkman.

Weisman, S. R. 1988. "State in India Bars Fetus Sex-Testing." *New York Times* (July 20): 1, 6.

Weitzman, L. 1985. *The Divorce Revolution: The Unexpected Social and Economic Consequences for Women and Children.* New York: Free Press.

West, Robin. 1988. "Jurisprudence and Gender." *University of Chicago Law Review* 55:1.

——. 1990. "Equality Theory, Marital Rape, and the Promise of the Fourteenth Amendment." *Florida Law Review* 42:45–79.

Weston, Kath. 1991. *Families We Choose: Lesbians, Gays, Kinship.* New York: Columbia University Press.

Wexler, Joan. 1985. "Rethinking the Modification of Child Custody Decrees." *Yale Law Journal* 94:757.

Wharf, B. 1989. *Toward First Nation Control of Child Welfare: A Review of Emerging Developments in B.C.* Victoria: University of Victoria.

White, Deborah. 1985. *Ar'n't I a Woman? Female Slaves in the Plantation South.* New York: Norton.

White, E. Frances. 1990. "Africa on My Mind: Gender, Counter Discourse, and African-American Nationalism." *Journal of Women's History* 2:73.

White, Julie. 1993. "A New Standard for 'Family Values' and the Family's Relation to Work." Vanier Institute of the Family. *Transition* 23, no. 2: 8.

White, Lucie E. 1990. "Subordination, Rhetorical Survival Skills, and Sunday Shoes: Notes on the Hearing of Mrs. G." *Buffalo Law Review* 38:1.

——. 1993. "No Exit: Rethinking 'Welfare Dependency' from a Different Ground." *Georgetown Law Journal* 81:1961.

Wicks, Ben. 1988. *No Time to Wave Goodbye.* London: Bloomsbury.

Wigod, R. 1993. "Lesbian Couple Who Want Child Denied Sperm." *Vancouver Sun* (July 22): A1.

Wikler, D. and N. J. Wikler. 1991. "Turkey-Baster Babies: The Demedicalization of Artificial Insemination." *Milbank Quarterly* 69:5.

Wikler, Norma J. 1986. "Society's Response to the New Reproductive Technologies: The Feminist Perspectives." *Southern California Law Review* 59, no. 5: 1043–57.

Williams, Joan C. 1989. "Deconstructing Gender." *Michigan Law Review* 87:797.

——. 1990. "Sameness, Feminism, and the Work/Family Conflict." *New York Law School Law Review* 35:347.

——. 1991. "Gender Wars: Selfless Women in the Republic of Choice." *New York University Law Review* 66:1546.

Williams, Lucy A. 1992. "The Ideology of Division: Behavior Modification Welfare Reform Proposals." *Yale Law Journal* 102:719–46.

Williams, Patricia. 1988. "On Being the Object of Property." *Signs* 14:5–24.

——. 1991. *The Alchemy of Race and Rights: Diary of a Law Professor.* Cambridge: Harvard University Press.

Williams, Raymond. 1989. "Desire." *What I Came to Say.* London: Radius.

Williams, Wendy W. 1982. "The Equality Crisis: Some Reflections on Culture, Courts, and Feminism." *Women's Rights Law Reporter* 7:175.

——. 1984–85. "Equality's Riddle: Pregnancy and the Equal Treatment/Special Treatment Debate." *New York University Review of Law and Social Change* 13, no. 2: 325–80.

Willke, J. n.d. *Did You Know.* Quoted in Frances Olsen, "Unraveling Compromise." *Harvard Law Review* 103 (1989): 105, 128.

Wilson, William Julius. 1987. *The Truly Disadvantaged: The Inner City, The Underclass, and Public Policy.* Chicago: University of Chicago Press.

Wingerter, Rex B. 1987. "Fetal Protection Becomes Assault on Motherhood." *In These Times* (June 10–23): 3, 8.

Wisconsin State Journal. 1990. "Illegitimacy Biggest Killer of Our Babies." (February 9): 11A.

Wittgenstein, Ludwig. 1953. *Philosophical Investigations.* Trans. by G. E. M. Anscombe. New York: Macmillan.

Woliver, Laura R. 1988. "Review Essay: The Equal Rights Amendment and the Limits of Liberal Legal Reform." *Polity* 21, no. 1: 183–200.

———. 1989a. "The Deflective Power of Reproductive Technologies: The Impact on Women." *Women & Politics* 9, no. 3 (November): 17–47.

———. 1989b. "New Reproductive Technologies: Challenges to Women's Control of Gestation and Birth." In Robert Blank and Miriam K. Mills, eds., *Biomedical Technology and Public Policy*, pp. 43–56. Westport, Conn.: Greenwood.

———. 1990. "Reproductive Technologies and Surrogacy: Policy Concerns for Women." *Politics and the Life Sciences* 8, no. 2 (February): 185–93.

———. 1991. "The Influence of Technology on the Politics of Motherhood: An Overview of the United States," *Women's Studies International Forum* 14, no. 5: 479–90.

Wood, Betty. 1987. "Some Aspects of Female Resistance to Chattel Slavery in Low Country Georgia, 1763–1815." *History Journal* 30:603–9.

Yeo, Stephen. 1988. "Difference, Autobiography, and History." *Literature and History* 4, no. 1: 37–47.

Zinn, Maxine Baca. 1989. "Family, Race, and Poverty in the Eighties." *Signs* 14:856–72.

BIOGRAPHIES

Marie Ashe is Professor of Law at Suffolk University School of Law in Boston, Mass., and has written extensively about legal regulation of female gender and female sexuality. Her work includes: "Zig-Zag Stitching and the Seamless Web," *Nova Law Review* 13 (1989); "Inventing Choreographies: Deconstruction and Feminism," *Columbia Law Review* 90 (1990); "Abortion of Narrative: A Reading of the Judgment of Solomon," *Yale Journal of Law and Feminism* 4 (1991); "The 'Bad Mother' in Law and Literature: A Problem of Representation," *Hastings Law Journal* 43 (1992); and " 'Bad Mothers, 'Good Lawyers,' and 'Legal Ethics,' " *Georgetown Law Journal* (1993).

Martha Albertson Fineman is the Maurice T. Moore Professor of Law at Columbia University in New York City. She is a 1975 graduate of the University of Chicago Law School. She clerked for Luther M. Swygert of the Seventh Circuit Court of Appeals. Professor Fineman began teaching in 1976 at the University of Wisconsin Law School, and in 1984 she developed the Feminism and Legal Theory Project at Wisconsin. The project is now located at Columbia Law School and is devoted to fostering interdisciplinary feminist work on law and legal institutions. In addition to numerous articles and book chapters on feminism, family law, and the regulation of intimacy and sexuality, Professor Fineman is the author of *The Neutered Mother, the Sexual Family and Other Twentieth-Century Tragedies* (New York: Routledge, 1995) and *The Illusion of Equality: The Rhetoric and Reality of Divorce Reform* (Chicago: University of Chicago Press, 1991). She is a contributor and co-editor of a number of collections of papers from the Feminism and Legal Theory Project, including *The Public Nature of Private Violence* (New York: Routledge, 1994), and *At the Boundaries of Law: Feminism and Legal Theory* (New York: Routledge, 1991).

Kate Harrison was an Associate in Law at Columbia Law School in 1990–1992 and thereafter worked for a New York law firm. Since returning to Australia in

1994 she has worked at the Legal Aid Commission of New South Wales, and as a consultant. She holds a degree in law from the University of New South Wales, a Masters in Law from Columbia Law School, and a Ph.D. in politics from the University of Sydney.

Isabel Karpin is a lecturer in law at the University of Sydney, Australia. She graduated from Sydney University with a Bachelors of Arts and Law in 1987, received an LL.M. from Harvard in 1991 and is currently completing her J.S.D. at Columbia. Her research and teaching interests lie in feminist legal theory, reproductive technology, health law, and law and popular culture.

Marlee Kline is an Associate Professor at the Faculty of Law, University of British Columbia, Canada, where she teaches feminist legal theory, social welfare law, and property. She received a B.A. in psychology from Simon University in 1982, a B.A. in jurisprudence from Oxford in 1984, an LL.B. from Dalhousie Law School in 1985, and an LL.M. from Osgoode Hall Law School in 1991. Her research is focused on the impact of child welfare law on the First Nations, the ways that law is implicated in interactive relations of race, gender, class, and sexual identity, and on family-related issues within feminist legal theory. She is currently involved in examining the impact of child welfare law on various Black communities in Canada, as part of a larger interdisciplinary research project with six other feminist scholars that is entitled "Challenging the Public/Private Divide: Women, Law, and Social Change."

Nancy K. Miller is Distinguished Professor of English at Lehman College and the Graduate School, CUNY. Her most recent book is *Getting Personal: Feminist Occasions and Other Autobiographical Acts* (Routledge, 1991). She is currently working on a project about contemporary memoirs and dead parents.

Mary Jane Mossman is a Professor of Law at Osgoode Hall Law School of York University in Toronto, Canada. She has written extensively on issues about women in the legal profession and family law, and was recently retained to provide research about women lawyers by the Canadian Bar Association's Task Force on Gender Equality in the Legal Profession. She was a Visiting Adjunct Professor at Columbia Law School in the 1992 fall semester.

Barbara Omolade heads the B.S. Education degree program for early childhood educators at the City College, Center for Workers Education, an evening college program for working adults. Her research specialization is single mothers and the issues of gender in the Black community. She is the author of the forthcoming *The Rising Song of African American Women*, a collection of published and original essays to be published summer 1994 by Routledge Press.

Nina Perales is a staff attorney with the Puerto Rican Legal Defense and Education Fund (PRLDEF), a national legal organization founded to protect the civil rights of Puerto Ricans and other Latinos. Ms. Perales coordinates the Latina Rights Initiative, a PRLDEF project focused on race and gender discrimination against Latinas. Her work includes litigation and advocacy in the area of Latina economic empowerment, as well as the areas of health and domestic violence. Ms. Perales graduated from Brown University in 1986 and is a graduate of Columbia University Law School.

Dorothy E. Roberts is a professor at Rutgers University School of Law–Newark, where she teaches courses on criminal law and civil liberties. She has written and lectured extensively on the interplay of race, gender, and poverty in legal issues concerning motherhood and reproduction. Her articles have appeared in *Harvard Law Review, University of Chicago Law Review, Social Text, Essence,* and the *New York Times.* Professor Roberts is currently writing a book tentatively entitled *Race, Reproduction, and the Meaning of Liberty,* during a fellowship at Harvard University's Program in Ethics and the Professions. She received her B.A. from Yale University and her J.D. from Harvard Law School. Professor Roberts is the mother of three children.

Ruthann Robson is Professor of Law at the City University of New York's School of Law, teaching in the areas of constitutional law, feminist legal theory, and sexuality and the law. Her work has been primarily focused on the possibilities of a specifically lesbian legal theory and appears in the book *Lesbian (Out)Law: Survival Under the Rule of Law* (Ithaca: Firebrand Books, 1992) as well as in numerous articles in law reviews, periodicals, and anthologies. She is also the author of two collections of lesbian fiction and a forthcoming novel about a lesbian attorney who represents lesbian mothers.

Carol Sanger is a Professor of Law at Santa Clara University, where she teaches contracts, family law, and feminist jurisprudence. Her research focuses on how law affects decision making within the family, particularly around the issue of family composition. She has written on this issue in the contexts of immigration, the emancipation of minors, and custody. Professor Sanger has been a visiting scholar at the Institute for Research on Women and Gender at Stanford University and a visiting professor at Stanford and Columbia Law Schools. Among her publications, many of which investigate the regulation of motherhood, is the forthcoming book *Separating from Children.*

Ann Shalleck is a professor at the American University, Washington College of Law, where she started and directs the Women and the Law Program. As part of this program, she has developed an annual workshop on Women's Rights and the Law School Curriculum and a program on Women and International Law. Professor Shalleck's writings are in the areas of clinical law and feminist theory; they include "Clinical Contexts: Theory and Practice in Law and Supervision," *New York University Review of Law and Social Change* (1993–94); "Constructions of the Client Within Legal Education," *Stanford Law Review* (1993); "The Feminist Transformation of Lawyering," *Hastings Law Journal* (1992); and "Feminist Legal Theory and the Reading of *O'Brien v. Cunard*," *Missouri Law Review* (1992). She served on the District of Columbia Task Force on Gender Bias in the Courts, as well as the Advisory Committee on Implementation of the Task Force Report. She is a 1971 graduate of Bryn Mawr College and received her J.D. from Harvard Law School in 1978.

Reva Siegel is Professor of Law at the Yale Law School, where she teaches courses in the fields of contracts, constitutional law, civil rights law, and feminist and critical race theory. Her work examines questions of civil rights from a legal-historical perspective. Her publications include: "Reasoning from the Body: A Historical Perspective on Abortion Regulation and Questions of Equal Protection," *Stanford Law Review* 44, no. 2: 262–381; "Home as Work: The First Woman's Rights Claims Concerning Wives' Household Labor, 1850–1880," *Yale Law Journal* 103, no. 5: 1073–217; and "The Modernization of Marital Status Law: Adjudicating Wives' Rights to Earnings, 1860–1930," *Georgetown Law Journal* 82, no. 7: 2127–211.

Marty Slaughter is an Associate Professor at Cardozo School of Law, Yeshiva University, New York City. She received a J.D. from the University of California, Berkeley, in 1987 and a Ph.D. in English from the University of Wisconsin in 1967. She has published articles on the First Amendment rights and a book for Cambridge University Press on seventeenth-century language theory. Professor Slaughter is currently working on Constitutional protections for cultural groups.

Joanna Weinberg is a 1972 graduate of Harvard Law School, and received an LL.M. from Columbia Law School in 1980. She received a B.A. in sociology from Brandeis University in 1968. She is an Associate Adjunct Professor in the Department of Social and Behavioral Sciences, University of California, San Francisco, and also teaches at Hastings College of the Law in San Francisco. Professor Weinberg has published articles on issues relating to women and the welfare system, focusing on the impact of the welfare state on women, and on health policy issues relating to midlife and older women. She is currently completing a book on women and the welfare state in the twentieth century.

Laura R. Woliver received her Ph.D. from the University of Wisconsin, Madison, in 1986. She has written numerous articles on women's rights, civil rights, legal issues, and activism. She is the author of *From Outrage to Action: The Politics of Grass-Roots Dissent* (Urbana: University of Illinois Press, 1993). She is a political science professor at the University of South Carolina, Columbia.

Gender and Culture
A Series of Columbia University Press
Edited by Carolyn G. Heilbrun and Nancy K. Miller